T5-COA-924

Anne Teresa De Keersmaeker / Rosas 2007–2017

Editor
Christian Dumais-Lvowski

Texts
Gilles Amalvi
Floor Keersmaekers

Photography
Anne Van Aerschot
Herman Sorgeloos

ACTES SUD
Mercatorfonds

Distributed by Yale University Press,
New Haven and London

Cover
Keeping Still — Part 1 (2007)
Photo
Herman Sorgeloos

Dear Anne Teresa,

Ten years, thirteen pieces: from *Keeping Still — Part 1* to *Mitten wir im Leben sind/Bach6cellosuiten*, from Ann Veronica Janssens's evanescent lights to the chiaroscuro of Bach's Cello Suites, from medieval music to Gérard Grisey's spectral formulas, these pieces cover a repertory that spans from the fourteenth to the twentieth century. Ten years, thirteen pieces that dialogue with Bach's solo pieces, Mahler's late-blooming romanticism, and Brian Eno's post-rock. With Shakespeare, Mozart, Rilke. Shakespeare with Brian Eno. Rilke with Salvatore Sciarrino's *Opera per flauto*. Mahler with Jérôme Bel. Bach with Boris Charmatz. With the outside, the open air, the light of dawn. With the temporality of exhibition spaces. With walking, singing, and silence. Ten years of explorations during which you put your vocabulary, your writing, your dancer's body to the test anew. And, already, a question: Confronted with this profusion of movements, music, styles, what was your compass, and what's ours? Yours: Beyond the affinities for this or that work, this or that piece of music, this or that dancer, what running thread is secretly weaving its way through these pieces? What questions, obsessions, and systems of deciphering the world through dance are at work there? During this ten-year sequence, what links the music, the words, and the bodies? And how do they nourish, reflect, and contaminate one another? Most importantly, does this sequence make sense to you? Is it the bearer of an inflection, a transformation, a gap—in the way of creating, of treating the music, of composing the choreography? And, simultaneously, a way of transmitting Rosas's repertory, of putting it back into play? And, on our side: How are we to look at this architecture of movements in the time of its elaboration? How are we to untangle the singularities, mark the ruptures and continuities, and thus situate these pieces in the larger body of your work since your first choreography, *Fase*, in 1982?

Differently put: Can we regard these ten years as a coherent aesthetic and temporal whole, that is, as a "period" marked by an inflexion, like a sentence with its commas, semicolons, and breath? Can we detect a more profound logic at work in it than simply an arbitrary cut in time? How is the dynamic that informs this period different from that of the previous decade? What new problems, questions, and resolutions does it contain? And when did it start, exactly? Was it in 2007, with *Keeping Still* and your return to the stage? With the appearance of the principle "my walking is my dancing," which reconfigures the experience of movement through walking? How, precisely, do we measure such a period? What parameters, what way of *counting* or measuring time, are we to use? In *Clio*, Charles Péguy wonders about the multitude of intertwined times that contribute to forming the temporal construct that we call a *period*: "Look into your memory. What you will see—what you do see—there is that the flow, the event of the real, is not homogenous, that time is hardly singular. . . . Is it not evident that events are not homogeneous, that they are perhaps organic in the sense that they have what are called in acoustics antinodes and nodes, peaks and troughs, a rhythm, perhaps some regulation, tension and release, periods and epochs, axes of vibration, moments of agitation, crisis points, monotonous plains and suddenly suspension marks."[1]

Ten years, thirteen pieces. More than one a year, we might think, were we to adhere to a linear and chronological view of time, to solve for the average while disregarding singular durations, accelerations, blocs. When we look more closely, though, what we see, as it happens, are precisely these nodes, these tensions, these releases: in the titles, the dates. The titles say: Keeping still. Bits of time. The song. Three farewells. Waiting (*en atendant*). They say something about a stop, a pause. A time for questions, for asking them again. "How is movement produced in the body? What possible relation is there between improvisation and writing? Between dance and music?" Basic questions, opening questions, that provided the material for the exchange with Alain Franco during the making of *Zeitung* (2008). Is that what it is about? A new start, but a start midway through the journey, a start on the go, so to speak? About a return to the start that doesn't efface anything of what has already taken place? A start that stops and restarts?

The pieces that mark the start of this period followed each other at the rhythm of one a year. But then there were leaps: two years between *Cesena* (2011) and *Partita 2* and *Vortex Temporum*, both from 2013. Then another two years before *Golden Hours*, the exhibition *Work/Travail/Arbeid*, and *Die Weise von Liebe und Tod des Cornets Christoph Rilke*, all from 2015. Three projects in the same year: a sharp acceleration. And there again: nodes, tensions and releases, as if moments of research were followed by moments of effervescence; as if moments of solitude, silence, crisis were succeeded by resolutions that took the form of vast group compositions. These cycles, oscillating between profusion and scarcity, weave between them two necessities that correspond to two simultaneously convergent and contradictory temporalities: the need to affirm a "sovereign" writing, and the desire to subject it to the unpredictable bodies of the performers, to accidents, to the asperities of new musical or literary materials, to the questions raised by other interlocutors, be they artists, musicians, or choreographers. "The goal," you say, "is for the writing to exist in itself. That requires a search for the laws that govern the organization of time and space, laws that go beyond the temporary and the anecdotal, both of which are linked to contingencies. It's thanks to the performers that the idea can be embodied, but, in the end, the horizon for this writing is for it to be able to exist for itself."

1 Charles Péguy, *Clio* (1931), in *Temporal and Eternal*, trans. Alexander Dru (Indianapolis: Liberty Fund, 2001).

We might say that dance, for you, exists in two forms. One is inscribed in duration and proceeds from a writing and a mode of composition; this is the form that links the first forays into Steve Reich's music to the experimentations at the outer edges of movement that you weave around Bach's suites. The form that relies on geometry, the golden section, and the mathematical constructions that we find inscribed, like a secret signature, at the heart of every piece. There is also, at the same time, the dance that exists only in the present of the encounter, before the alterity of the music or text, which imposes another relation to space, time, and movement. Each treated work calls forth a specific choreographic response, which weds itself to the characteristics of that work and offers an in-depth treatment not only of its structure, but also of the aesthetic and philosophical questions it raises. This *variety*, these clear leaps in time and style—far from being an aesthetic *dérive* attuned to prevailing affinities—seem rather to stem from the relentless pursuit of a question that you approach through different angles. I saw most of these pieces with the intuition that what was at stake in them was something of the progressive enmeshing of these two dimensions: the long time of the work and the present time of creation. As the beginning of a reflexive moment, a slide toward a more porous way of handling the structures of dance—one that is, perhaps, less subservient to the grids of writing. Or of a writing that offers itself more to *being read*. A writing that, in laying bare its rules and its erasure, allows us to see the draft underneath the score and affords more space to the principle of uncertainty.

I look at the photographs, trying to find some signs that would shore up this intuition. Usually, photos only yield fragmentary clues; that is true of dance in general, and even more so of a dance that is about flux and passing, and inhabited by the question of music. Before these still, silent images, what remains? Anne Van Aerschot and Herman Sorgeloos reveal leaning, suspended bodies. Silhouettes, alone or in groups. Some in familiar attitudes, others solemn, dressed all in black. Groups that walk or run. Here a piano, there a violin, a cello, a flute: lots of instruments, lots of dancers circling around the instruments. Slowness, momentum, alterities that coinhabit. An empty space there, an orchestra here. Varied colors, lights with changing tonalities. The detail of a hand, the frozen movement of a run, the line of an arm, the line of a group of dancers. In 2009, Boris Charmatz, in *50 ans de danse*, put the photographs of a book about the work of Merce Cunningham end to end. Starting with these choreographic snapshots, Charmatz restores the arrangements, the transitions, and forces the movement between stopped forms. Putting each of the states that make up this book side by side, what type of dance would we see materialize before us? What would this unfolding tell us about your writing, its transformations, about the action of time in your oeuvre?

It is difficult for photographs to tell us something about time—to express the juxtaposed temporalities that intertwine, not just in a dance piece but also between pieces. To materialize the shape of duration: the hiatuses; the intervals that light and body formulate in *Keeping Still*; the voids and sudden accelerations of *The Song*; the leaps from Bach to Schönberg in *Zeitung*; the upswing of the rhythm during the courante in *Partita 2*; the slowness that settles into the bodies in *En Atendant*; the gradual increase of the light in *Cesena*; the whirlwind of instruments in *Vortex Temporum*, which sketches the eye of the storm absorbing duration; the time of silent reading (which differs radically from the time of hearing or looking) that invades *Die Weise von Liebe und Tod des Cornets Christoph Rilke*. Still, the photos reveal a movement of flux and reflux: a constant oscillation between "lessness" and proliferation, solitude and multitude, movement and stasis. This oscillation is accentuated by the fact that the images reveal few figures, few clearly identifiable choreographic forms. What we see, rather, are silhouettes in waiting—between two states, two moments, hovering on the threshold. Photos that show or demonstrate little, that don't carve a brand name on the marble, don't put a signature on every gesture. That don't allow us to say with every image: "Yes, of course, that's Anne Teresa de Keersmaeker." Photos that by the same token avoid the "catalogue of gestures" effect by putting the stress, instead, on that which resists sense or capture—the sensation of a passage that has taken place, or is about to take place.

Looking at these photographs as a continuous unfolding, another sign appears: your body, your silhouette. It appears across this whole long sequence at regular intervals, every two or three years. Like a metronome, it insists, it returns. There it is: alone, feeling its way as if in the dark in *Keeping Still — Part 1*; alone still, though accompanied by the Ictus ensemble and Jérôme Bel, in *3Abschied*; with Boris Charmatz and Amandine Beyer in *Partita 2*; with Michaël Pomero and Chryssi Dimitriou in *Die Weise*; and, lastly, like a hyphen linking each of its solos in *Bach6cellosuiten*. What does this presence tell us? What is the sense of this physical engagement in your work—of this return of your own body to the question of work?

I have the impression that if anything in this ten-year sequence *makes sense*, if anything in it articulates the slide from one period to another, it plays itself out at the level of your body as a node, as the point around which revolve the plural temporalities of an oeuvre elaborated over the course of some thirty-five years. In its resurgence, this body operates simultaneously as a concentration of time and a vector of reflexivity. A sensible presence, it is also an *index* pointing toward two essential dimensions: the work of time, and the time of work. First as a body, as a dancer's body susceptible to aging, it materializes the way in which duration operates within the work, it transforms its perception and its becoming by actualizing it.

By the same token, it puts its finger on the singularity that accompanies the choreographic art, its *fatum* and its promise. The choreographic art is *always already past* while also being, at each of its occurrences, irremediably present. In this sense, your body operates like a third term that goes beyond the apparent tension between sovereign writing and the contingencies of the interpretation—beyond the tension, crystallizing and materializing it, incorporating without fetishizing, empathizing, or putting particular emphasis on it. This presence does not signal the authenticity or legitimacy of *the choreographer*. It is not a signature placed on an original. It does not affirm mastery or underline an *aura*. Nor is it—by an effect of reversed fetishism—a body that shows itself in its aging, in the wisdom of its maturity. It's more like a body that returns after an absence to resolve a problem that had been left in suspense.

We can map out several major periods, each of them marked by a certain use of your own body—acting simultaneously within the economy of your work, and as a more general demonstration of the various regimes of the choreographic. First, the foundation, the invention of a language: "At the very beginning, when I started choreographing, in the 1980s, I would dance myself: all the danced movements came from my own body. I was twenty then—I was searching for a language. I wanted to keep that very close to me, pressed up against my own body, literally." That was followed by a time—oriented more toward composition and deepening the relation to music—during which the writing grew more abstract: "I did four pieces in which I danced myself; after that, for various reasons, I needed to step back, and I worked more as the choreographer. After a while, though, I started dancing again. But it had been a long time since I had worked in the studio with this question: What is my dance, my way of dancing today?"

This question, "What is my dance?" is the one you asked again in *Partita 2*, in the duo with Boris Charmatz that we can see as a distant echo of the duo in *Piano Fase*. *Piano Fase*: two women, of equal size and look, dance in unison to a composition for piano. *Partita 2*: a man and a woman, one tall, the other short, dance slightly off rhythm. Now and then they synchronize with the music, but only to better distance themselves from it—not as an objective, a goal to be achieved, but as a passage, a threshold, a crossing that is constantly being restarted. That's where I discovered your work. I knew *Fase*, *Rosas Danst Rosas*, *Achterland*; younger, I had seen *Drumming*. But it was really in the studio with Boris Charmatz and Amandine Beyer, during the rehearsals where Bach's music would start playing, stop, start again, where it would pass from violin to voice and from voice to steps, that I encountered, in your dance, the question of *work*: a dance that shows itself in its labor, its effort, its line, and its errancy. That question is present in the time of the laboratory—the work of rehearsing, creating—and also in the final result, on stage. The tremble of a dance that continues searching and that gives itself to vision on the edges—of the music, of the rhythm, of geometric spirals.

In a text about *Partita 2*, I discussed the place left to the spectator to construct his or her own relation to the music and the dance: "How to dance to a piece of music without *subtracting* it from the spectator? Without robbing her of the multitude of possible dances it contains: the movements it engenders, the physical intensities that course through it? How to dance without confiscating the images summoned by the music? To dance while leaving holes, gaps, while leaving the possibility of pursuing it further? The presence of your body in this redefinition of the relation between dance and music seemed to put the finger on a form of incompleteness, on a porosity that displaces both the formal structure of movement and its sensible apprehension: through this deferred agreement, this perennially readjusted and re-launched relation to rhythm, *Partita 2* presents something like the incapacity of the body to *realize* the music, to render it fully visible. The claim that 'my walking is my dancing' takes on a singular value: walk, yes, but to mark; dance as a certain way to mark the steps, to beat the measure through one's own pulse, one's own rhythm. If the metronome posits an absolute value, the body, for its part, imprints a value that is relative to the space: a value scaled to its measure, one that has to be measured against disorder, the irregular, the *too much* and the *not enough*. It is perhaps not by chance that this dimension of incompleteness affirmed itself after the work with Jérôme Bel on *3Abschied*. Faced with Mahler's *Das Lied von der Erde*, an imposing lyrical work, they had to find ways to *de-complete* the total character of that symphony; find strategies to keep fusion at bay and to unsettle the oceanic feeling of Mahler's music. In *3Abschied*, the dancing body is no longer the focal point; instead, it becomes the marker that makes it possible to adjust the distance between itself and what surpasses it: neither dominant nor dominated, the dancing body inaugurates an intermediary position."

I discovered your work when this intermediary position—which runs through *Keeping Still*, *3Abschied*, and *Partita 2*—was being formulated, and today I am connecting it to the reappearance of your body in the work. That's also where I discovered *A Choreographer's Score*, the series of books, each devoted to a specific production or productions, in which you lay out the conditions of appearance of your work by analyzing the physical and geometric principles that ground it. In them, we see you in front of a blackboard, tracing spirals, columns, and numbers with chalk, articulating the relation between phrases, working out their duration and spatialization, then stopping to give body to the equation you've just traced. This intermediary position situates itself at the junction between the formal clarity of the idea and its passage through the body—between the grid and the flesh, geometry and play. Your body, I realize as

I scan the photographs, becomes a border—the intersection between the different dimensions of the oeuvre, as well as between the different elements that participate in the choreographic creation. A border between text, music, and dance, the realness of flesh and the ideation of forms, discourse and composition. A node that holds together invention and its interpretation, archive and transmission, repertory and experimentation.

This body is no longer, as had been the case at first, a body that *invents* its language, but rather a body that puts this language anew to the test of the work—not afraid to make it stammer, to subject it to other languages and other intensities in order to keep it alive. A sign that exposes the work, this body is also the point through which the formalism attached to your system of composition *de*-completes itself. That is how we can reread the oscillation, operative across this entire period, between large group compositions like *Cesena*, *Vortex Temporum*, *Golden Hours*, and *Così fan tutte* (2017) and the pieces where you dance, where you lay bare the structure by showing yourself in the process of grappling with an idea and giving it form. What gets established between these two zones of creation is a porous relation, a relation of correspondences, akin to that between the sketch and the canvas: the different states of singing in *3Abschied*—until you yourself sing "Der Abschied"—and the crystalline singing of the Ars subtilior in *En atendant*; the variations of walking in *Partita 2* that return to form a line in *Golden Hours*; or, indeed, the text, the question of knowing what dance might do with an articulated language, the text that, as you say "returns regularly, and allows new horizons of creation to emerge. Although it is sometimes visible on the surface, at other times it digs itself more deeply, in ways that make it less immediately apparent." At each stage, a question transfers itself, is adjusted, and finds a new formal resolution that establishes both a point from which it can be relaunched and a place of sedimentation.

Deep down, your body acts like a resolution to the contradiction that confronts every choreographic oeuvre: to abide, to inscribe itself in time without being frozen into a dead archive. These ten years correspond to the moment when the question of the "oeuvre" was formalized as such: as an aesthetic whole based on common rules, an always-expanding repertory to be reactivated continuously, and as a nonhomogeneous block of duration shot through by divergent intensities. Your body is simultaneously the *guarantor* and the unquantifiable and unmeasurable, the principle of uncertainty that relaunches the work. It is interesting to note that the reappearance of your body took place on the one hand in a dance production, *Keeping Still*, and on the other in the space of the museum—a site of preservation, of historical inscription and validation—with the reprise of *Violin Fase* at New York's Museum of Modern Art in 2011. The entry into the museum marks, simultaneously, a deposit, a form of safekeeping indispensable for the survival of the ephemeral art that is dance, as well as (through the subjection of your body to the gaze as it inscribed the traces of its steps on the sand, gradually revealing geometric forms) a resistance to the paradigm of museification. The movement, its trace, and its idea, summed up in a gesture that summons and conjures disappearance at one and the same time.

This desire for an inscription in space and time that does not result in the *mummification* of the work appears most clearly in the exhibition *Work/Travail/Arbeid*. Through the process of stretching out the choreographic material of *Vortex Temporum*, *Work/Travail/Arbeid* renders the work visible in all of its different dimensions: genetic (how it is invented), architectonic (how it is organized), physical (how it is spent), and relational (how it forges links). Insinuated into the articulation of these different strata is a dimension that gives substance and meaning to the exhibition's title. What is put to work here, what is exhibited in its radical uncertainty, its tentativeness, is the blind spot materialized in space: the point of the gaze. From where, and how, do we look at these bodies at work? A question that we could formulate more generally: From where, and how, do we look at choreographic work in the process of being formed?

In the open space of *Work/Travail/Arbeid*—with no stage, backstage, or specified space of representation—the dancers are visible in each of their states at every stage of the work: preparation, appearance/performance, activity, rest, recovery time, vacancy. Incidentally, this baring functions less as an image of the studio or of a work in progress than as a *dilation* of the work: the possibility to observe, at once, the nuances and the interstices, the passages, akin to the principles of modulation or dilation of a sound in time that are the ground of Gérard Grisey's spectral music. Pushing this analogy further, we could say that the *spectral* character of *Vortex Temporum* is made palpable, in *Work/Travail/Arbeid*, by the intertwining of activities in time and the modulation of states, which generate an effect of *persistence* in time. To experience this exhibition and its duration is to perceive a dance in decantation. Motifs are diffused, propagated; a phrase or movement returns, reappears, for a few minutes, a few hours, even a few days later, at the end of its cycle. The geometric construction based on the golden section is invested here with a more diffuse, even relative, value. It symbolizes the friction of temporalities: the temporality of the instant, of the microsecond, and the imperceptible temporality, because not within reach, of the cycle. In this sense, the spirals traced in chalk on the floor no longer concern only the motion of stable bodies (the dancers) whose movements obey the order of the composition; they also integrate and interpret the movement of unstable bodies (the visitors), whose presence generates a noise that disturbs the structure.

The spirals are no longer the symbol of a sovereign mathematical order but the sketch of a "chaosmos," the affirmation of a "world made up of divergent series."[2]

Because of its dilated time made of interweaving cycles, and its way of embracing the instability of a reality subject to entropy, this exhibition occupies a peculiar position in the productions of the last ten years. Because there is a change of medium, and with it the inversion of the museal logic into a vector of creation, and also because the work is put on display, this time, *without your body*. Or, rather, with it, but on the sides, above, on the margins. Also presented at WIELS, in parallel to *Work/Travail/Arbeid*, was the solo *My Breathing Is My Dancing*, which was exhibited as an experiment, a new field of research that relaunched the notion of "my walking is my dancing" and displaced the movement of walking toward the more sustained impulse of breathing. This incision within the territory of *Work/Travail/Arbeid* is what is taken up anew and formalized in *Die Weise von Liebe und Tod des Cornets Christoph Rilke*. There again: "nodes, peaks and troughs, a rhythm, perhaps some regulation, tension and release, periods and epochs, axes of vibration, moments of agitation, crisis points, monotonous plains and suddenly suspension marks."

The question that launched this text was about the logic at work during this period. Perhaps one of the specificities of this time is that, strictly speaking, it is not a *sequence* with a beginning and an end, but a *vortex temporum*, a space for the interweaving of the contradictory temporalities that flow through your evolving oeuvre. Through the resurgence of your body, this logic becomes visible, but also elusive. It ramifies itself in a multitude of rhizomes that overflow it, and that keep it from being petrified as repertory or museum piece.[3] I started writing this letter after seeing *Mitten wir im Leben sind/Bach6cellosuiten*; I left the theater wondering about the question of desire, of research, and of their being put back into play. What are you doing, what are you searching for, and how do you reconcile that search and this desire? "Mitten wir im Leben sind," the Lutheran dictum that you chose to put in the title (it is, likewise, Pina Bausch's epitaph), is about life, about the "middle of life," about being at a crossroads, like a distant echo of the opening line of Dante's *Divine Comedy*: "Nel mezzo del cammin di nostra vita" (Midway upon the journey of our life). This middle—*mezzo*, *mitten*—does not have absolute value; it is there wherever the question of knowing what comes after manifests itself. I asked myself this question. Indeed, I asked you this question during an interview: What comes after Bach's Cello Suites? Let me ask it again, more broadly this time: What comes after? How to go on?

Bach's Cello Suites oscillate between the popular dance and the funeral march, between lithe spirals and the austerity of a memento mori. And you chose to dance the most crepuscular of the six: suite number five, with its minor accents made up of sudden flights and returns to gravity. You are there for the sixth as well: you return with the other dancers, one body among others. You are not a center or a periphery—perhaps a middle? A middle that moves, that changes trajectory. A middle that moves so as to open up space, melt, fade? The flickering of your presence, does it mark an elision, a passage, like a dance entwined with a *farewell to dance*? I don't know. What comes after?

Gilles Amalvi

P.S. When I listen to music, especially Bach, and even more especially the Cello Suites, I don't see bodies. I close my eyes and I follow the trajectory of the notes in my head. I notice movement, maybe, but on the edges: an abstract movement, an uncoiling of lines. To be honest, that was the first thing I wanted to ask you: Where do these bodies come from, how do they appear, how do you give them form? And, listening again to Jean-Guihen Queyras's recording while writing, the bodies come back, they *re-turn*. They come back unannounced, like fluid specters. They add themselves to the music, slip into its interstices. Not as an illustration, not in the way the faces of a film come back when we hear its soundtrack, but like markers, fulcrums, *élans*. As if, with the music, they were in their midst . . .

---

2 Gilles Deleuze, *The Fold: Leibniz and the Baroque*, trans. Tom Conley (Minneapolis: University of Minnesota Press, 1993), 137.
3 Among these "rhizomes" we can cite the program *Re:Rosas*, which grants access to the "source code" for *Rosas Danst Rosas*, allowing anyone and everyone to appropriate it; or the various reprises of *Zeitung*, which became *Re:Zeitung* with the students at P.A.R.T.S., and then, following the addition of a new part written by Louis Nam Le Van Ho, *Zeitigung*.

Dance and Its Traces
A conversation with Anne Teresa De Keersmaeker

The book in your hands opens a window onto the pieces produced by the dance company Rosas over the last ten years. The start of that period coincides with a turning point: thenceforward, Anne Teresa De Keersmaeker's oeuvre started to be driven by new questions, interests, and findings.

In a sense, this book offers a possible answer to the question: How can dance leave traces? By its very nature, any traces left by this art form fade. "Beyond YouTube, it's a fact that dance audiences and the greater public have relatively few opportunities to see repertoire pieces—not just Rosas's works, but works of dance history in general," says De Keersmaeker. "Historic key pieces like *Appalachian Spring* by Martha Graham, *Trio A* by Yvonne Rainer, *Café Müller* by Pina Bausch, or *Set and Reset* by Trisha Brown are not easily accessible. Watching a recording in no way compares to the collective and immediate experience of dancers and audience sharing space and time in a live performance. Rosas, however, consistently revisits performances from the repertoire. This is true not only of *Fase* (1982), which has remained an active part of the company's program, but also of *Rosas danst Rosas* (1983), *Achterland* (1990), *Verklärte Nacht* (1995), *Drumming* (1998), *Rain* (2001), *A Love Supreme* (2005), and *Zeitung* (2008).[1]

Photographs preserve traces left by dance. They stop time and capture the dance at points where the eye can't pause and linger during the performance itself. Anne Van Aerschot and Herman Sorgeloos, resident photographers at Rosas, offer an exceptional and limpid glimpse into the company's dance universe. They are intimately familiar with De Keersmaeker's choreographic language, and they have perceptively captured on film the evolution of that language over the past ten years.

Five Anchor Points

In 2017, surveying the past decade of her work, De Keersmaeker identified five underlying anchors: time and space, working with dancers, the observation of nature, the Eastern concept of energy, and, lastly, the art of writing. "These factors already played a role in the earlier work, but less consciously so." The turning point ten years ago, then, was not at all a radical parting with the past, but rather an explicit surfacing of these principles and sources of inspiration.

De Keersmaeker considers the essence of dance to be the organization of movement in time and space. The framework of time is largely provided by the art that the choreographer describes as her first partner: music. When working on a performance, she uses the structural and compositional qualities of the score as a guide: "Since I started my journey, I have looked for as many different strategies as possible to fully explore and deepen the relationship between dance and music. The movement vocabulary of a choreography and the internal logic of its grammar are often established on the ground provided by the music."

The process of organizing the space is usually guided by mathematical principles (the golden ratio, the magic square, the Fibonacci sequence) and geometric figures.[2] Already in her first solo piece, *Violin Phase* (1982), De Keersmaeker used a circle as the basic pattern for the choreography, and the importance of geometries and mathematics has only increased over time. Those who visited the exhibition *Work on Paper* (2015) at BOZAR, Brussels, or are familiar with Rosas's publications, are aware of the role that complicated drawings of linked spirals, circles, stars, and polygons in various ratios play in the company's creative process. These same drawings are marked on the floor of the studio and stage to serve as references for the dancers. "In addition to the space in which the dance takes place, there is of course also the space delineated and occupied by the dancing body: dance as a moving architecture, grafted onto a vertical and a horizontal axis. The magic square, or three-dimensional volumes like a dodecahedron, may help organize this moving architecture."[3]

Then there are the dancers. "Nobody is a blank sheet. A dancer's body has a story that is unique to it, and the person has unique mechanical, sensory, emotional, social, intellectual, and spiritual dimensions. As a choreographer, the conglomeration of all those different dimensions is your working material. In other words, your writing is connected to every facet of the corporeal and psychic personality of each dancer. Part of your work goes on in your head, but you are just as engaged in what happens between the dancers: you attend to the physical space, and the mental and emotional space. You give shape even to the non-tangible, and understand the body as a carrier of emotions. Creating a performance is an intensive social process, and it is important to choose the right people. Not just for the way they interact among themselves, but also because you need them to help you look for answers to the central question."

The third aspect to have emerged as a strong anchor in De Keersmaeker's work in the past

---

1 In the case of *Verklärte Nacht*, *A Love Supreme*, and *Zeitung*, it is more accurate to speak of rewriting than revisiting, since each of these iterations underwent some change.
2 The magical square is subdivided into nine smaller squares of equal size, each of which contains a number from 1 to 9, so that the sum of every line across three squares (horizontal, vertical, and diagonal) is always fifteen. It is also a symbolic representation of the nine energies associated with the "nine-star ki," a form of astrology based on the doctrine of qi and the I Ching.
3 The dodecahedron is a spatial figure composed of twelve identical pentagons, twenty vertices, and thirty edges.

decade is observation of nature, and the ways in which the sciences—physics, astronomy, biology—articulate the way we see nature. "Is there any such thing as a natural order in the universe and, if so, how can that be embodied in a performance?" Primarily she examines the extent to which the human body—her work material—is a universe unto itself, a microcosm that reflects the laws of the macrocosm. As a reference point she takes Leonardo da Vinci's *Vitruvian Man*, which stresses the artist's commitment to the articulation of mathematics and science through art. "When I talk about the observation of nature, that includes the observation of the body. I try to understand how the order of nature presents itself in the human body, how the mechanics of human movement work, and how natural laws like gravity manifest themselves in dance."

In these investigations De Keersmaeker is strongly influenced by Eastern concepts of energy, including yin-yang theory, which defines all that is tangible around us as energy materialized, as born from infinity and ultimately destined to return there. Existence opening and closing like a spiral. All that is perceptible is therefore in continuous transformation under two complementary forces, two polarities considered as an opening and a closing. "These laws also manifest in our bodies. The simplest examples are breathing and the beating of our hearts. Everything in nature is characterized by it—consider images of a hurricane or of the Milky Way. That spiral is the fundamental DNA of every movement. By studying nature and its energetic patterns, I am trying to develop a style of writing in dance that reflects nature's order and chaos and connects the material with the immaterial."

The dancing body can also act as a tangent between the abstract and the concrete, resulting in a choreographic work. "Dance allows you literally to embody the most abstract ideas. With the body as a starting point, you work with what is closest to you, with the most individual and at the same time the most universal carrier of meaning." Although this offers unique possibilities, it also means that the writing always *requires* being embodied. "Since it coalesces with the body, what you write for dance can never be as conclusive as it is in music, for instance, to say nothing of the visual arts. So there is a limit to how much you can hold on to and spell out as a choreographer: you have to convey it to the dancers, and they shape and interpret it."

As a performance art, dance must be embodied time and again. In that respect, De Keersmaeker believes that making a piece and performing it are two sides of the same coin. "After the rehearsals, a new working process starts the moment you begin the performance. That is when the performance really starts to exist. And its existence continues to be in constant evolution."

Back to Basics: *Keeping Still* and *Zeitung*

When asked how the thirteen works of the last decade are connected, De Keersmaeker is reluctant to answer at first. It is difficult to reduce the questions that were asked in the making of those pieces, and the answers that resulted, to a few lines. "The encounter with Ann Veronica Janssens sometime in 2007 was really important. What fascinated me about her work from the start was its clear, brilliant, transparent minimalism—a lightness that is at the same time very concrete. The way she deals with the perception of light and matter demonstrates a radical elegance."

The encounter led to their collaboration on *Keeping Still* (2007), in which the performer Robert Steijn also participated. De Keersmaeker considers the performance a key moment: "The circumstances you work in are very defining for the materials that are created. There is daylight in a studio, but you have to transfer what you have created to the 'black box' of the theater. We wanted to examine what laws govern our perception from that angle, and the way light sculpts the space is a crucial aspect in this. By adding mist, the light in *Keeping Still* gained materiality, carving out the space in an architectural-sculptural sort of way. Over the course of the performance, the relationship between what was seen and what was heard changed continuously. The performance starts in extreme darkness, like before the beginning of time, with nothing more than a child's voice reading a text. What follows is a large plane of light cutting through that darkness and dividing the space in two. Then the main theater light switches on and, finally, the space fills with mist, completely changing the way it is perceived. It is a sort of cyclical movement: extreme darkness yields to sculptural light, which yields to a general lighting, until the space closes in on itself again through mist." A certain threat emanates from that rising fog, expressive of De Keersmaeker's concern over the increasing devastation of the Earth. The performance was inspired by the text of the Earth Charter,[4] and by Gustav Mahler's song cycle *Das Lied von der Erde*. The music is a tribute to the beauty of the Earth and to its inevitable, inexorable vulnerability and transience.

The study of movement that started with *Keeping Still* (assisted by David Hernandez) continued into the next performance, *Zeitung* (2008). Here, too, it meant a return to the essence, that is to say, to the fundamentals of movement in the human body. The basic concept is that the body contains three centers from

---

[4] According to EarthCharter.org, the Earth Charter is "an international declaration of fundamental values and principles for the advancement of a just, sustainable and peaceful global society." The charter's text, the fruit of a six-year global consultation process at the initiative of the Earth Council and Green Cross International, was finally approved in March 2000 at a UNESCO assembly.

which movement originates: the head, the chest, and the pelvis. From there, the dancers set out to develop movement materials. "It was a study of human mechanics, in the process of which we observed how such natural laws as gravity are expressed in movement." To turn the findings into a choreography, De Keersmaeker decided to explore the boundaries between improvisation and composition. "Improvisation really is 'instant composition'; you make choices on the spur of the moment, without the possibility of repeating them immediately afterward. That said, the framework of an improvisation *can* be repeated: the choreographic guidelines can be precise enough to give improvisation a fixed foundation. The writing then becomes a kind of specified improvisation, establishing an evolving architecture within a certain time and space."

Zeitung was the first collaboration between De Keersmaeker and pianist Alain Franco. "I knew Alain through his work with the Ictus ensemble, and I had been to a concert of his where he played music by Bach, Webern, and Schönberg. Using this selection of music, he developed a structure to reflect on time. It occurred to me that this could be a good starting point for exploring the relationship between dance and music."

The Song and *3Abschied*

Keeping Still and *Zeitung* proved to be pivotal points in the history of the company, foundations for the ten years that followed. For *The Song* (2009) De Keersmaeker continued her collaboration with Ann Veronica Janssens, and Michel François, also an artist, joined them. "After *Zeitung*, I asked Alain Franco: 'What music, apart from Bach, lends itself well to dance?' Laughing, he answered: 'The Beatles.'" Taking *The White Album* (1968) as a framework, De Keersmaeker, Janssens, and François created a performance that was stripped in every possible way of nonessential layers. The goal was to distill the basic elements of the organization of movement in time and space. "What remained was the 'objective matter,' the raw building blocks of a performance: light, sound, time, the space of the theater, the moving body within it, and so on." One guiding principle was silence: save for a few moments, there is not a second of music to be heard. *The White Album* may have served as a hidden template, but it did not supply an audible soundtrack. De Keersmaeker worked with a foley artist, who dissected, amplified, or punctuated the movements of the dancers with impromptu sound effects. Other than that, the only sound came from the dancers' walking, running, and breathing. Figuratively speaking, the performance is embedded in silence: in the sense of stillness and deceleration, and in the sense of a blank space imbued with unwritten possibilities and stories.

The ten dancers in *Keeping Still*—nine men and one woman—started from the basic questions in *Zeitung* about the way movement originates in the head, the torso, and the pelvis to develop more complex phrases and produce counterpoints that involved several dancers in different constellations.[5] In so doing, they played with notions of horizontality and verticality, challenging gravity and looking to flight as the ultimate dance form. For their part, Janssens and François created a blank space onstage: a totally white surface, with a reflective foil hanging from the rafters above it, acts as the central light point in the field of vision, and constitutes a strong base geometry delineating the dancing area.

The Song was followed, in 2010, by *3Abschied*, a collaboration with the French choreographer Jérôme Bel. With him, De Keersmaeker continued with the sixth and final part of Mahler's *Das Lied von der Erde*, which had already played an important role in *Keeping Still*. Mahler's song cycle is based on centuries-old Taoist poetry, and "Der Abschied," the last part, is about death, symbolized by dusk. The prevailing sentiment of the song is not despair, however, but acceptance and salvation. Music about death: Is that something you can dance to? De Keersmaeker and Bel effectively put the query to the audience in the first part of the performance. But *3Abschied* is not at all exclusively about that question. "Apart from my continuing need to express my concern for the planet, there was also the desire to work with the most basic instrument we have: the voice. *Keeping Still* was grafted onto the relationship between dance and music; in *The Song*, we went looking for the sound of movement and the movement of sound. And yet, the body itself also holds an instrument in the shape of the voice. Singing is the simplest, most natural way to make music."

What led De Keersmaeker to Bel was the desire to find a partner with whom to share the core question of whether one can dance death. Their exploration of the boundaries of dance and what it can incorporate led them to challenge Daniel Barenboim's idea that it is impossible to dance "Der Abschied."[6] The result of their collaboration, *3Abschied*, is a radical and conceptual dance concert in which De Keersmaeker, as Bel puts it, dances from the entrails of the music, from its source. And not just in the foreground, but also among the musicians: she touches them and interacts with their music-playing bodies. At the end of the performance it becomes very clear where the title comes from. Yet the question the performance started with turns out not to have one conclusive answer. De Keersmaeker and Bel explore three

---

[5] "Phrase" refers to a fixed series of successive and interrelated movements that have a clearly defined start and finish.

[6] Daniel Barenboim is an Argentinean Israeli pianist and conductor. In the first part of *3Abschied*, De Keersmaeker tells the audience about her meeting with Barenboim, in which he expressed his reservations about her idea to choreograph "Der Abschied."

possible ways to deal with a parting ("Abschied" means "Farewell"). In the first parting, the musicians stop playing one by one and leave the stage, as in Joseph Haydn's "Farewell" symphony. In the second, they imagine (the acceptance of) death by collapsing on the floor or on their chairs, as if parting from life on the spot. In the third and final parting, De Keersmaeker sings, accompanied only by the piano. Her vulnerability is unmistakable; like the music, it wavers between solace and sadness. She dances and clears the space in the process. What remains is silence.

En Atendant and *Cesena*

En Atendant (2010) and *Cesena* (2011) came about at the invitation of the Festival d'Avignon. The city's rich history, and the special locations where the festival's performances are staged, played an important role in the creative process.[7] Given all this, De Keersmaeker chose Ars subtilior, a form of polyphonic music that flourished in the fourteenth century, especially at the papal court built in Avignon in that same era. Furthermore, the unique open-air setting inspired her from a visual point of view to use only the changing sunlight. "To that end, I worked with Michel François again for *En Atendant*, and with Ann Veronica Janssens again for *Cesena*. We went for opposites: *En Atendant* was staged at dusk, *Cesena* at dawn."

Her choice of the polyrhythmic Ars subtilior presented De Keersmaeker with a new challenge in her search for the relationship between music and dance. "The basic strategy of translating the musical counterpoint to movement involved parsing the music into different voices: the cantus line, tenor line, and countertenor line. The dancers were each assigned one of these lines. On top of that, we applied a principle that I call 'my walking is my dancing,' in which walking, the most elementary of human movements, marks the starting point of the choreography. In this case, and to the extent that it was possible, we equated one step to one note."

Additionally, De Keersmaeker worked with principles based on Eastern philosophical concepts of energy to organize the moving architecture of the dancing body. As explained in the *Choreographer's Score* for these two productions, Tao, yin and yang, the concept of qi as life force (together with what it teaches about its transformation), the magic square, the golden ratio, and the Fibonacci sequence all played a role in the way De Keersmaeker organized the three-dimensional performance space.[8] In different ways, they served as the structure and the evolution of the performance (not only temporally, but also with a view to the different constellations of dancers and the order in which they appear) and provided measures for dealing with the body as a collection of parts in very specific proportions.

"Finally, the city's history and the music provided a fruitful framework in which to help the dancers make choices and enrich their movements. This *imaginarium*—made up of stories, images, symbols, and characters drawn from fourteenth-century artistic, scientific, historical, and philosophical sources—added a narrative element to the performance and made everything more colorful." Historic references are also evident in the title, *Cesena*, which refers to the north Italian city that revolted against the ecclesiastical authorities in 1377, resulting in the ruthless murder of its entire population.[9]

A significant difference between *En Atendant* and *Cesena* is the role of the music. "*En Atendant* is built around the song 'En atendant souffrir m'estuet,' which provides the leitmotif of the performance. *Cesena*, conversely, has no recurrent musical theme: the performance consists of ten scenes paired to about as many songs. Björn Schmelzer, the artistic director of the vocal ensemble graindelavoix, came up with a musical dramaturgy inspired by the history of the papal palace in Avignon and the Western Schism."

These two performances also show a different relationship between dancers and musicians. *En Atendant* has eight dancers (three women and five men) backed by a flutist, plus three musicians (including one singer) from the Cour et Coeur ensemble. The singer and dancers operate relatively independently, with the result that there is room for music and silence, for group choreographies, solos, and duets. In *En Atendant* the musicians play the music and the dancers shape the choreography; in *Cesena*, conversely, these boundaries fade, and the singers dance and the dancers sing. Together they form a cast of no fewer than nineteen, all of whom remain onstage for the duration of the performance, like one big ensemble. The composition of the group of dancers and singers changes with every "tableau": it falls apart, gets divided, individuals now split off, and now are pulled toward the shared center, at which moments they resemble a single great moving body. Meanwhile, as opposed to *En Atendant*, which fades into darkness, the light and brilliance continually increase. *Cesena*'s performers and audience leave the night behind and raise their heads to the rising sun.

---

[7] The locations include, among others, the Celestine cloister (where *En Atendant* was performed), the Carmelites cloister, and the Cour d'honneur of the Palace of the Popes (where *Cesena* was performed).
[8] Anne Teresa De Keersmaeker and Bojana Cvejić, *En Atendant & Cesena: A Choreographer's Score* (Brussels: Rosas and Mercatorfonds, 2013).
[9] Cardinal Robert of Geneva, who ordered the slaughter, was later elected to the papacy as Clement VII by the French cardinals, and acted as the first antipope to reside in Avignon and challenge the papacy in Rome. His election marked the start of the Western Schism, the name given to the conflict within the Catholic Church between popes and antipopes. It lasted from 1387 to 1417, and naturally the music of that era often refers to these historic events.

Vortex Temporum and Work/Travail/Arbeid

In 2013, De Keersmaeker created a performance for seven dancers and six musicians called *Vortex Temporum*, after the eponymous composition (1994–96) by Gérard Grisey. "The idea started brewing in 2006, when I attended a concert of the Ictus ensemble, who were playing this key work of spectral music. I was fascinated by the way *Vortex Temporum* visualizes different versions and perceptions of time by the richness of the sound, and the many nuances with which Grisey colored his composition. The music of *Vortex Temporum* does not immediately hold an invitation to dance—as, say, Bach's music does. Even so, I found it rich in movement."

De Keersmaeker's approach to this music was twofold. On the one hand, she fell back to the way she had worked with Béla Bartók's string quartet in 1984, and with Ludwig van Beethoven's *Die Grosse Fuge* in 1992: writing out measure by measure, almost on the principle of "one note, one step." On the other hand, she also returned to the method she had used with Ars subtilior. As she had done while working on *En Atendant* and *Cesena*, De Keersmaeker peeled apart the different voices and linked each dancer individually to a single instrument. The six musicians (flute, clarinet, piano, cello, violin, and viola) each paired up with a dancer, or in the case of the piano, with two dancers. Starting from one basic phrase, directed toward the points of the magic square, each dancer constructed his or her own basic phrase, which was then tuned as much as possible to the lines of his or her instrument. In addition, the physical movements exerted by the musicians in the act of playing their instruments were a direct source of inspiration for the development of the movement vocabulary. Indeed, the musicians themselves are included in the choreography: onstage with the dancers, they are integrally part of the performance.

In its final shape, *Vortex Temporum* is divided into four chapters. In the first, music and dance are separated: the musicians play alone, eventually disappearing to make room for the dancers, who, arranged in a half circle, dance in silence, barely moving from the spot. One dancer stays behind and enters into an intense dialogue with the piano. What follows is a spirited and intriguing choreography of dancers and musicians: they move through the space, running and walking, following a circle that is forever shifting to the sliding tones of the music. Finally, the musicians retreat to the back and the choreography, assuming the shape of a vortex, seizes control of the stage.

During the rehearsal process for *Vortex Temporum*, De Keersmaeker was contacted by the artistic director, Dirk Snauwaert, and senior curator, Elena Filipovic, at WIELS, a center for contemporary art in Brussels. They invited her to imagine a performance in the form of an exhibition and an exhibition in the form of a performance. "The thought process about the exhibition soon made its way into the creation process of *Vortex Temporum*. Because we were pulling that layered music apart voice by voice, we arrived at a kind of drawn-out, 'diluted' time. That form of time seemed much more suitable for a museum concept than the 'condensed' time of a performance in the 'black box.'" Temporally and spatially, *Vortex Temporum* lends itself well to the atypical setting—for dance—of a gallery space. The organization of movement following ground patterns based on circles and spirals makes the work less bound to the frontal perspective of the theater, and ideal for a space in which the audience is free to roam.

The exhibition was on "display" at WIELS for nine weeks. Open to the public for seven hours a day, the show-performance followed not a seven-hour but a nine-hour cycle that De Keersmaeker developed for the occasion. As a result, people could come at the same time each day and see something different. Additionally, the composition of the group of performers changed every hour. "The music was opened up, as it were. The various individual lines of the musicians, linked to a dancer, were shown separately from each other, both as solos and in combinations. This separation of voices was characteristic of and crucial to the working process of *Vortex Temporum*, and yet it could not be shown in the final performance, in which all the voices come back together and everything is condensed anew." Hence the project's title, *Work/Travail/Arbeid*: a dissection of De Keersmaeker's working process.

Because the perspective in the exhibition space is not exclusively frontal, as it is in the "black box" of the theater, the distance between the stage and the audience vanishes. What emerges in the "white cube" is an opportunity to move among the dancers, to see the choreography from all angles, to be as close to it or as far away from it as one wishes. The audience also comes and goes as it pleases because, unlike with a conventional performance, there is no real beginning or end. In other words, the "white cube" offers the audience liberties rarely, if ever, offered by the "black box" of the theater. Performers and audiences alike found themselves reconsidering their relationship. Dancers had to find ways to deal with visitors crossing their paths or joining in the dance; visitors had to decide for themselves what perspective they liked best, and how to relate to the dance that they shared the space with.

After its nine weeks at WIELS in 2015, *Work/Travail/Arbeid* enjoyed shorter stints at the Centre Pompidou in Paris, Tate Modern in London, the Museum of Modern Art in New York, MUDAM in Luxembourg, and the Volksbühne in Berlin.

Golden Hours (As you like it) and Die Weise von Liebe und Tod des Cornets Christoph Rilke

Golden Hours (As you like it), which premiered in January 2015, was a performance inspired by the 1975 album *Another Green World* by ambient music pioneer Brian Eno. "People's most direct relationship with music is often through pop music. The combination of music with the poetic quality of lyrics, the theatrical aspect of performance, and, generally speaking, the pulse of pop is what makes this sort of music very danceable." De Keersmaeker explains that she chose the song "Golden Hours" as the opening piece and title of the performance because she has a soft spot for its simultaneously light, humorous, and melancholy character, and for Eno's quirky sound experiments. More importantly, though, the lyrics are about the perception of time, a persistent theme for De Keersmaeker.[10] She incorporated the ideas of the lyrics into the choreography, and the song plays on a loop at the start of the performance, which opens with the entire dance group walking, at an extremely slow pace, toward the audience and then away from it. "This is where the principle that my walking is my dancing is put on display in its purest form. The steady progress refers to fixed, regular, chronometric time. After the introduction, the dancers break away from this continuity in ways that are much more kinetically expressive, and that change the perception of time."

It is at this point that William Shakespeare's *As You Like It* starts. This play follows the musical prologue, and is the subtext of the choreography. De Keersmaeker felt that Eno's "Golden Hours" dovetails with a number of key elements of *As You Like It*: the notion of time, play with gender, play with language. She also saw a connection to her environmental concerns. "The Arden woods represent a harmonious existence in balance with nature. Shakespeare juxtaposes that to the urbane court weighed down by humankind's relentless ambition to dominate nature and, in so doing, destroy it." But the dancers don't recite the text of the play; apart from the musical intermezzos, the performance takes place in silence. "In a sense, I used Shakespeare's text in the same way I normally approach music: as the origin or instigator of movement. With *As You Like It*, I wanted to further examine the principle that my walking is my dancing, hence the choice of a literary genre that is necessarily not intended to be read in silence, but to be enunciated." De Keersmaeker was guided by several questions: "How can a thought, intention, image, or idea that is usually uttered via the spoken word, generate movement? How do we create meaning and express what we want to communicate through movement?"

Die Weise von Liebe und Tod des Cornets Christoph Rilke (2015) is based on the eponymous work by Rainer Maria Rilke from 1899, and is likewise a performance with a text at its foundation—not a play this time, but a poetic, mysterious tale about a young soldier, a standard-bearer, who goes to war and is killed on the battlefield after an unexpected night of passion. This time the text *is* declaimed, by De Keersmaeker herself. As she delivers and enacts the words, the text is projected on a large screen behind her. With this piece, De Keersmaeker returned not only to a text that she had known and cherished for twenty-five years, but also to a more recent interest in the relationship between breathing and voice. "If walking is an elementary human movement, then breathing is even more vitally so, really. It is a movement that, like every other manifestation of energy, according to Eastern philosophies, opens and then closes again. Breathing gives life to the voice and, in so doing, literally brings out what lives inside. Your voice is unique, inextricably linked to your identity as an individual."

Spurred on by that idea, De Keersmaeker found the perfect accompanying music in Salvatore Sciarrino's *Opera per flauto*. That composition, rather than being grafted onto a melody, is grafted onto the physical aspect of breathing in and blowing out in order to produce sound. It conjures an ominous and tense atmosphere that seems to be hinting at the hardships, and ultimate fate, that await the young Cornet. The flutist Chryssi Dimitriou plays alone, unaccompanied by dance. The dance, in a prologue performed by Michaël Pomero, precedes the music, after which a part of the text is projected. The opening, in sum, is a simple exposition of the three elements that bring this performance together: dance, sound/breath/voice, and text. Then it's Dimitriou's turn, playing alone and, when she is finished, Pomero returns, accompanied by De Keersmaeker. Together they continue drawing the pattern that Pomero had already started tracing on the clay floor, in a choreography in which they unmistakably interact, though without ever touching.

They transition to the text and, at one point, De Keersmaeker finds herself alone onstage. She embodies Rilke's work in both dance and voice. "I wanted to explore how word and movement can affect each other but also how they can retain their identities in the process. The goal was to tune the internal logic of both dance and text in such a way that they add to and cultivate each other." The end of the performance, the death of the Cornet, finds De Keersmaeker standing in a pool of dark-red light. And with the transition from the dramatic death of the son to the terse notification of his death to the mother, the scene again illuminates in white light. Although clear-cut, the ending feels open, like a question mark that, in the current atmosphere of war and violence, clings forebodingly to the audience.

Cosi fan tutte

"At that point in my career, it was most definitely the greatest challenge I had ever accepted," De Keersmaeker says about her direction of and choreography to Wolfgang Amadeus Mozart's *Così fan tutte*, a work that sits somewhere between *opera buffa* and *opera seria*. Its story goes as follows: The enlightened thinker Don Alfonso, eager to prove that

---

10 A sample of the lyrics: "The passage of time is flicking dimly up on the screen . . . How can moments go so slow / Several times / I've seen the evening slide away / Watching the signs / Taking over from the fading day."

reason is life's only true guiding principle, makes a bet with two young soldiers, Guglielmo and Ferrando. Aided by the clever and emancipated maid Despina, Don Alfonso comes up with a test of love: the two men are to disguise themselves as Albanians and attempt to seduce one another's fiancées, thus testing their faithfulness. The fiancées, Fiordiligi and Dorabella, both yield to their seducers, hence the title: *così fan tutte* ("that is what all women do").

It is not too surprising that the opera has come to be regarded as sexist and misogynistic. But De Keersmaeker has a more nuanced take on it: "*Così fan tutte* has a musical-dramaturgical logic that creates a wonderfully cultivated tension between text and music, one that goes far beyond sheer anecdote. For instance, Don Alfonso's conclusion in the finale is not given momentum by the music; quite the contrary. Conversely, the music of the arias sung by the women suggests that more profound emotions and considerations are at play within them than are evident at first sight—emotions and considerations that place them above the men on those fronts. And still, it does turn out that the men's freedom, granted because of their disguises, makes their own loyalty and dedication less evident and confronts them with confusing choices."

Above all, De Keersmaeker feels that Mozart's opera is a reflection on loss, parting, and longing. "In spite of its comical character, the music gives *Così fan tutte* a melancholic undertone, one that elevates it to a more abstract—almost existential, you could say—level of deeply human questions and experiences that exceed the plot of the opera. I tried to use the dance in such a way that it aligns with the tension between text and music." The music comments on the libretto, and De Keersmaeker, in much the same way, considered the choreography as a complementary, autonomous voice (indeed, a visible voice) that adds something that is impossible—or at least much more difficult—for text and sound to convey. Whereas in the past she had associated dancers to instruments, in *Così fan tutte* she links them to singers.

Under her direction, the opera opens with all twelve performers arranged in a half circle. The image conveys a state of rest, harmony, and balance from which the story is allowed to develop. Dancers and singers, all dressed in black, execute the same opening phrase, thus eliminating the distinction in their roles. As the opera progresses, their connection manifests itself in different ways: sometimes the movements are grafted directly onto the music, sometimes they emphasize an aspect of the text, sometimes they create enough distance from music and text to allow the dance to add a layer of meaning of its own. The minimalist scenography of Jan Versweyveld, stripped as it is of all unnecessary ballast, brings this interaction to the fore. The light, clear and pure at the beginning, underlines the important moments by switching to intense colors as the experiment unfolds. The colors guide the idea of transformation as if it were an alchemical process. And not a reversible one: even though order is ostensibly reestablished at the end of the opera, in reality there is no turning back the clock, and what was will never return, can never be undone.

Partita 2 and *Mitten wir im Leben sind/Bach6Cellosuiten*

A central characteristic of De Keersmaeker's oeuvre is the fact that it alternates between work for larger groups, and performances for smaller casts in which she herself dances. *Partita 2* and *Mitten wir im Leben sind/Bach6Cellosuiten* fall into the latter category. These creations both use Bach's music, specifically pieces for a solo instrument (violin and cello, respectively), and the music is played live onstage.

De Keersmaeker underlines her love for Bach: "His work is truly unique in the history of Western music. What I find fascinating about his compositions is the masterful fusion of the concrete and the abstract, a particular, sensitive layering of formalism and structure and mathematical patterns with deeply human, emotional, and spiritual dimensions." Moreover, the danceable character of the violin partitas and the Cello Suites are particularly inviting to a choreographer.[11] "Although writing choreographies to such masterpieces is a great challenge, and one that I approached with some reticence. It was a quest for *how* to write, how to find a choreographic answer to that music."

In the case of *Partita 2* (2013), she embarked on this quest with French choreographer and dancer Boris Charmatz and violinist Amandine Beyer. Beyer rendered Bach's second partita and provided the dancers with an analysis of the music during rehearsals. The process included distilling a bass line, which De Keersmaeker then subjected to the "my walking is my dancing" principle. To take the choreography further, she attuned that principle to the different parts of the partita. "In the *allemande*, the dancing is walking, which turns into running in the *courante*; the *sarabande* reveals long and diagonal lines, and the relentless *chaconne* propels the dancers forward in concentric circles."

De Keersmaeker distinguishes two lines in the way she and Charmatz approached the partita: "On the one hand, we wanted to uncover the structure of the partita, its underlying basic layer, as this would allow us to stay close to the music. On the other hand, there was an impulsive, corporeal reaction to the music, the process of being absorbed by it, the pleasure of dancing." These dimensions are explored during the performance by separating

---

[11] In both cases, the form and structure are derived from folk dances. The music that originally accompanied these dances eventually divested itself of its accompanying function, and came to exist as a musical genre in its own right.

them. In the first part, the violinist plays in total darkness, which allows for the purest form of listening, since there is not the slightest extrinsic stimulus to distract. After that, we see the music in the dance, but we no longer hear it. Charmatz and De Keersmaeker dance in silence. The audience must avail themselves of their memory and of the choreography to add music to the experience. Following this twofold "exposition" (a process De Keersmaeker also used in *Vortex Temporum*), music and dance come together. Michel François's scenography gives the piece a plain setting: the prologue in the dark is followed by light dropping from a spotlight onto the scene, as if through a crack. The light is reminiscent of the line that shifts, slowly, across the face of a sundial as it marks the course of a day.

Four years later, in 2017, De Keersmaeker developed a choreography to Bach's Cello Suites. Revisiting Bach seems to have become more self-evident to her over the years. "Every time you analyze his work, his genius unfolds a little more, so that all you want to do is take your understanding to the next level." The choice of Bach's Cello Suites was also inspired by De Keersmaeker's encounter with the French cellist Jean-Guihen Queyras. As they discussed the idea of developing a work together, they quickly settled on the Cello Suites for the music. In the performance, each of the first four suites is linked to a different dancer. The dancer enters into a dialogue with Queyras, who plays in a different spot on the stage. "The right choice was very important in that. Each of the suites has a separate and specific 'color,' a base tone, and it was a matter of combining them with the personalities of the dancers in such a way that they would amplify each other." De Keersmaeker herself is less a protagonist than a master of ceremonies. She announces the suites with a gesture of her hand; with every dancer, she marks the floor pattern with colored tape; during the allemande, present in every suite, she joins the dancer and offers him or her the same phrase. As a result of their interaction, however, that phrase always turns out differently. The fifth and darkest suite, which Queyras plays without a dancer, marks a turning point, an unexpected question mark at the end of a sentence that moves into somber, contemplative territory. The sixth suite answers the fifth in the affirmative with a shift from the minor key to a major key, triumphant and festive, like a resurrection after a death. The sixth is the time for a group choreography, with all five dancers and De Keersmaeker onstage.

In a sense, De Keersmaeker built on her experience with *Partita 2* for this choreography. The bass line,[12] then as here, was an important factor, and, as with *Partita 2*, she was inspired by the popular dances on which the various suites were based. As such, the dance in the *courantes* is based on running, in the *sarabandes* on the slow tempo, and whirling movements express the energy of the *gigues*. That said, there is also a significant difference with *Partita 2*. "My walking is my dancing," the underlying principle of that choreography, is mostly a two-dimensional, horizontal movement. It is about occupying space by displacing weight. "I have since come to use a three-dimensional system, based on the horizontal and the vertical axes. Walking is the most elementary human movement, after breathing. And in walking, humankind distinguishes itself through the verticality of the spine. The horizontal axis is the social axis on which you reach out to others. It connects us to our fellow human beings. The vertical axis represents our relationship with the higher, spiritual dimension of existence. Much of our body language has to do with this verticality. Just consider what a straight back represents compared to a bent, closed posture."

By converging a formal principle with content that is emotionally or associatively charged, the dance reflects what happens in the music, and also provides it with an answer. De Keersmaeker will continue down this path of exploration into her next creation, again to music by Bach: in September 2018, her choreography to the Brandenburg Concertos is scheduled to premiere at the Volksbühne in Berlin.

Ashes to Ashes and, in between, Life

Alongside the new productions of the past ten years, Rosas has also been committed to revisiting various pieces of the repertoire, including *Rosas danst Rosas* (1983), *Achterland* (1990), *Verklärte Nacht* (1995), *Drumming* (1998), *Rain* (2001), *A Love Supreme* (2005), and *Zeitung* (2008). De Keersmaeker approached these "revivals" in different ways: sometimes the choreography remained intact, sometimes it underwent a thorough reworking, and sometimes it confronted the work of a related choreographer. Documenting the retakes—whether through dramaturgy, film, or photography—is as crucial as it is for the original performances. New performers add new elements and bring new qualities to the fore. "There is this tension between the fixed work and the fact that it always needs to be embodied again. The work is never mine alone. New dancers, in their turn, take it out of my hands and add something that I had not expected, and that I could not have given to the piece in the first place. I don't consider dance hermetically sealed, but a living organism in constant flux."

This makes it sound as though she is at peace with her medium's elusive character. Has she

---

[12] In keeping with the canon of baroque music, Bach never writes a note for a solo instrument that cannot be inscribed into the spirit of the figured harmony, which necessarily presupposes a bass voice, whether it is played or not, as the support for every possible melody. Starting with Beyer, and then more systematically with Queyras, De Keersmaeker has tracked the "invisible voice" of the bass, deducing it from an analysis of the melody, much in the same way as someone studies a painting to find its hidden diagonal lines.

ever envied artists who, working in other disciplines, produce fixed objects? "To me, dance celebrates human existence in all its ephemerality," she answers. "You have no choice but to accept that it disappears. It is precisely for this reason that I believe that dance is *the* most contemporary art. Consequently, the tension between the past, the present, and the future is considerable. You dance with your history in your body, with your experience of the now and looking to the future." As a corporeal art, the fate of dance is closely connected to that of humankind: ashes to ashes, dust to dust.

But between the ashes, there is life. And dance, for De Keersmaeker, is a way to relate, at once individually and collectively, to the world during that life. She underlines the importance of dance as an inter-human experience, and not just between the dancers, but also between the dancers and the audience. According to De Keersmaeker, that is the reason why, from the dawn of time, humans have danced to mark important occasions: to celebrate, to mourn. She raises this ritual aspect of dance when asked: Why the performing arts? What drives her as a choreographer and dancer to continue going for the stage? "It is in our nature to long for ritual, for shared experiences with other people in the same time and space. That is part of our quest for meaning. I like that a relatively simple event can have such a great intensity, can carry within itself so many possibilities."

And, finally, she looks ahead, to the future. "I am very preoccupied with the question of what I want to prioritize in the years to come," she admits. "Besides," she concludes, laughing, "there is still so much Bach."

Floor Keersmaekers

Keeping Still – Part 1 2007

Concept
Anne Teresa De Keersmaeker, Ann Veronica Janssens
In collaboration with
Robert Steijn
Dramaturgy
Claire Diez
Choreography
Anne Teresa De Keersmaeker in collaboration with David Hernandez
Music
Das Lied von der Erde (Der Abschied), Gustav Mahler, voice Kathleen Ferrier, the Wiener Philharmoniker conducted by Bruno Walter (1952)
Vocal coach
Lucy Grauman
Text
The Earth Charter, www.earthcharter.org
Voices
Kes Bakker, Anna Franziska Jäger, Anne Teresa De Keersmaeker
Artistic assistant
Anne Van Aerschot
Production
Rosas, La Monnaie / De Munt (Brussels)
Coproduction
Kunstenfestivaldesarts (Brussels)
Premiere
22.05.2007, Rosas Performance Space, Kunstenfestivaldesarts—Brussels

Pictures
Herman Sorgeloos

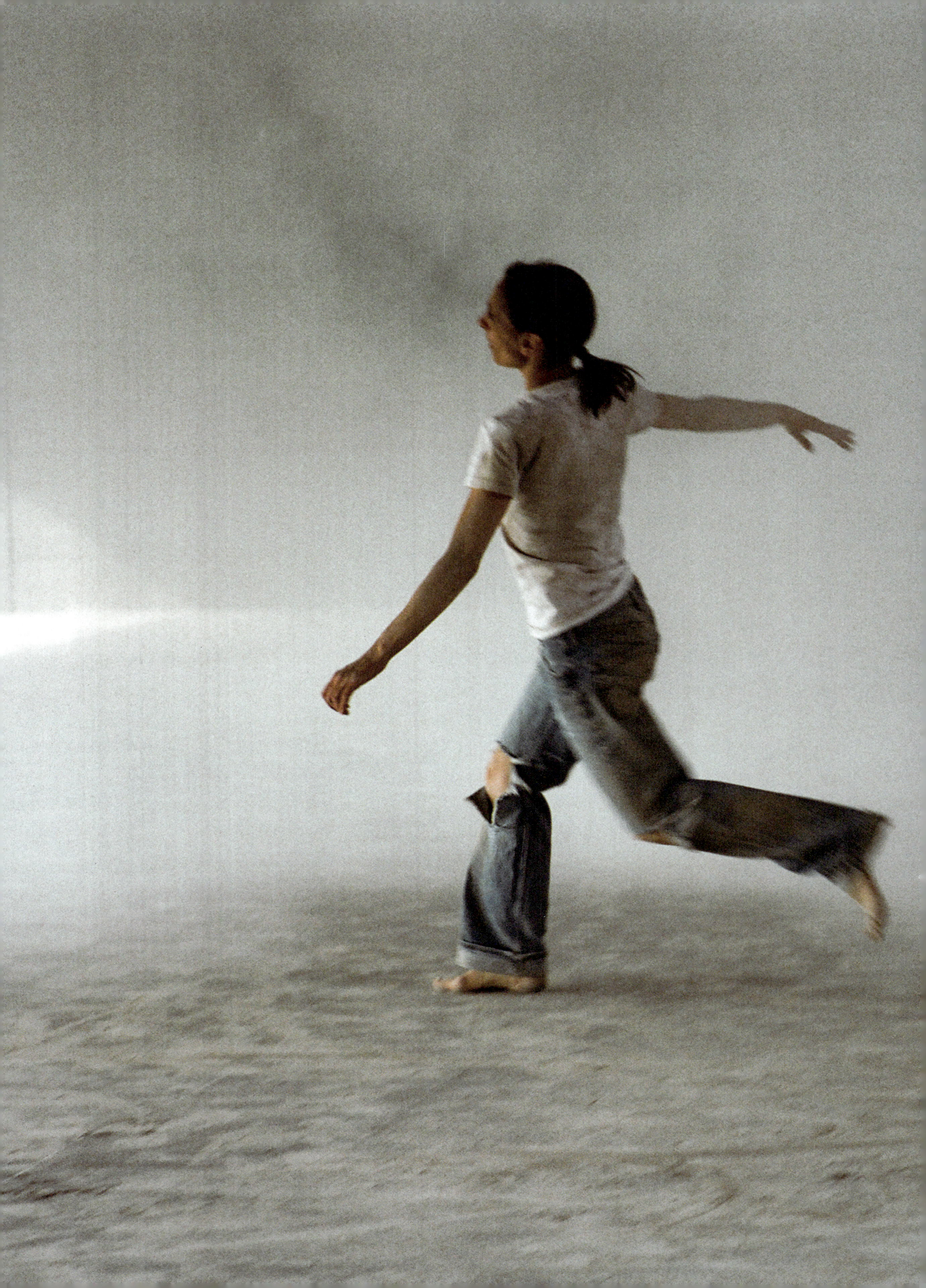

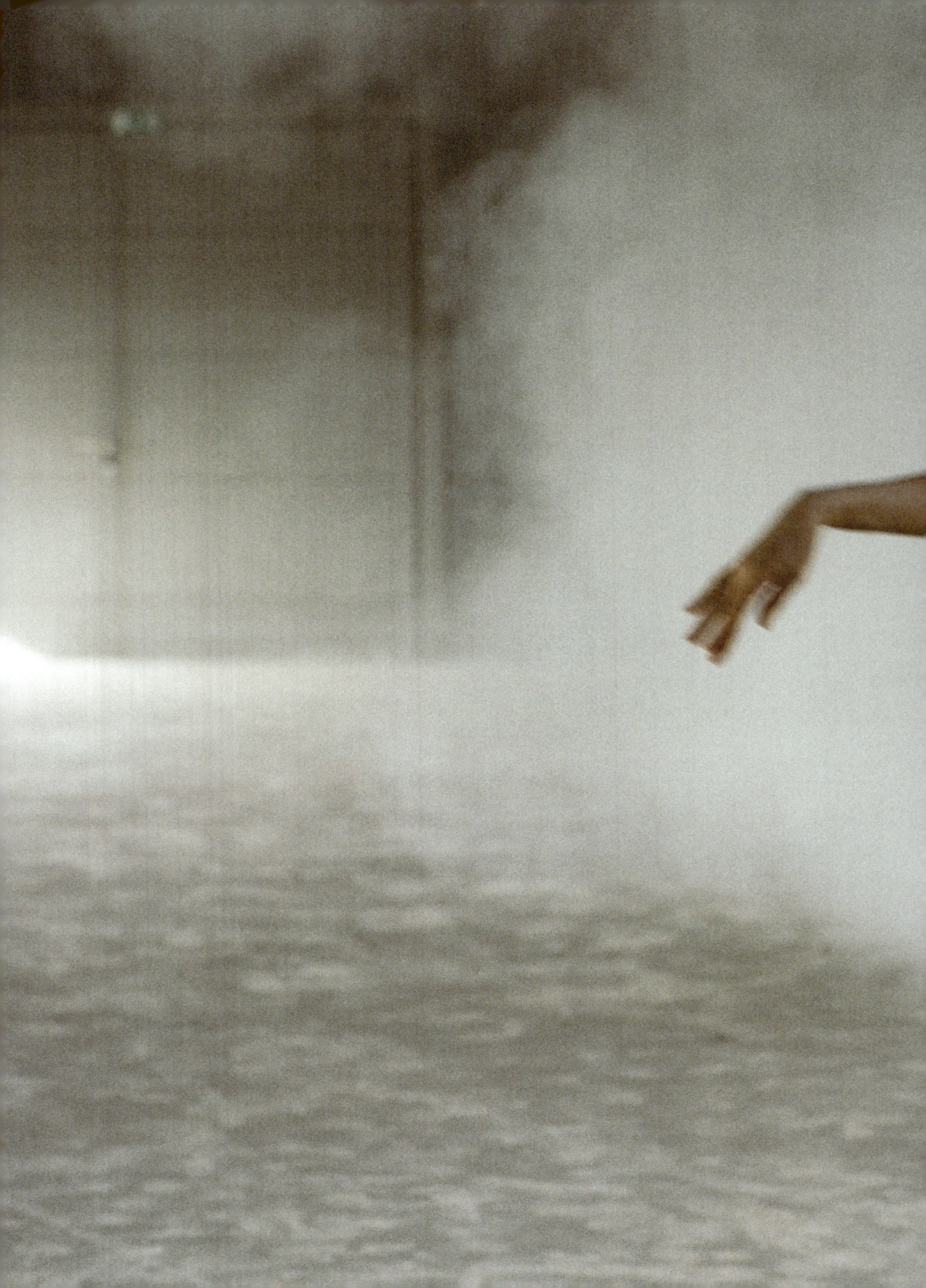

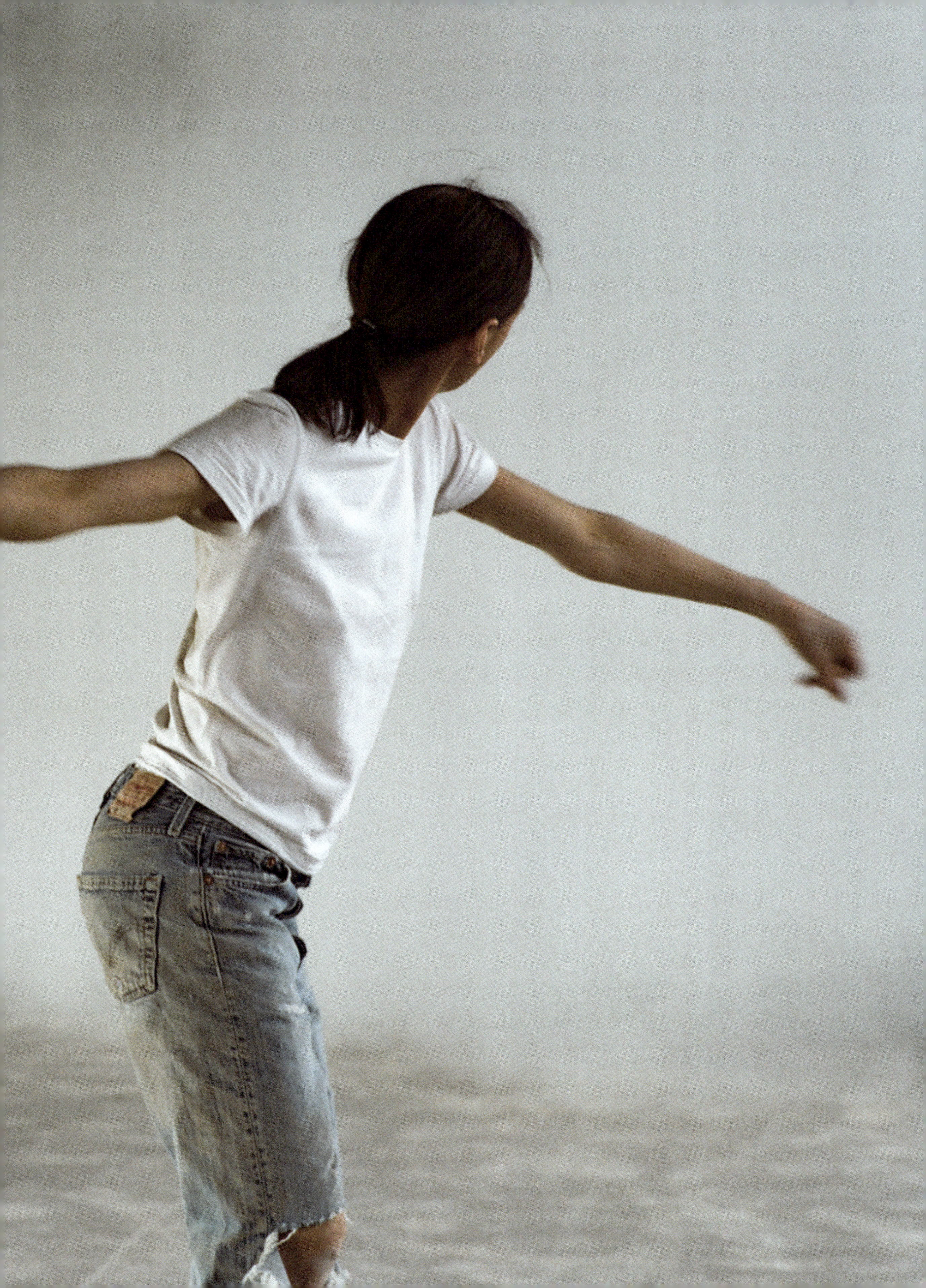

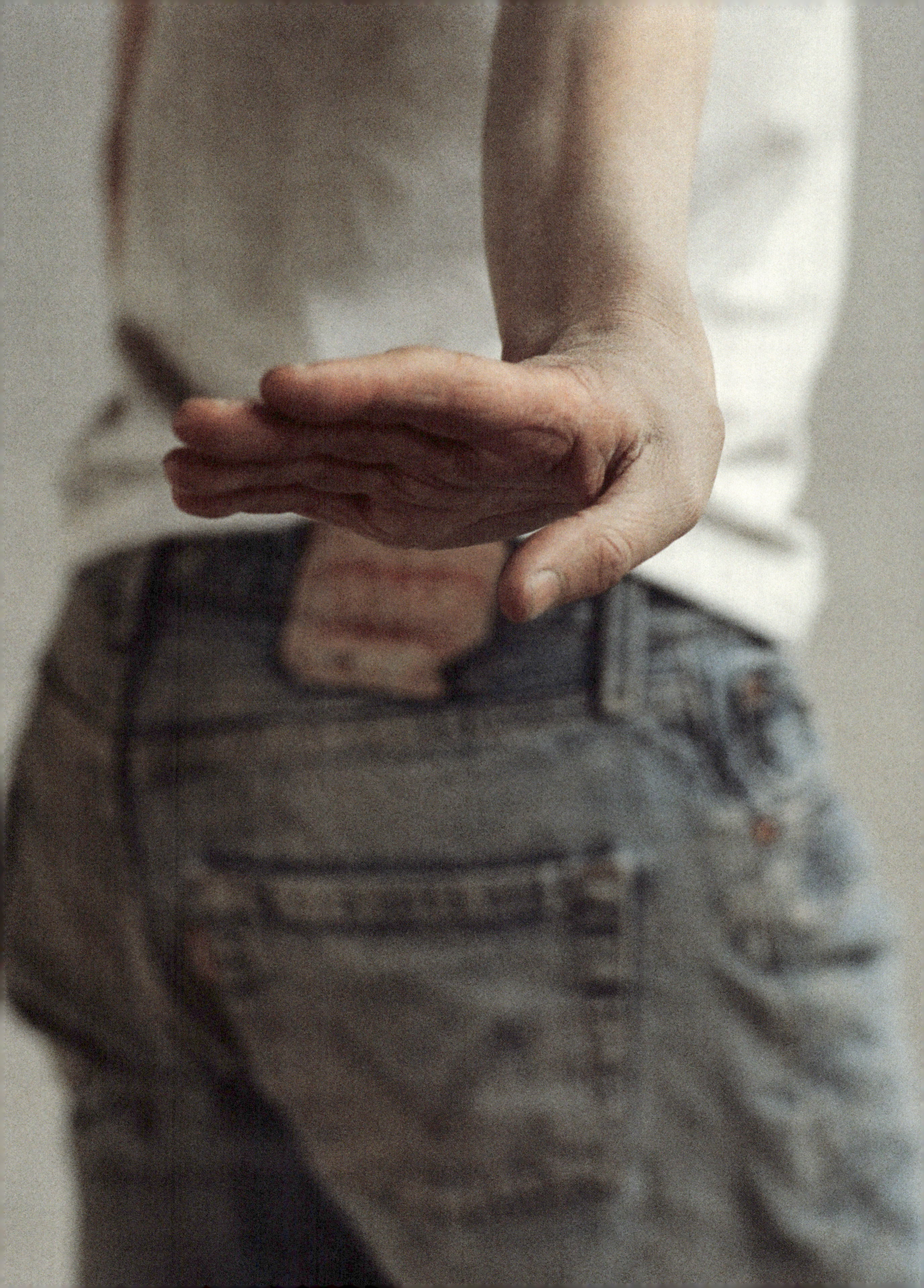

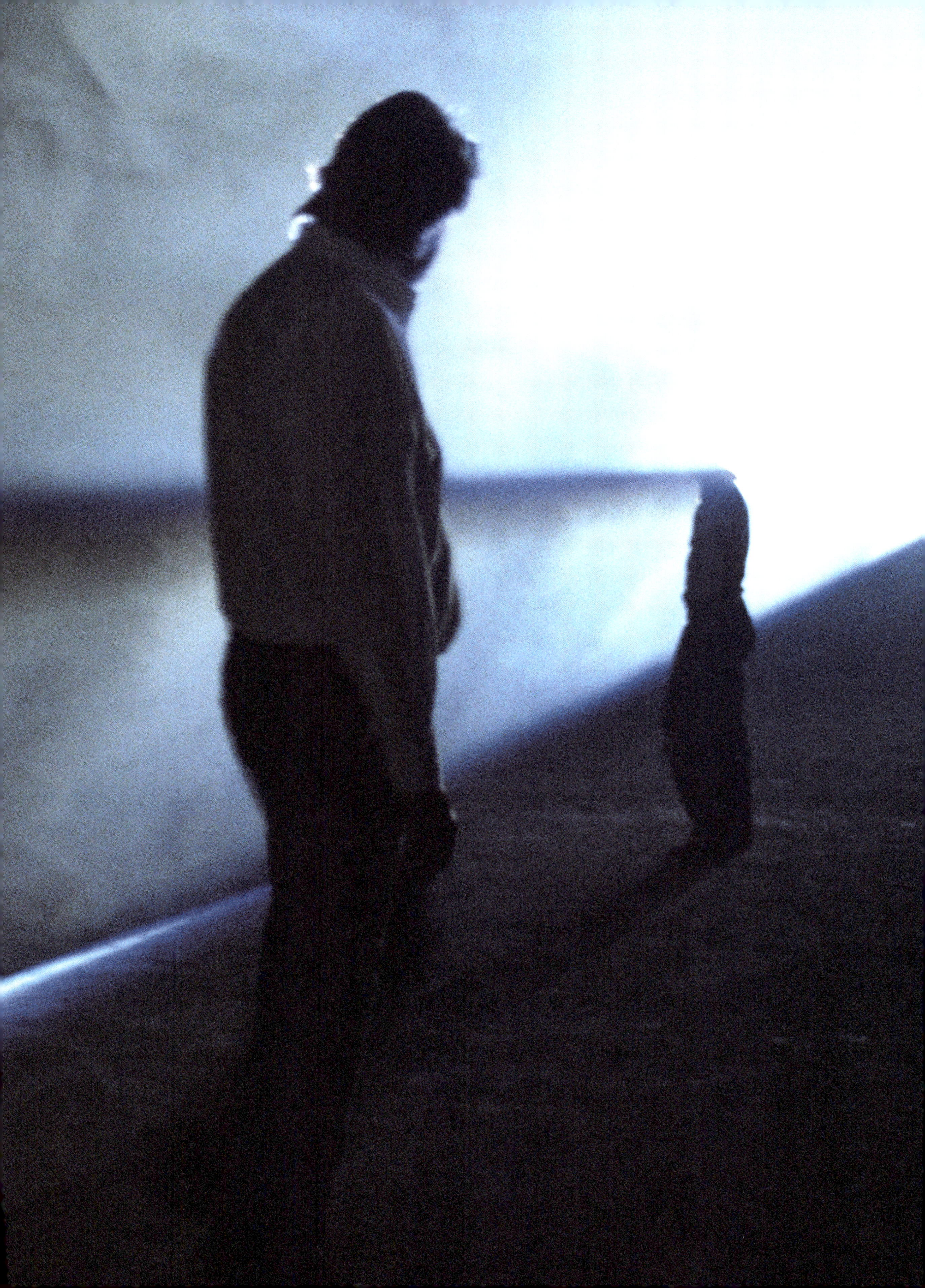

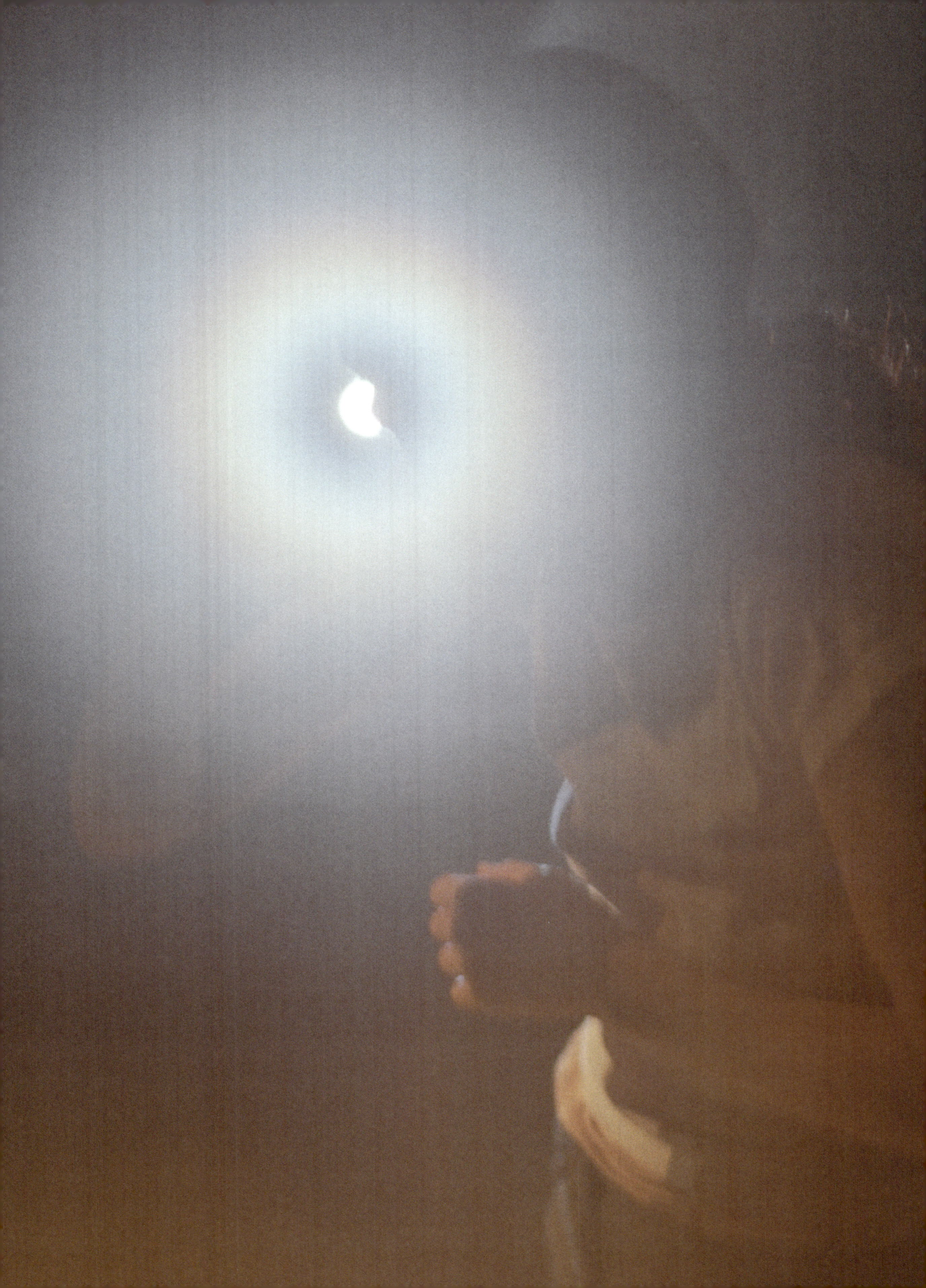

Zeitung 2008

Concept
Anne Teresa De Keersmaeker, Alain Franco
Choreography
Anne Teresa De Keersmaeker
Created with and danced by
Boštjan Antončič, Tale Dolven, Fumiyo Ikeda, Cynthia Loemij, Mark Lorimer, Moya Michael, Elizaveta Penkova, Igor Shyshko, Sandy Williams, Sue-Yeon Youn
Music
Johann Sebastian Bach, Arnold Schönberg, Anton Webern
Piano
Alain Franco
Dance vocabulary in collaboration with
David Hernandez
Set and lighting design
Jan Joris Lamers
Costumes
Anne-Catherine Kunz
Artistic assistant
Anne Van Aerschot
Sound
Alexandre Fostier
Production
Rosas
Coproduction
La Monnaie / De Munt (Brussels), Théâtre de la Ville (Paris), MC2 (Grenoble)
Premiere
11.01.2008, Théâtre de la Ville—Paris

Pictures
Herman Sorgeloos

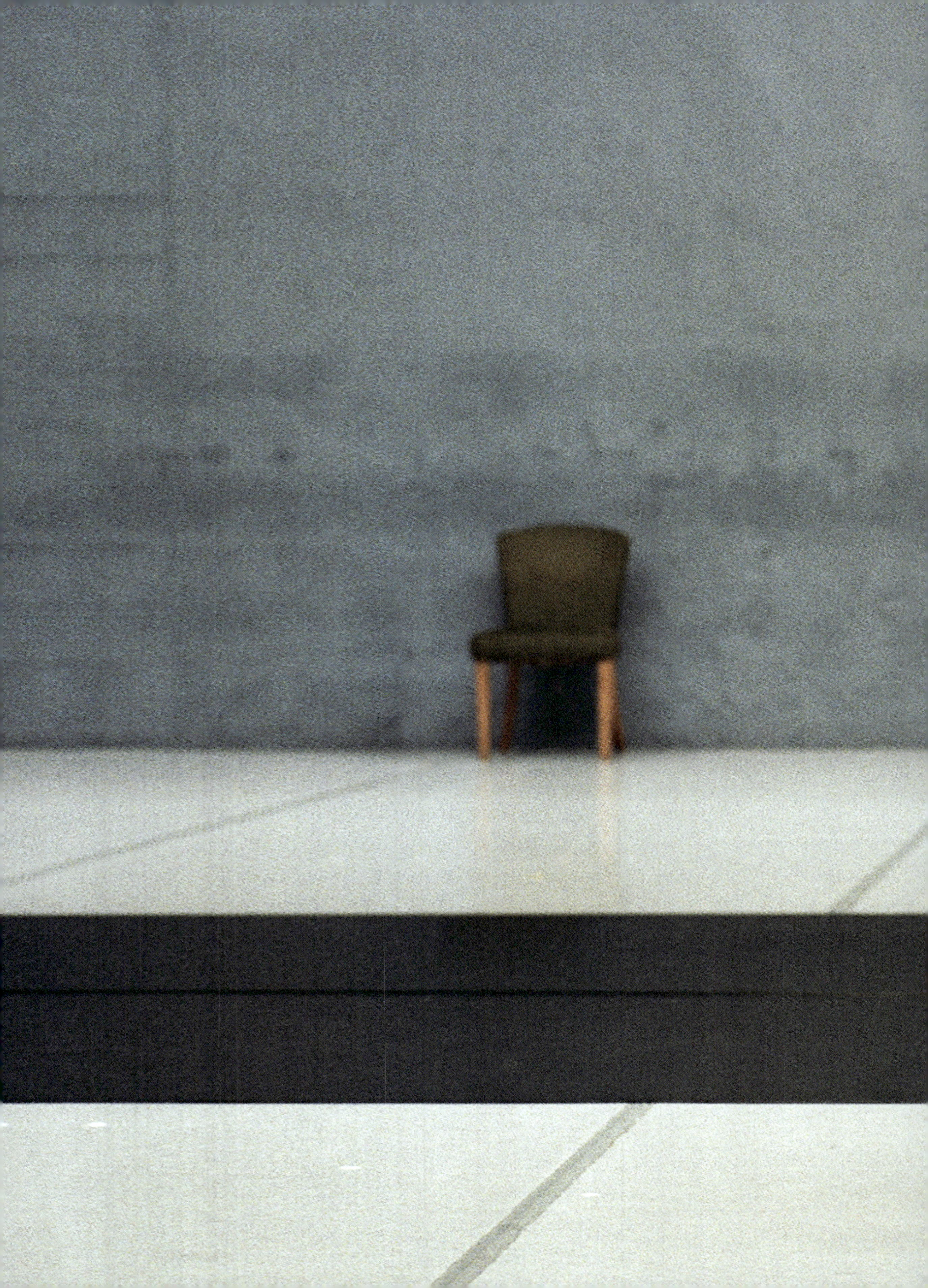

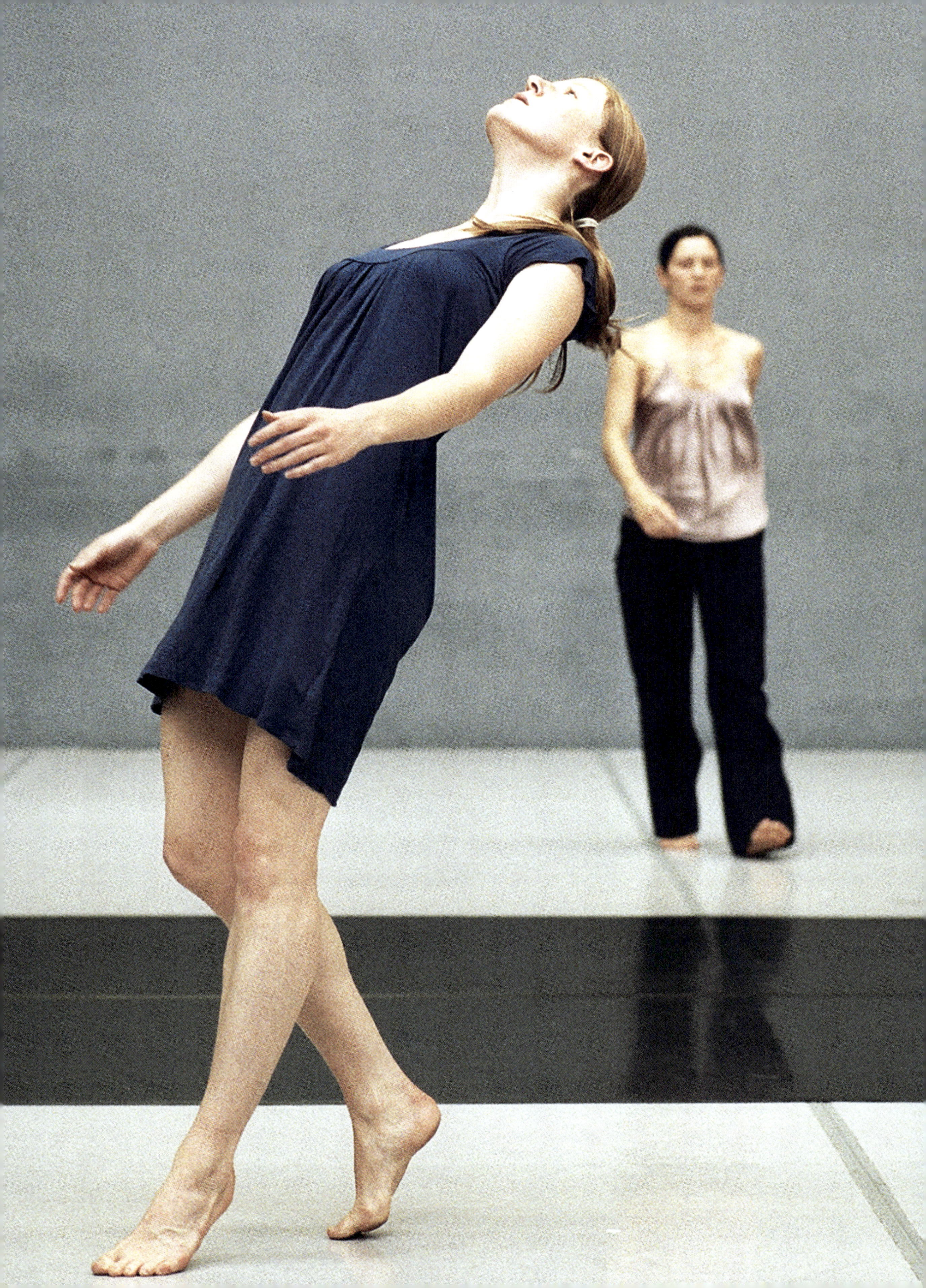

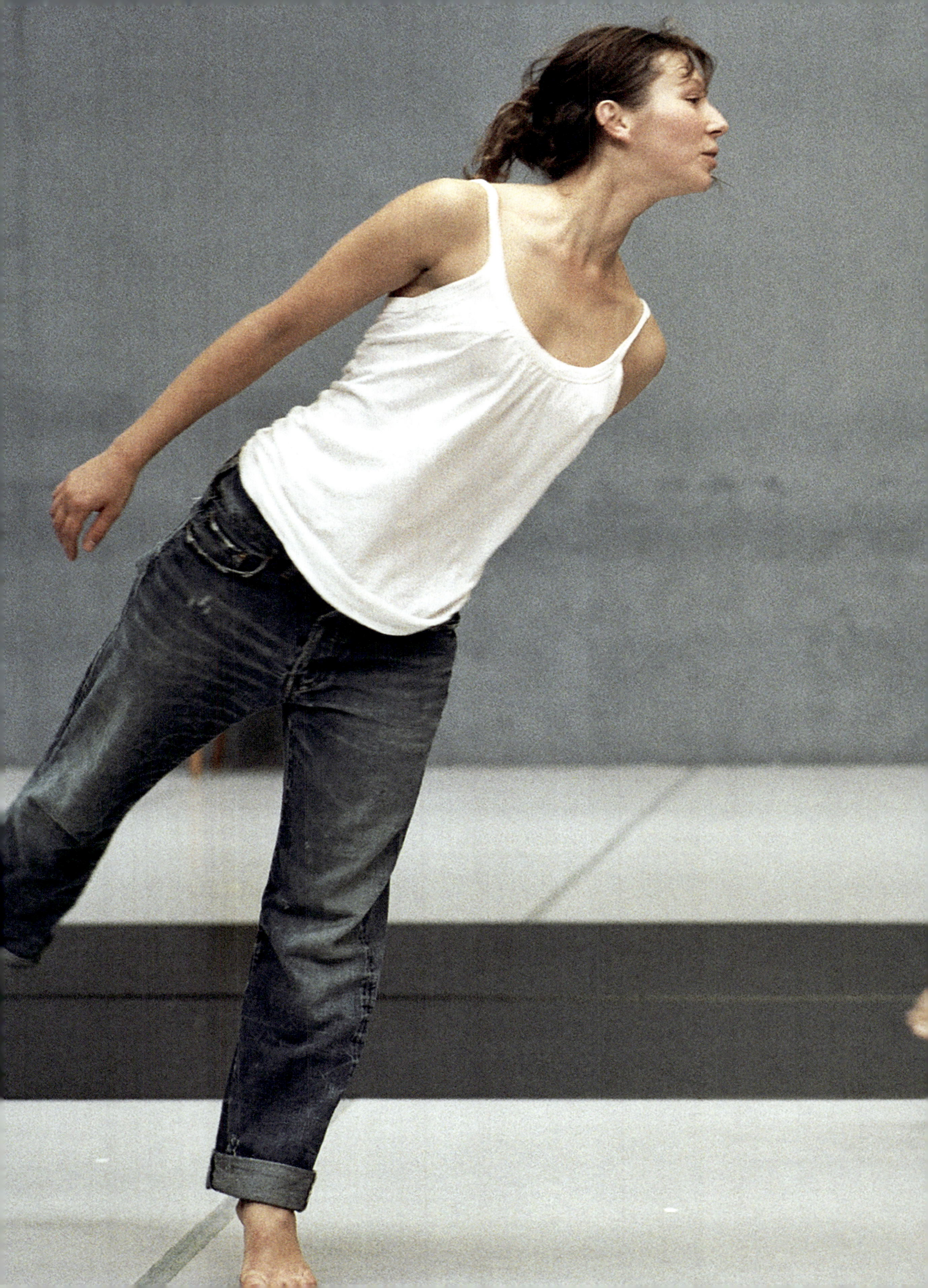

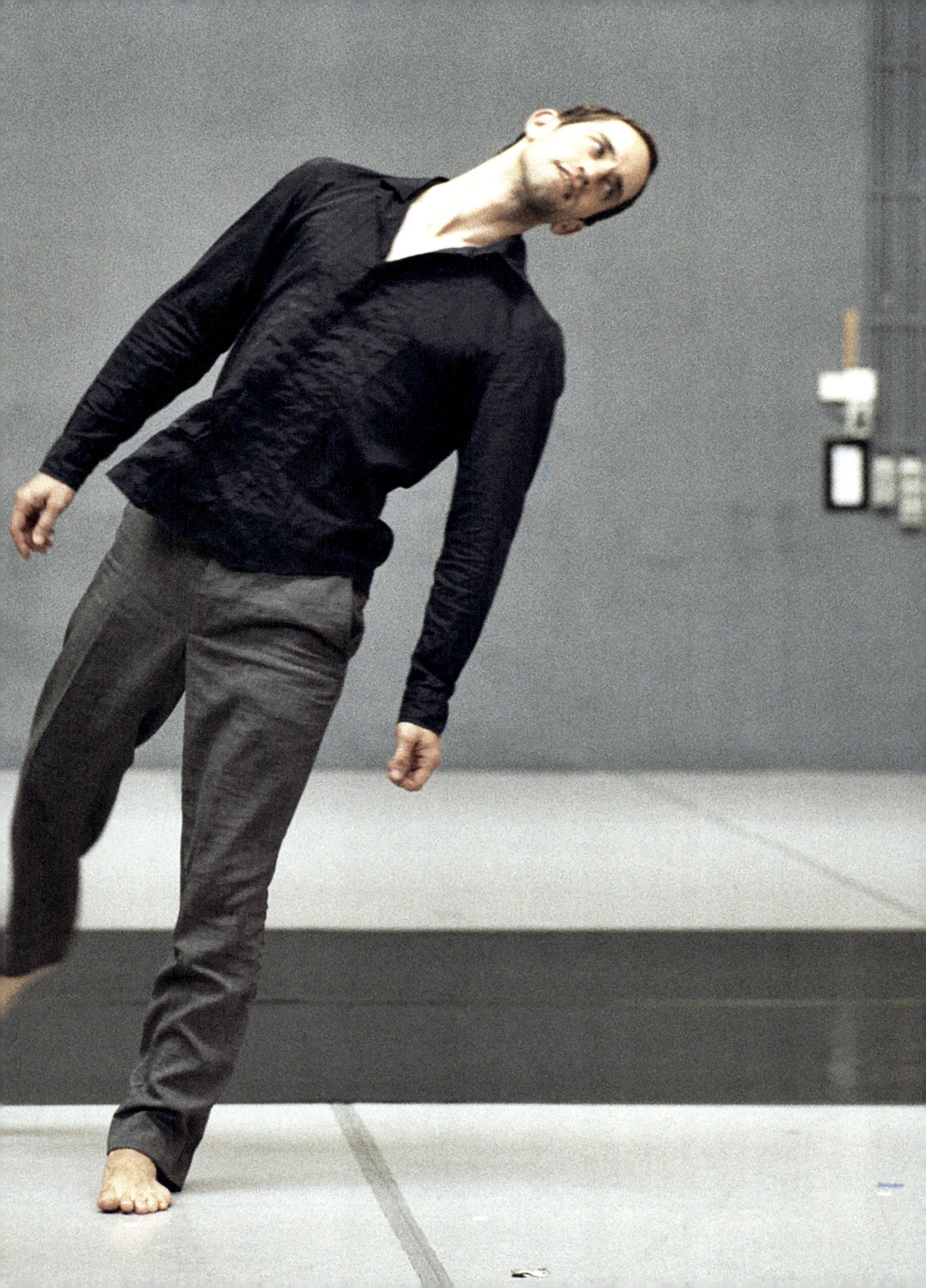

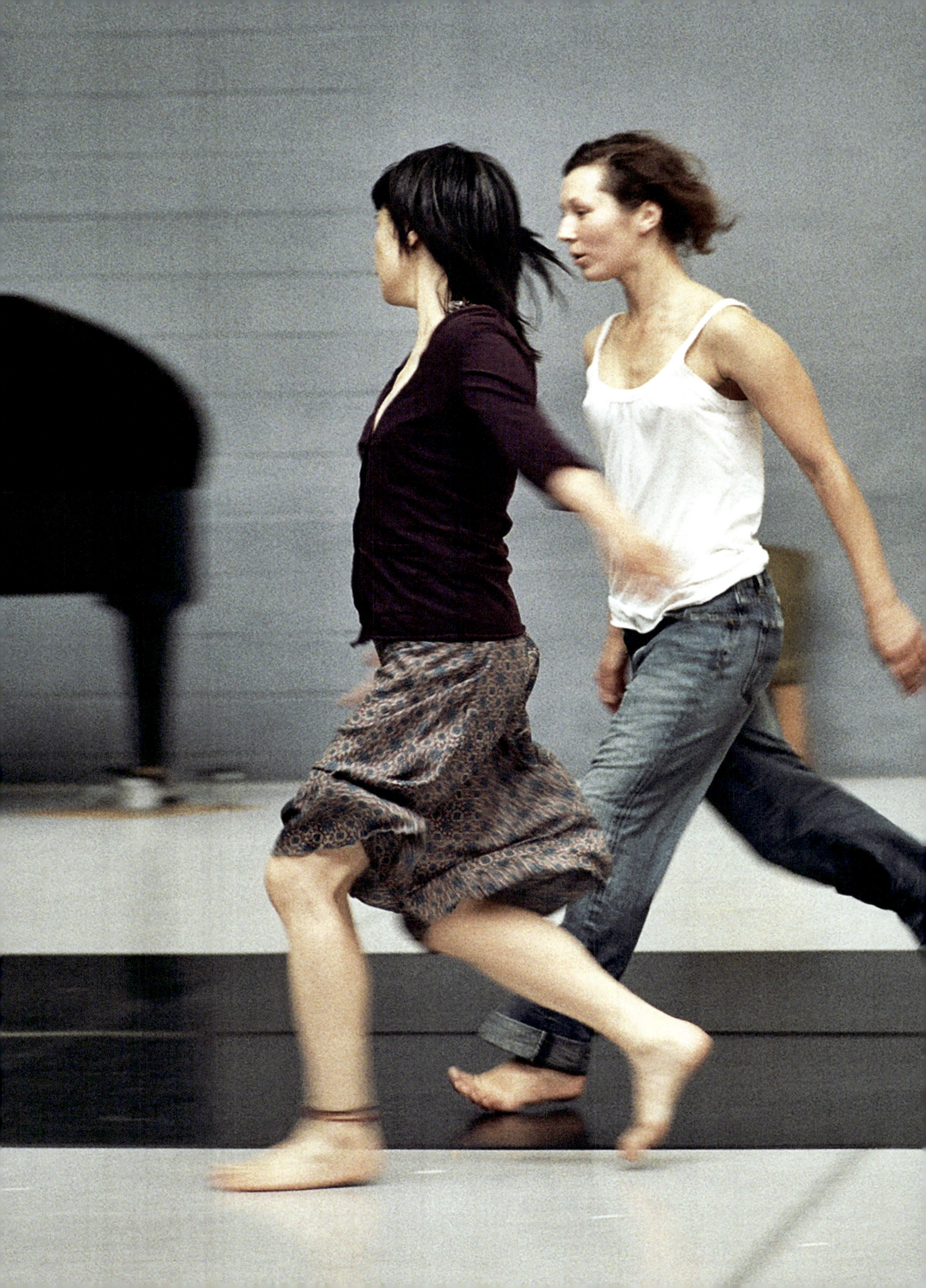

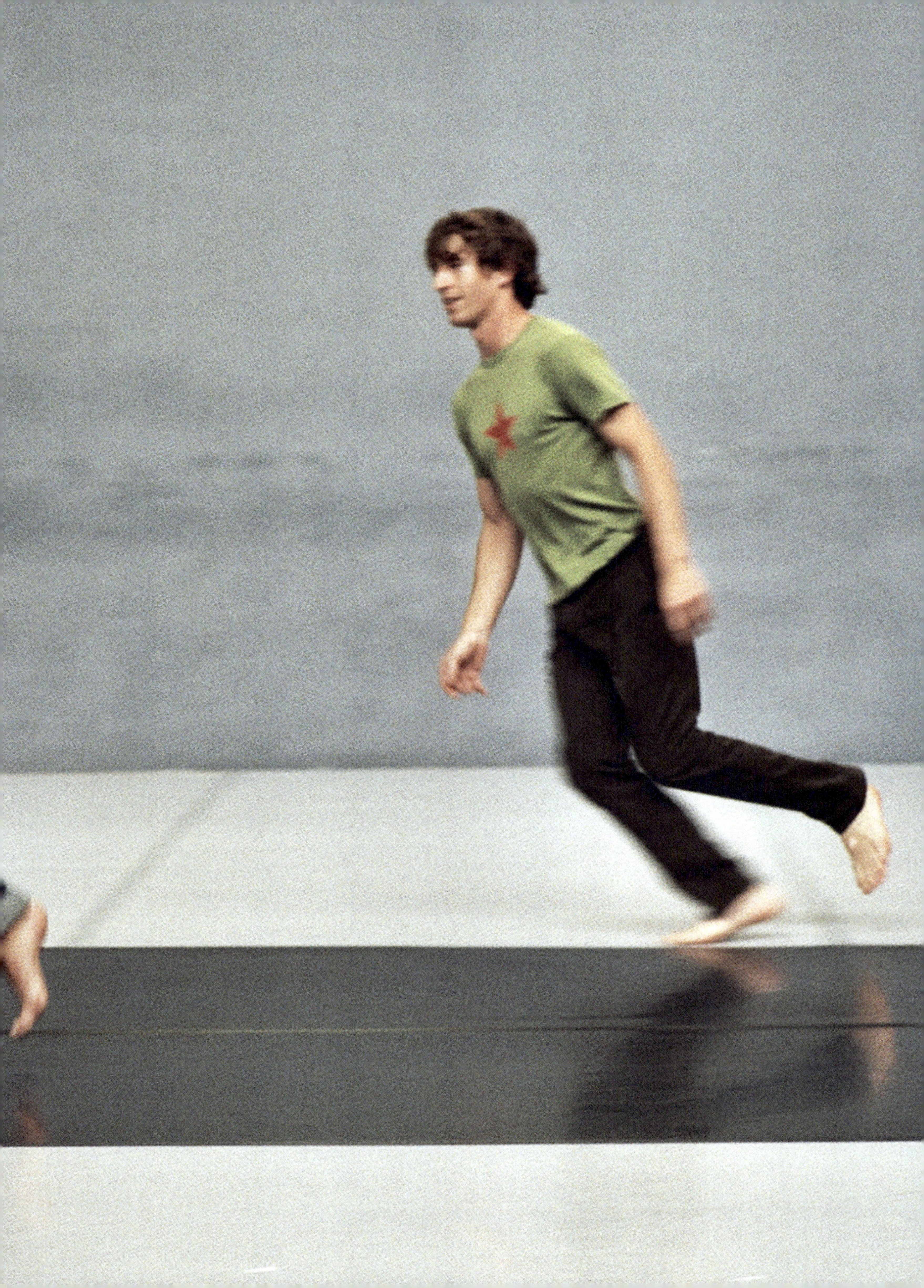

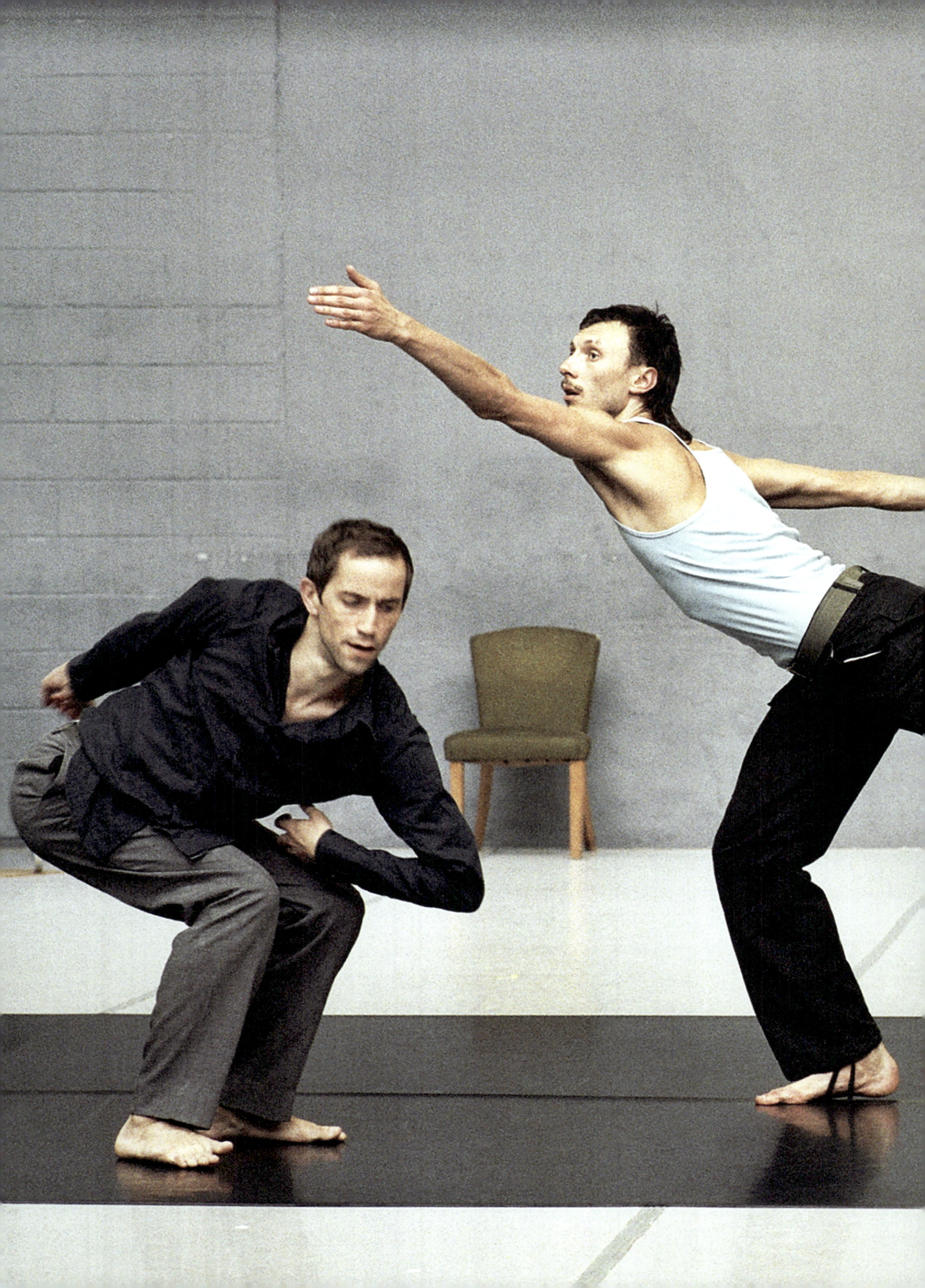

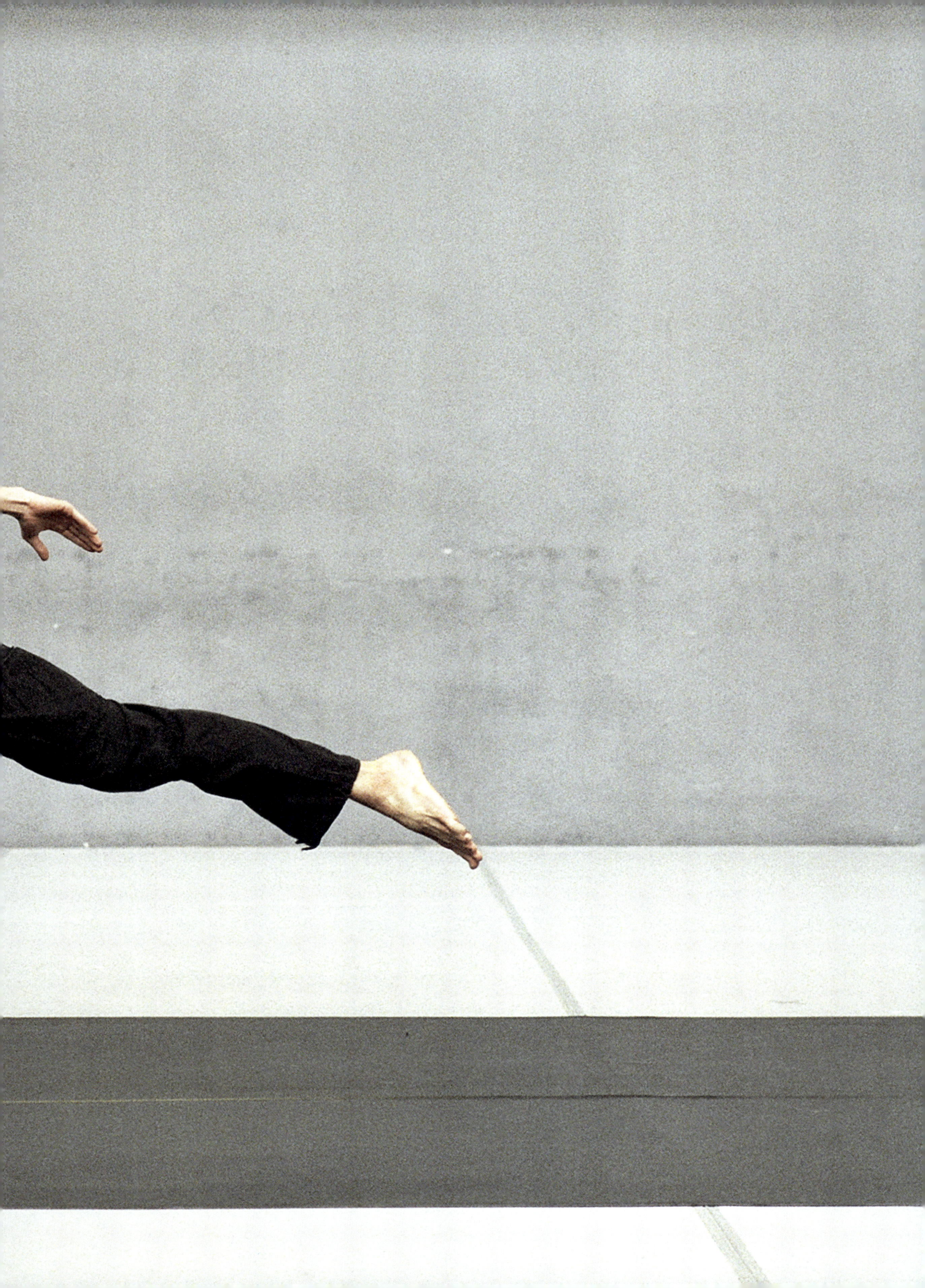

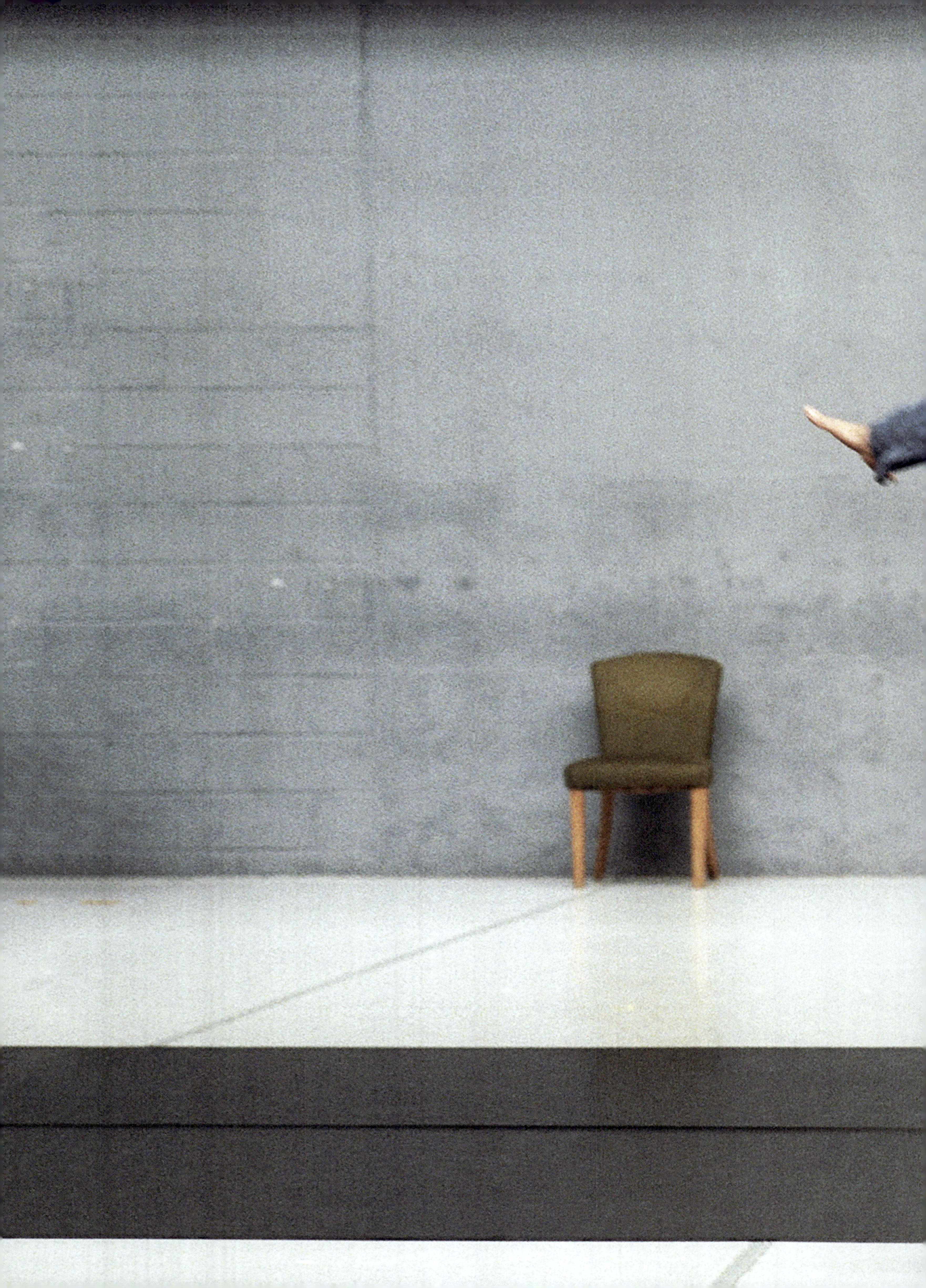

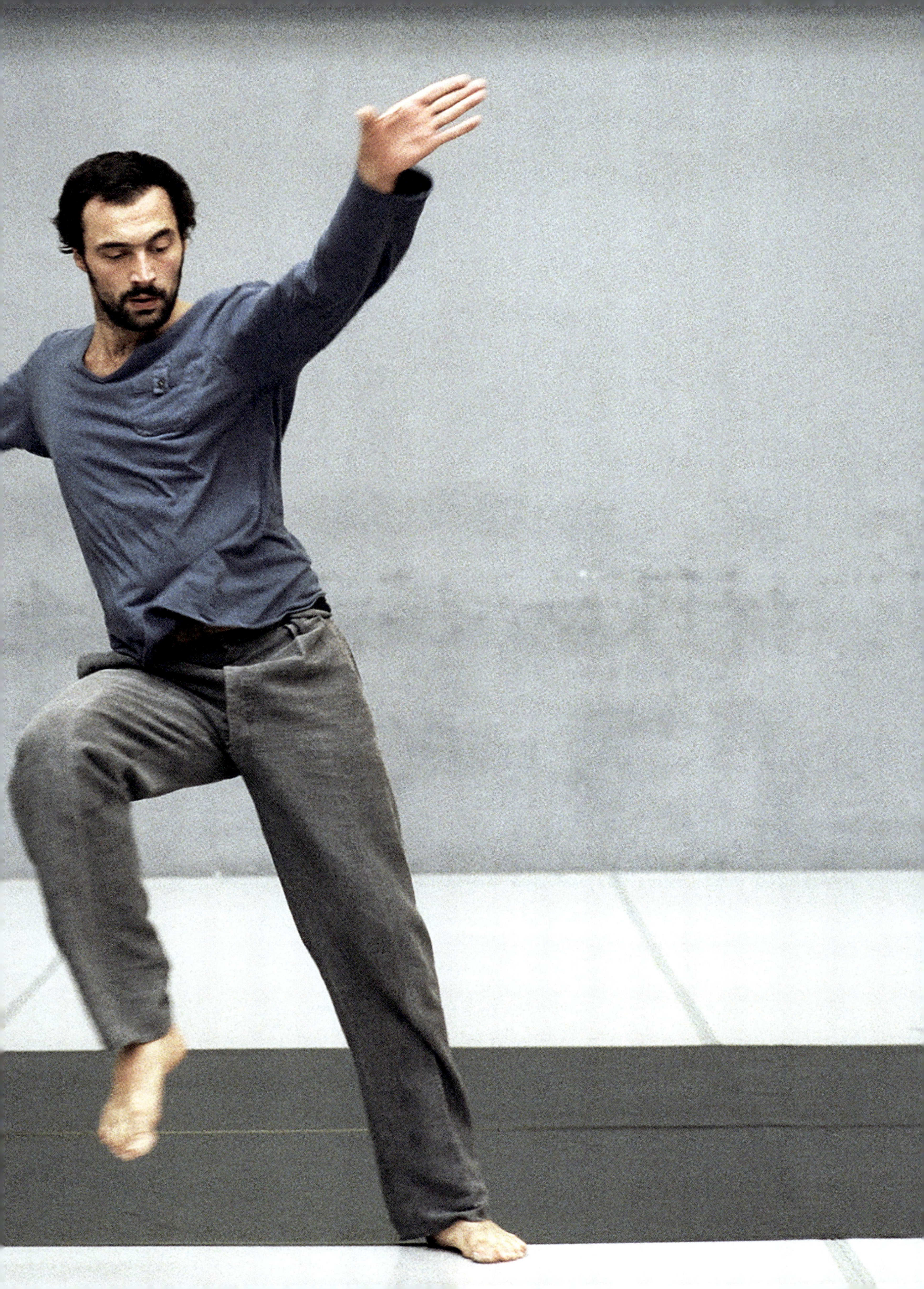

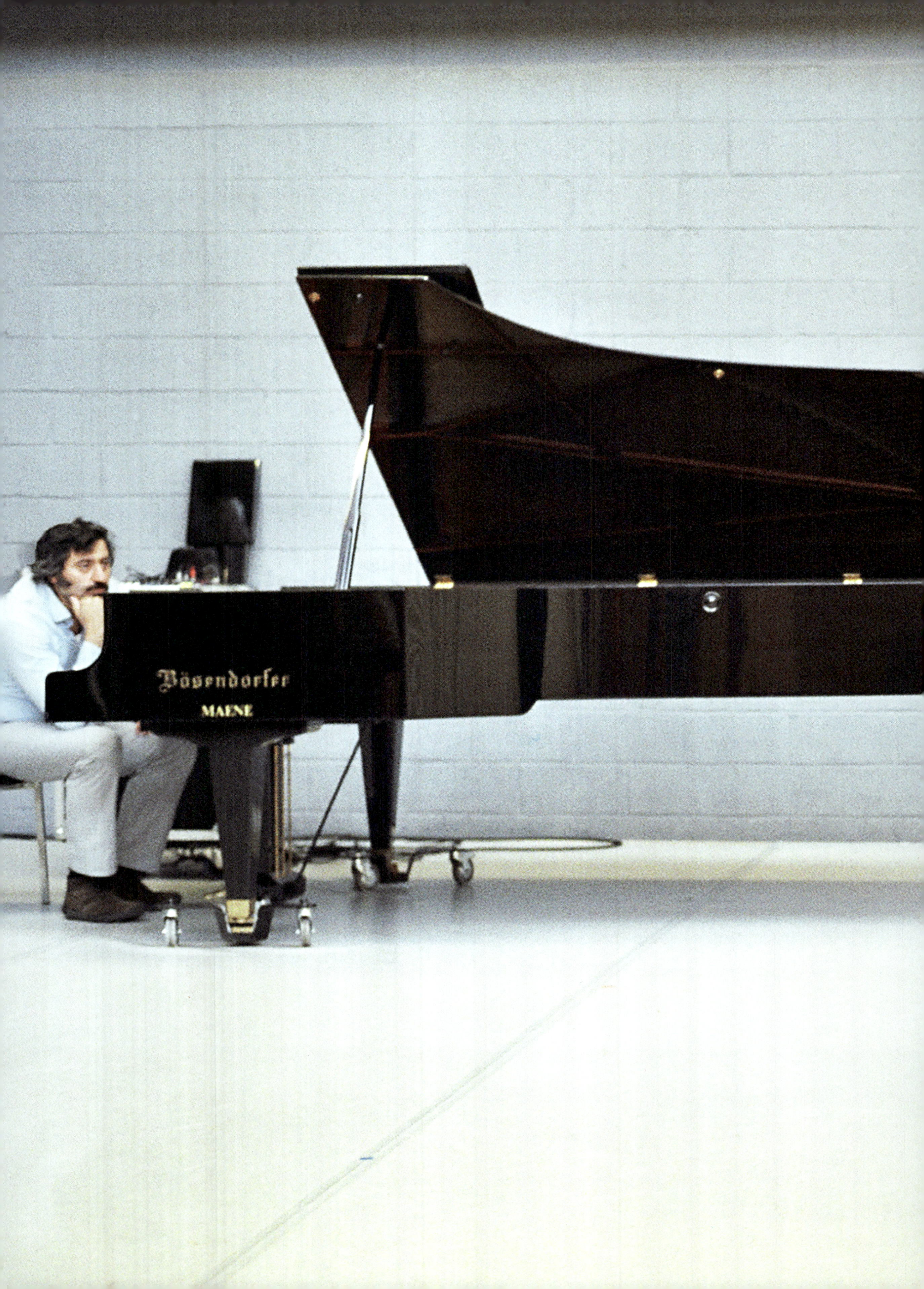
Bösendorfer
MAENE

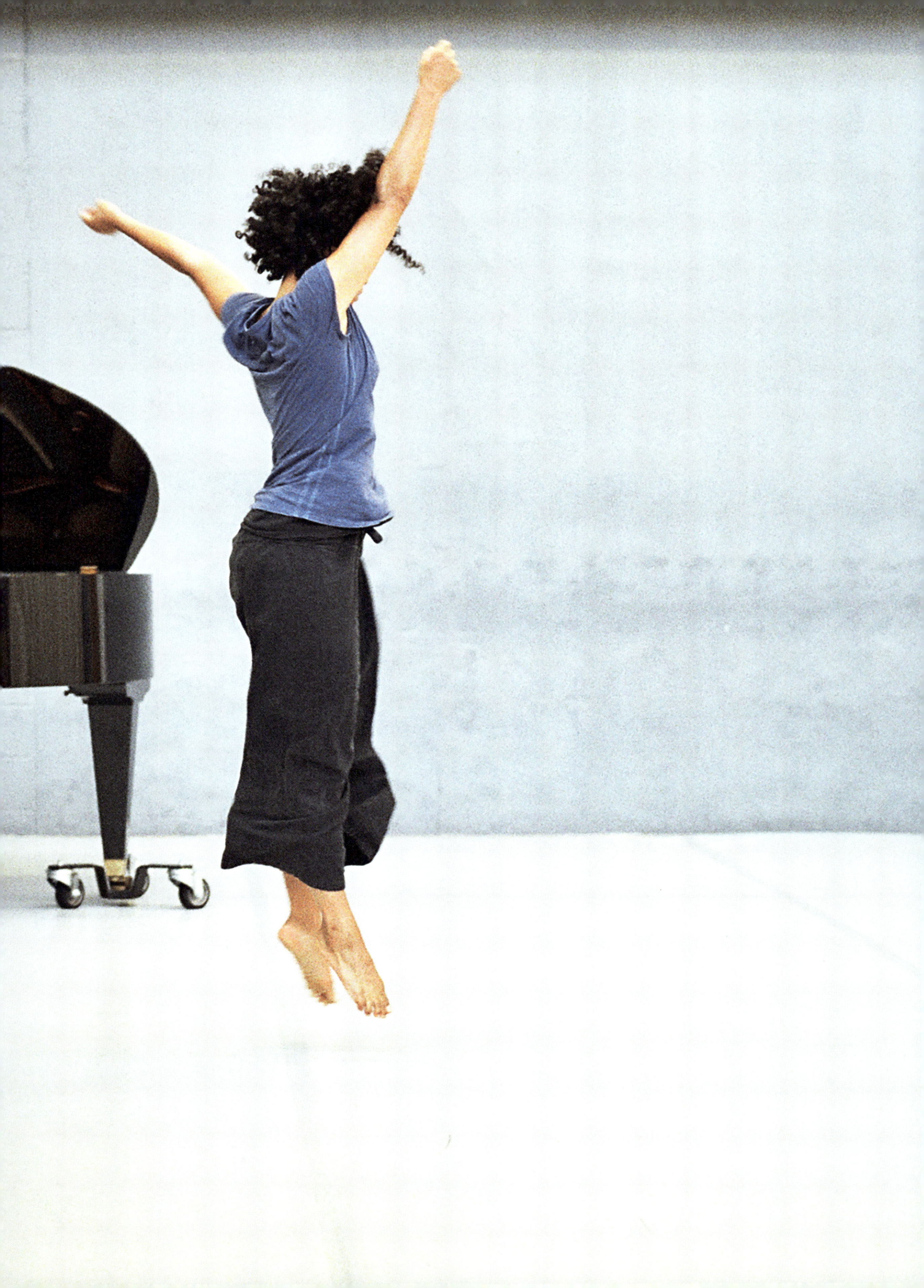

The Song 2009

Concept
Anne Teresa De Keersmaeker, Ann Veronica Janssens, Michel François
Choreography
Anne Teresa De Keersmaeker
Created with and danced by
Pieter Ampe, Boštjan Antončič, Eleanor Bauer, Carlos Garbin, Matej Kejžar, Mark Lorimer, Mikael Marklund, Simon Mayer, Michaël Pomero, Sandy Williams
Foley artist
Céline Bernard
Scenography
Ann Veronica Janssens, Michel François
Costumes
Anne-Catherine Kunz
Dramaturgy
Claire Diez
Musical advice
Eugénie De Mey, Kris Dane
Foley artist advisor
Olivier Thys
Artistic assistants
Anne Van Aerschot, Femke Gyselinck
Sound
Alexandre Fostier
Production
Rosas
Coproduction
La Monnaie / De Munt (Brussels), Théâtre de la Ville (Paris), Grand Théâtre de Luxembourg, Concertgebouw Bruges
Premiere
24.09.2009, Théâtre de la Ville—Paris

Pictures 1-4
Herman Sorgeloos
Picture 5
Michel François

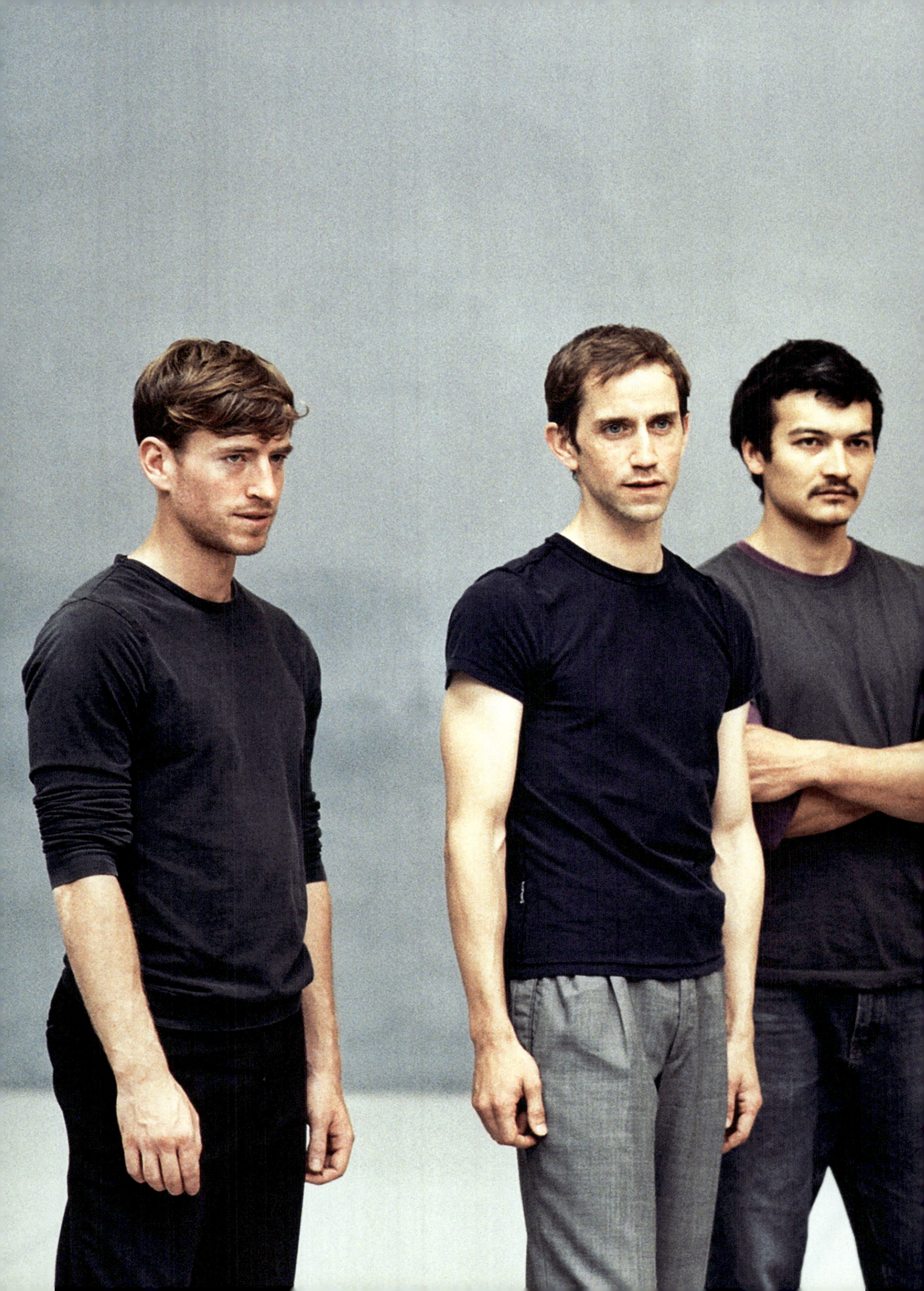

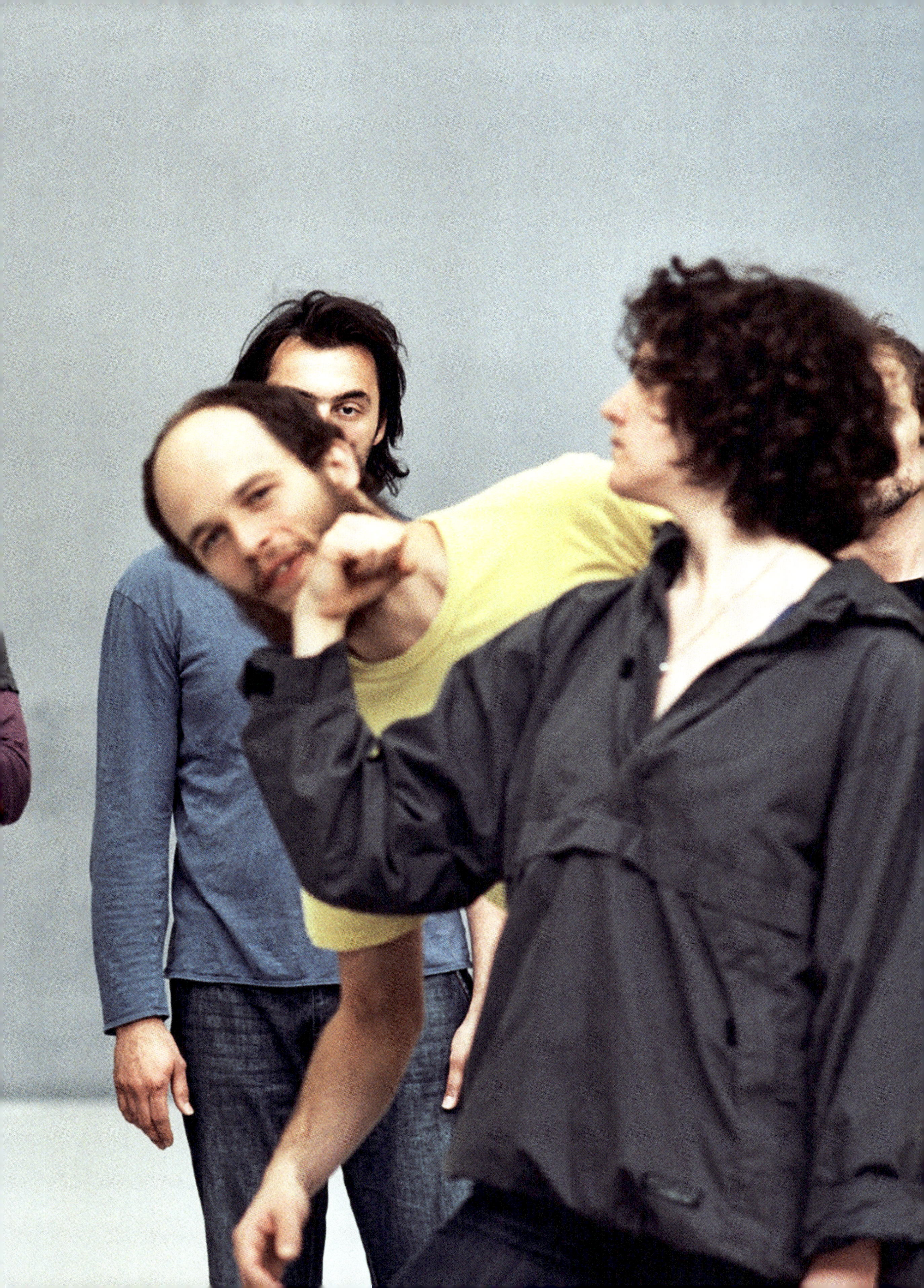

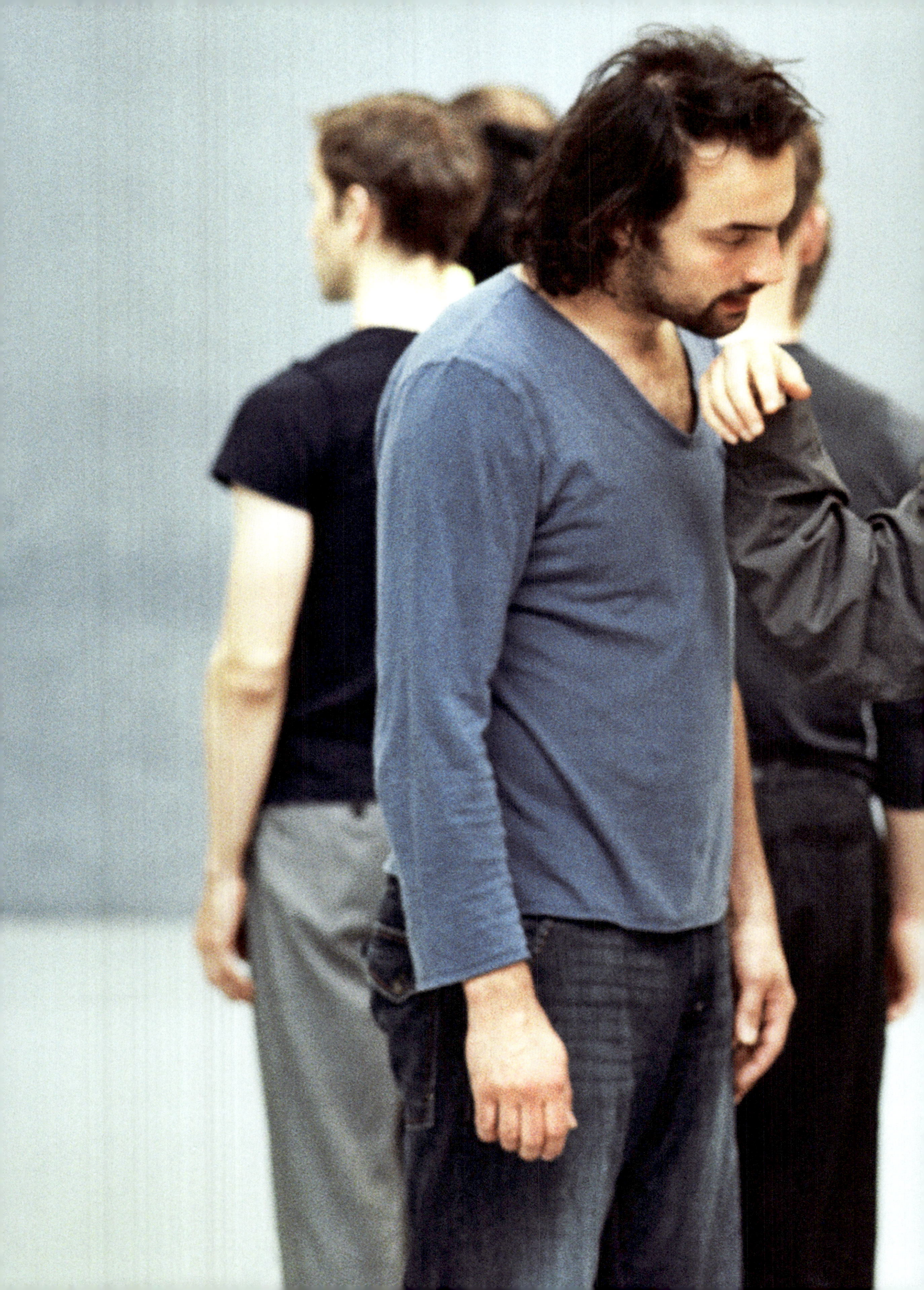

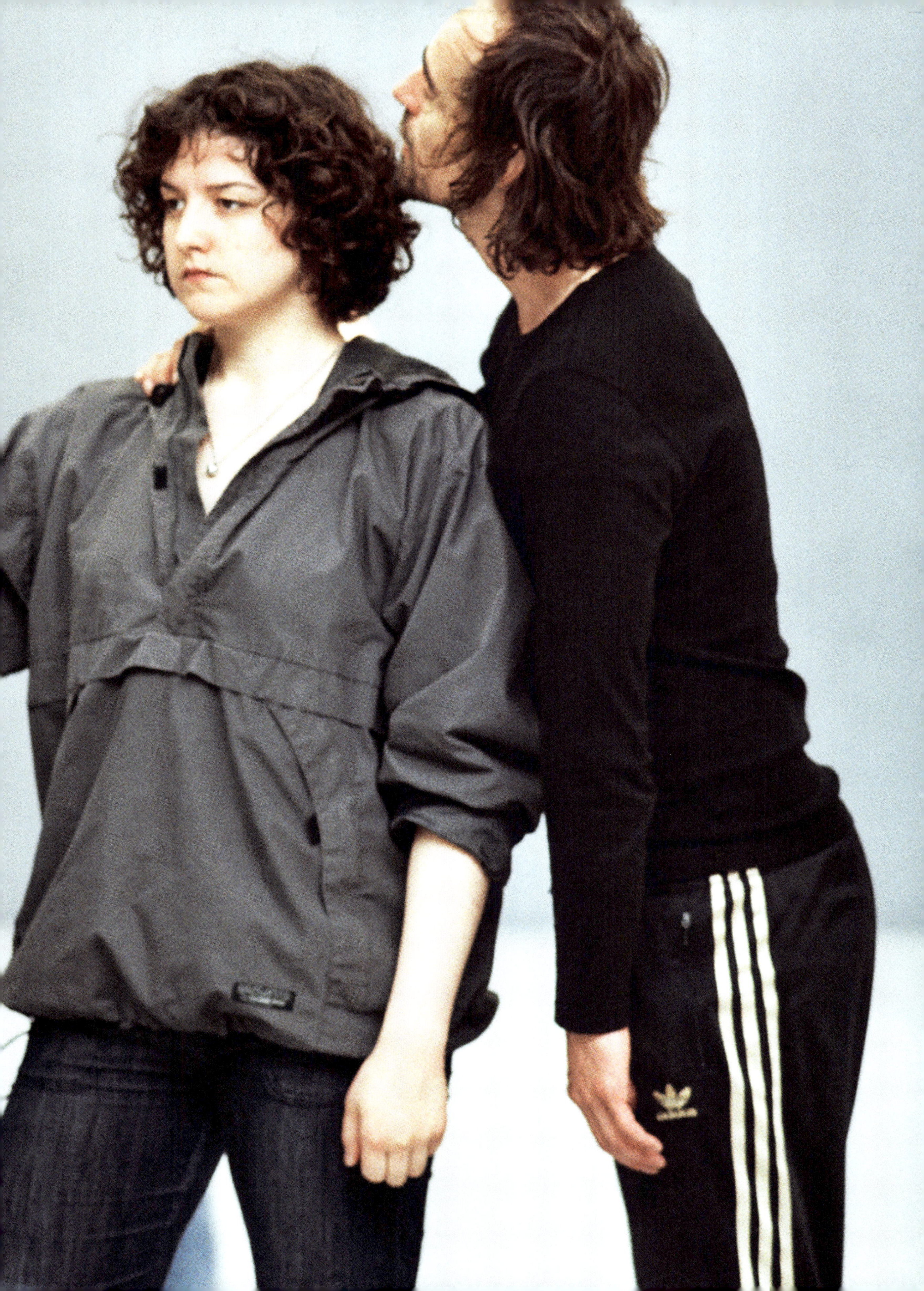

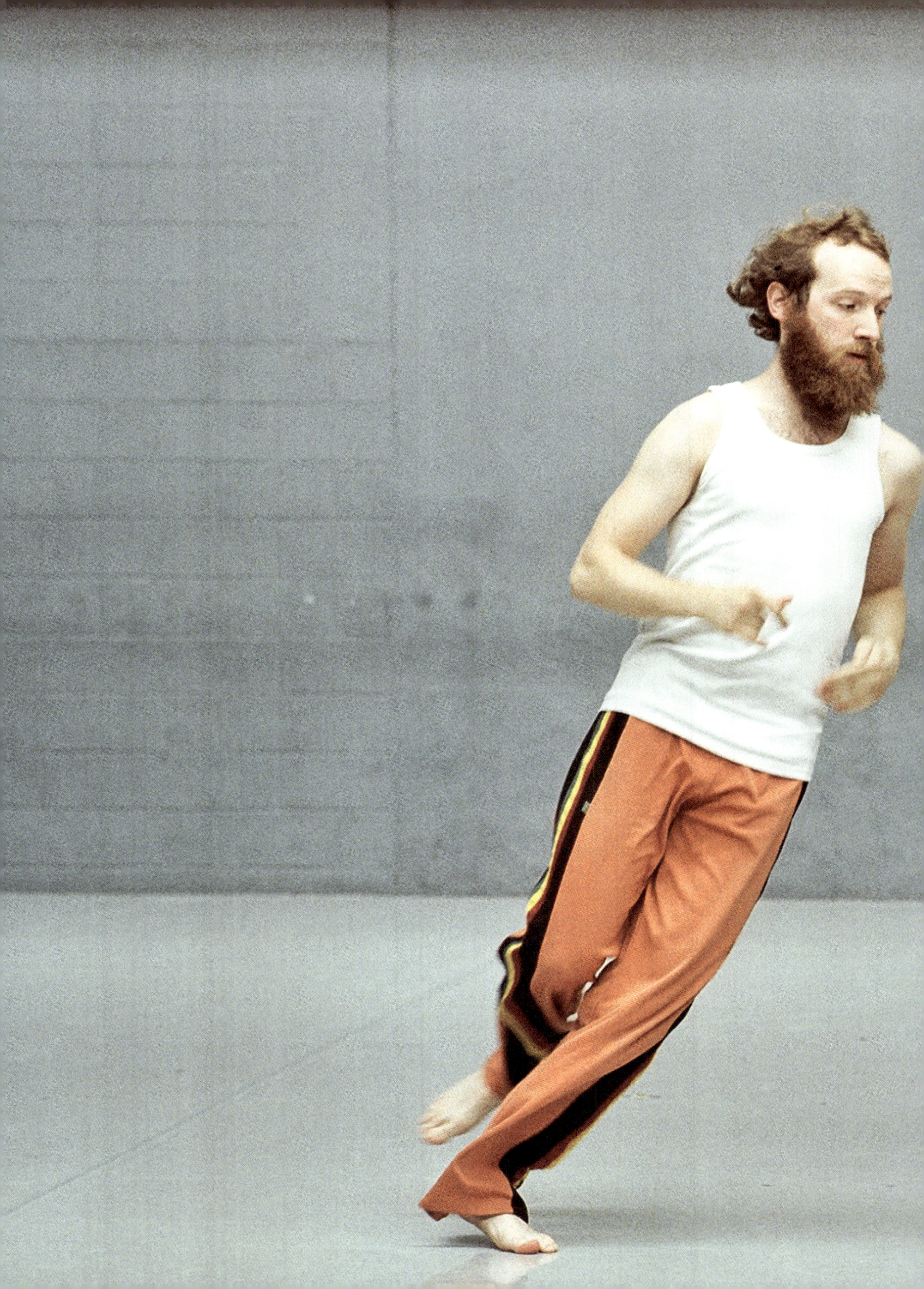

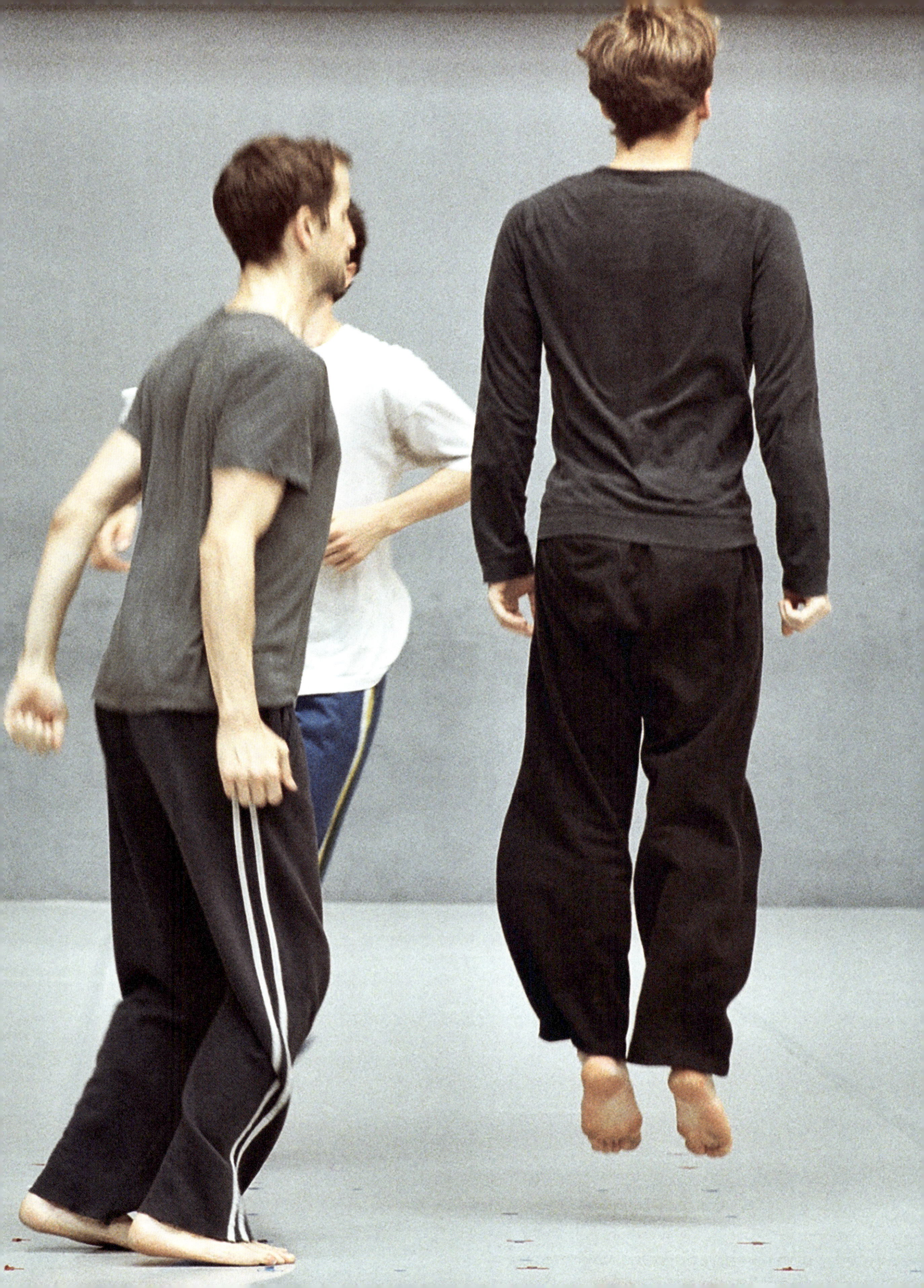

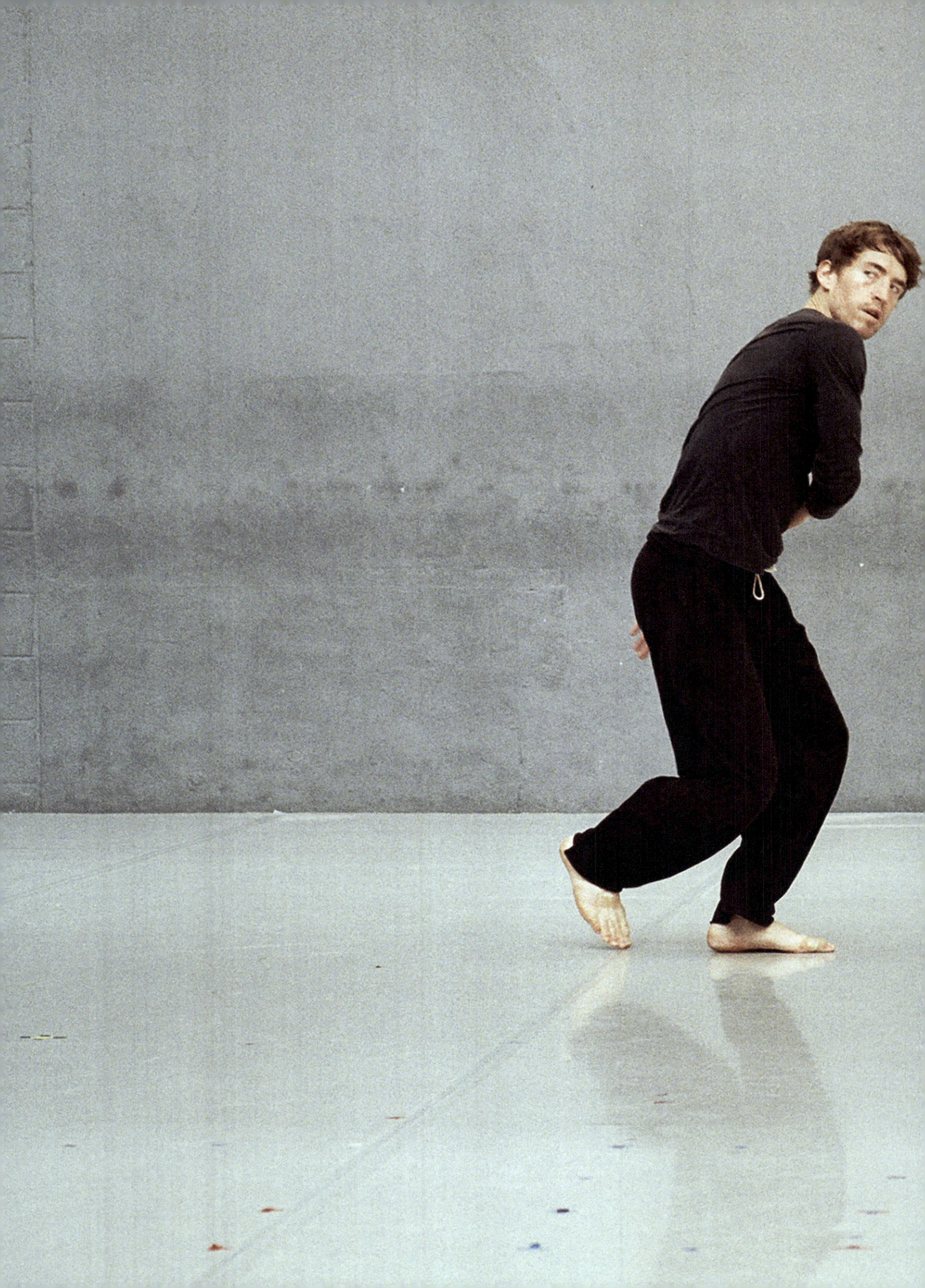

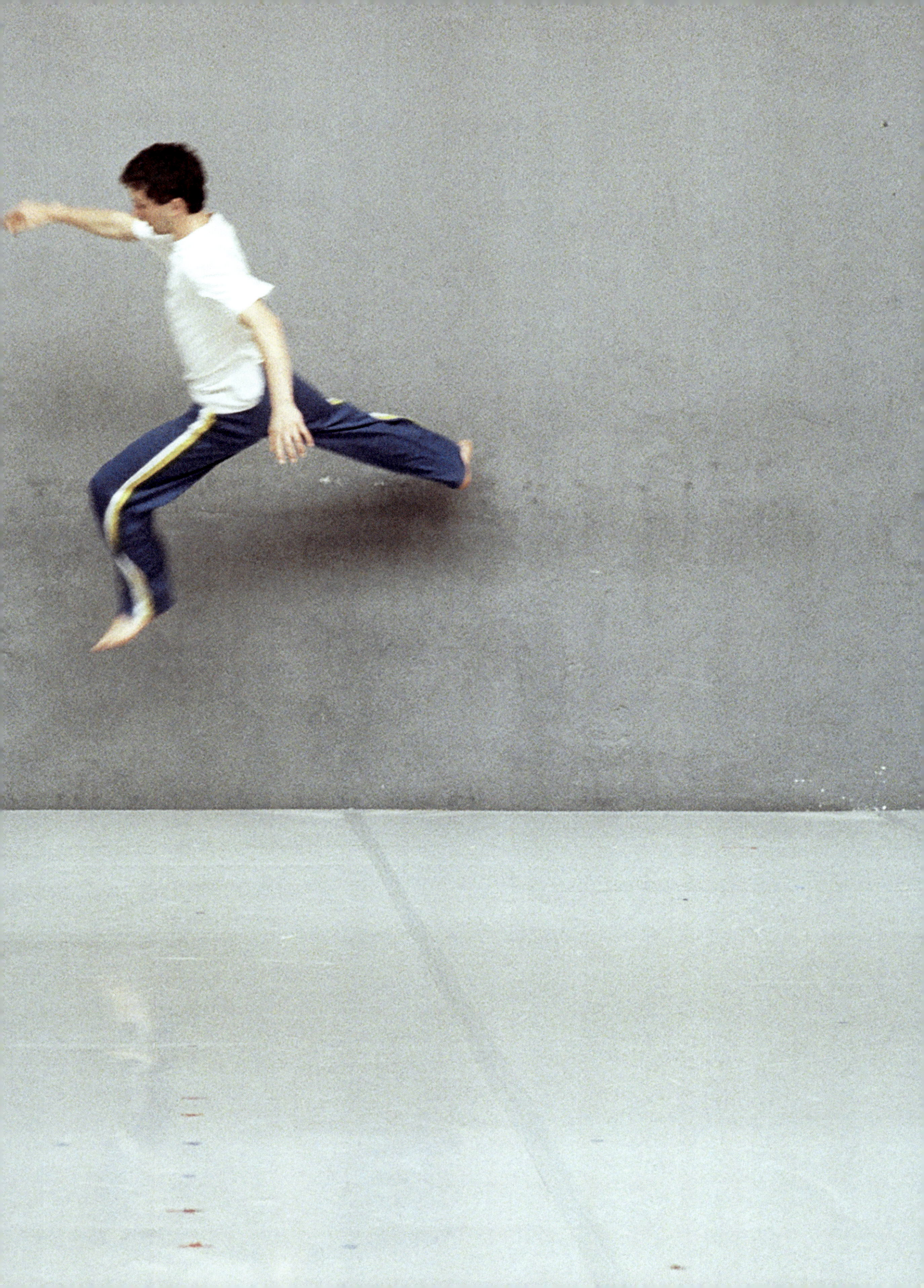

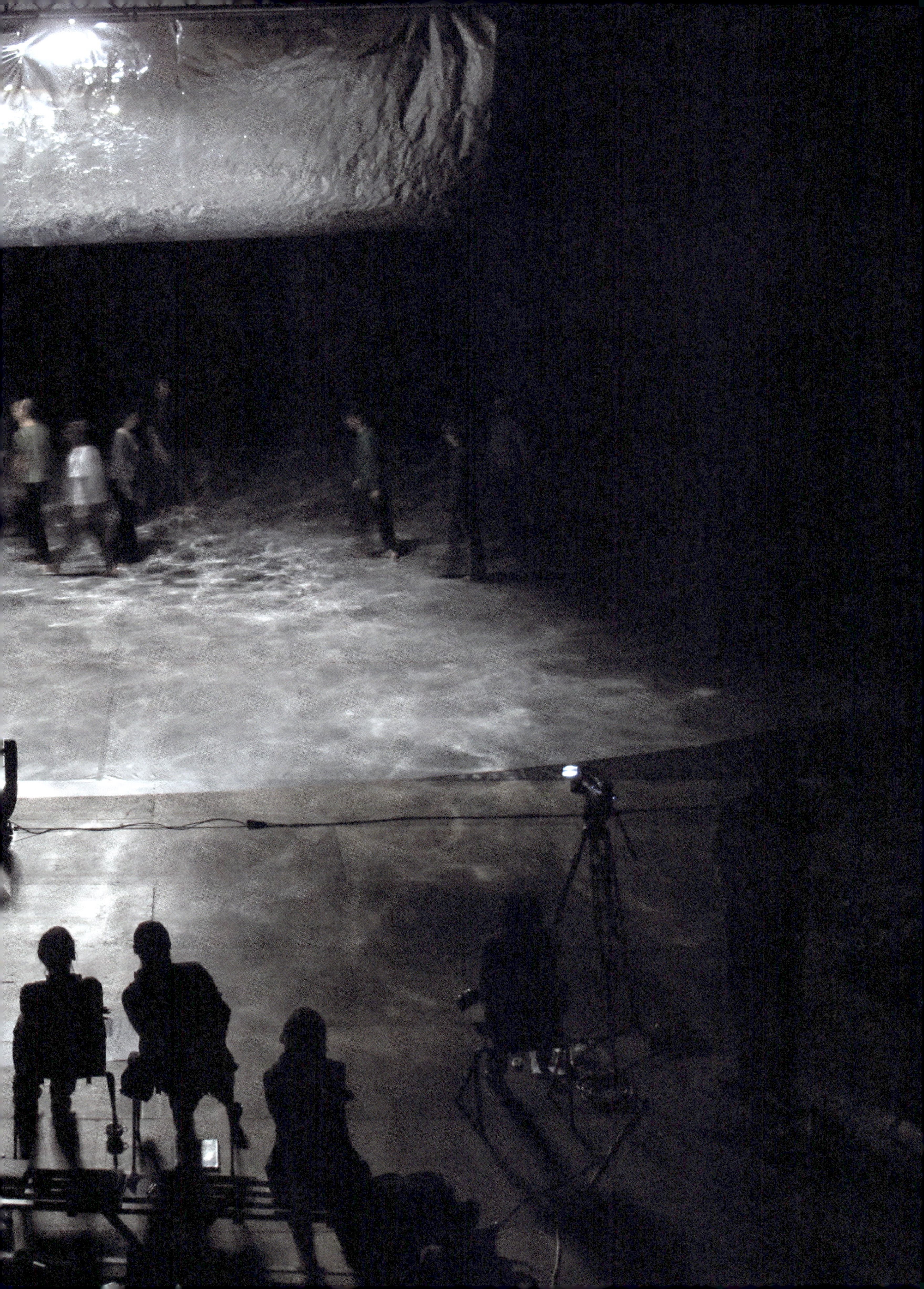

3Abschied 2010

Concept
Anne Teresa De Keersmaeker, Jérôme Bel
Danced by
Anne Teresa De Keersmaeker
Music
Das Lied von der Erde (Der Abschied), Gustav Mahler (Arnold Schönberg—transcription)
Musical direction
Georges-Elie Octors
Mezzo soprano
Sara Fulgoni / Ursula Hesse von den Steinen
Piano
Jean-Luc Fafchamps
Musicians
Premiere series Chamber music orchestra of La Monnaie / De Munt
Tour Ictus
Artistic assistant
Anne Van Aerschot
Production
Rosas
Coproduction
La Monnaie / De Munt (Brussels), Opéra de Lille, Sadler's Wells (London), Theater an der Wien, Théâtre de la Ville met het Festival d'Automne à Paris, Hellerau European Center for the Arts Dresden
Premiere
16.02.2010, La Monnaie / De Munt—Brussels

Pictures
Anne Van Aerschot

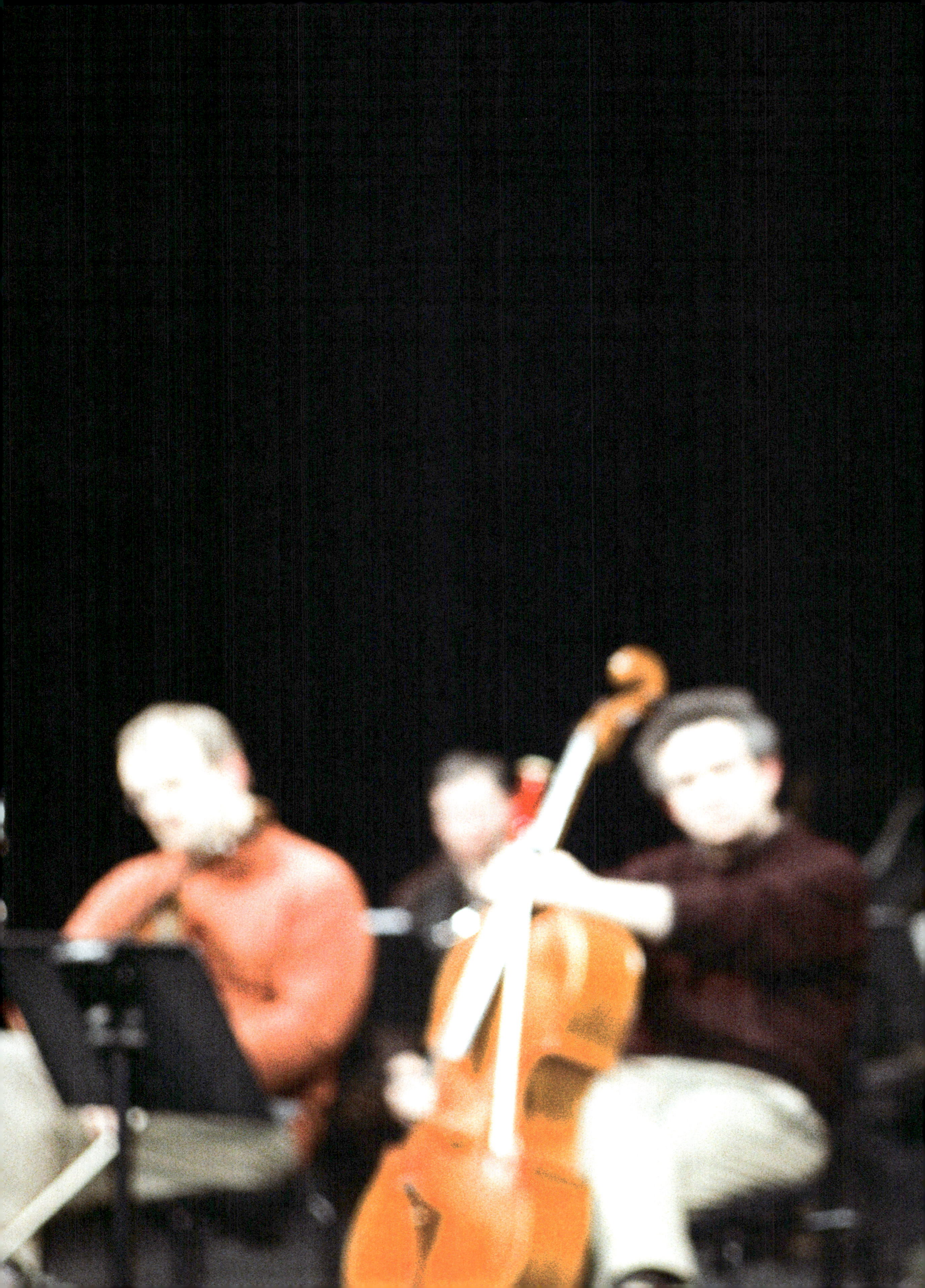

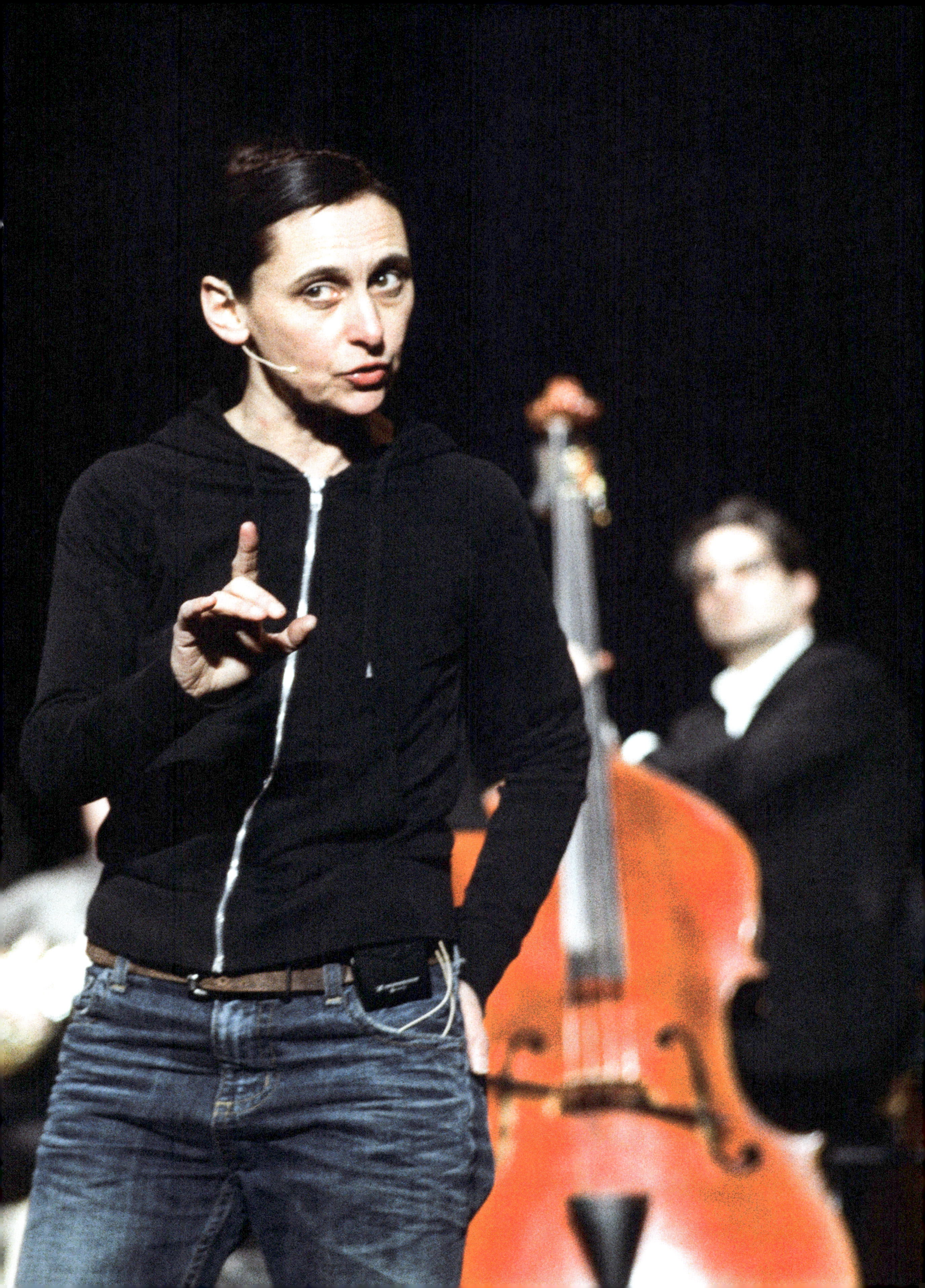

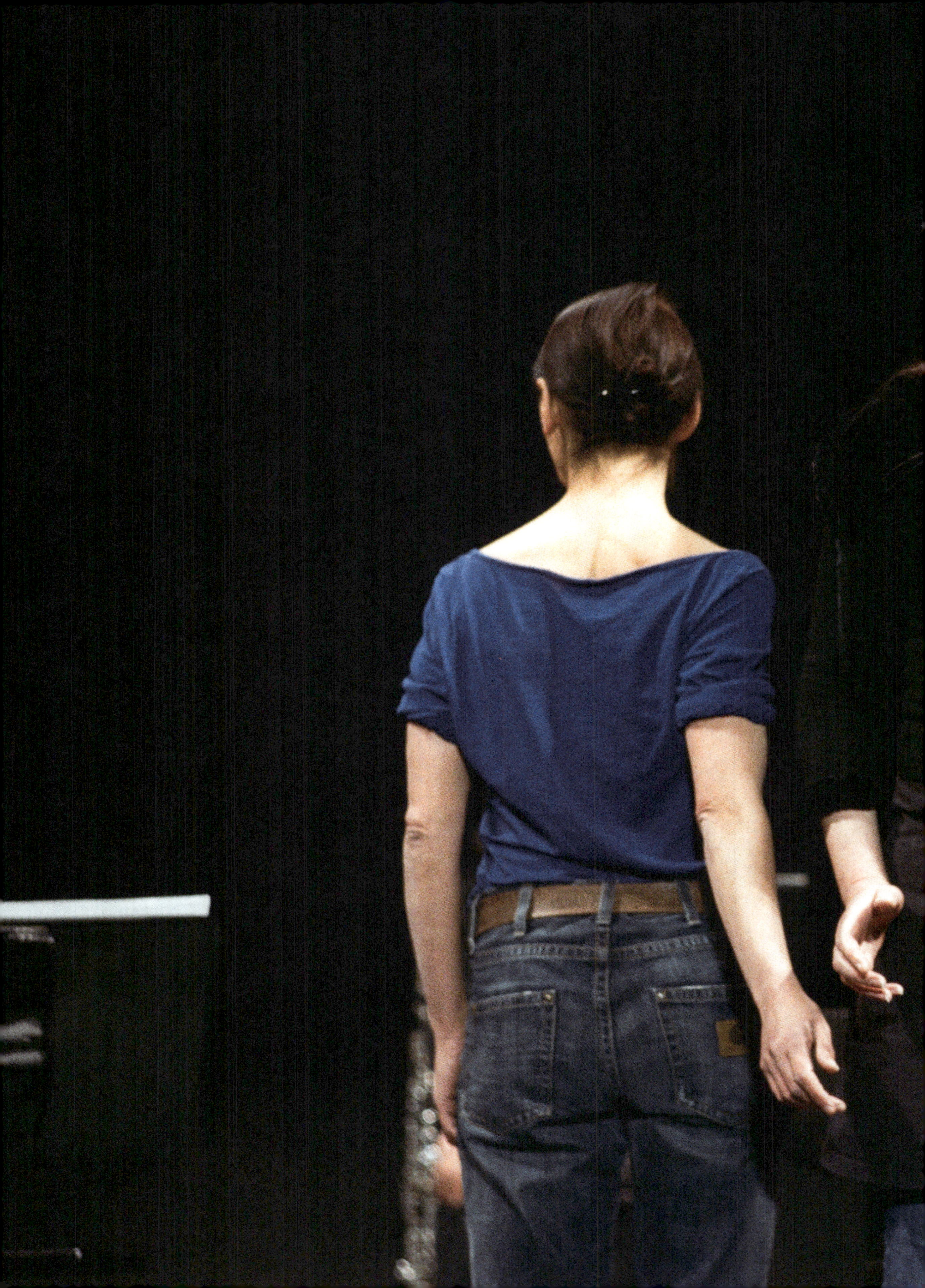

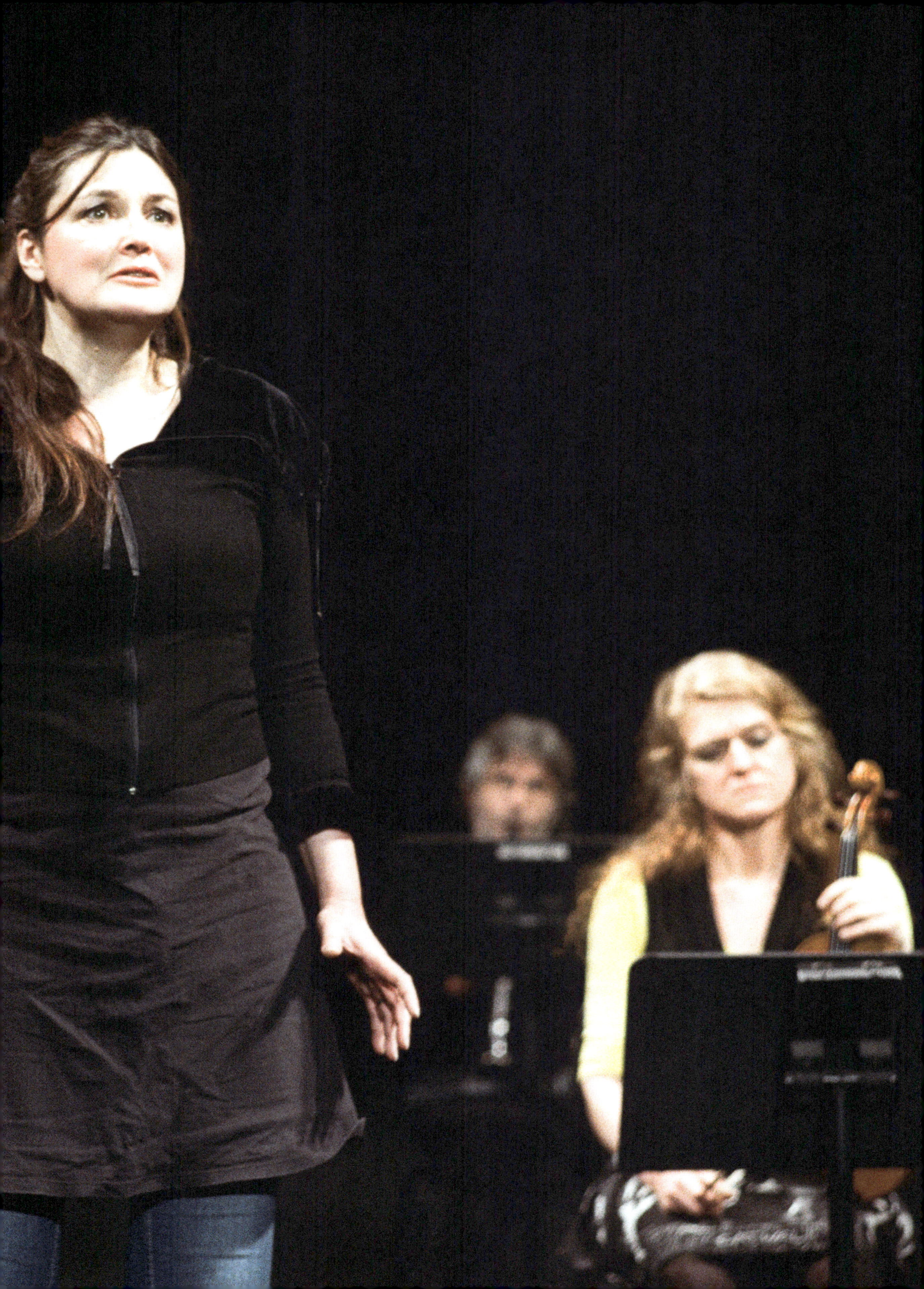

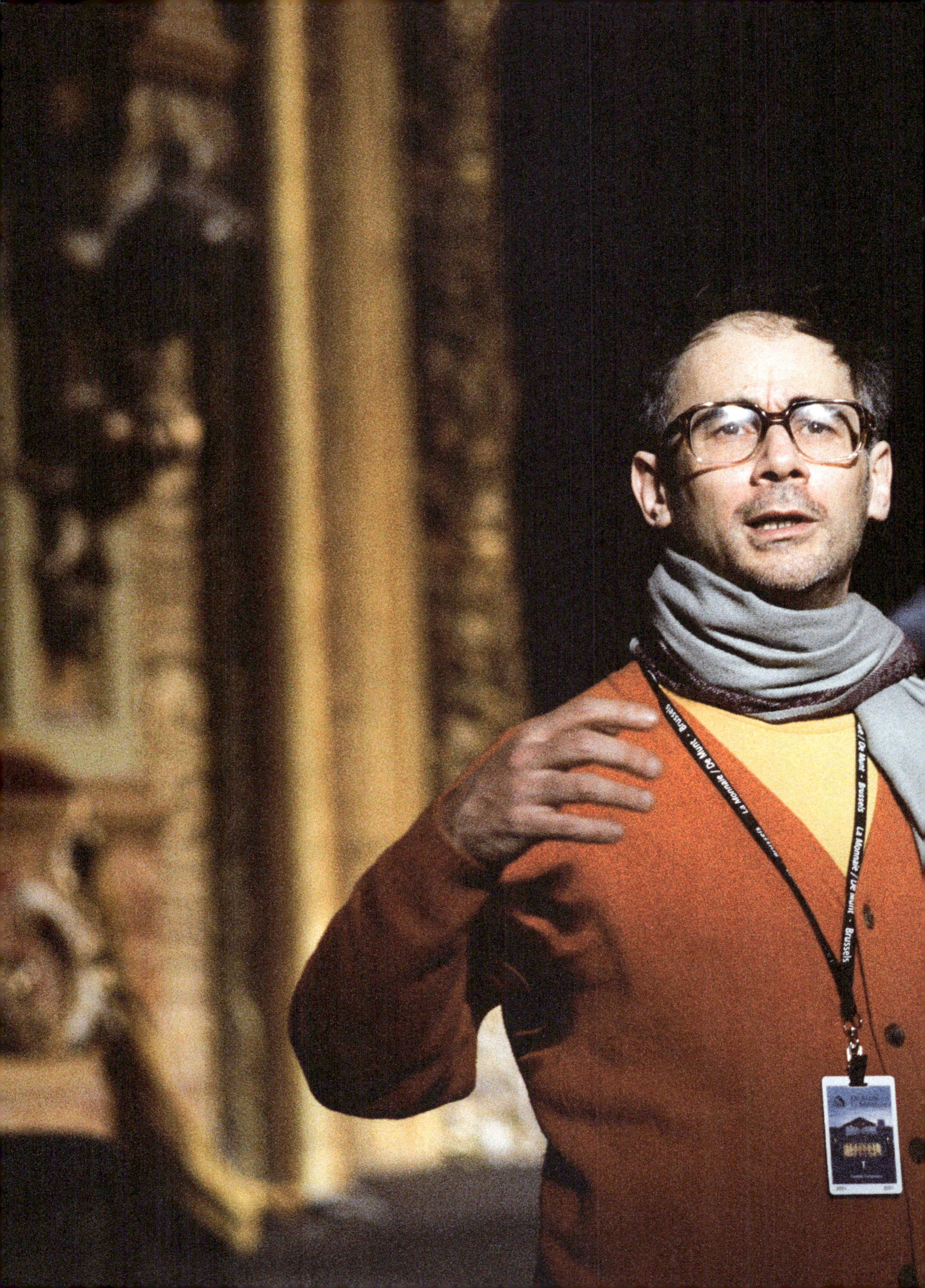
La Monnaie / De Munt · Brussels

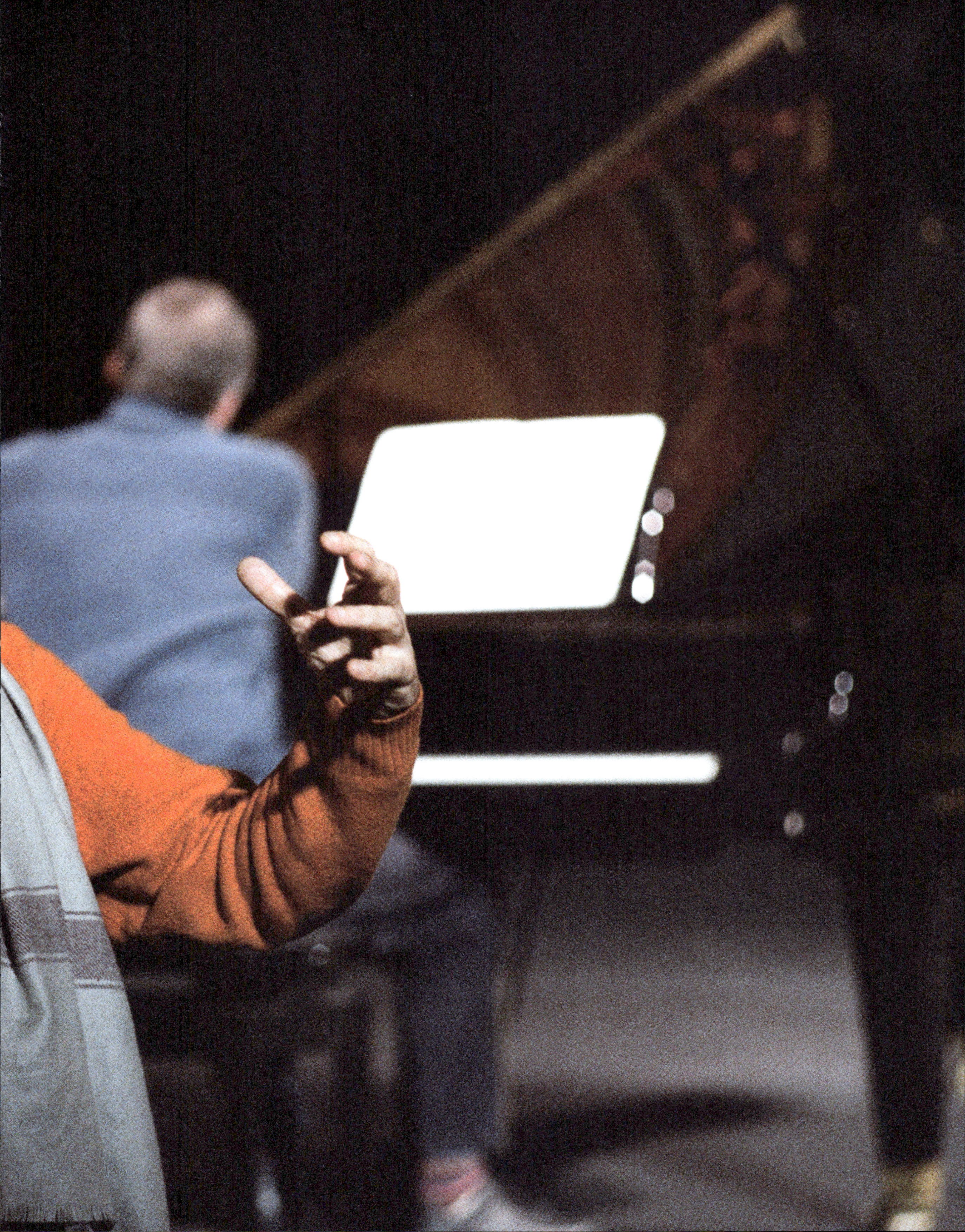

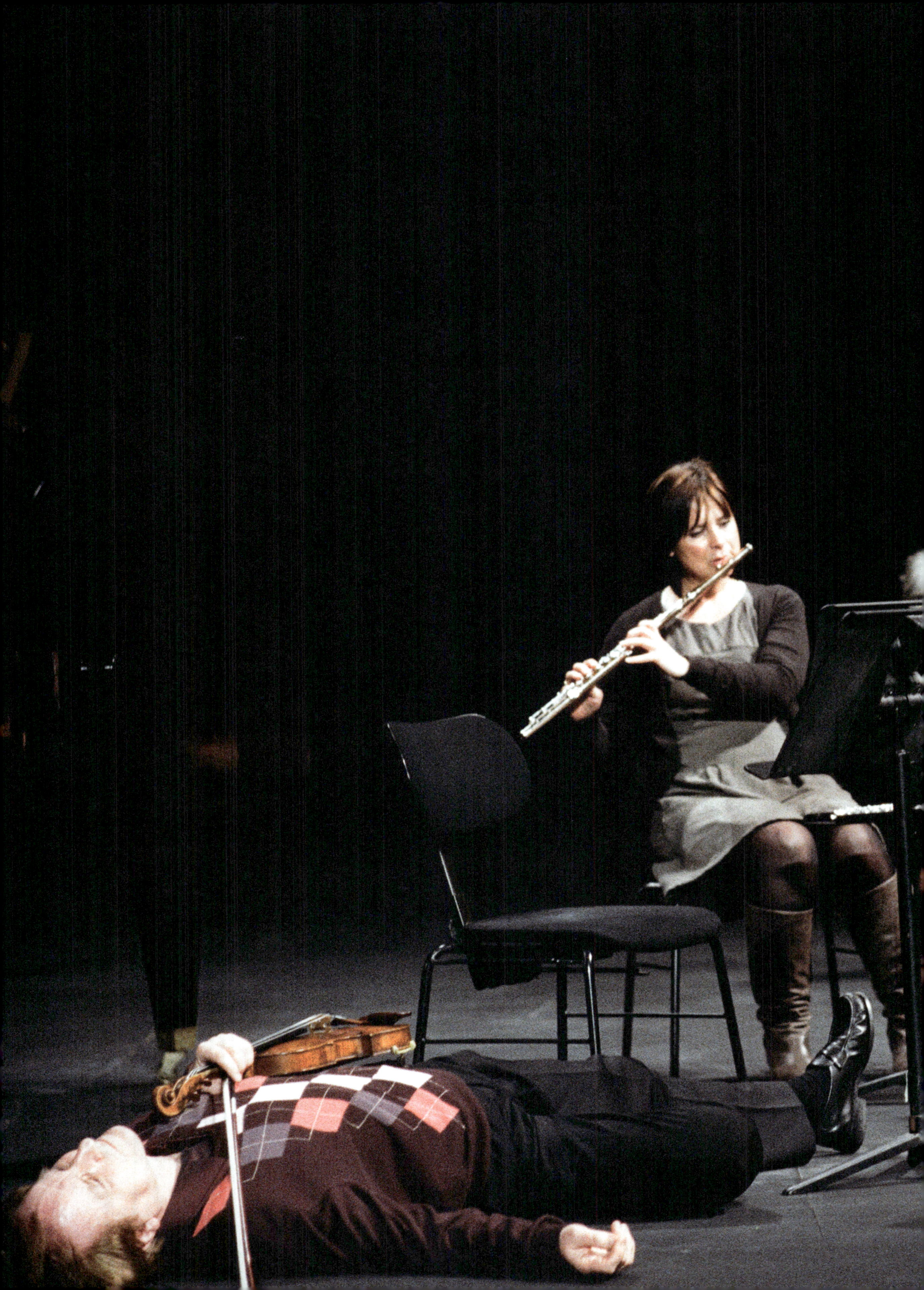

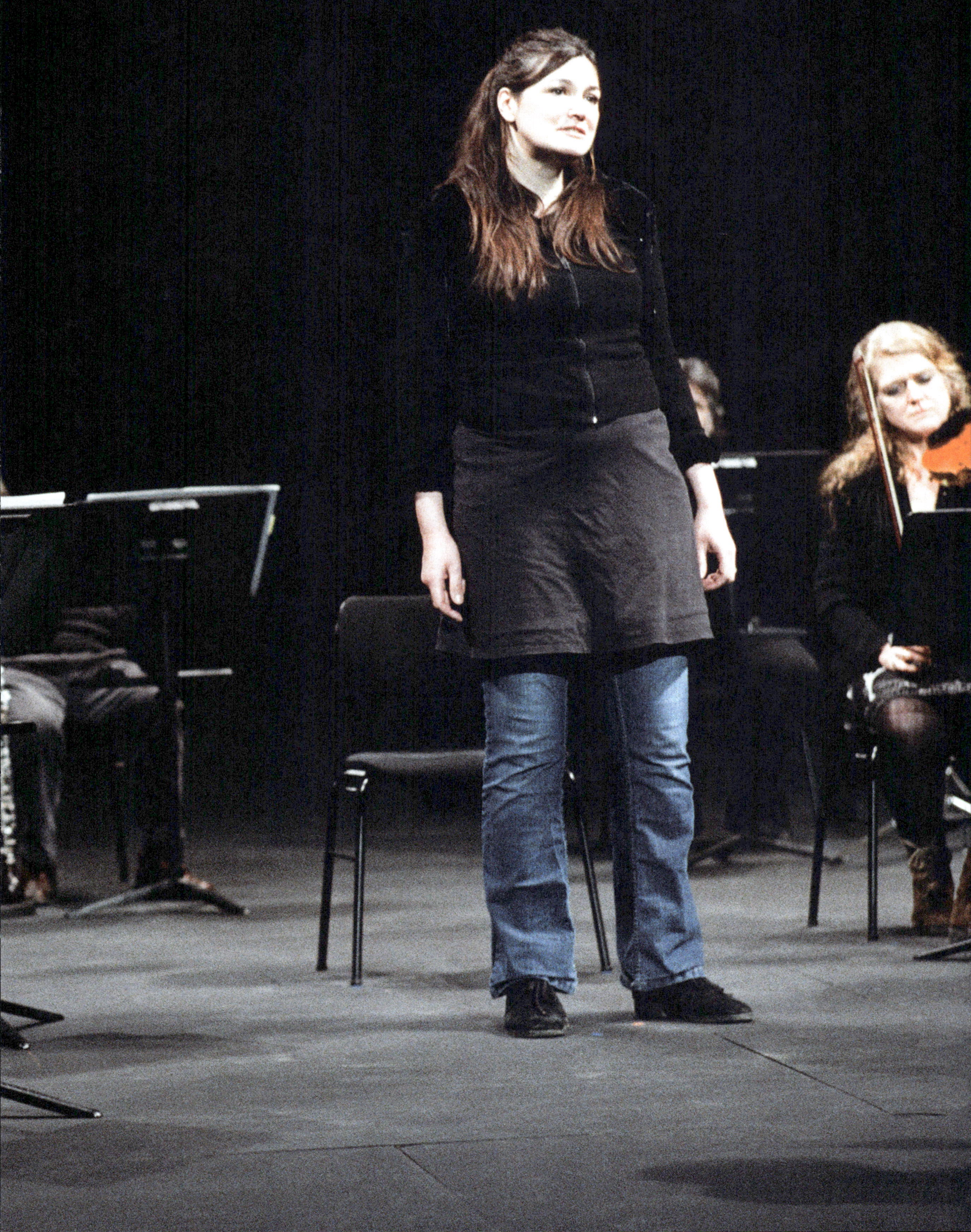

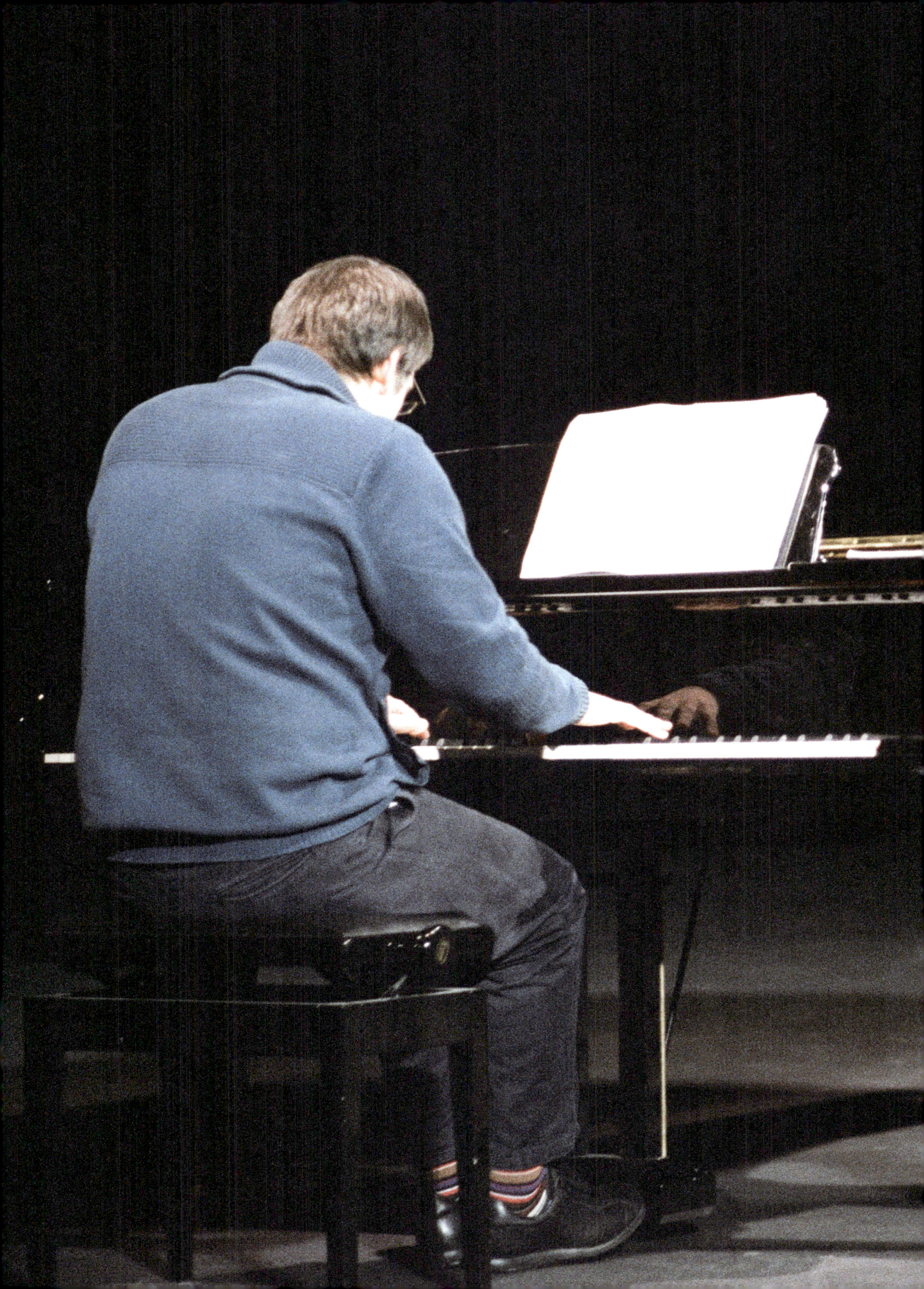

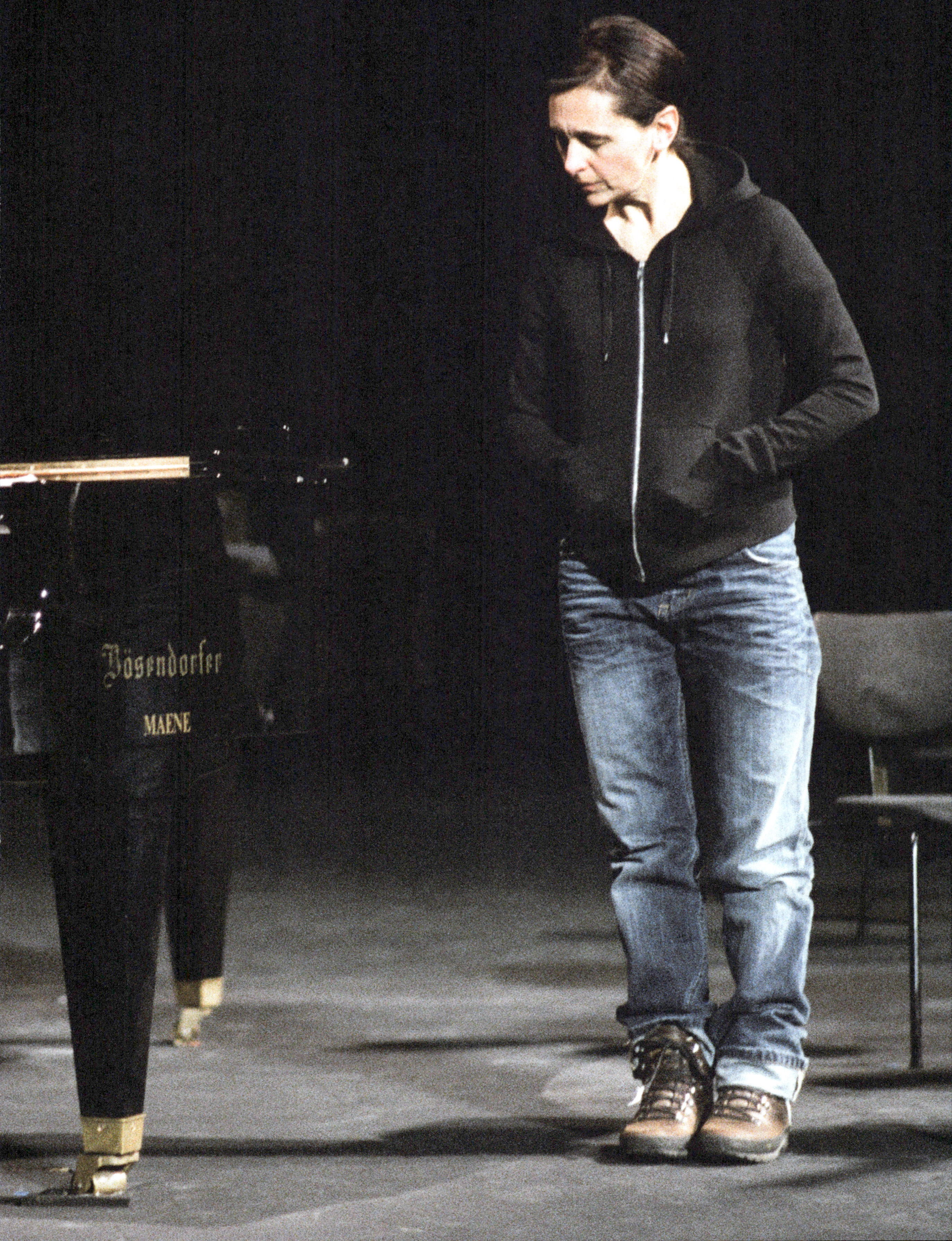
Bösendorfer
MAENE

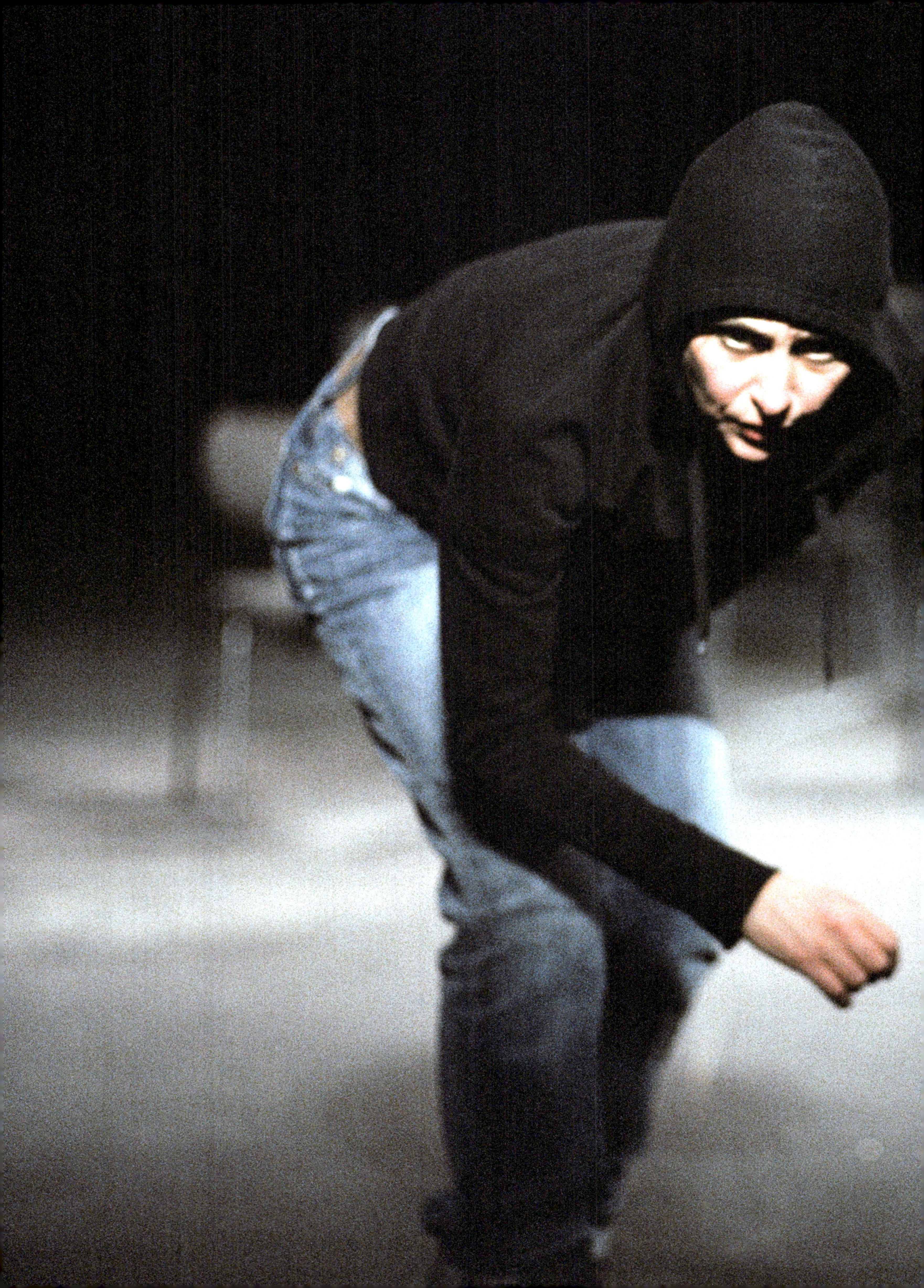

En Atendant 2010

Concept and choreography
Anne Teresa De Keersmaeker
Created with and danced by
Boštjan Antončič, Carlos Garbin, Cynthia Loemij, Mark Lorimer, Mikael Marklund, Chrysa Parkinson, Sandy Williams, Sue-Yeon Youn
Music
...L(ÉLEK)ZEM..', István Matuz
Ars subtilior:
En atendant, souffrir m'estuet (ballade), Philipoctus de Caserta
Estampie En Atendant 2, Bart Coen (2010)
Sus un' fontayne (virelai), Johannes Ciconia
Je prens d'amour noriture (virelai), anonymous
Esperance, ki en mon coeur, anonymous
Flute
Michael Schmid
Ensemble Cour et Coeur
Musical direction Bart Coen
Recorders Bart Coen / Thomas Baeté
Fiddle Birgit Goris / Dimos De Beun / An Van Laethem
Voice Annelies Van Gramberen / Els Van Laethem / Olalla Alemán / Poline Renou
Scenography
Michel François
Costumes
Anne-Catherine Kunz
Artistic assistants
Anne Van Aerschot, Femke Gyselinck
Production
Rosas
Coproduction
La Monnaie / De Munt (Brussels), Festival Grec (Barcelona), Grand Théâtre de Luxembourg, Théâtre de la Ville (Paris), Festival d'Avignon, Concertgebouw Bruges
Premiere
09.07.2010, Cloître des Célestins—Festival d'Avignon

Picture 1
Michel François
Pictures 2-9
Anne Van Aerschot

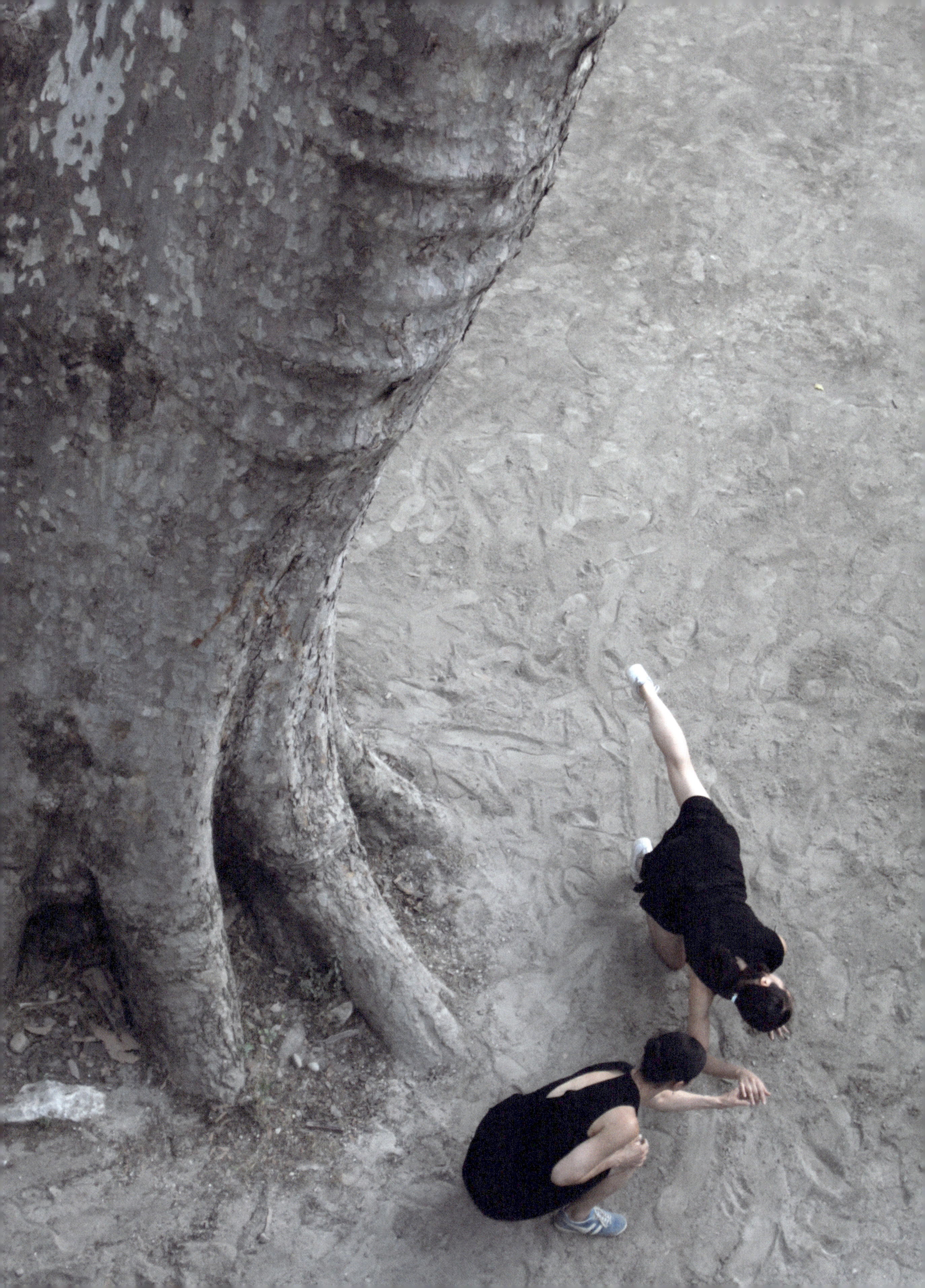

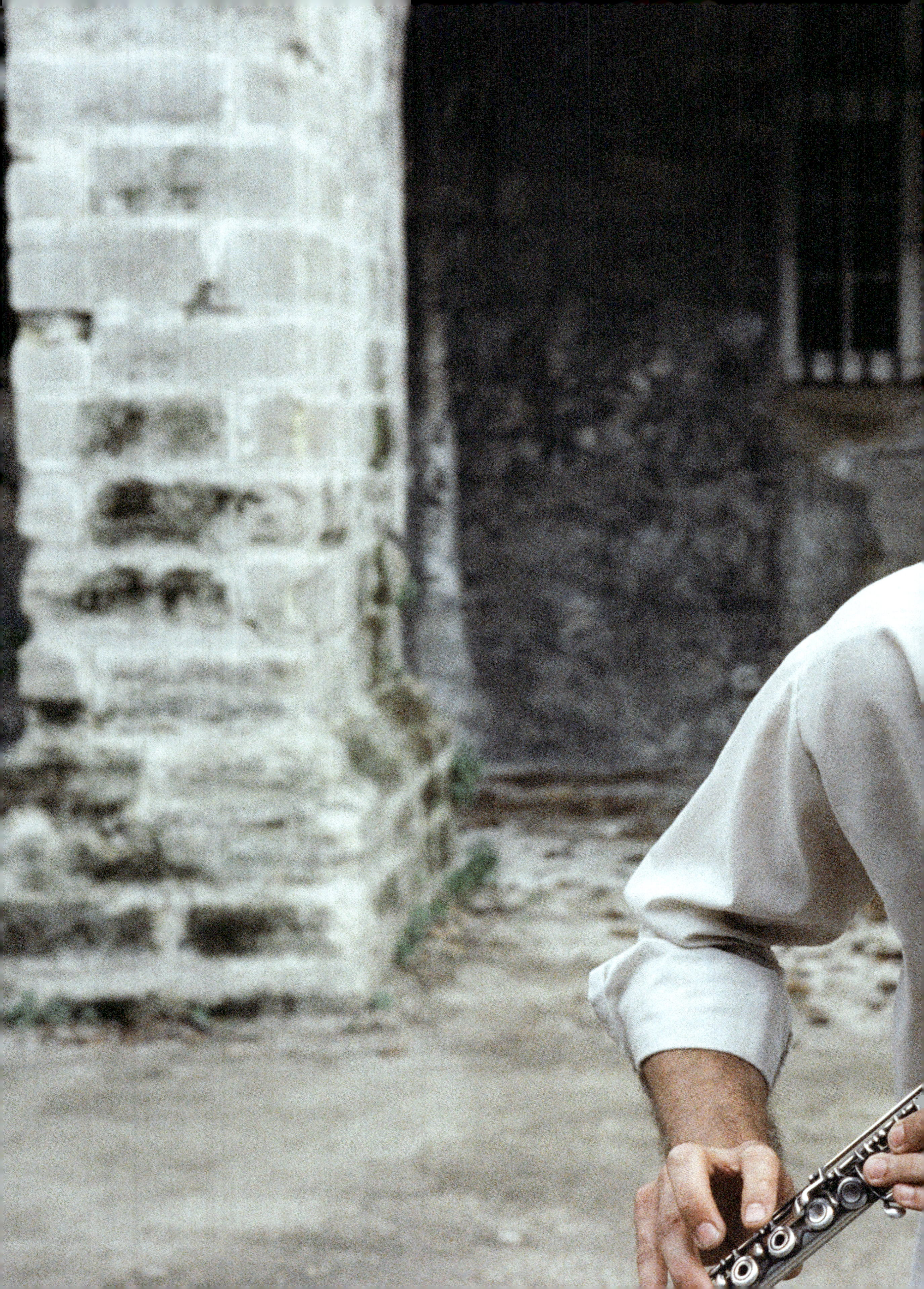

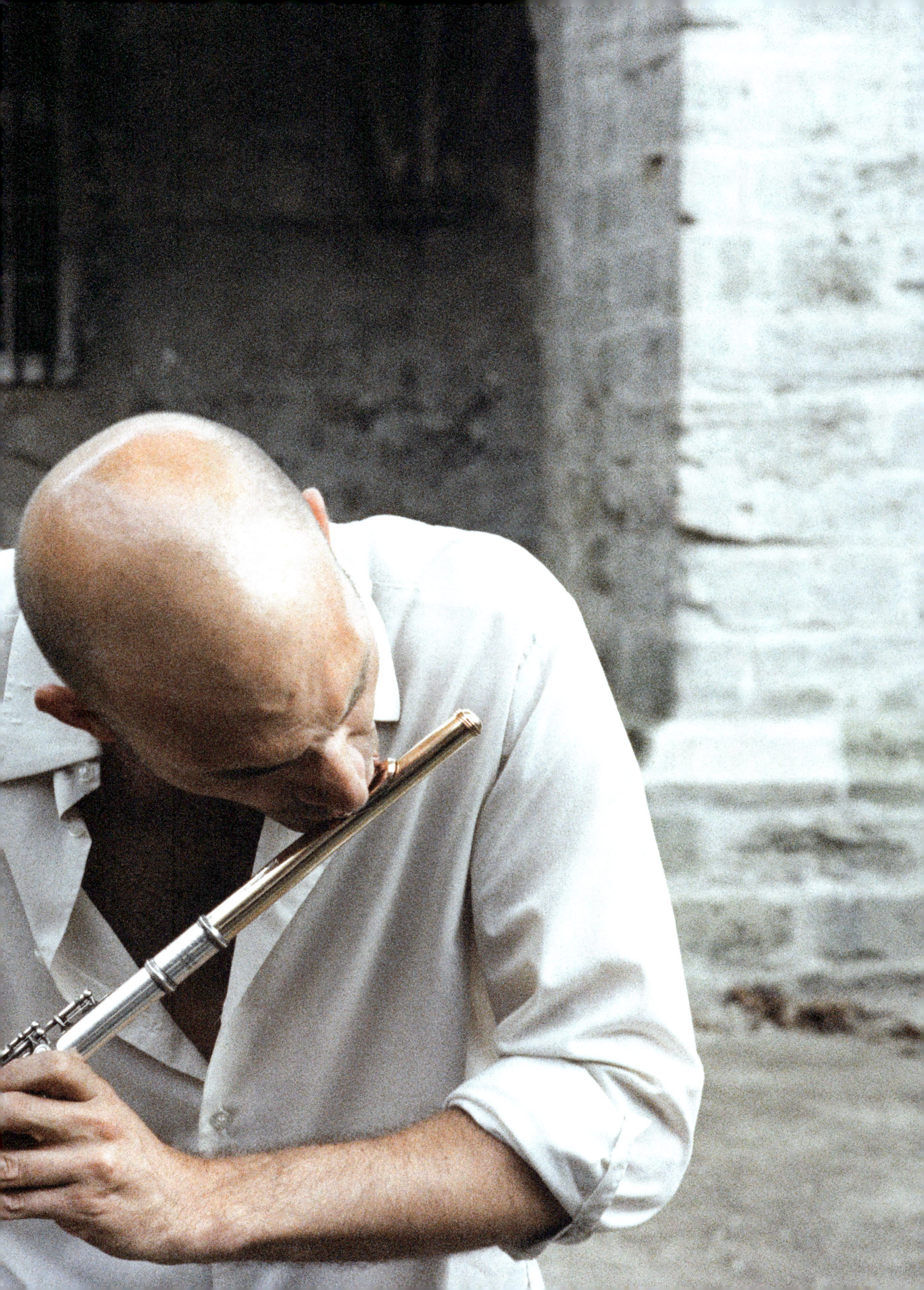

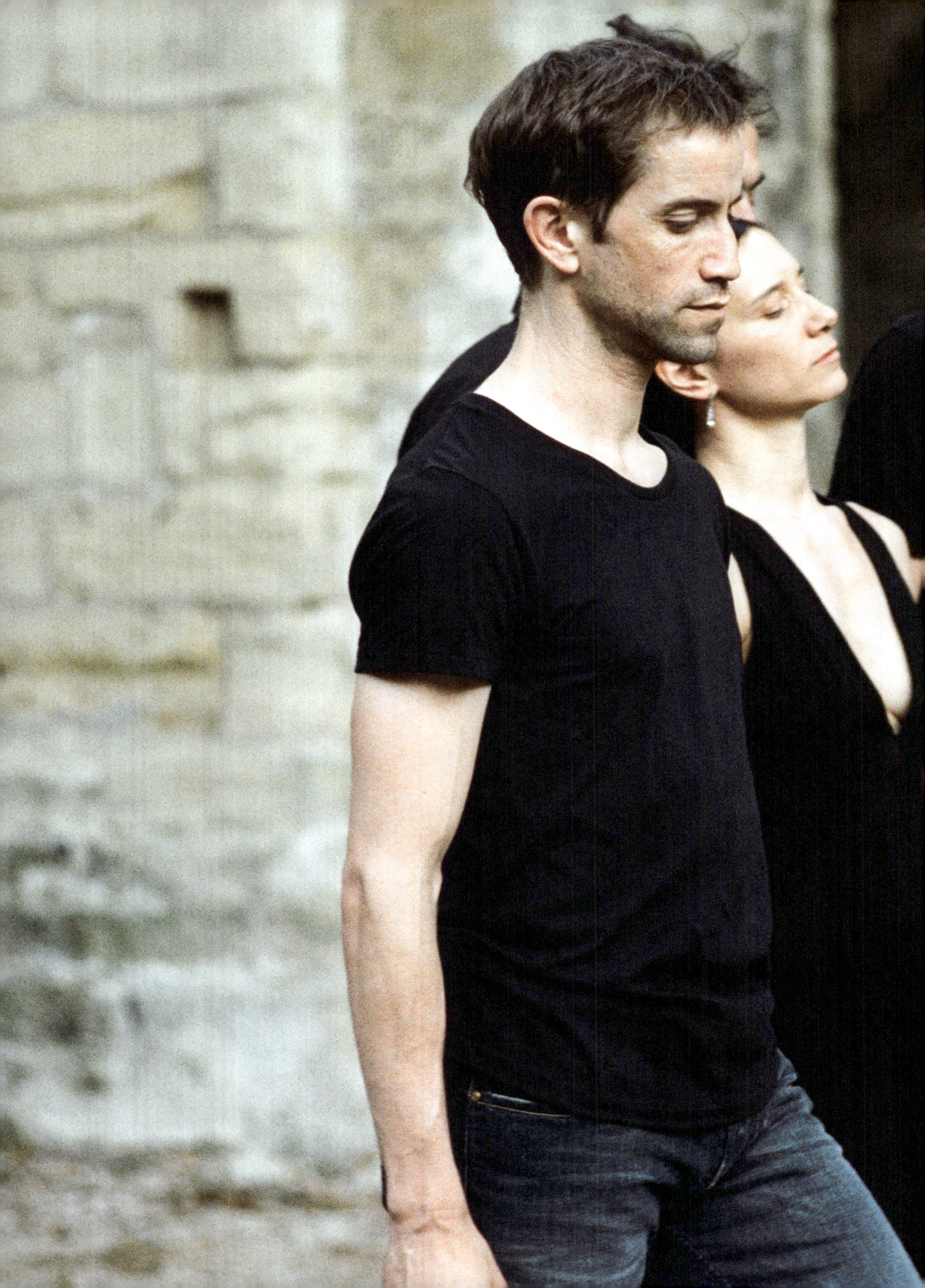

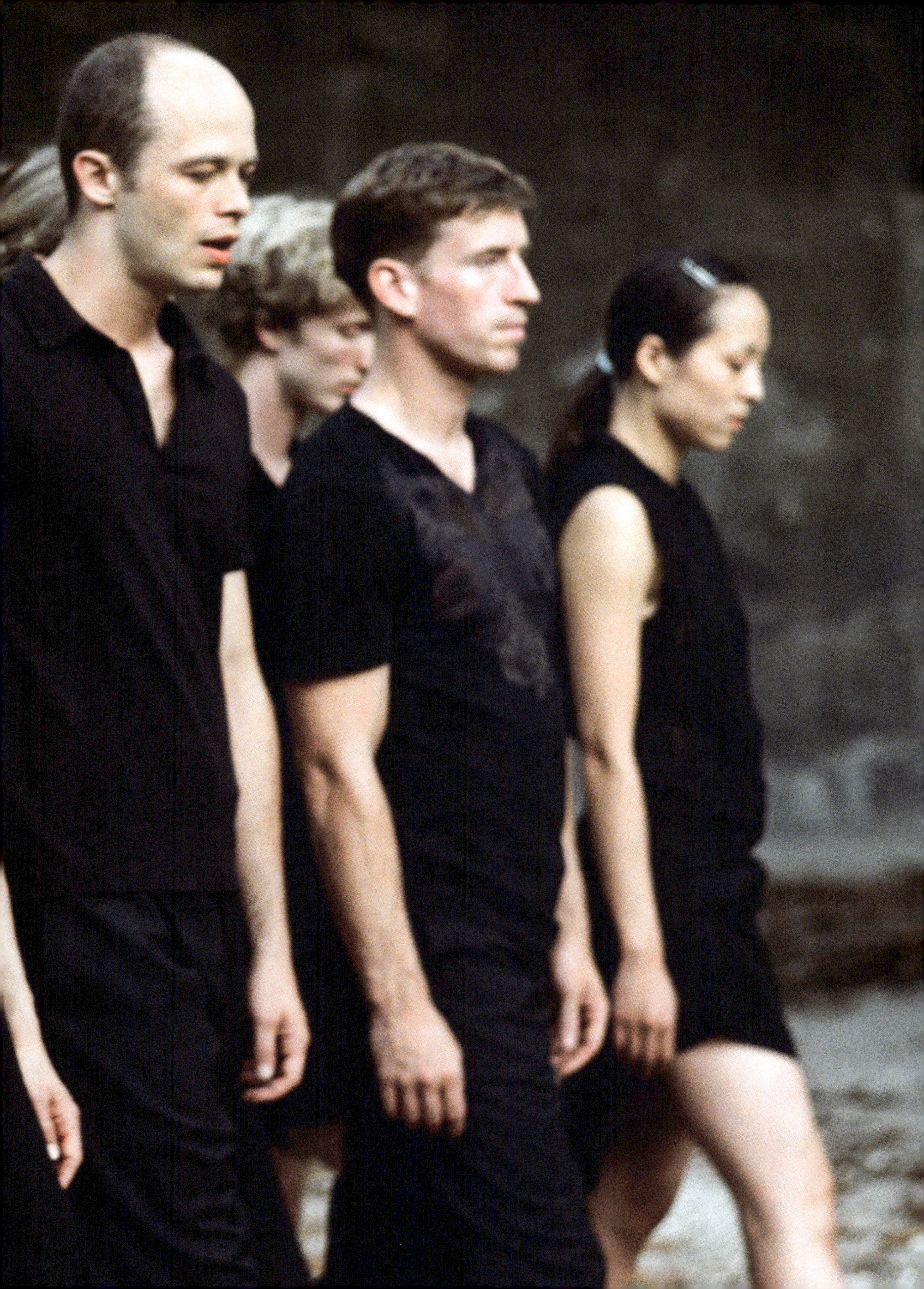

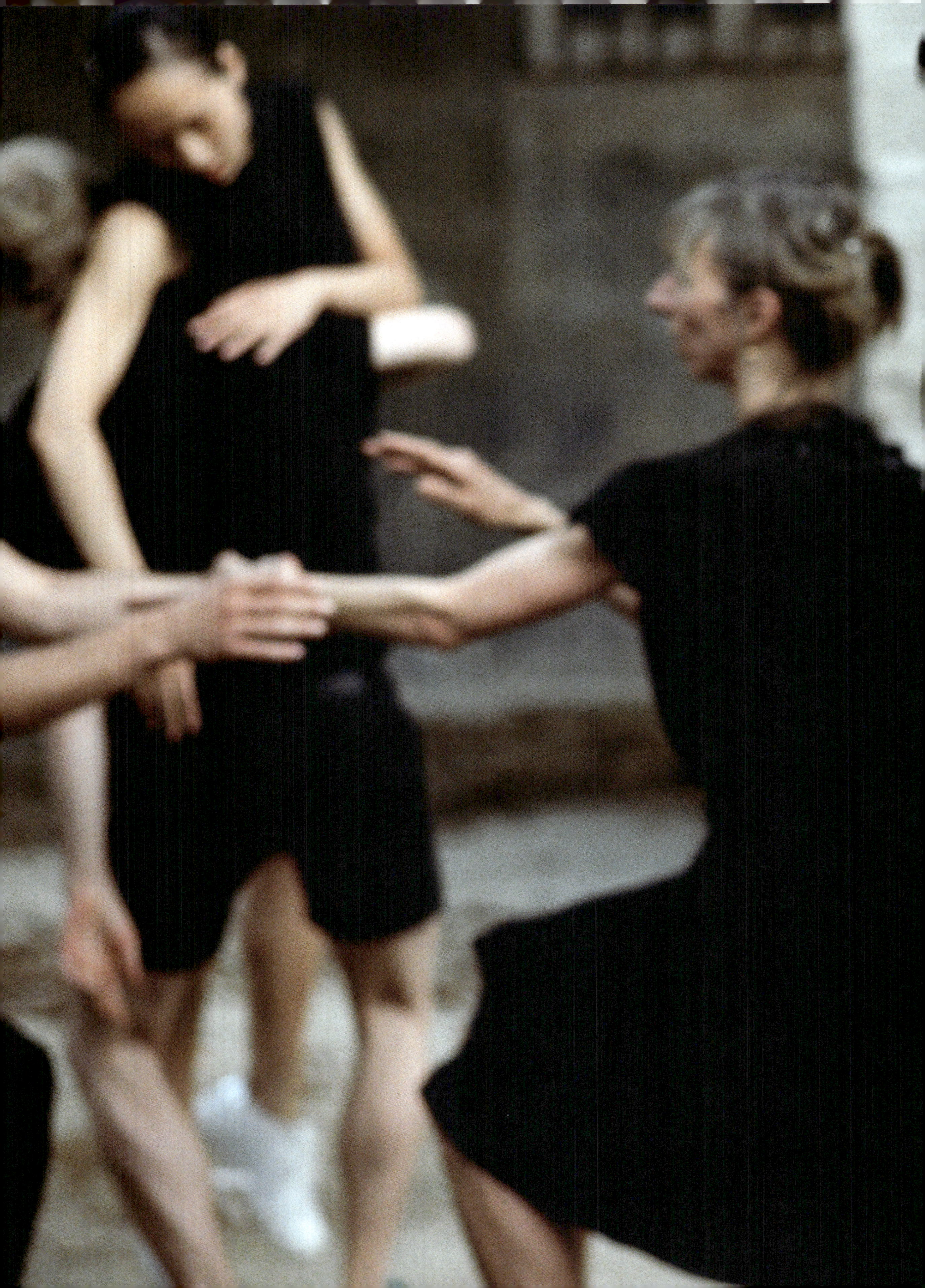

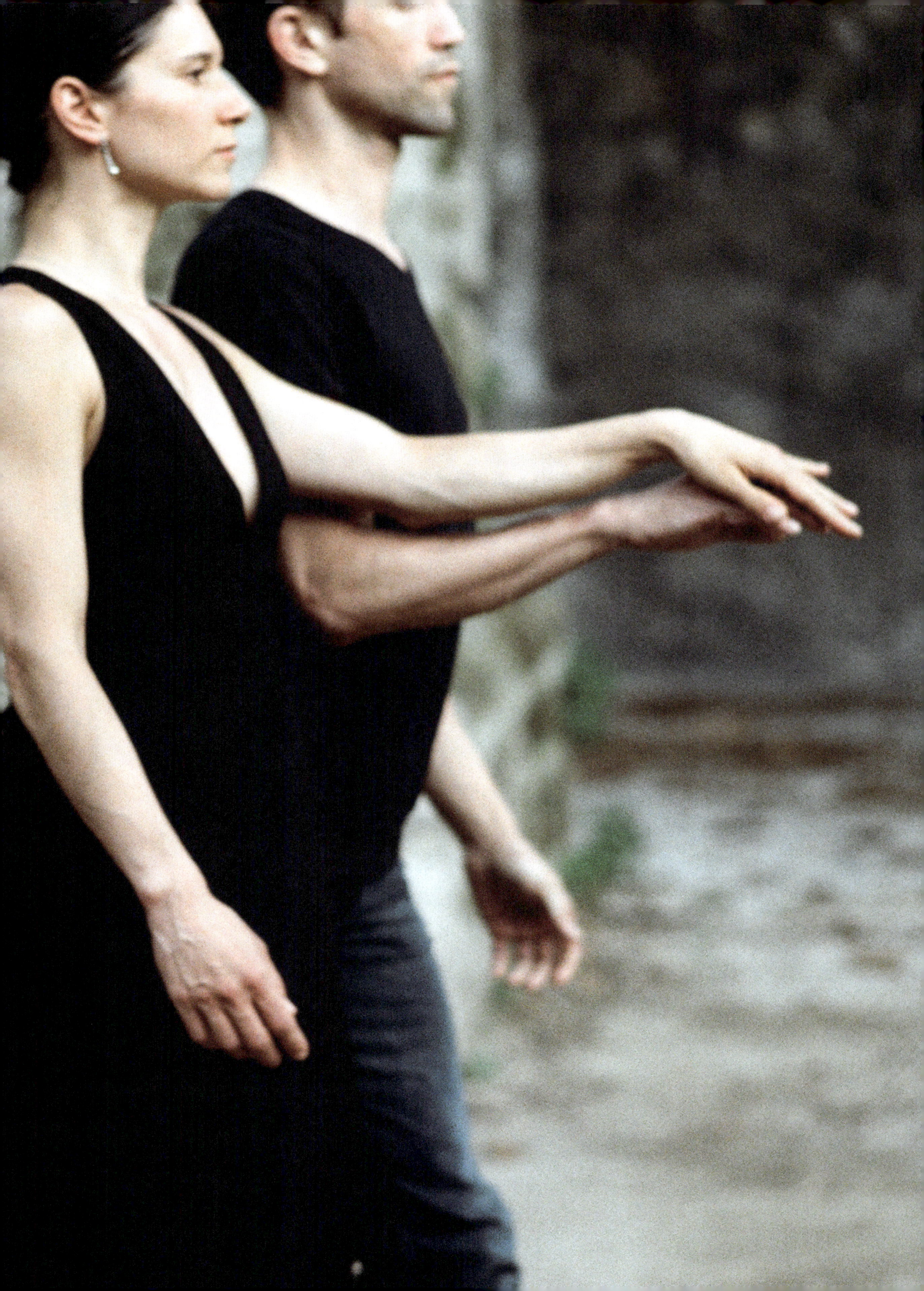

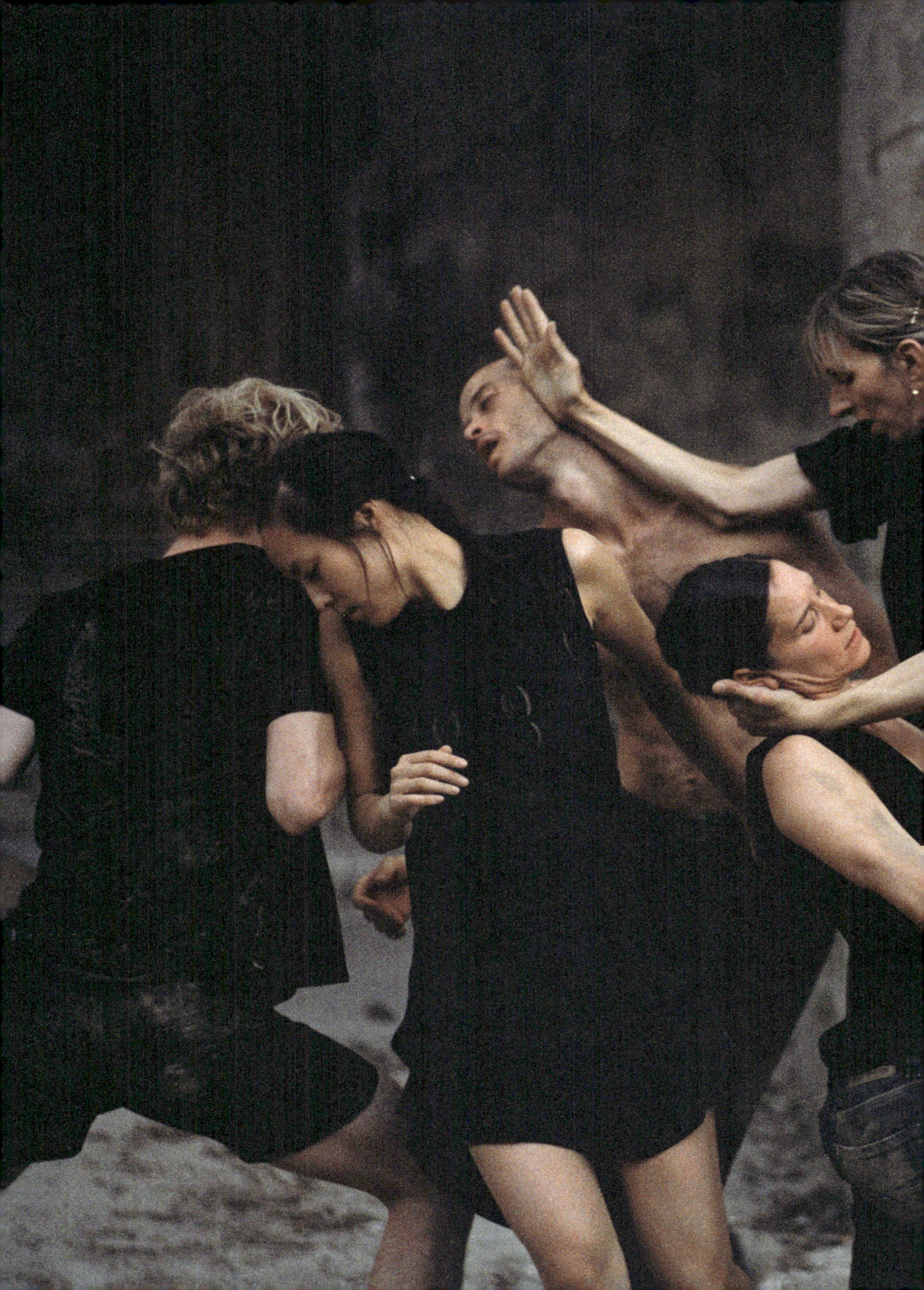

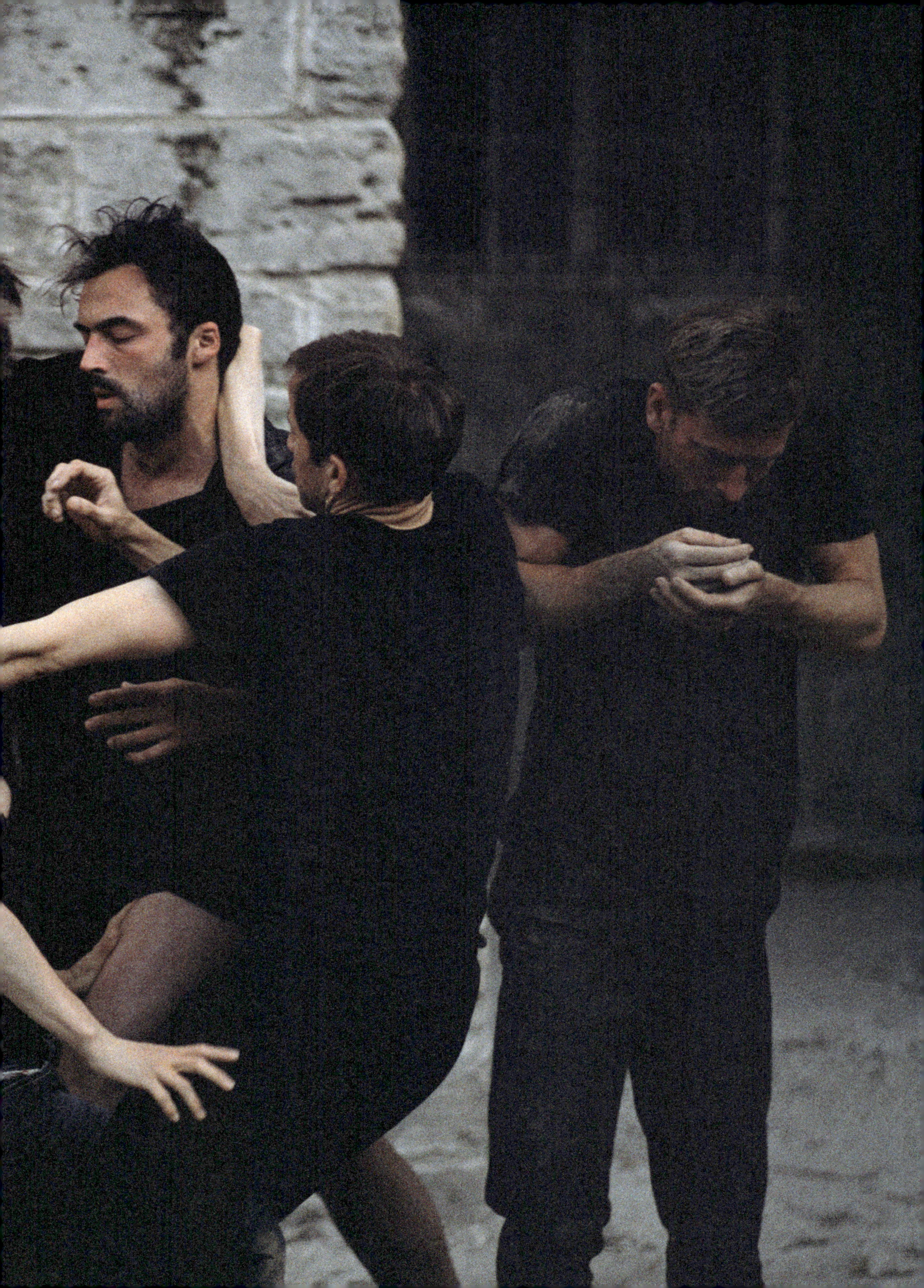

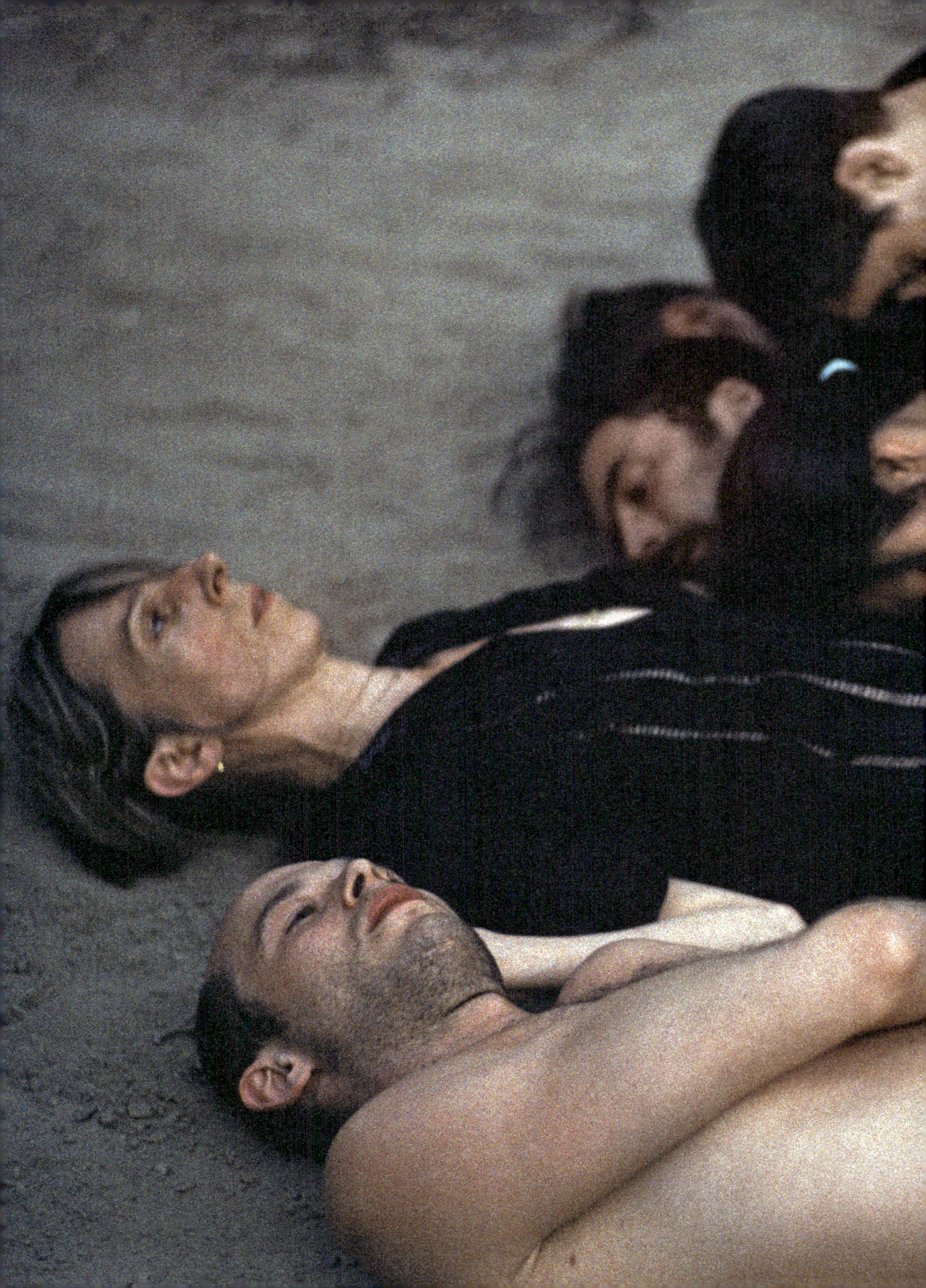

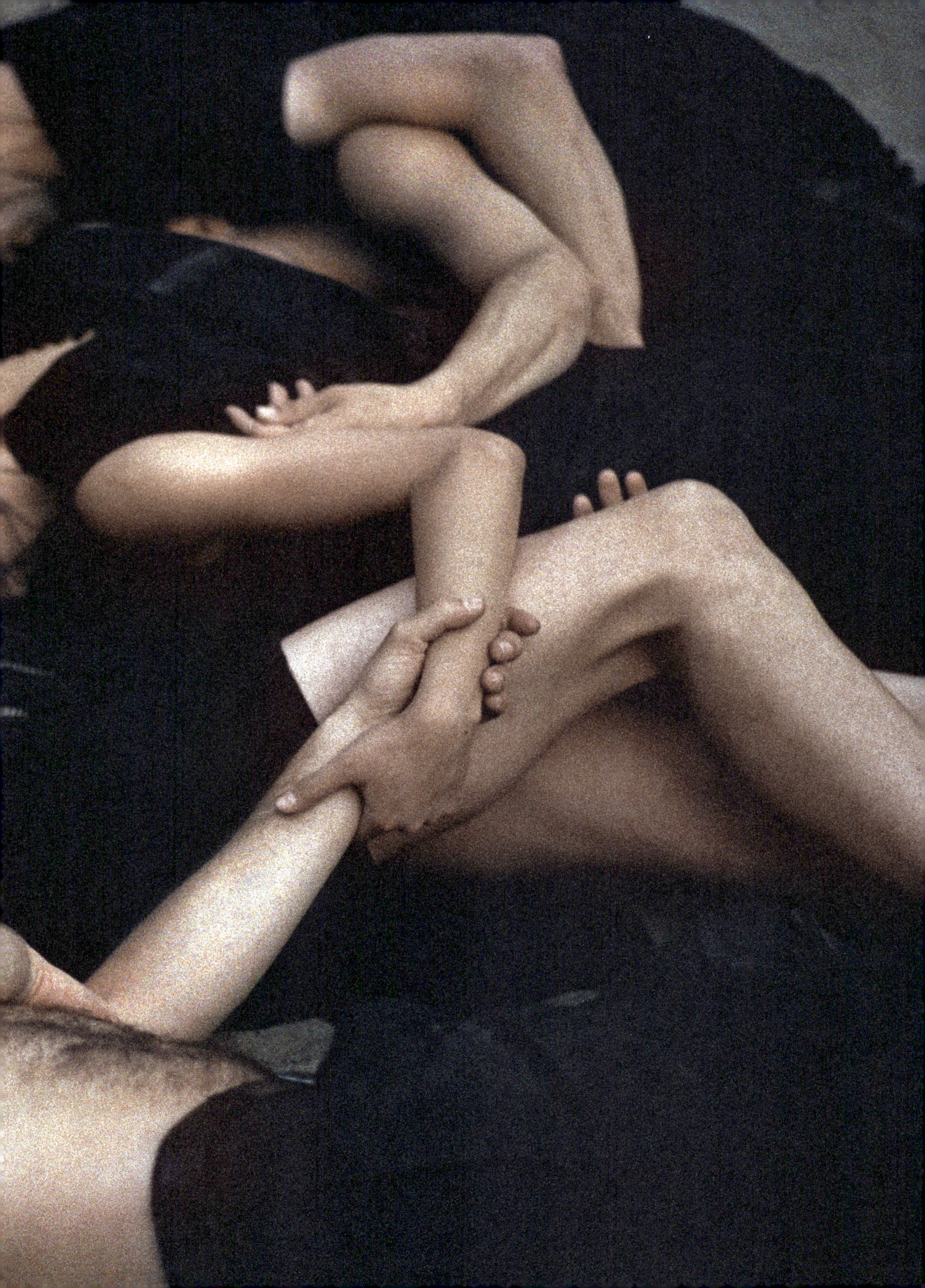

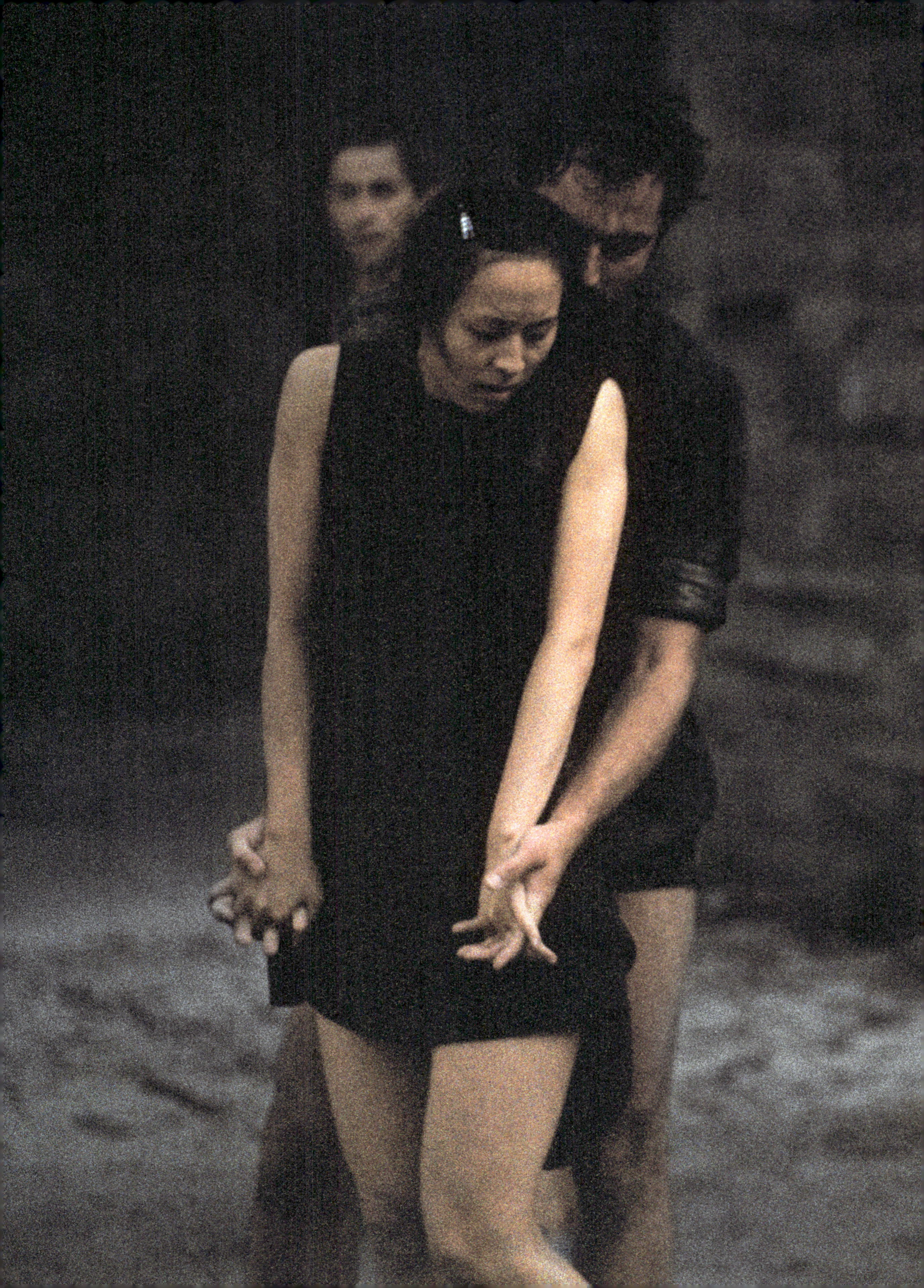

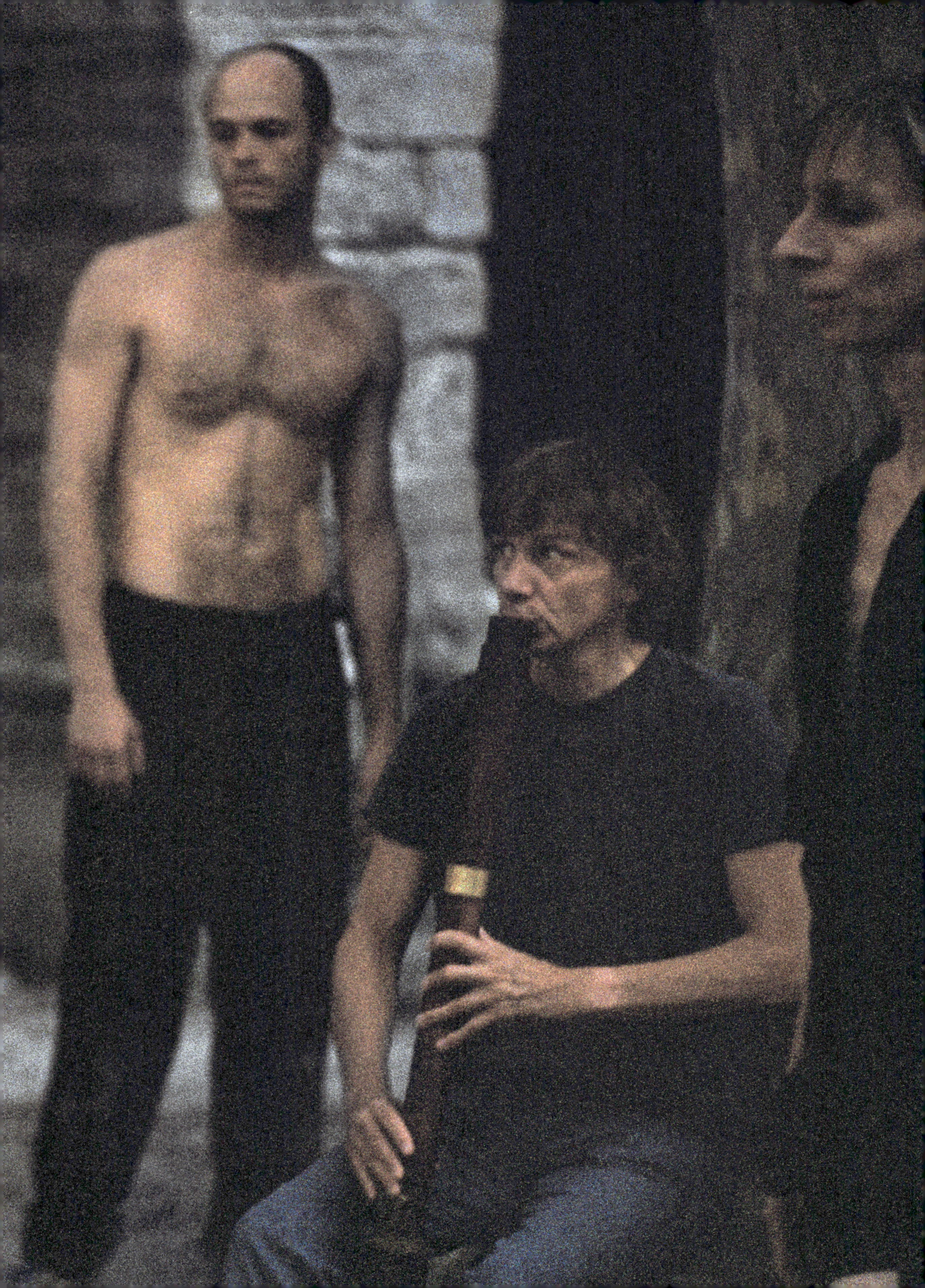

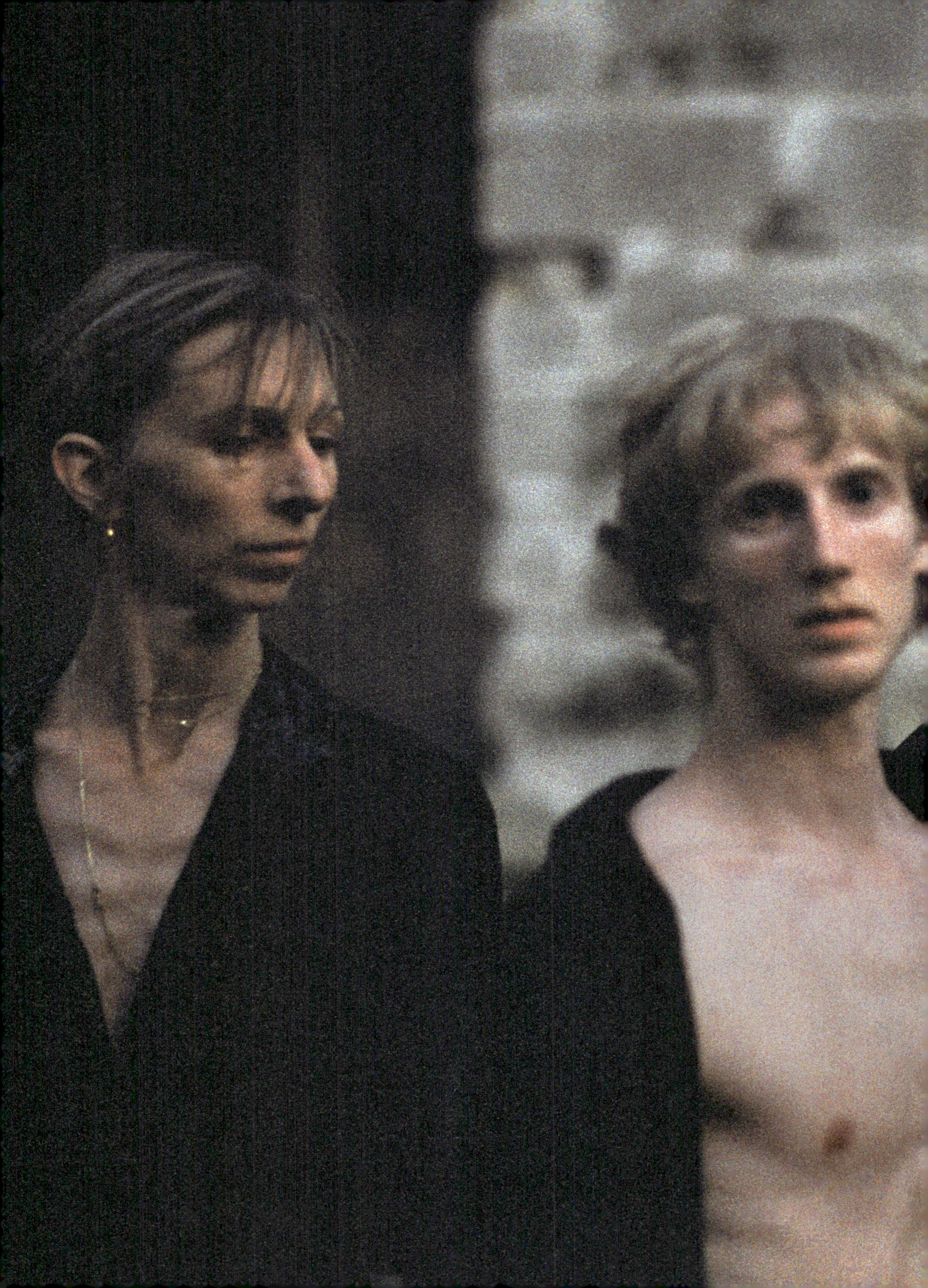

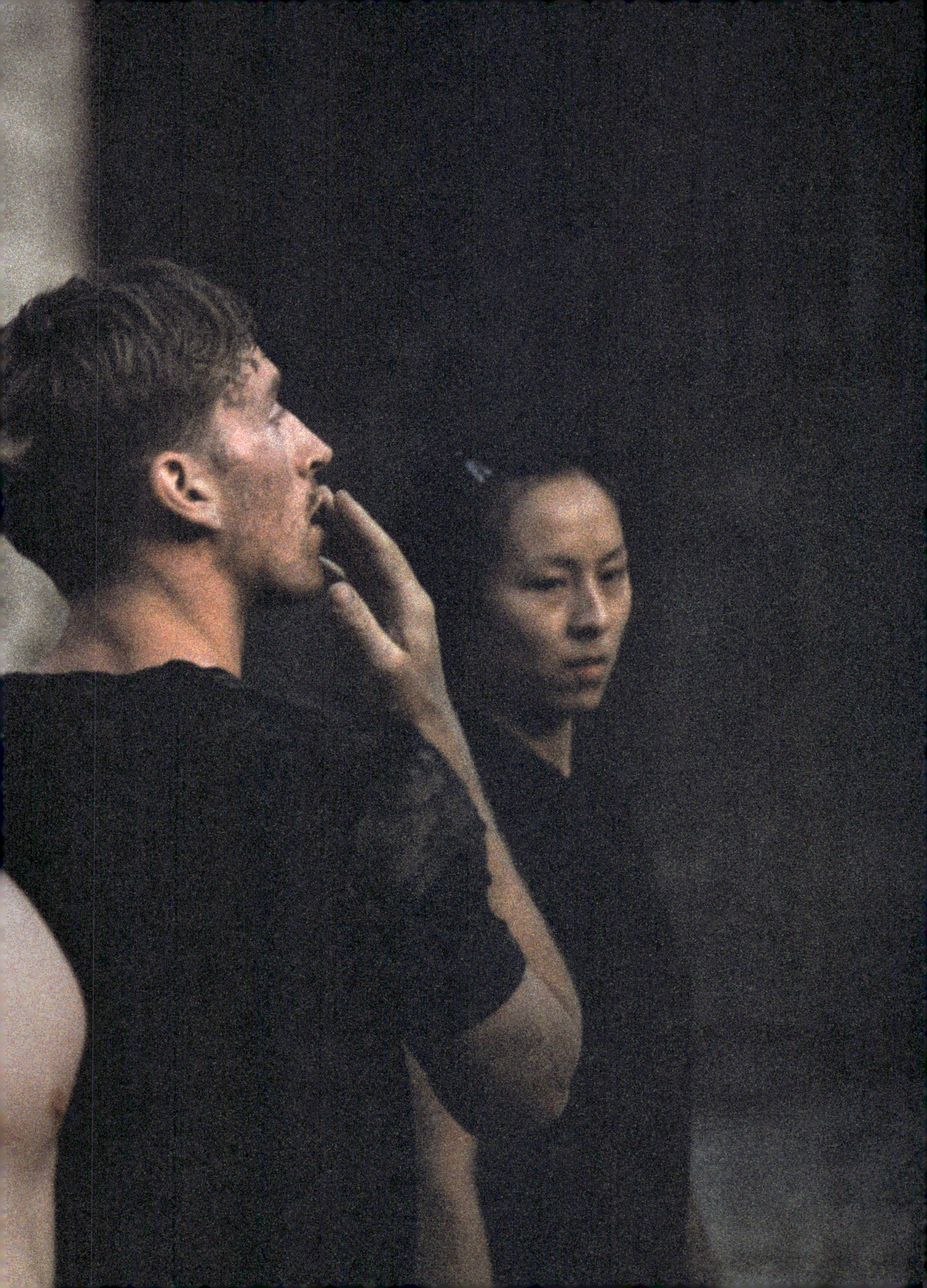

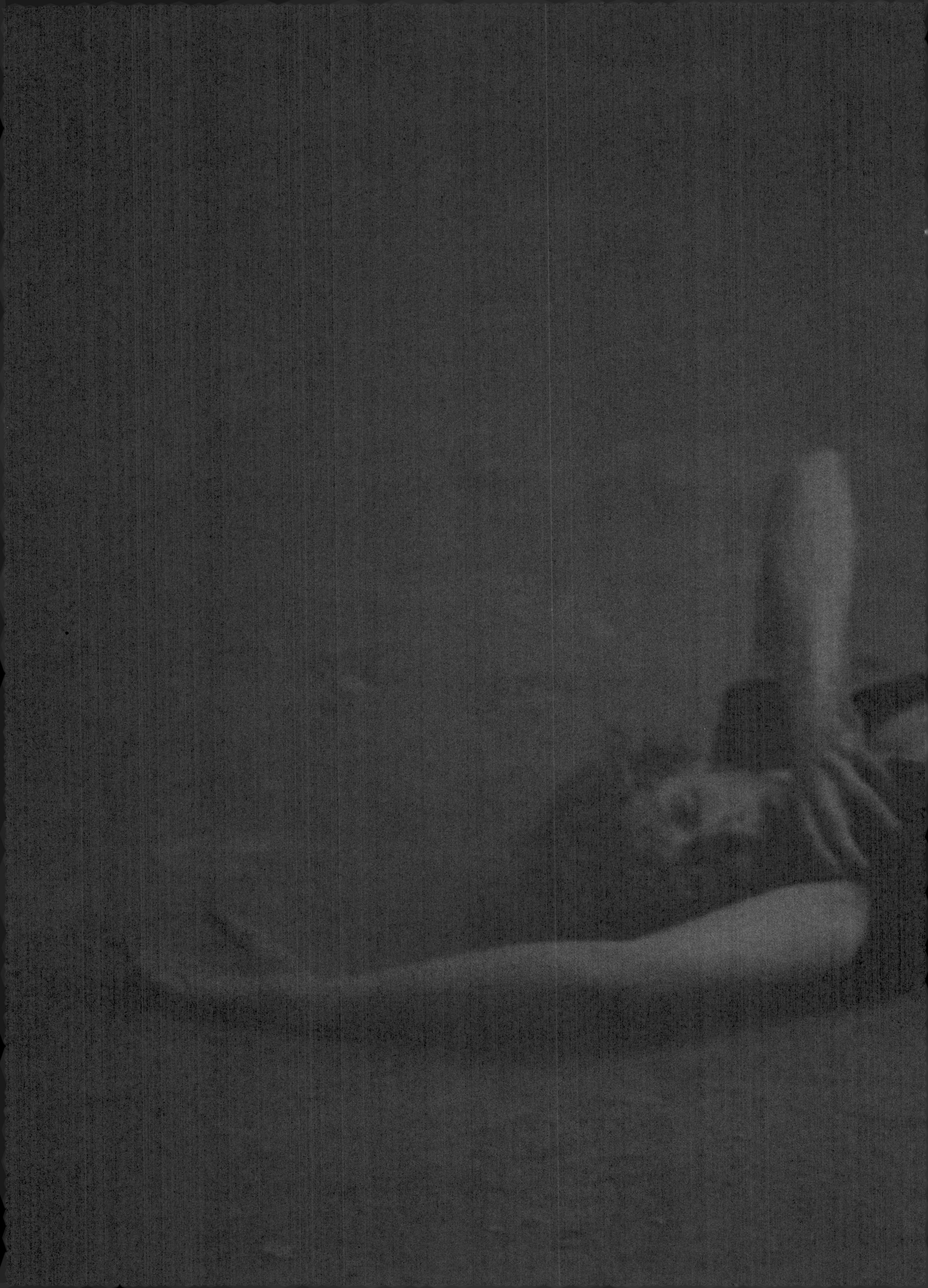

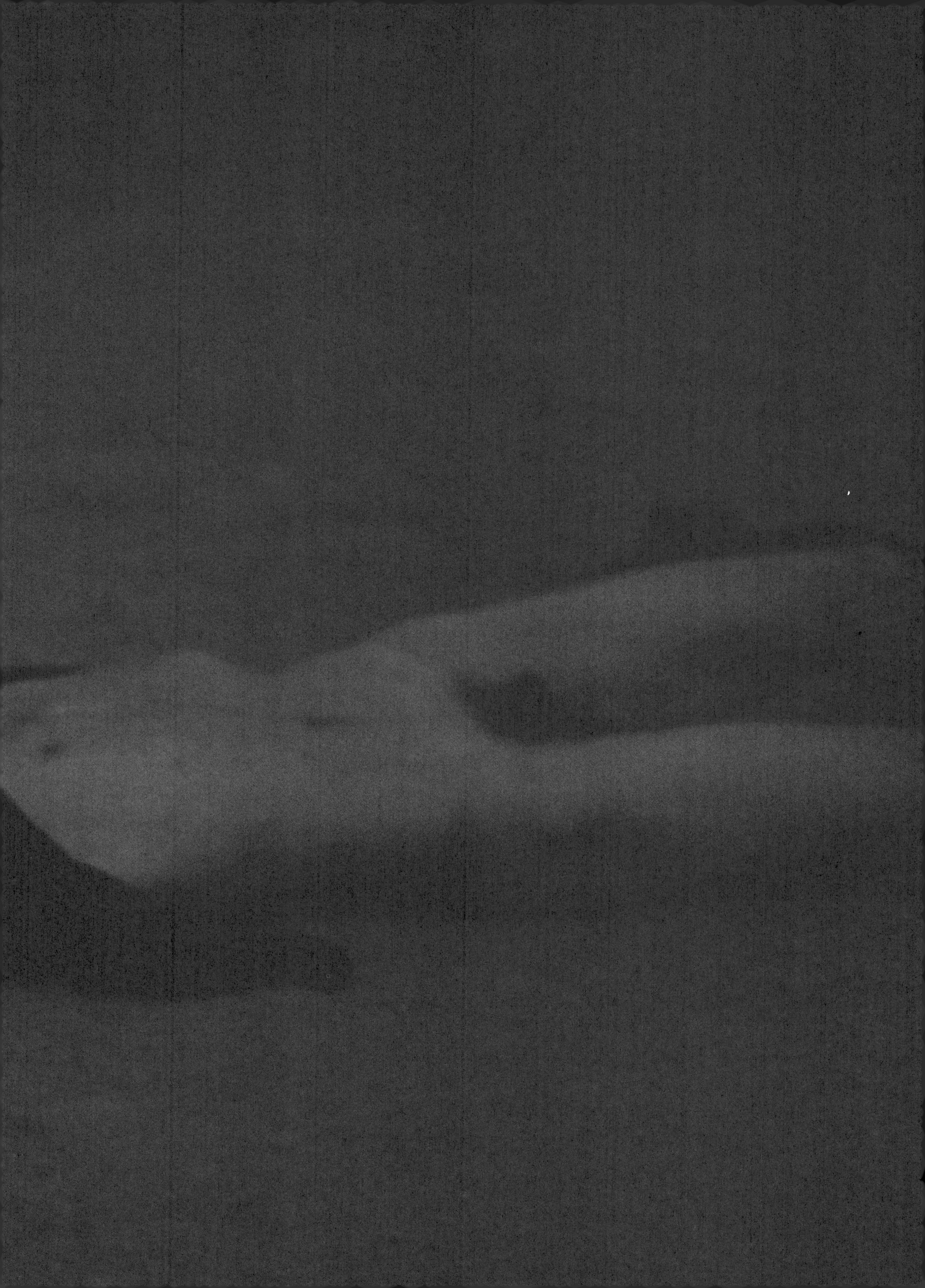

Cesena 2011

Concept
Anne Teresa De Keersmaeker, Björn Schmelzer
Choreography
Anne Teresa De Keersmaeker
Created with and danced by Rosas and graindelavoix
Olalla Alemán / Els Van Laethem, Haider Al Timimi, Boštjan Antončič, Aron Blom, Carlos Garbin, Marie Goudot, Lieven Gouwy / Joachim Brackx, David Hernandez, Matej Kejžar, Mikael Marklund, Tomàs Maxé, Julien Monty, Chrysa Parkinson, Marius Peterson, Michaël Pomero, Albert Riera, Gabriel Schenker, Yves Van Handenhove, Sandy Williams
Musical direction
Björn Schmelzer
Music
Ars subtilior:
Pictagore per dogmata / O Terra sancta / Rosa vernans, anonymous (Codex Chantilly)
Espoir dont tu m'as fayt partir, Philipoctus de Caserta (Codex Chantilly)
Corps femenin, Solage (Codex Chantilly)
Fumeux fume par fumee, Solage (Codex Chantilly)
Par les bons Gedeon et Sanson, Philipoctus de Caserta (Codex Chantilly)
Kyrie, anonymous (Ms Toulouse)
Inter densas / Imbribuis irriguis, anonymous (Codex Chantilly)
En attendant d'amer, Galiot (Codex Chantilly)
Le ray au soleyl, Johannes Ciconia (Codex Mancini)
Hodie puer nascitur / Homo mortalis firmiter, Jean Hanelle (Codex Torino)
Scenography
Ann Veronica Janssens
Costumes
Anne-Catherine Kunz
Artistic assistants
Anne Van Aerschot, Femke Gyselinck
Sound
Alexandre Fostier
Production
Rosas
Coproduction
La Monnaie / De Munt (Brussels), Festival d'Avignon, Théâtre de la Ville (Paris), Les Théâtres de la Ville de Luxembourg, Festival Oude Muziek Utrecht, Guimarães 2012, Steirischer Herbst (Graz), deSingel (Antwerp), Concertgebouw Bruges
Premiere
16.07.2011, Palais des Papes—Festival d'Avignon

Pictures 1-3
Herman Sorgeloos
Pictures 4-5
Michel François
Picture 6
Ann Veronica Janssens

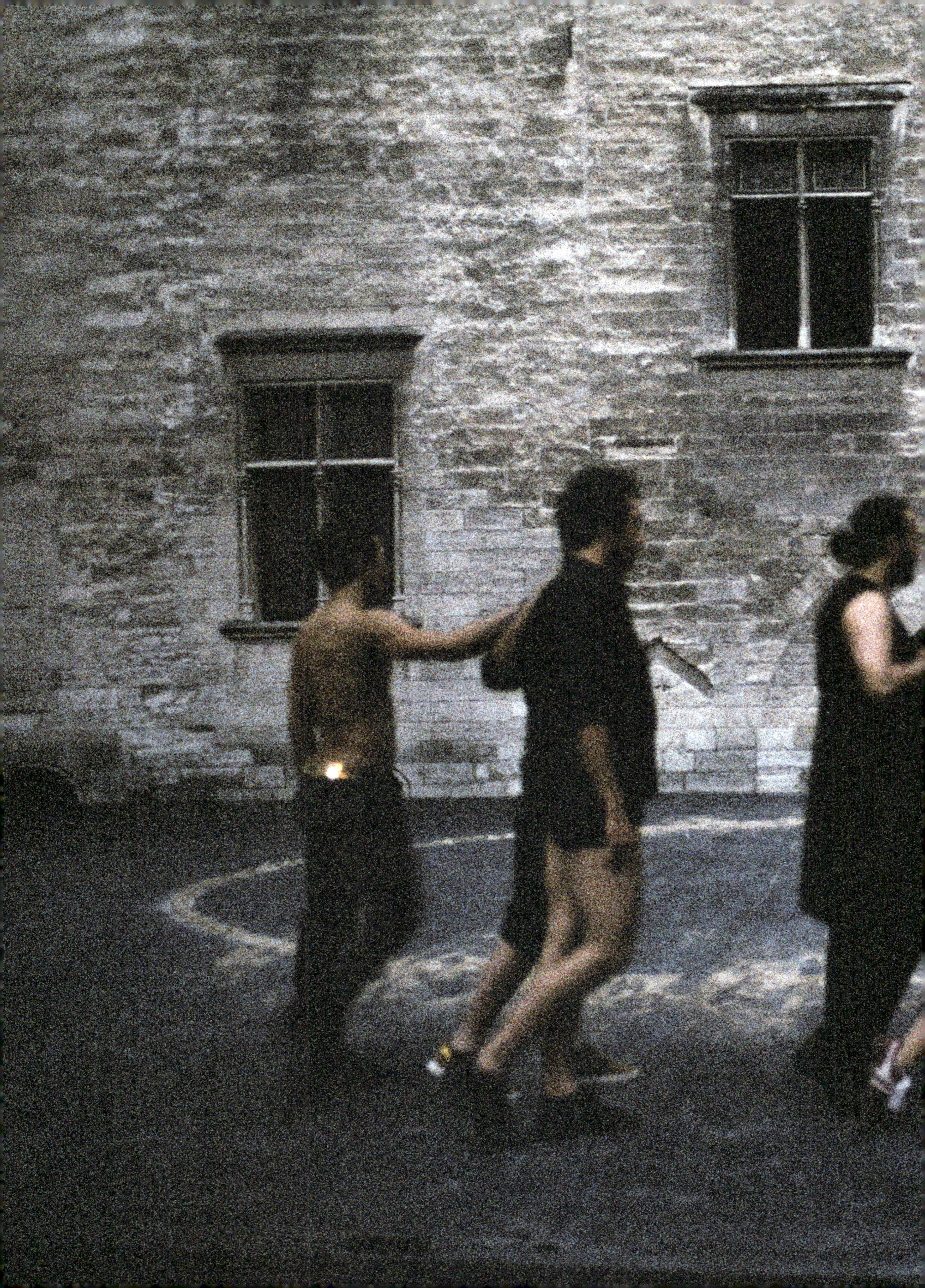

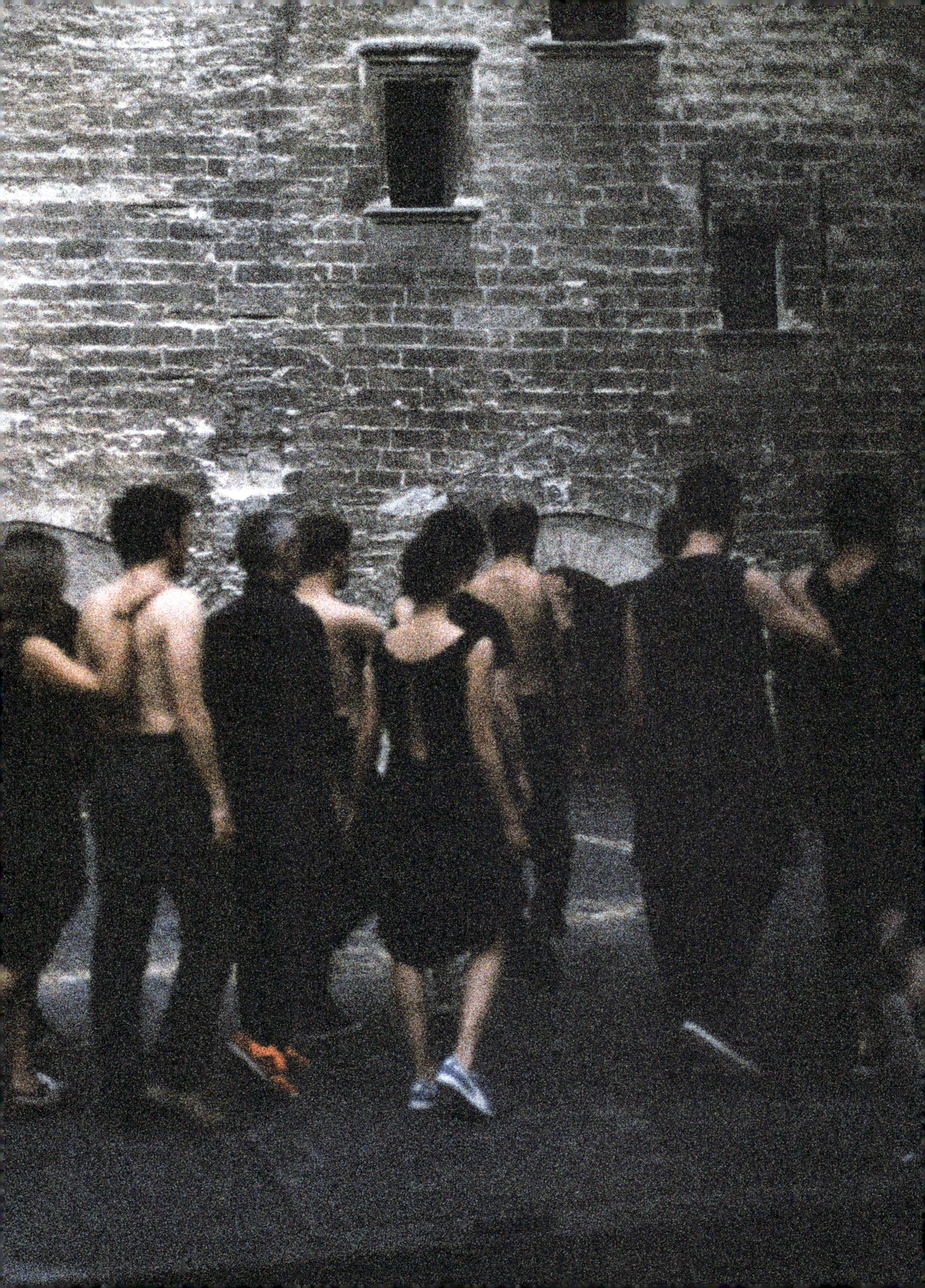

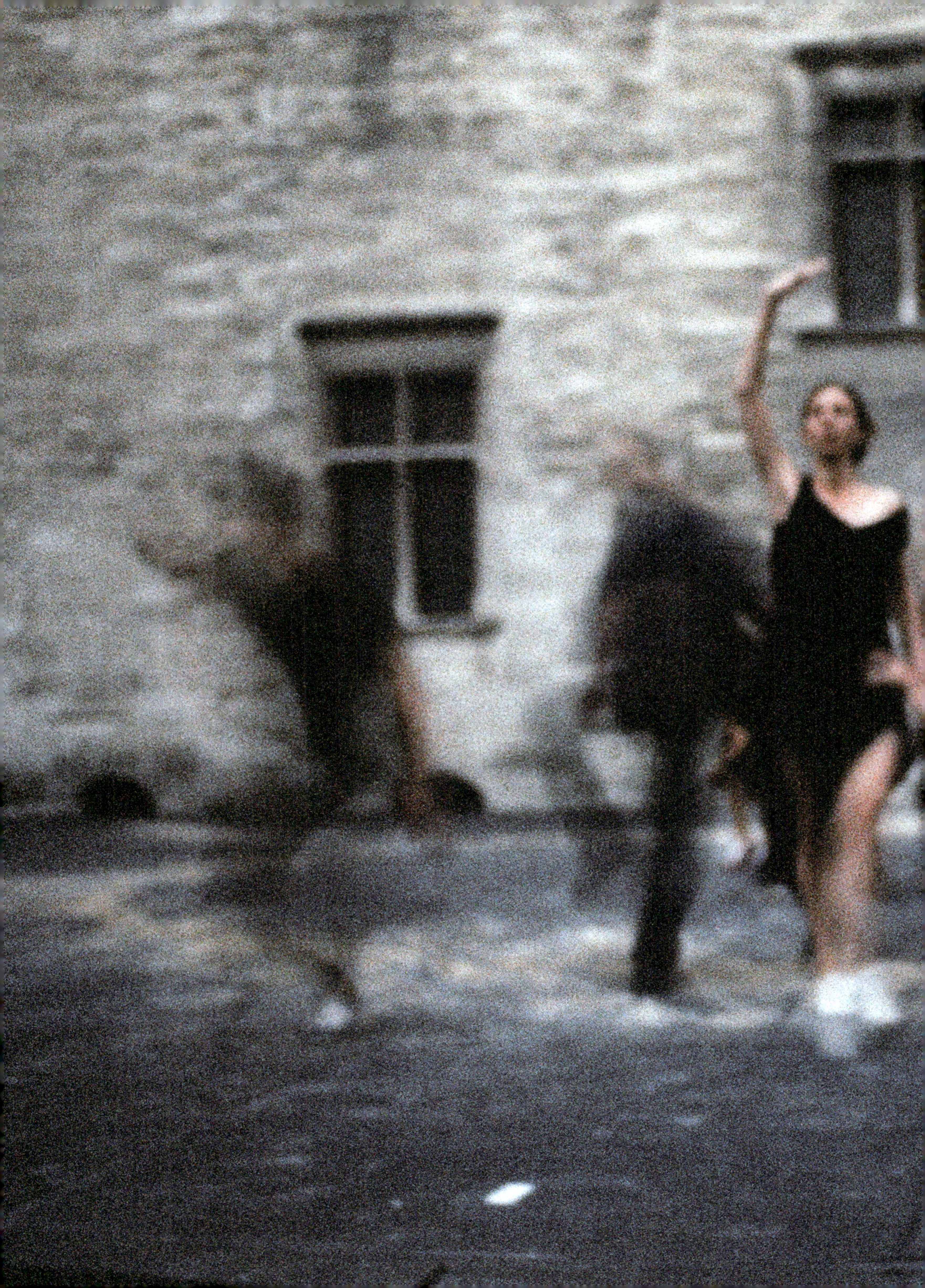

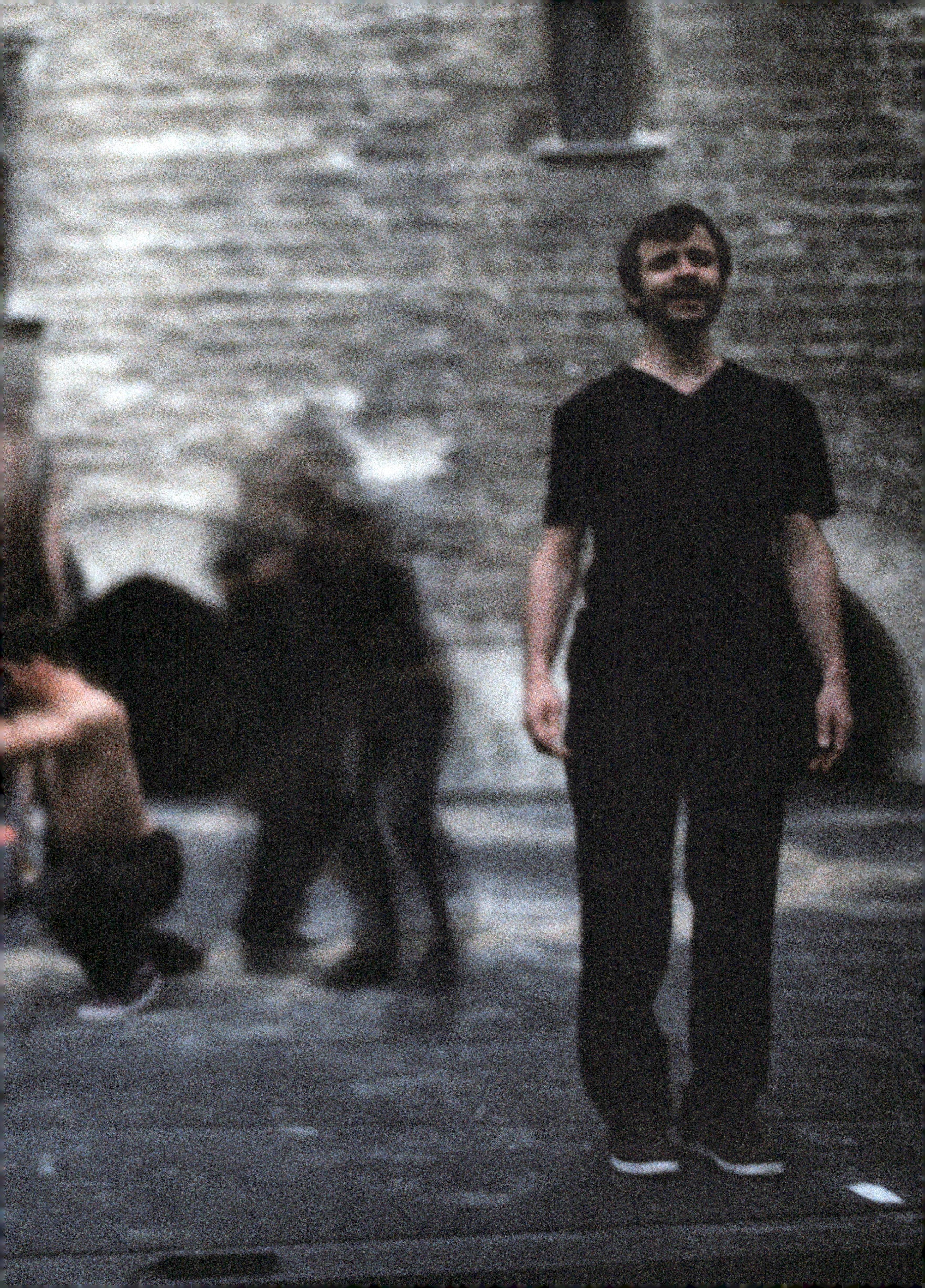

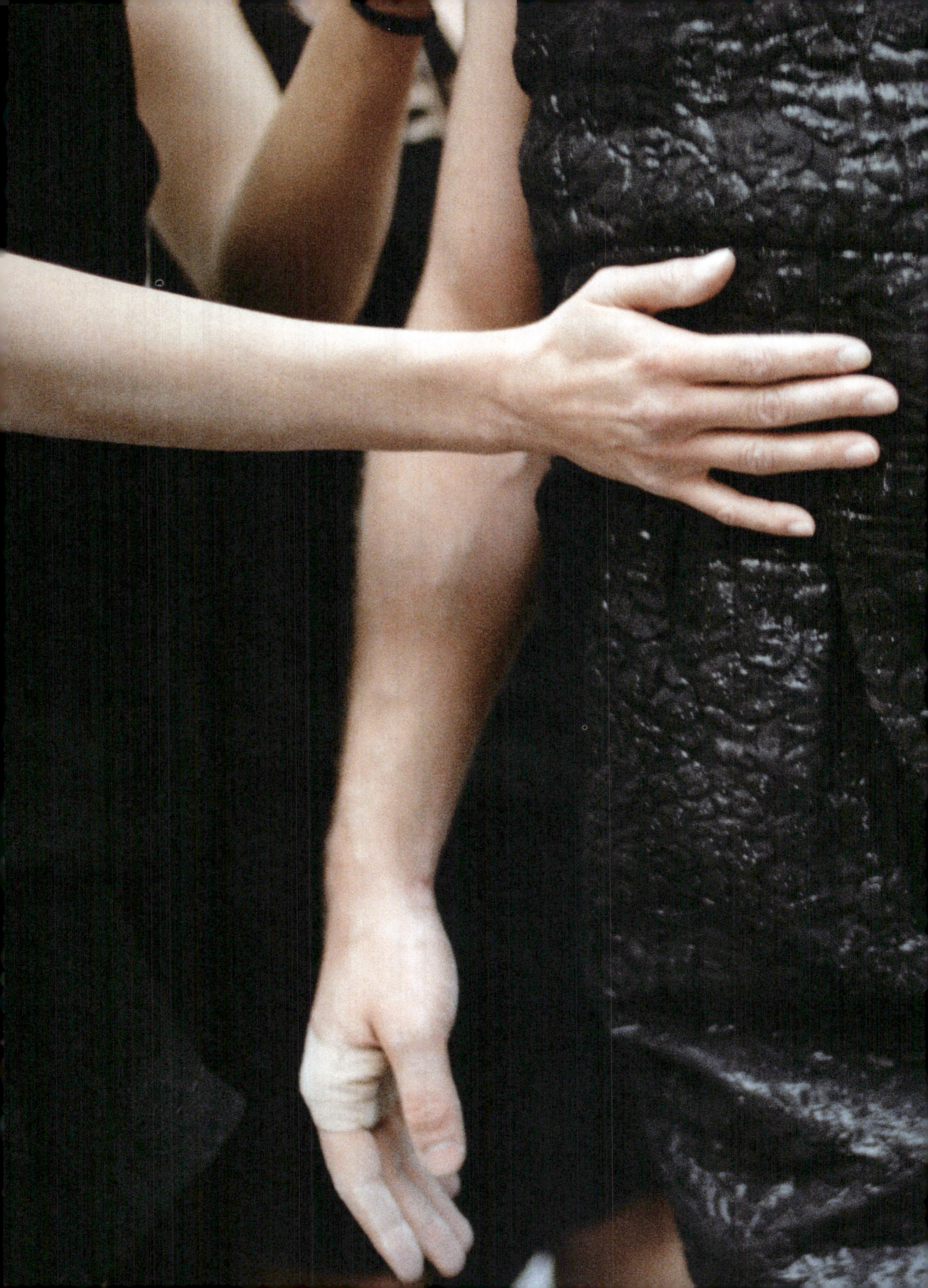

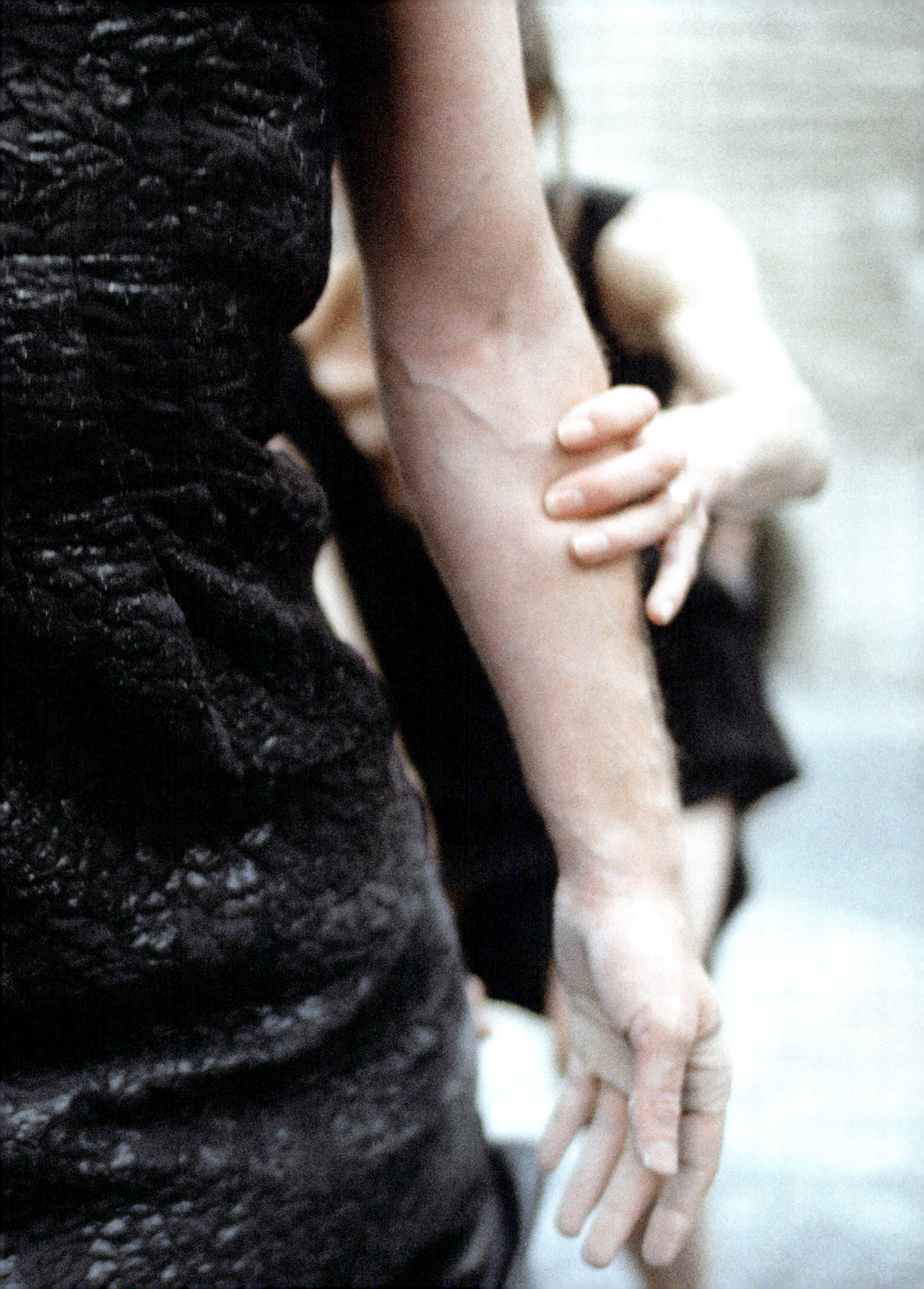

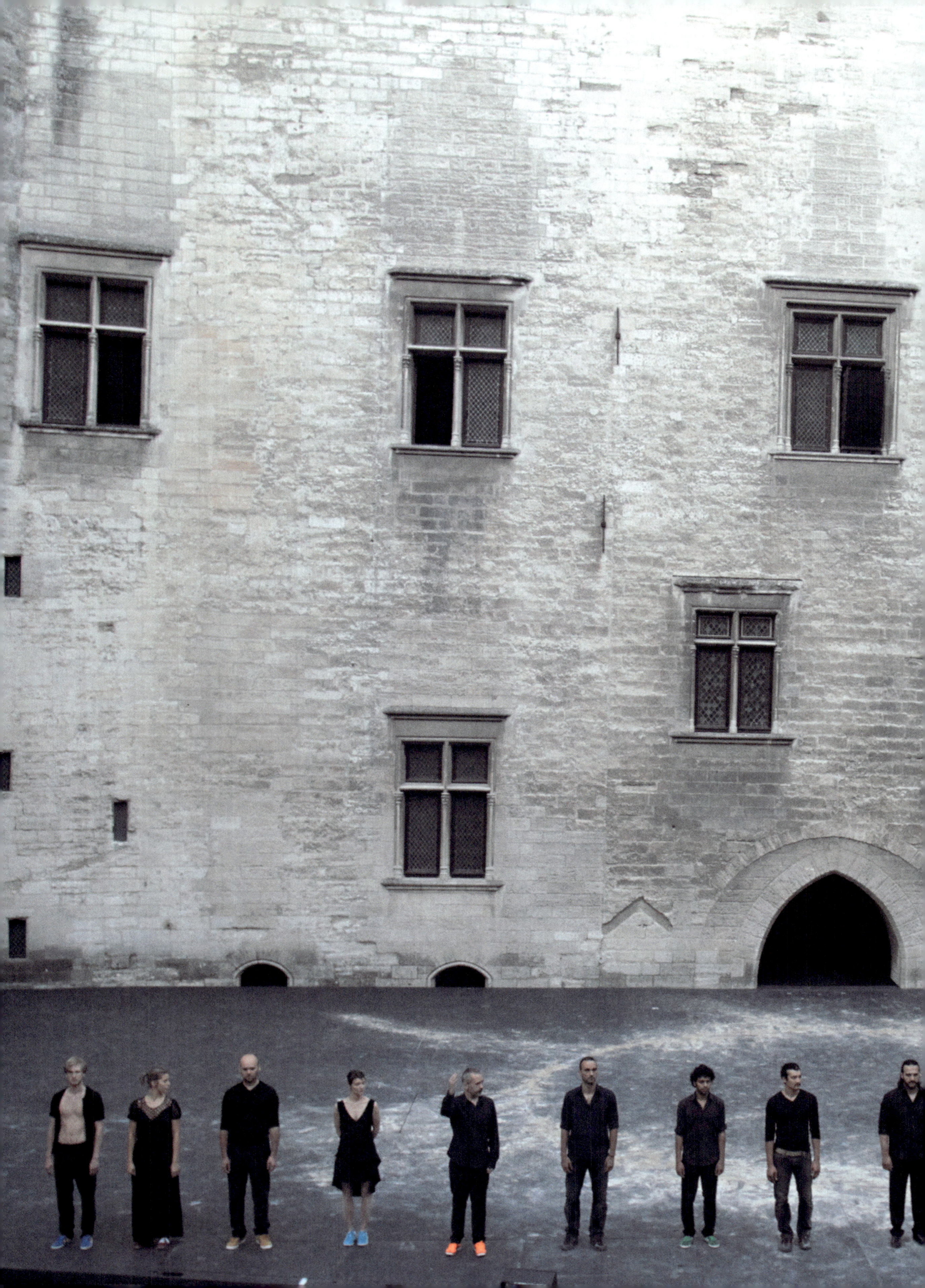

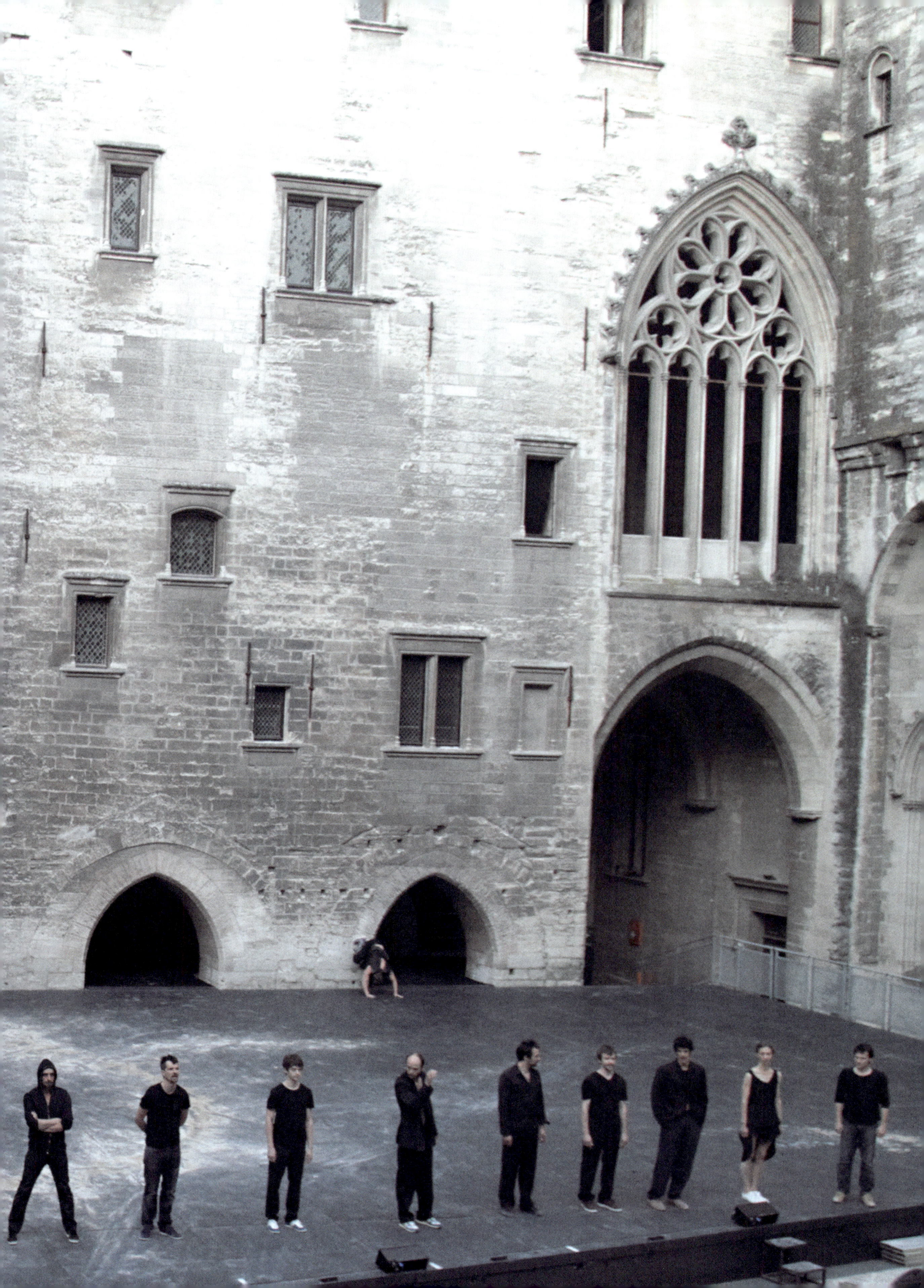

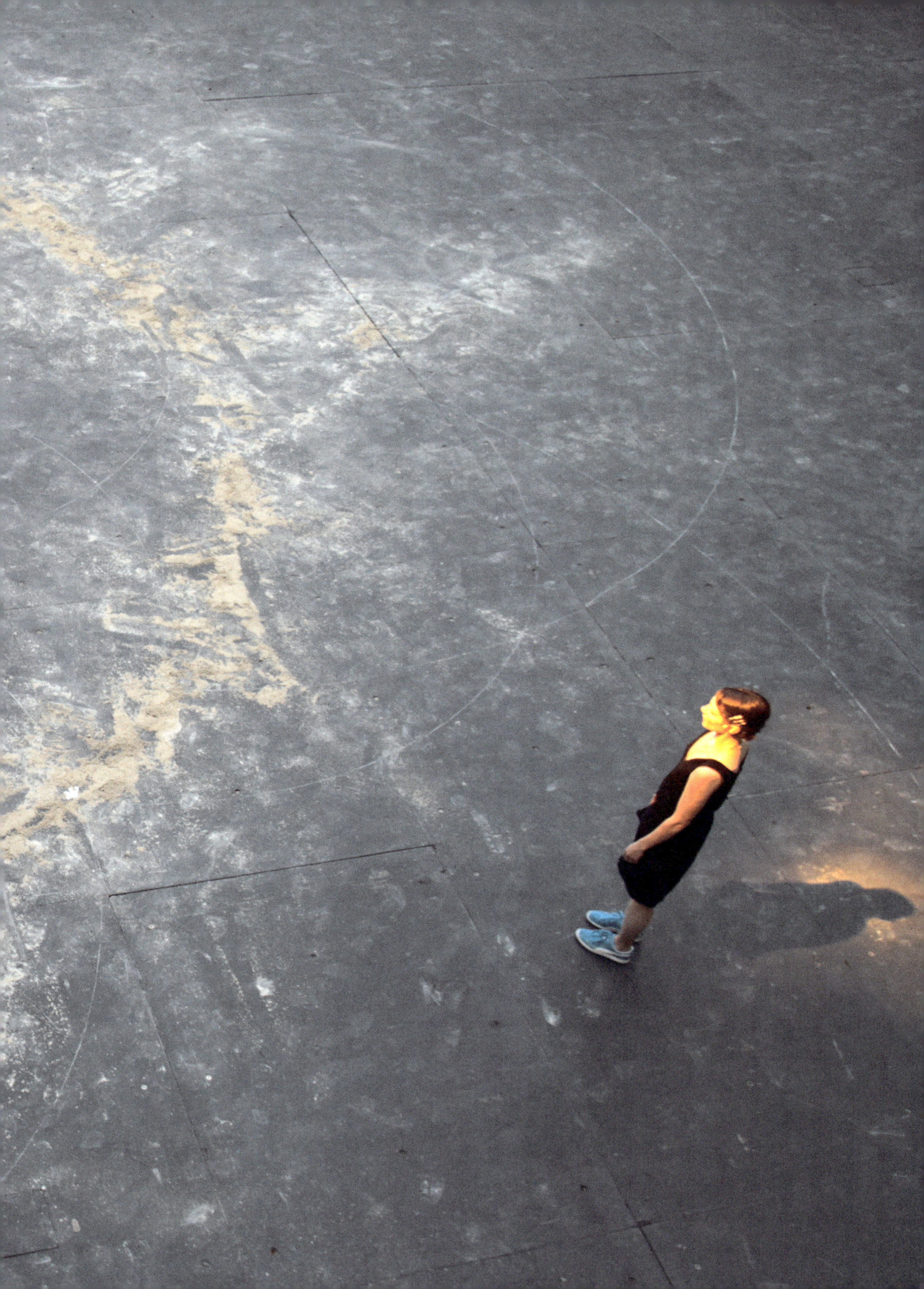

Partita 2 2013

Concept and choreography
Anne Teresa De Keersmaeker
Created with and danced by
Boris Charmatz, Anne Teresa De Keersmaeker
Music
Partita No. 2, Johann Sebastian Bach
Violin
Amandine Beyer / George Alexander Van Dam
Scenography
Michel François
Costumes
Anne-Catherine Kunz
Artistic assistant
Femke Gyselinck
Sound
Alban Moraud
Production
Rosas
With the support of
Musée de la danse—Centre chorégraphique national de Rennes et de Bretagne
Coproduction
La Monnaie / De Munt (Brussels), Festival d'Avignon, Les Théâtres de la Ville de Luxembourg, Kunstenfestivaldesarts (Brussels), ImPulsTanz (Vienna), La Bâtie—Festival de Genève, Berliner Festspiele, Théâtre de la Ville met het Festival d'Automne à Paris, Fundação Calouste Gulbenkian (Lisbon), Künstlerhaus Mousonturm (Frankfurt)
Premiere
03.05.2013, Kaaitheater, Kunstenfestivaldesarts—Brussels

Pictures
Anne Van Aerschot

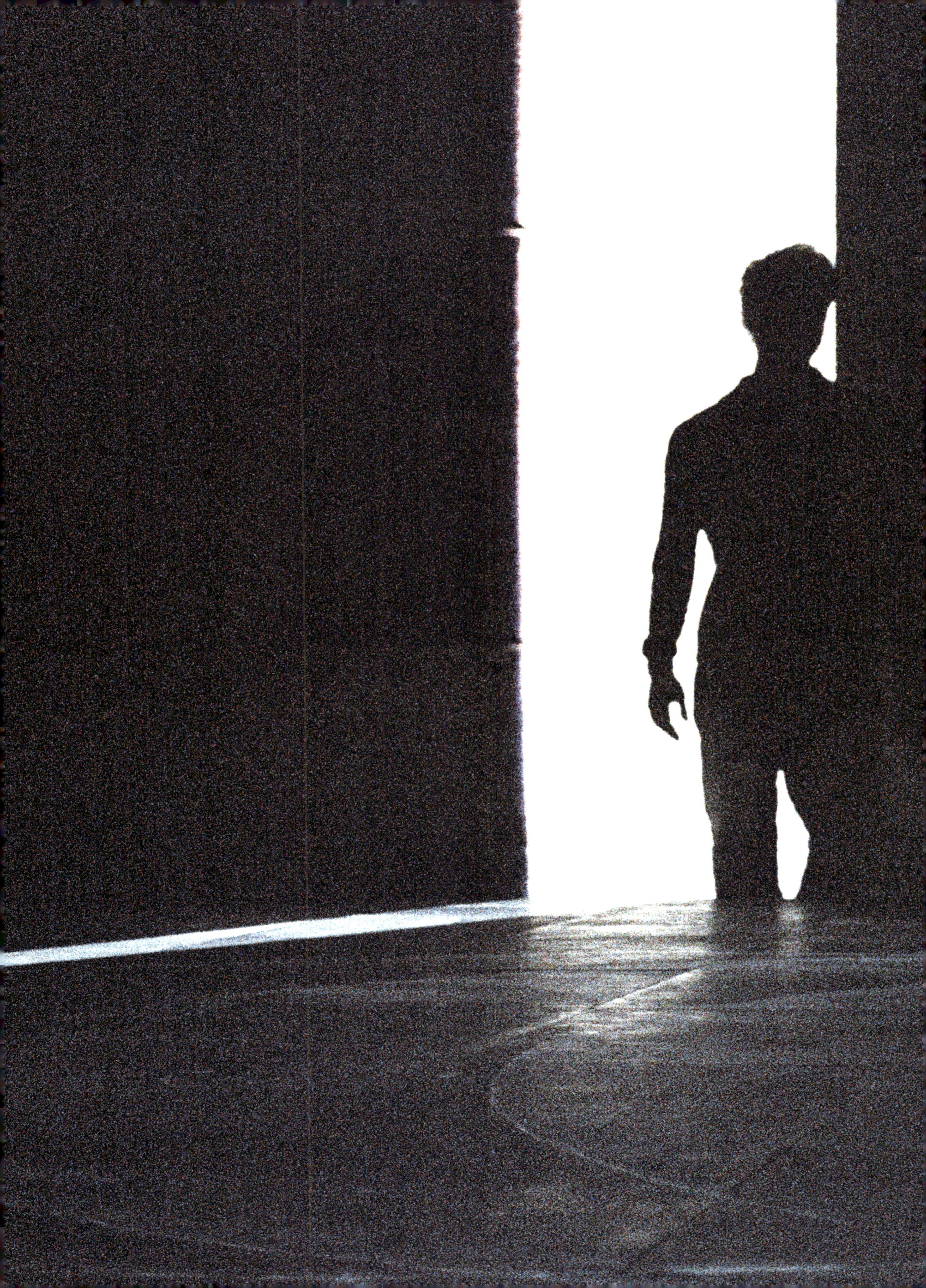

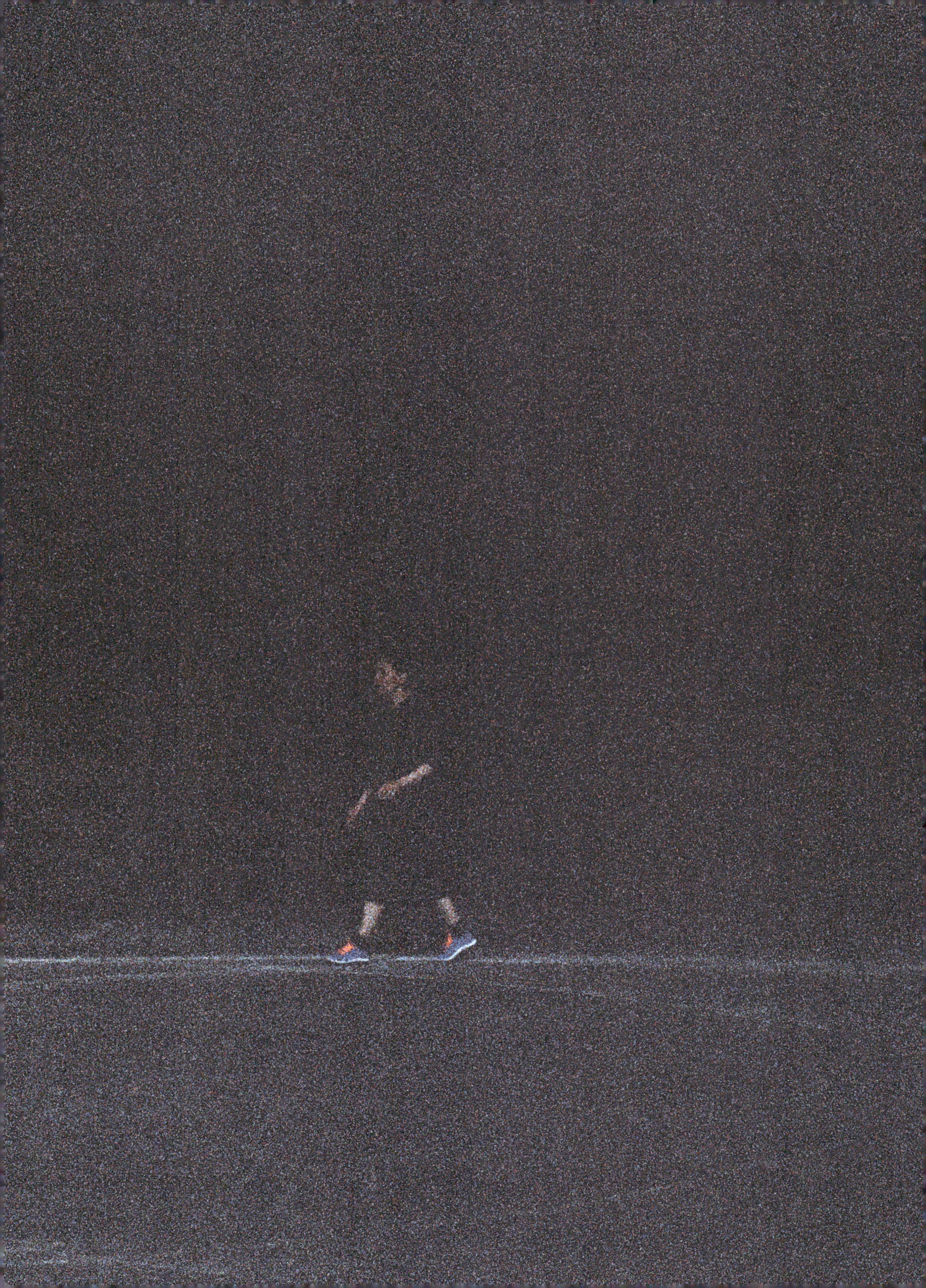

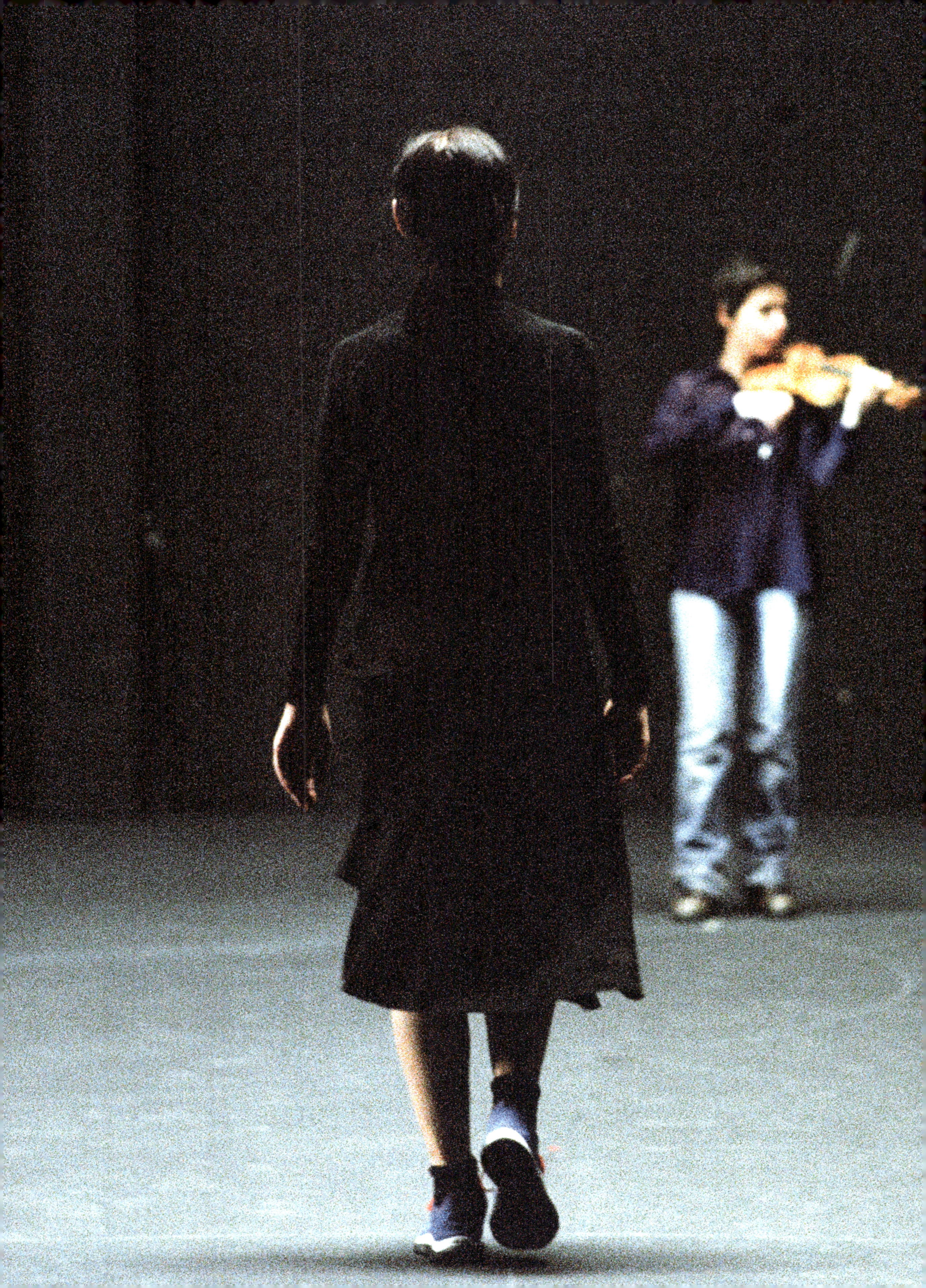

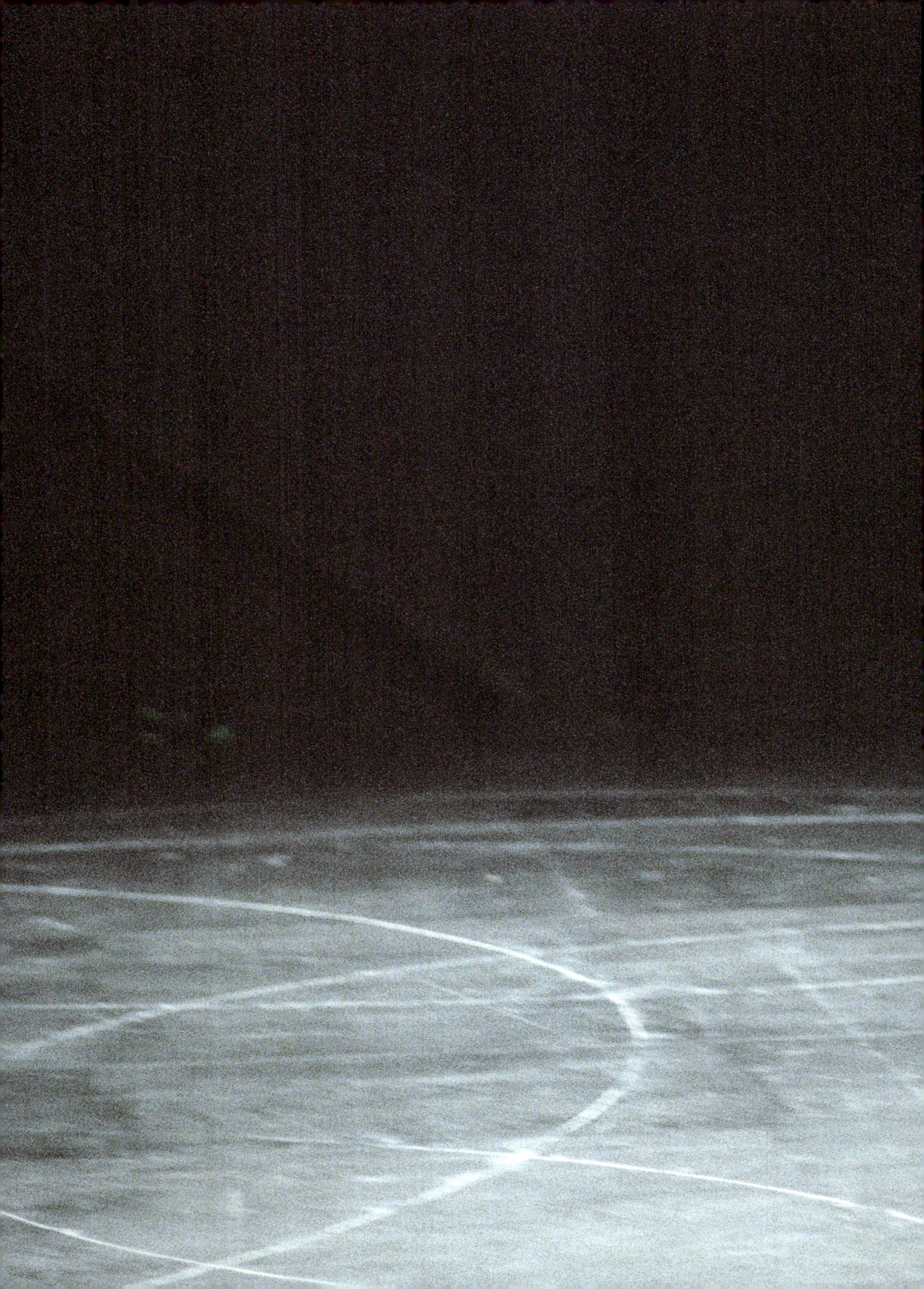

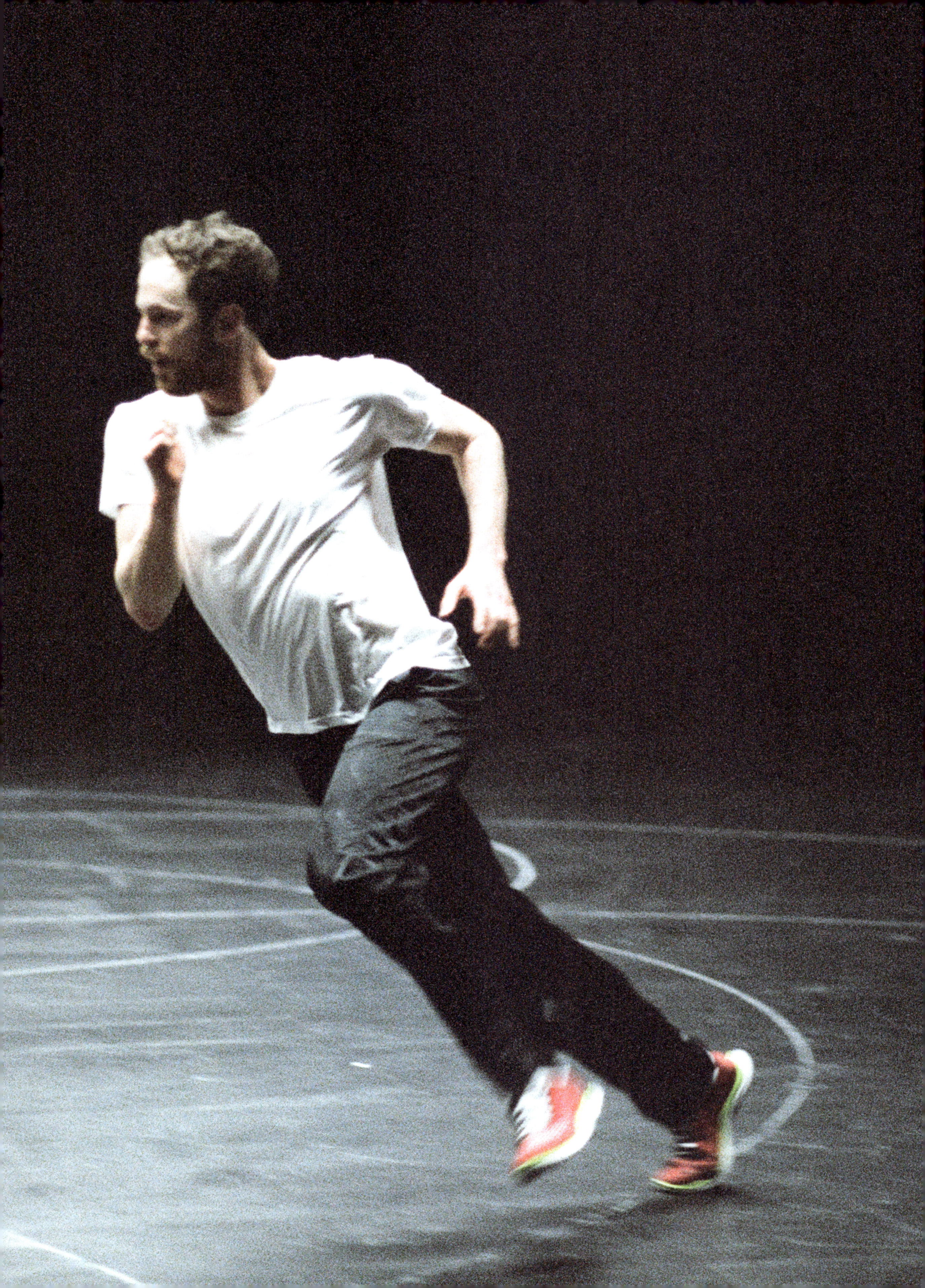

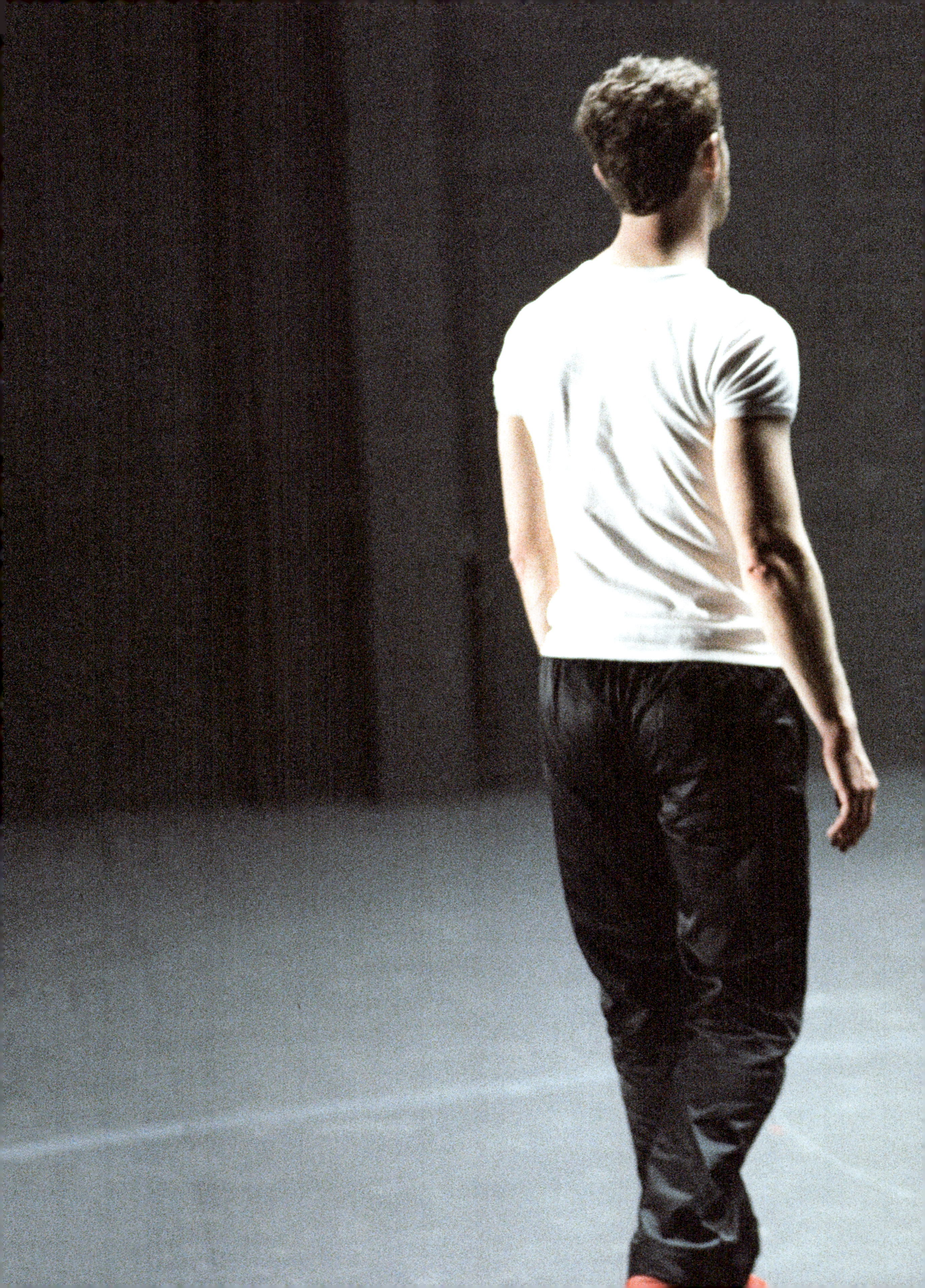

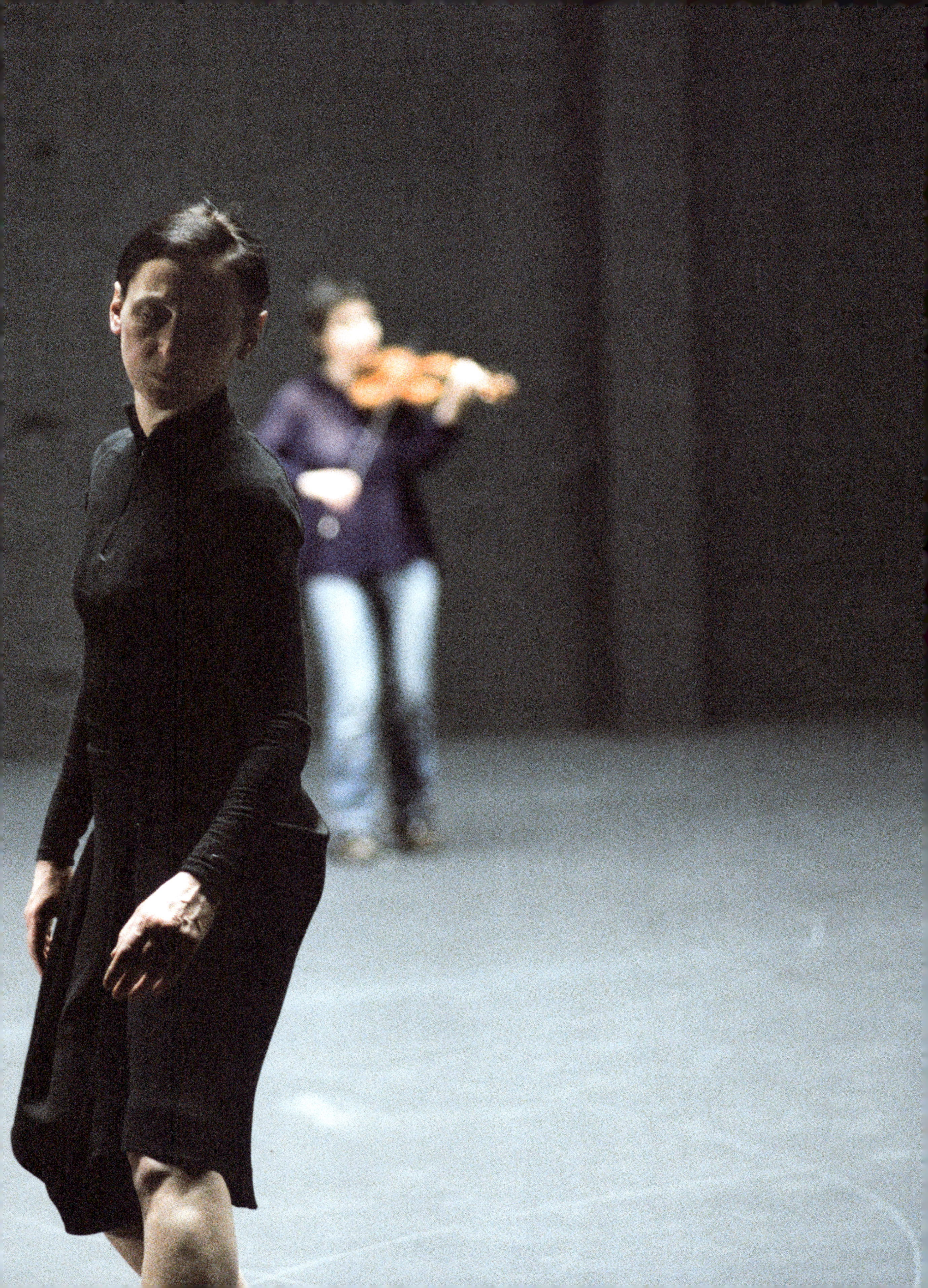

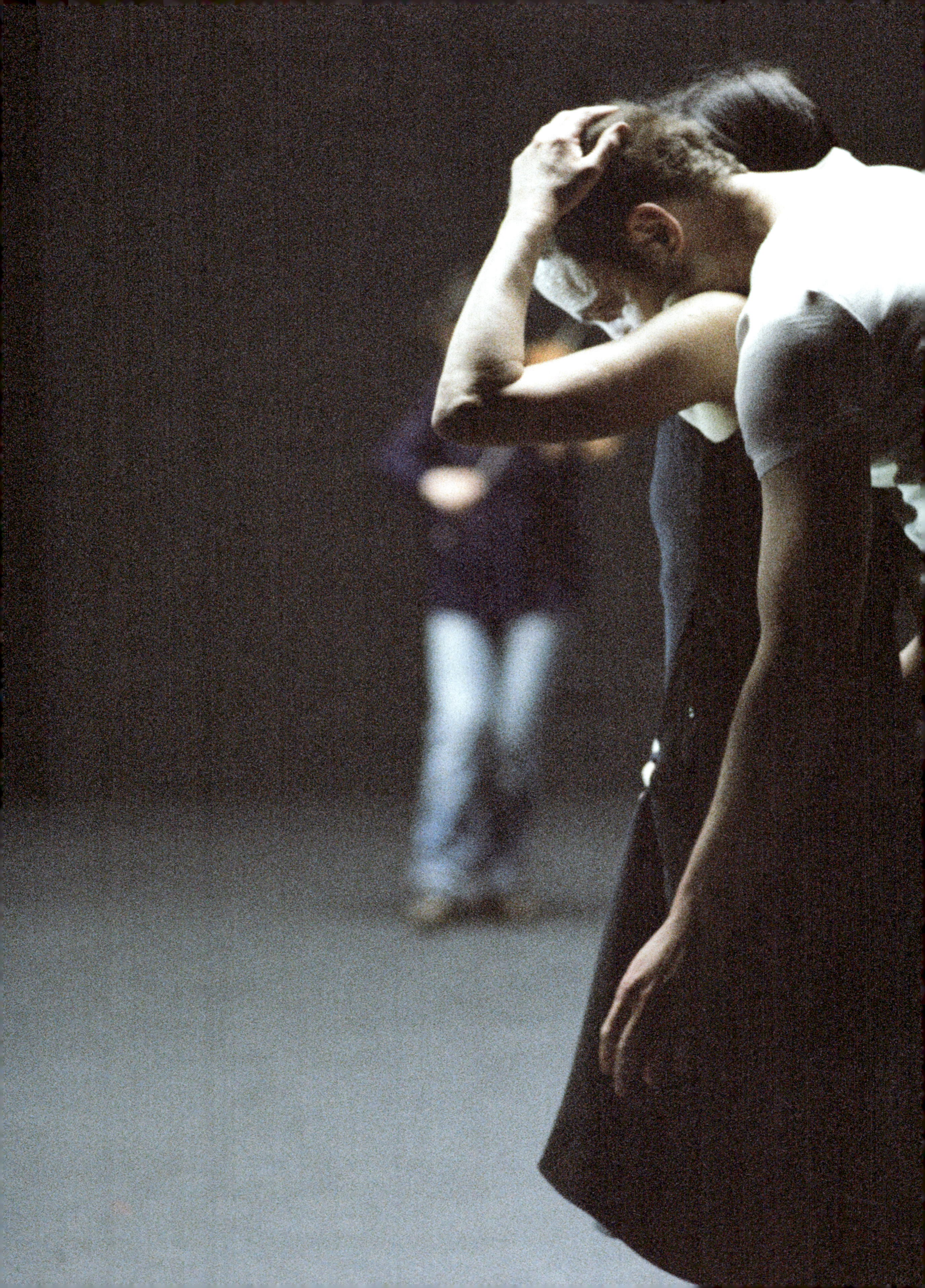

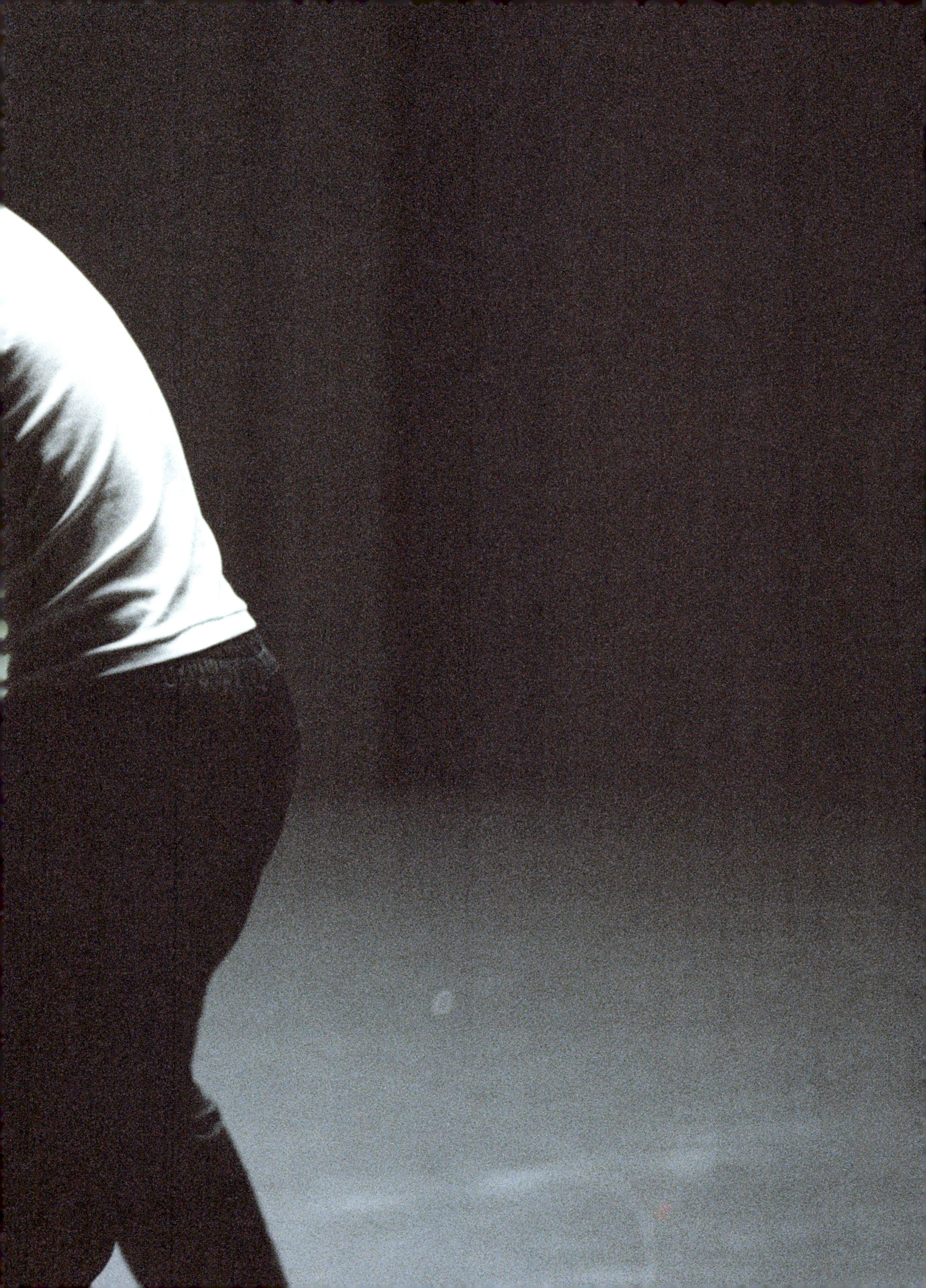

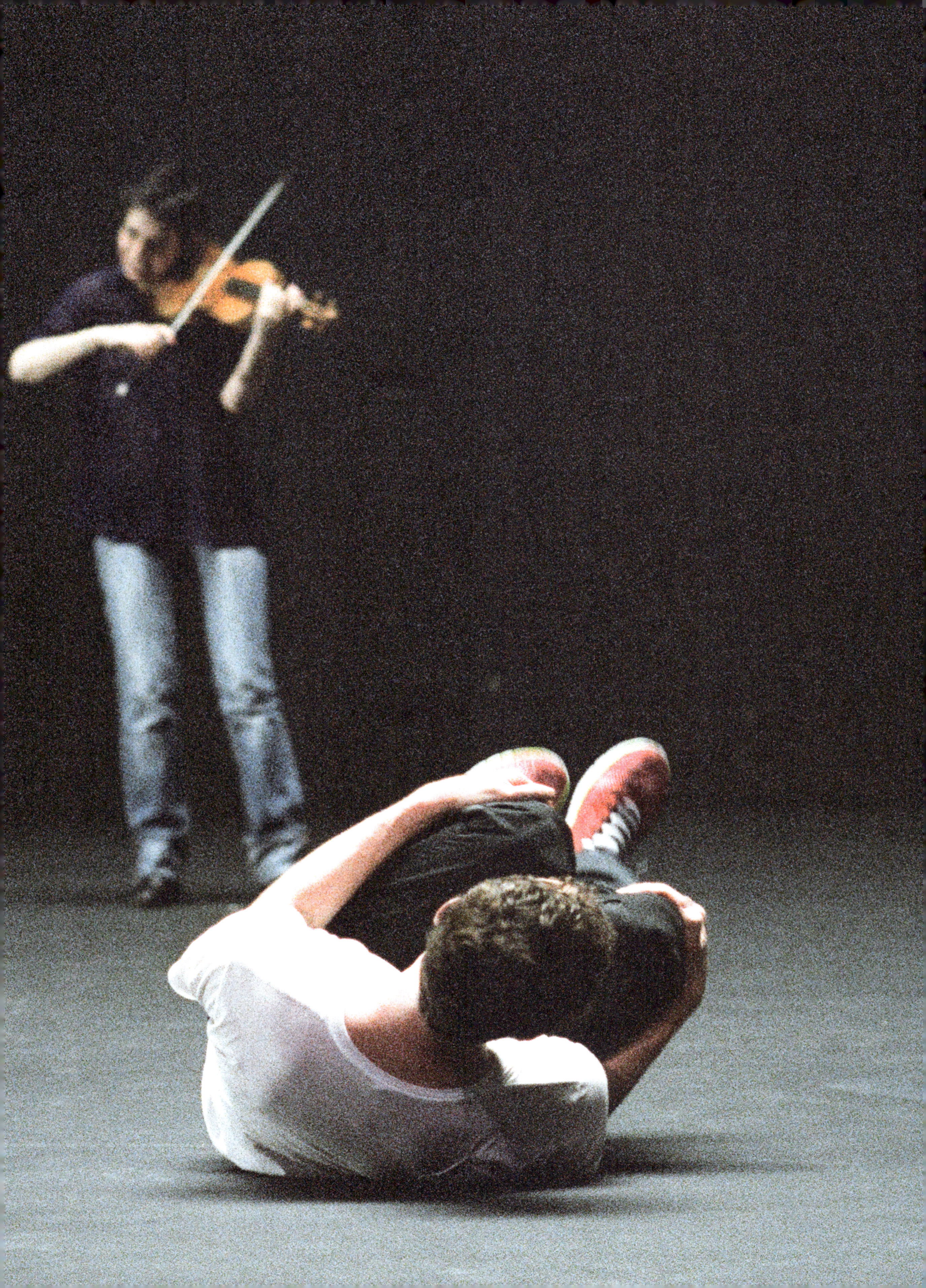

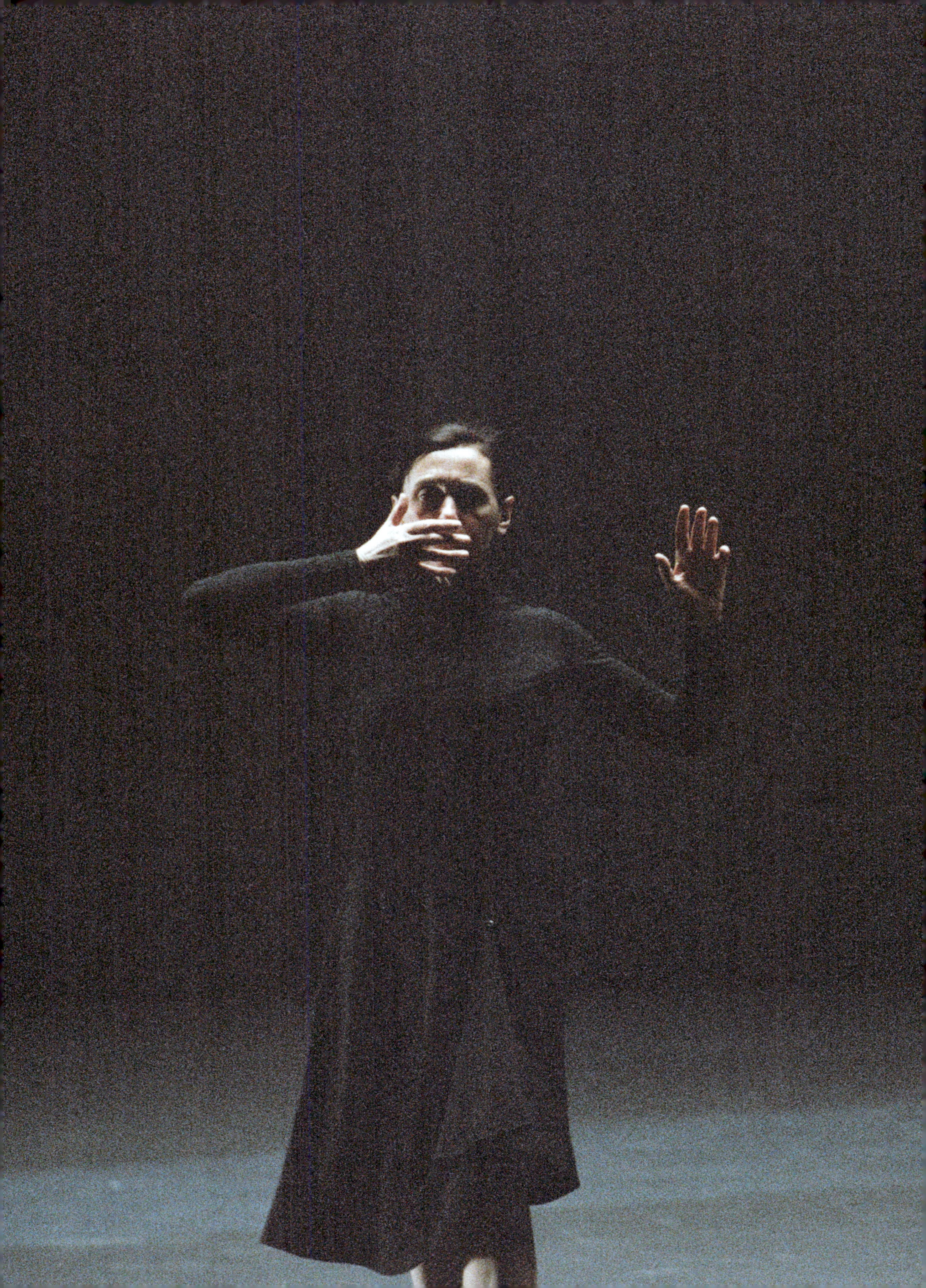

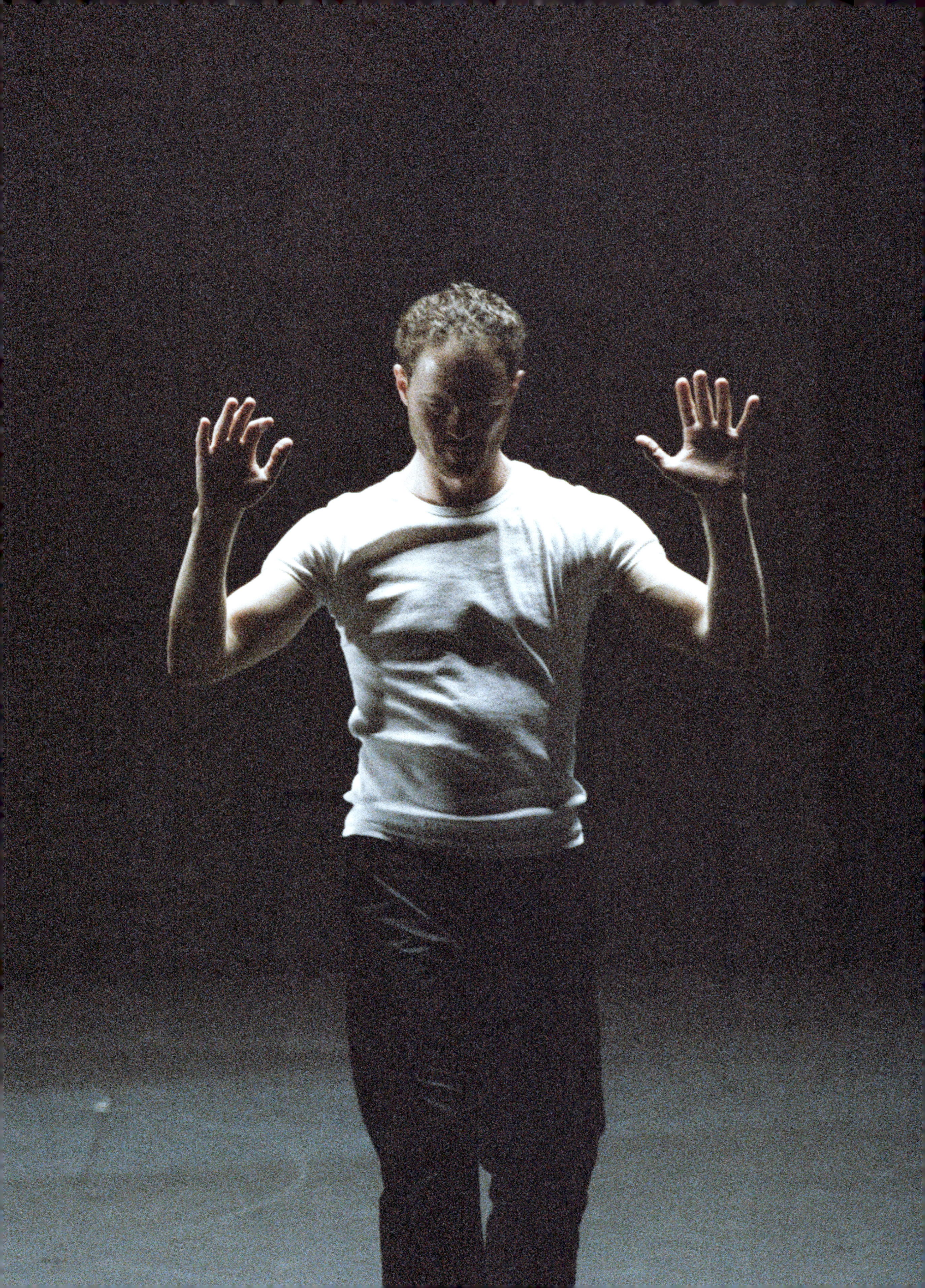

Vortex Temporum 2013

Concept and choreography
Anne Teresa De Keersmaeker
Created with and danced by
Boštjan Antončič, Carlos Garbin, Marie Goudot, Cynthia Loemij,
Julien Monty, Michaël Pomero, Igor Shyshko / Mark Lorimer
Created with
Chrysa Parkinson
Music
Vortex Temporum, Gérard Grisey (1996)
Musical direction
Georges-Elie Octors
Musicians
Ictus
Piano Jean-Luc Plouvier
Flute Michael Schmid / Chryssi Dimitriou
Clarinet Dirk Descheemaeker
Cello Geert De Bièvre
Viola Jeroen Robbrecht
Violin Igor Semenoff
Lighting
Anne Teresa De Keersmaeker, Luc Schaltin
Artistic advice—lighting
Michel François
Costumes
Anne-Catherine Kunz
Musical dramaturgy
Bojana Cvejić
Artistic assistant
Femke Gyselinck
Sound
Alexandre Fostier
Production
Rosas
Coproduction
La Monnaie / De Munt (Brussels), Ruhrtriennale, Les Théâtres de la Ville de Luxembourg,
Théâtre de la Ville (Paris), Sadler's Wells (London), Opéra de Lille, ImPulsTanz (Vienna),
Holland Festival (Amsterdam), Concertgebouw Bruges
Premiere
03.10.2013, Ruhrtriennale—Bochum

Pictures
Anne Van Aerschot

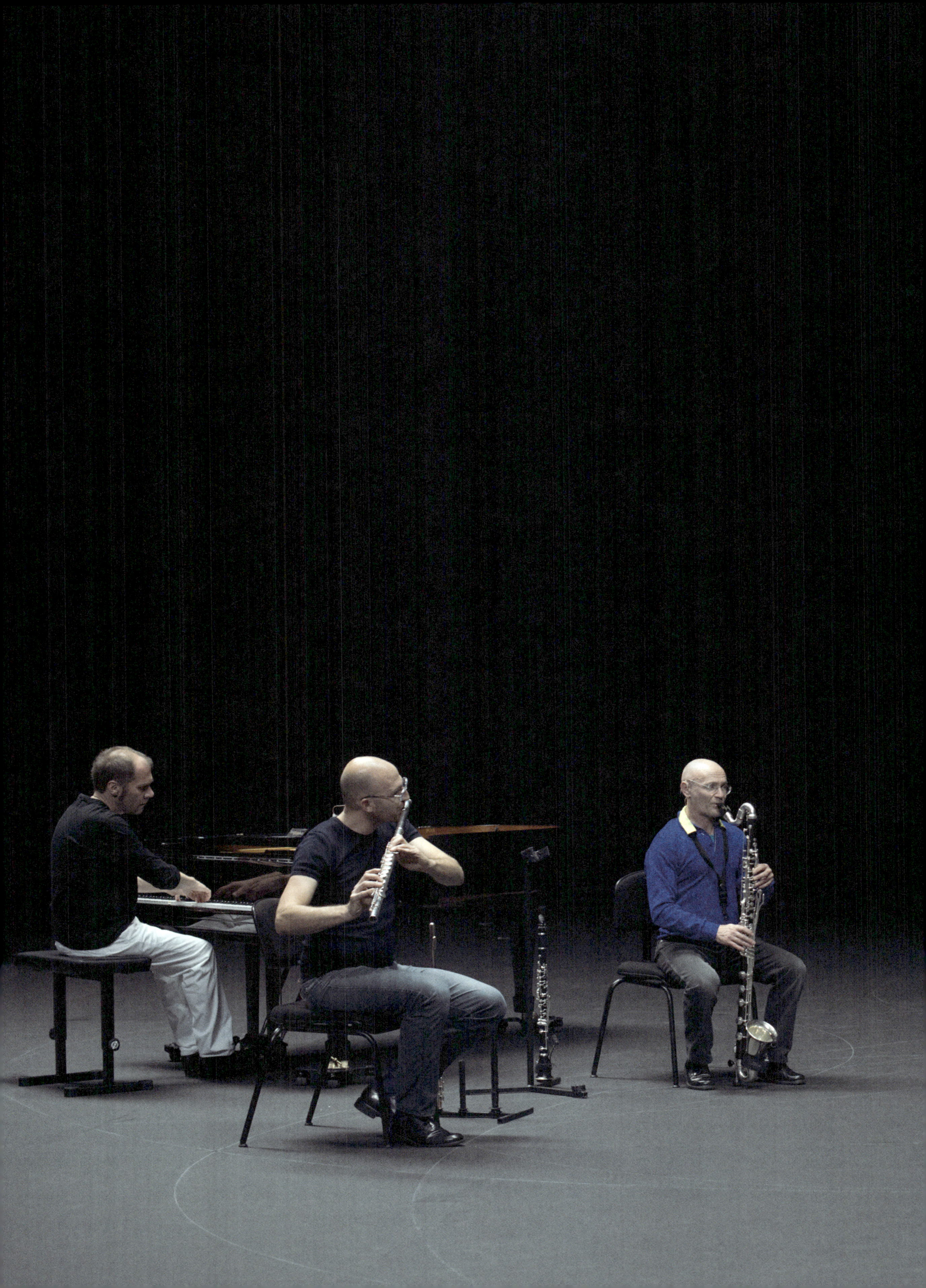

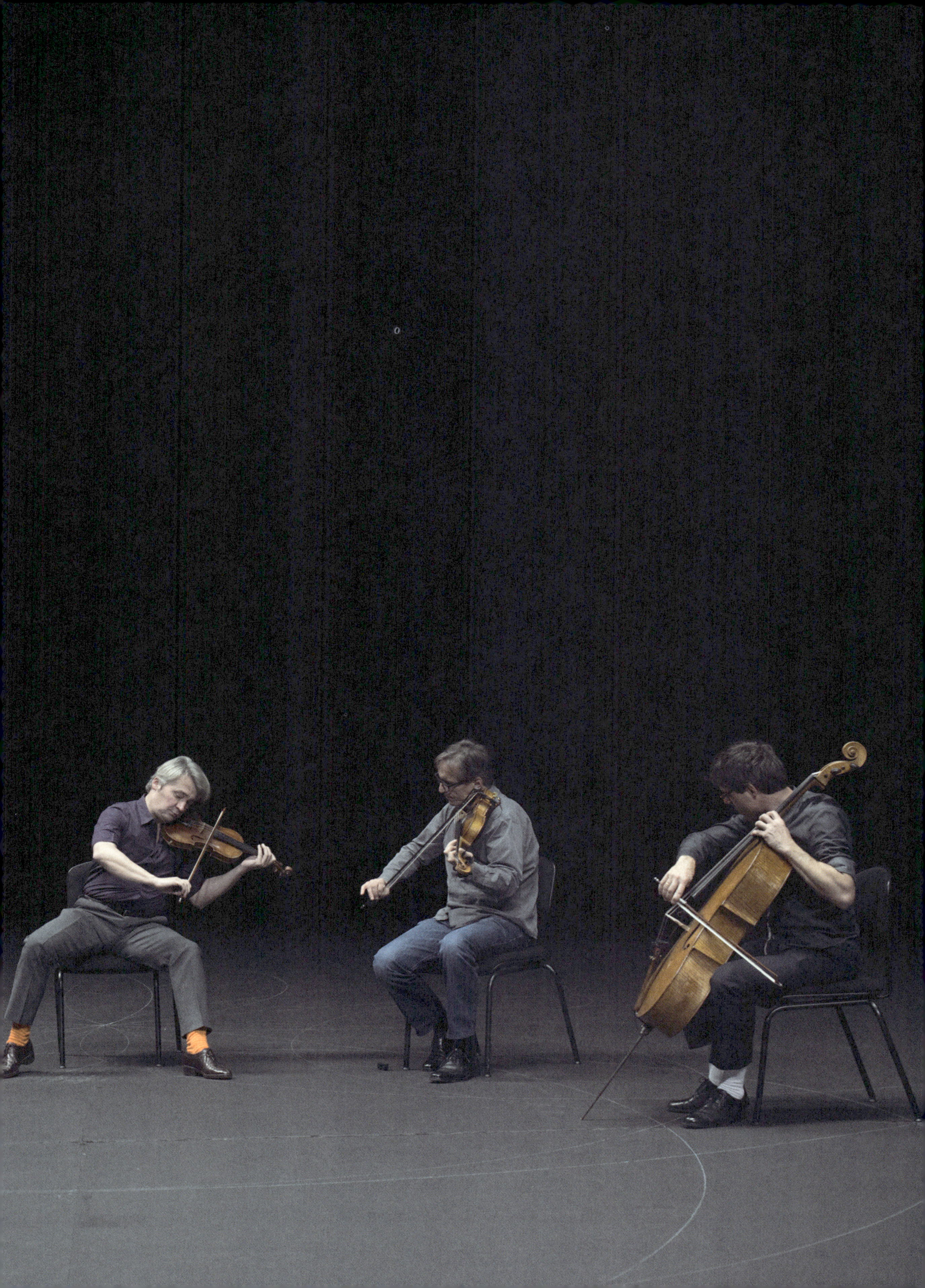

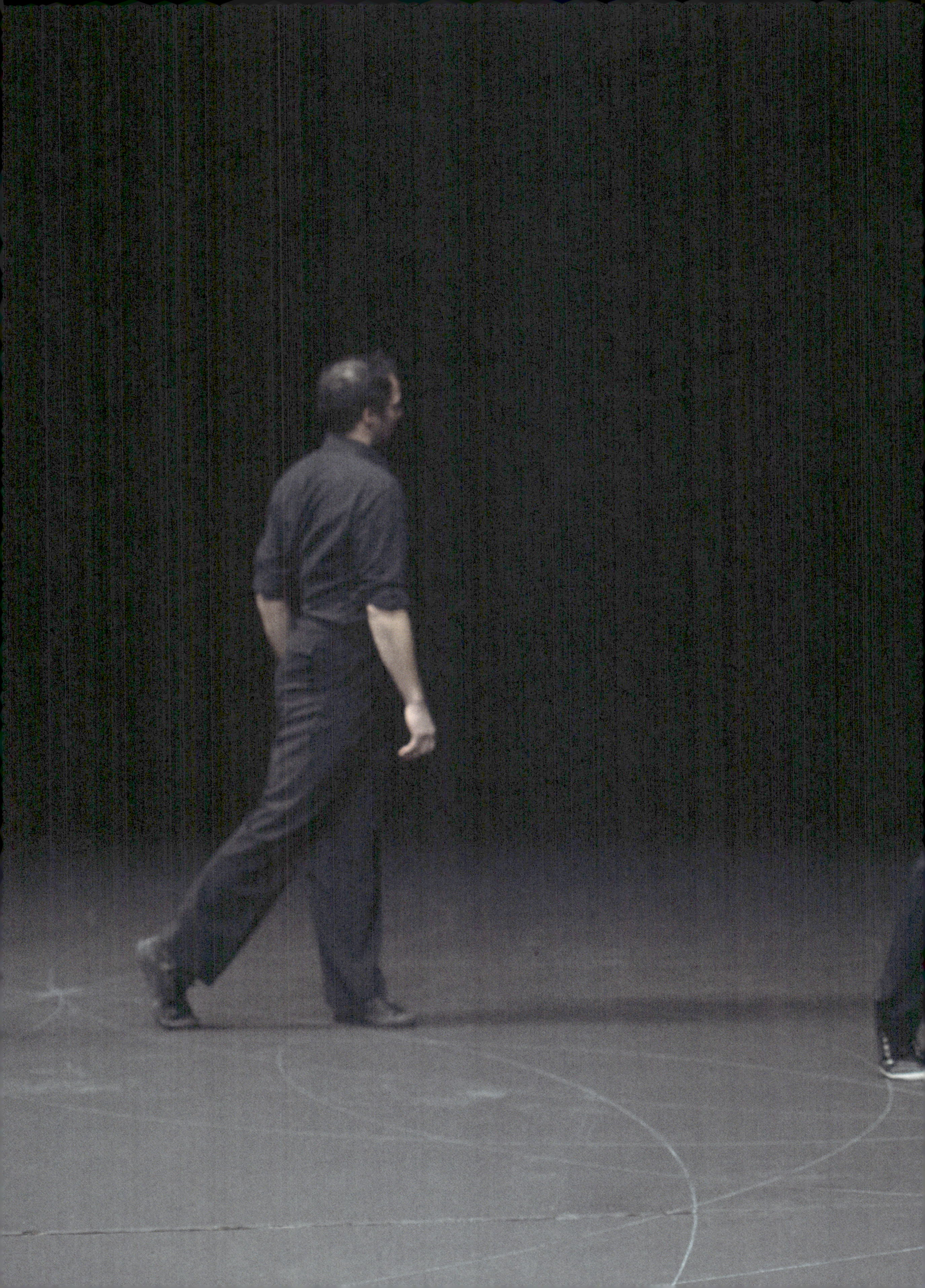

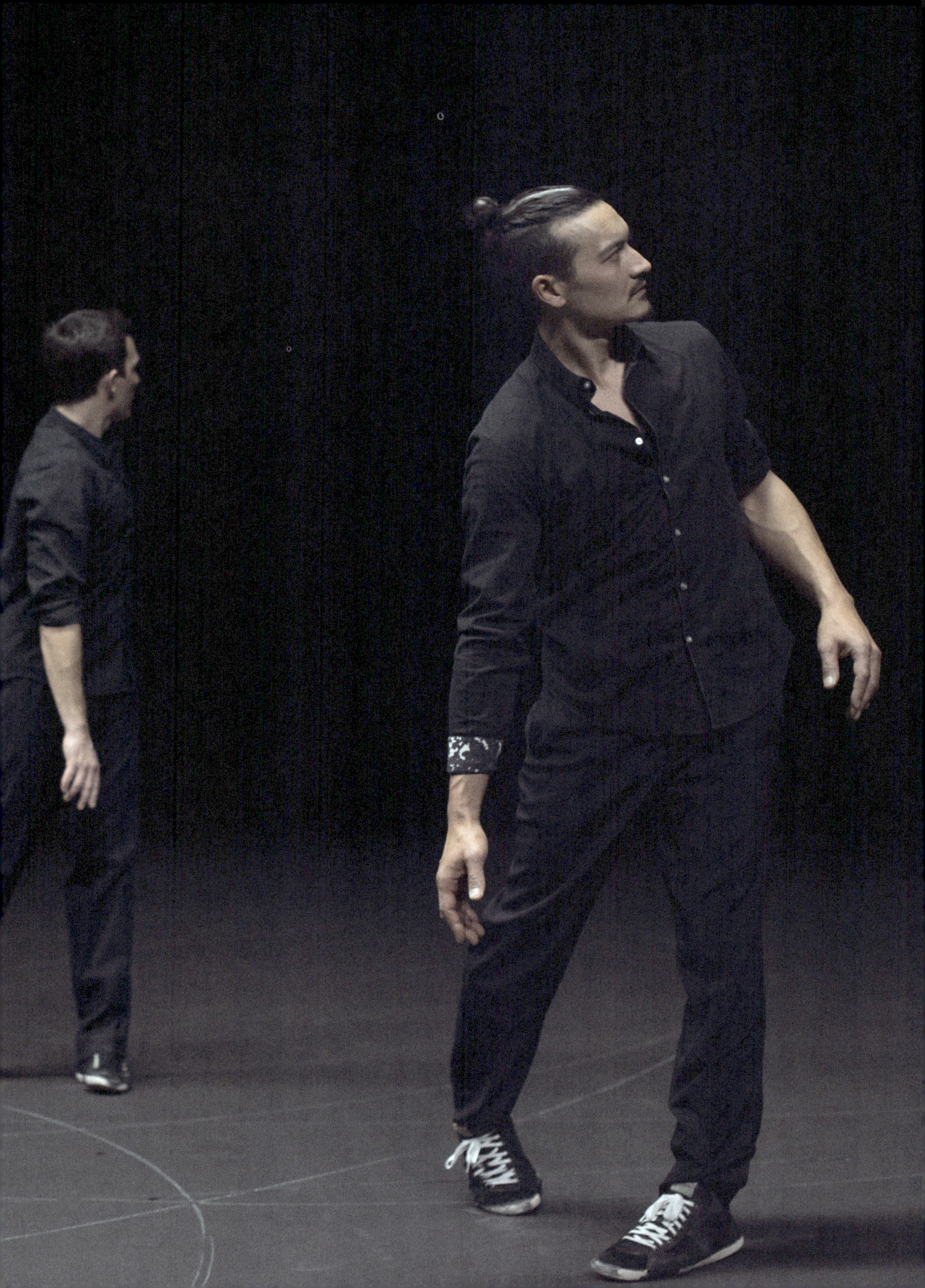

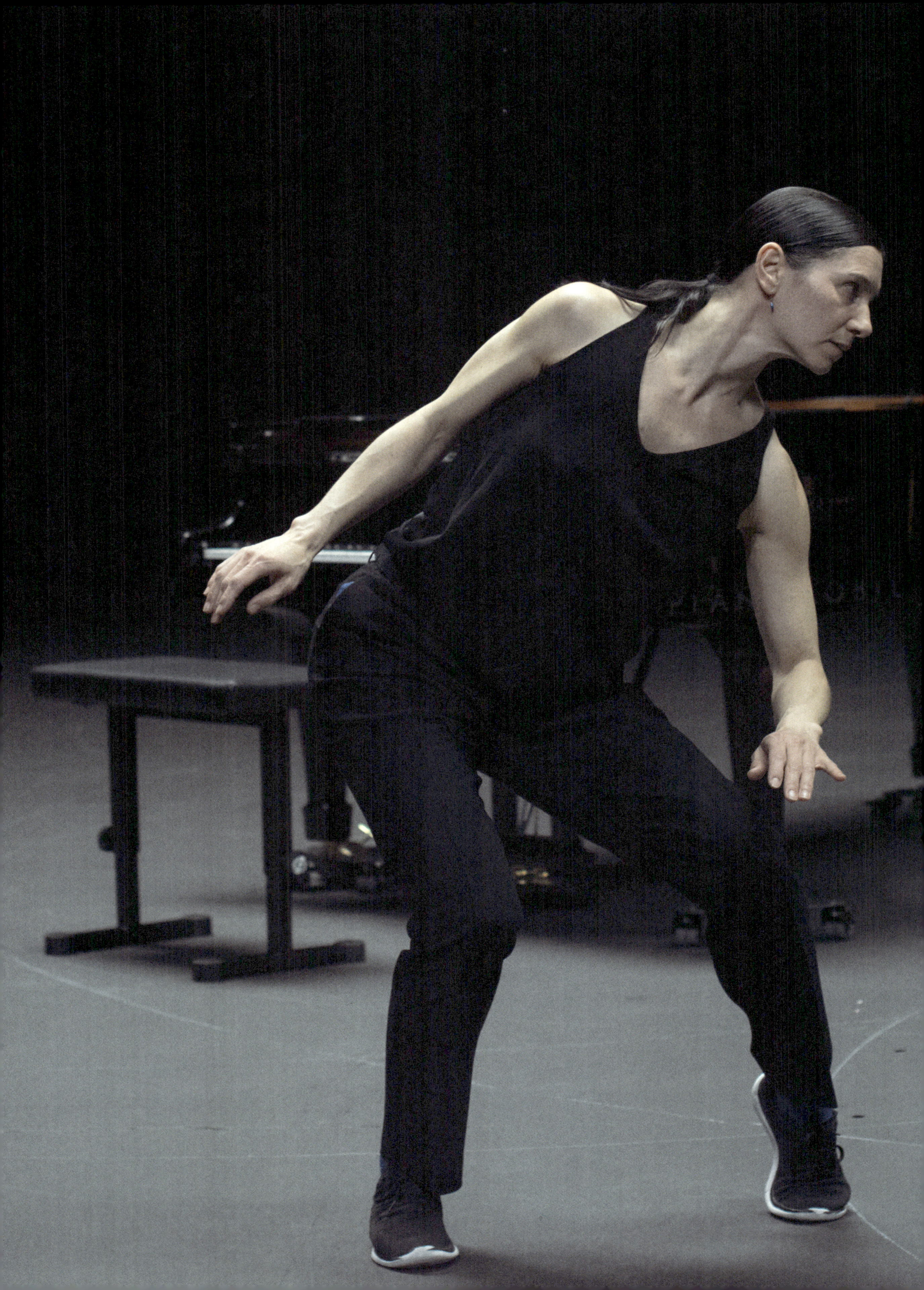

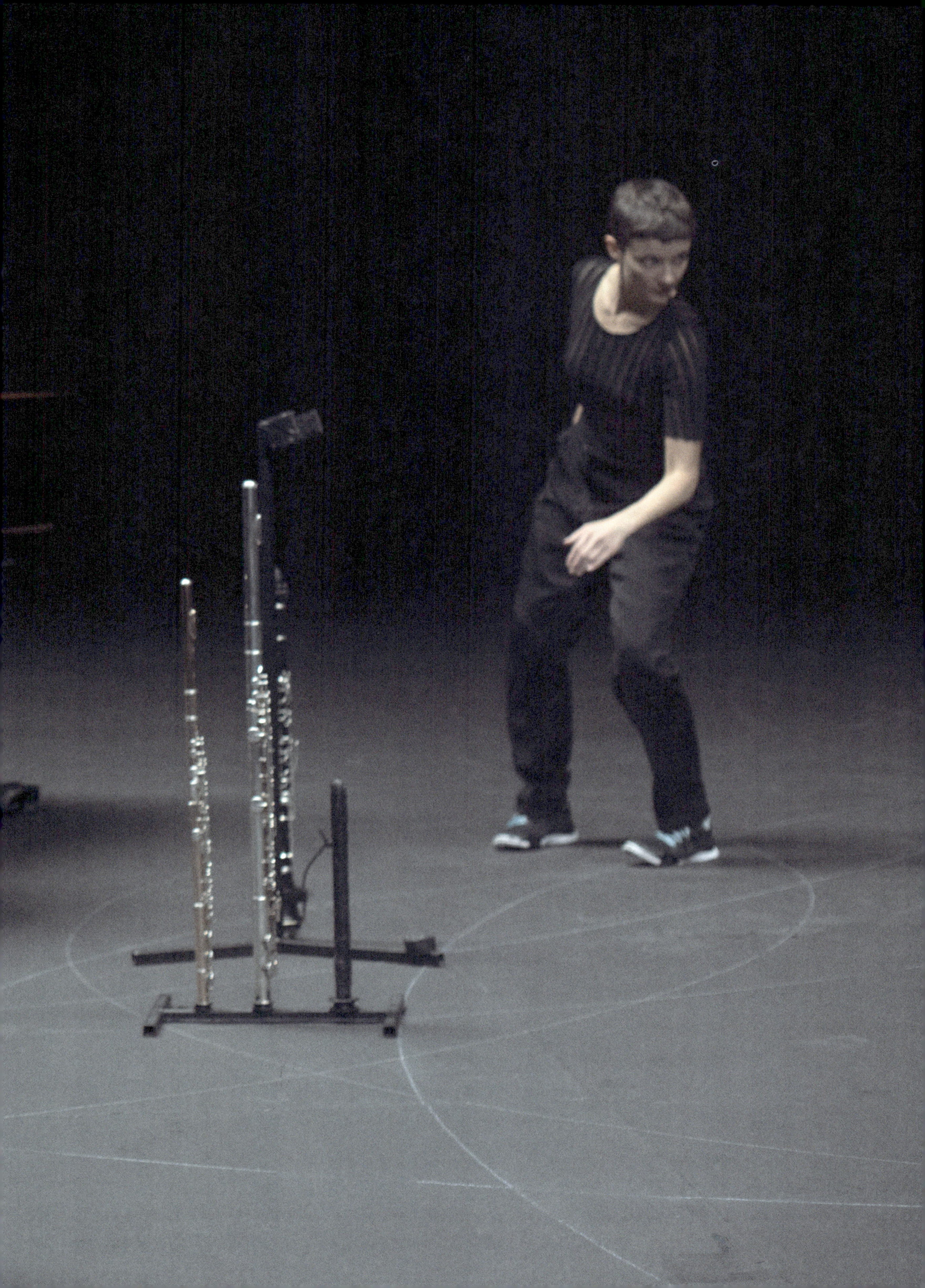

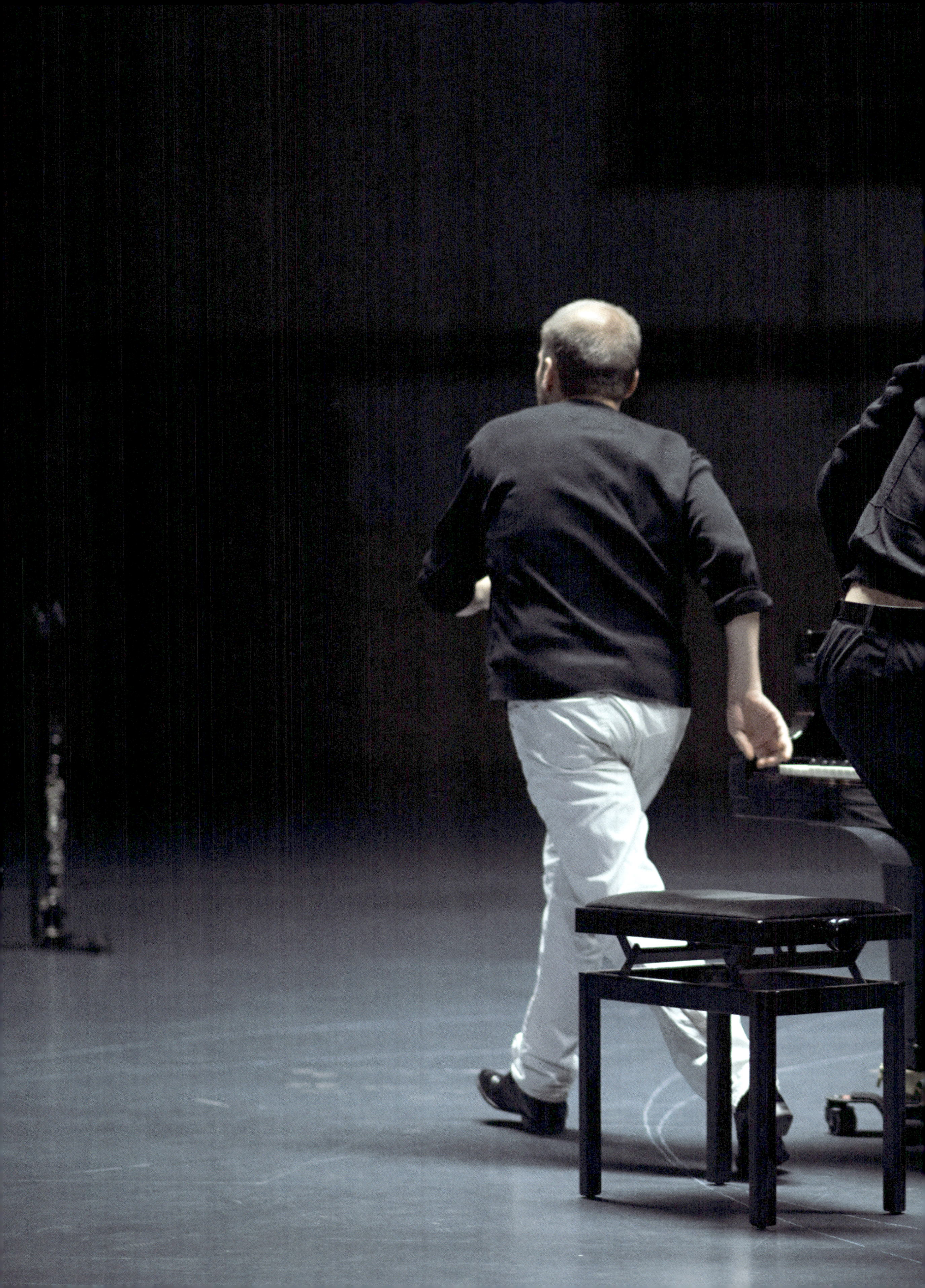

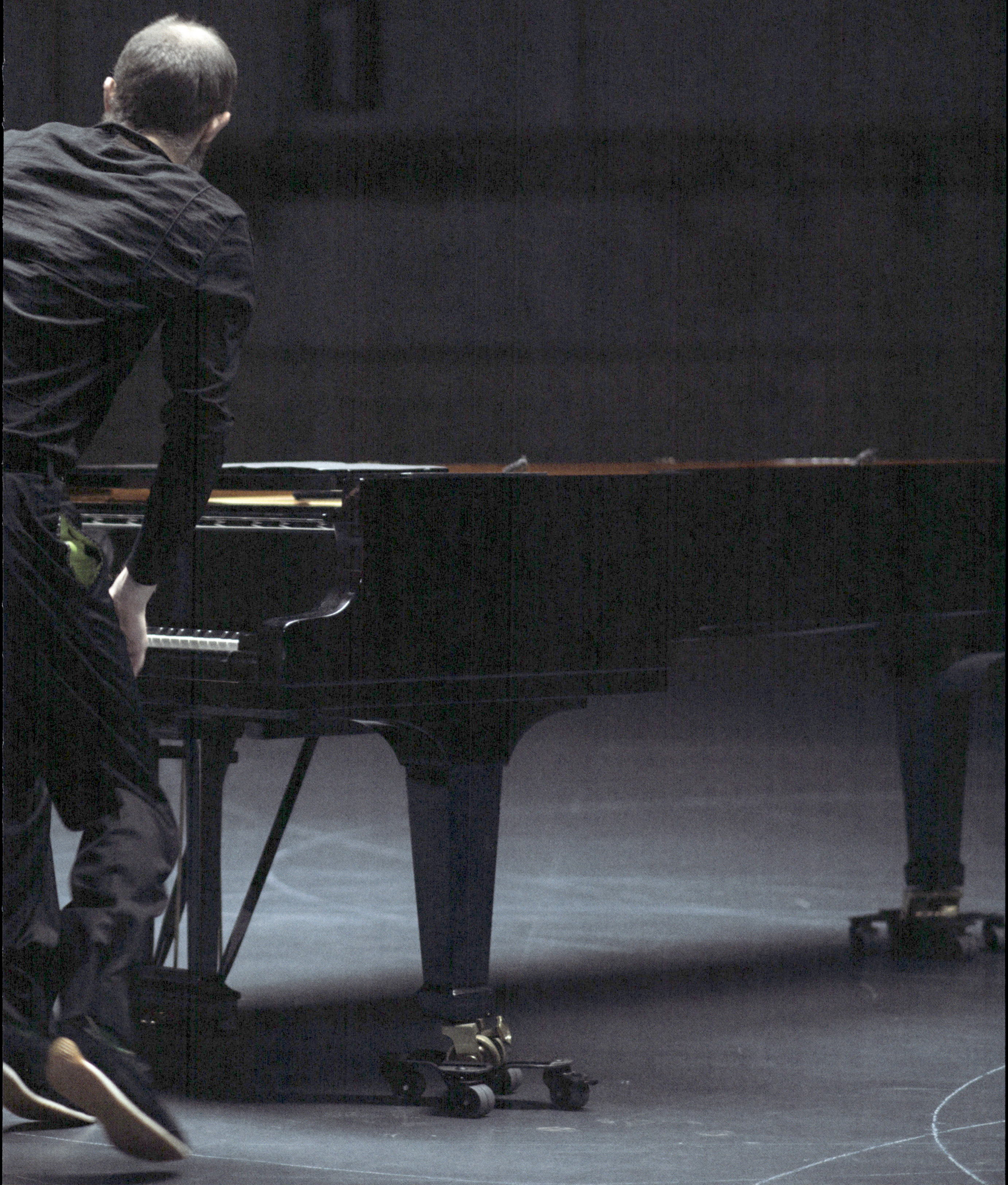

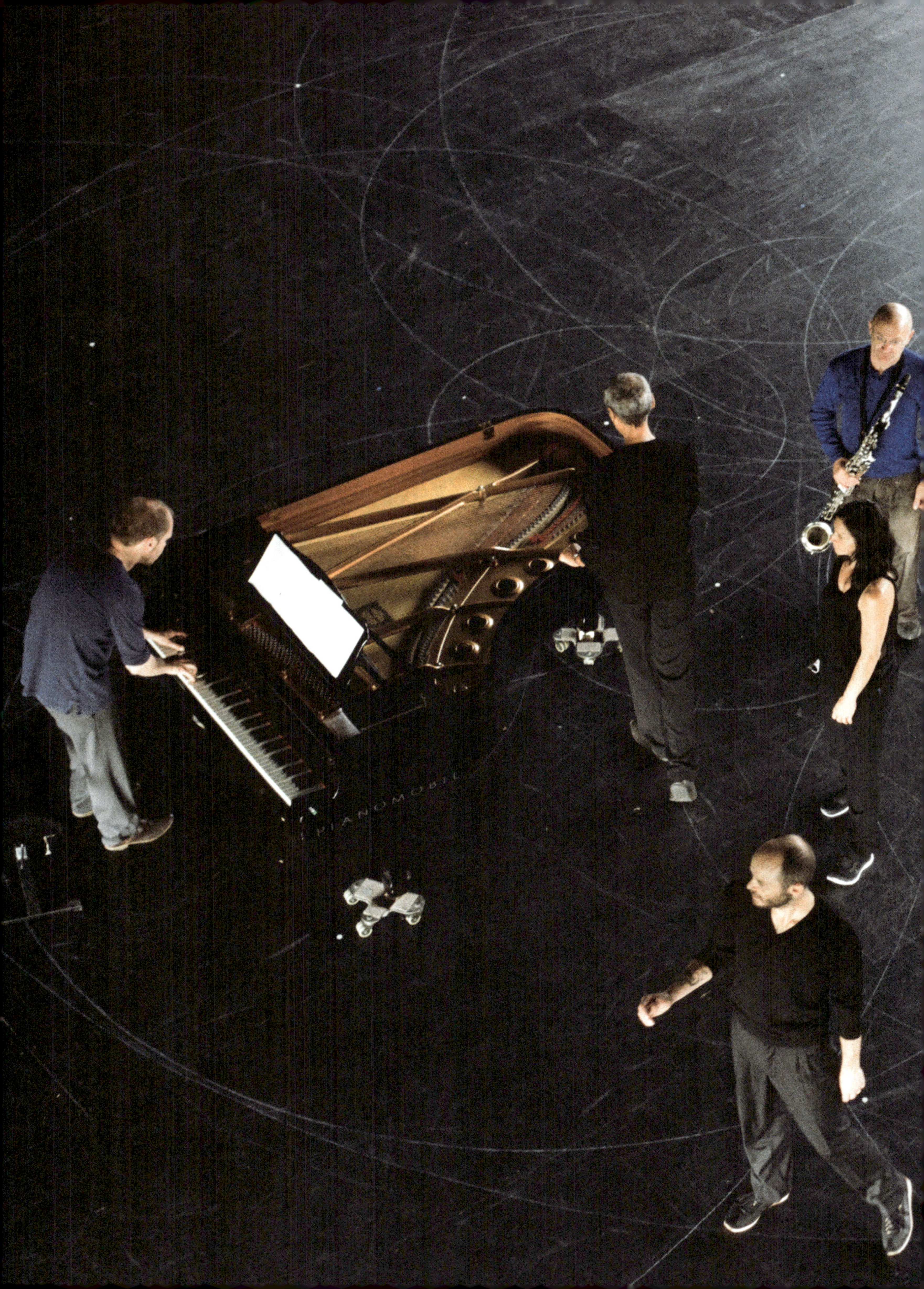
PIANOMOBIL

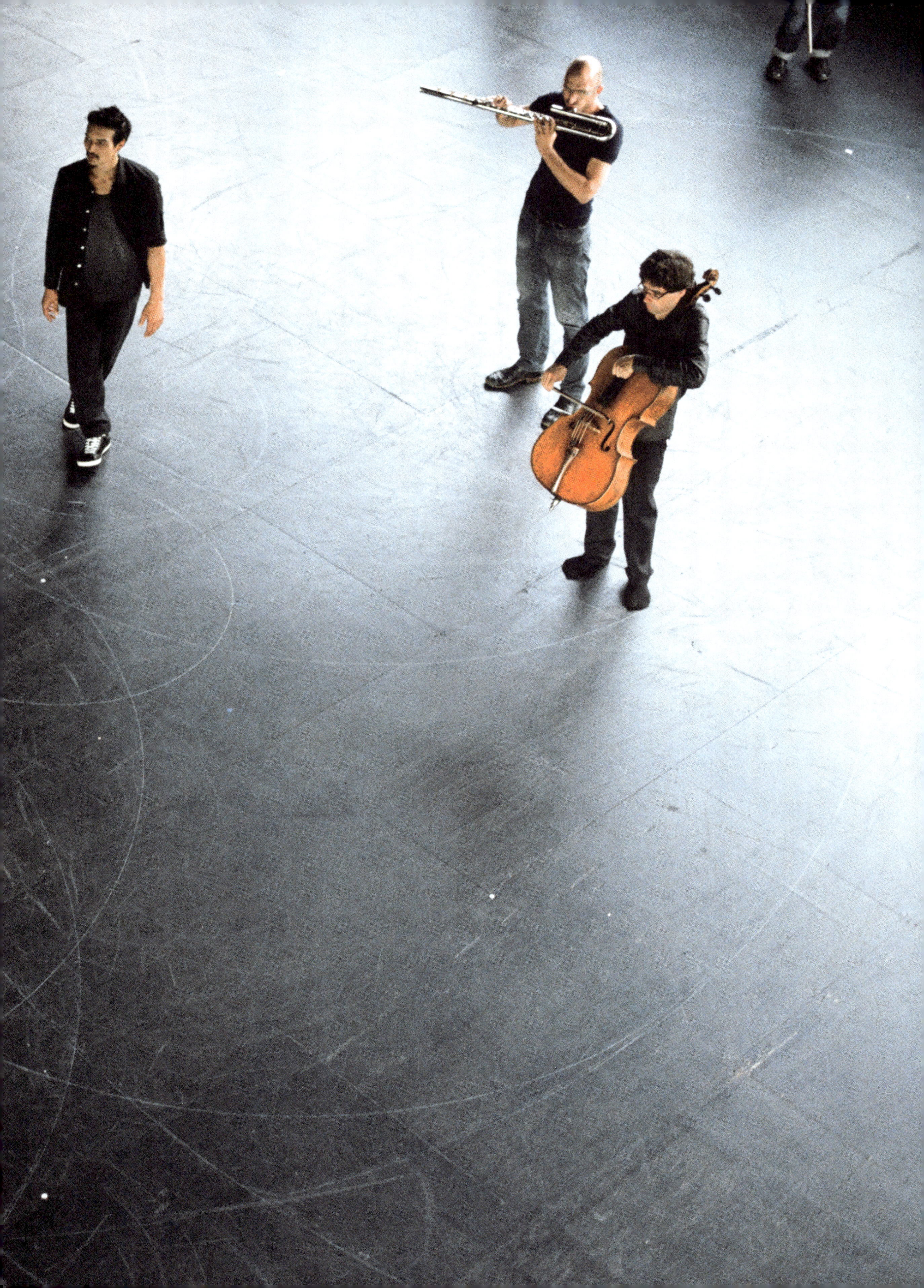

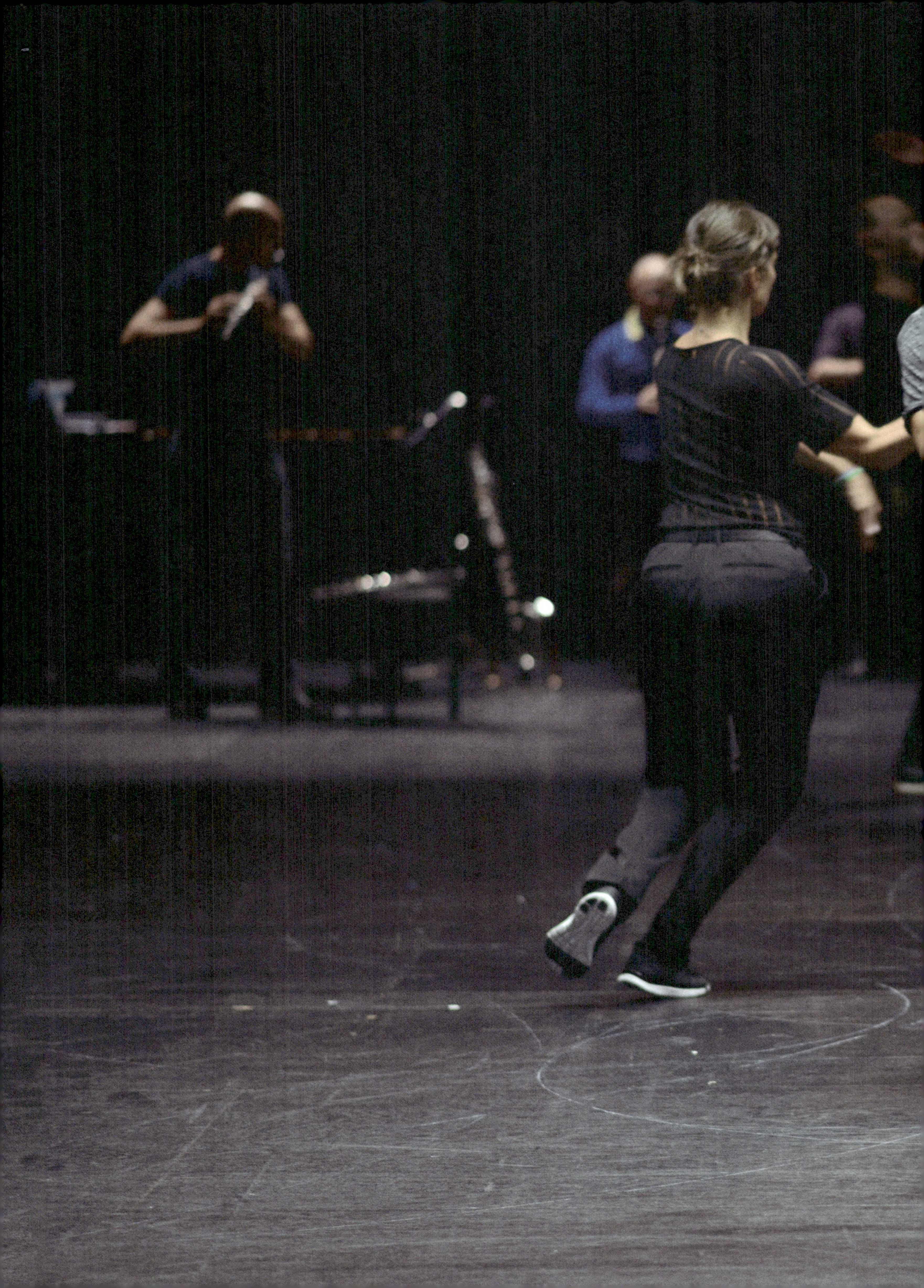

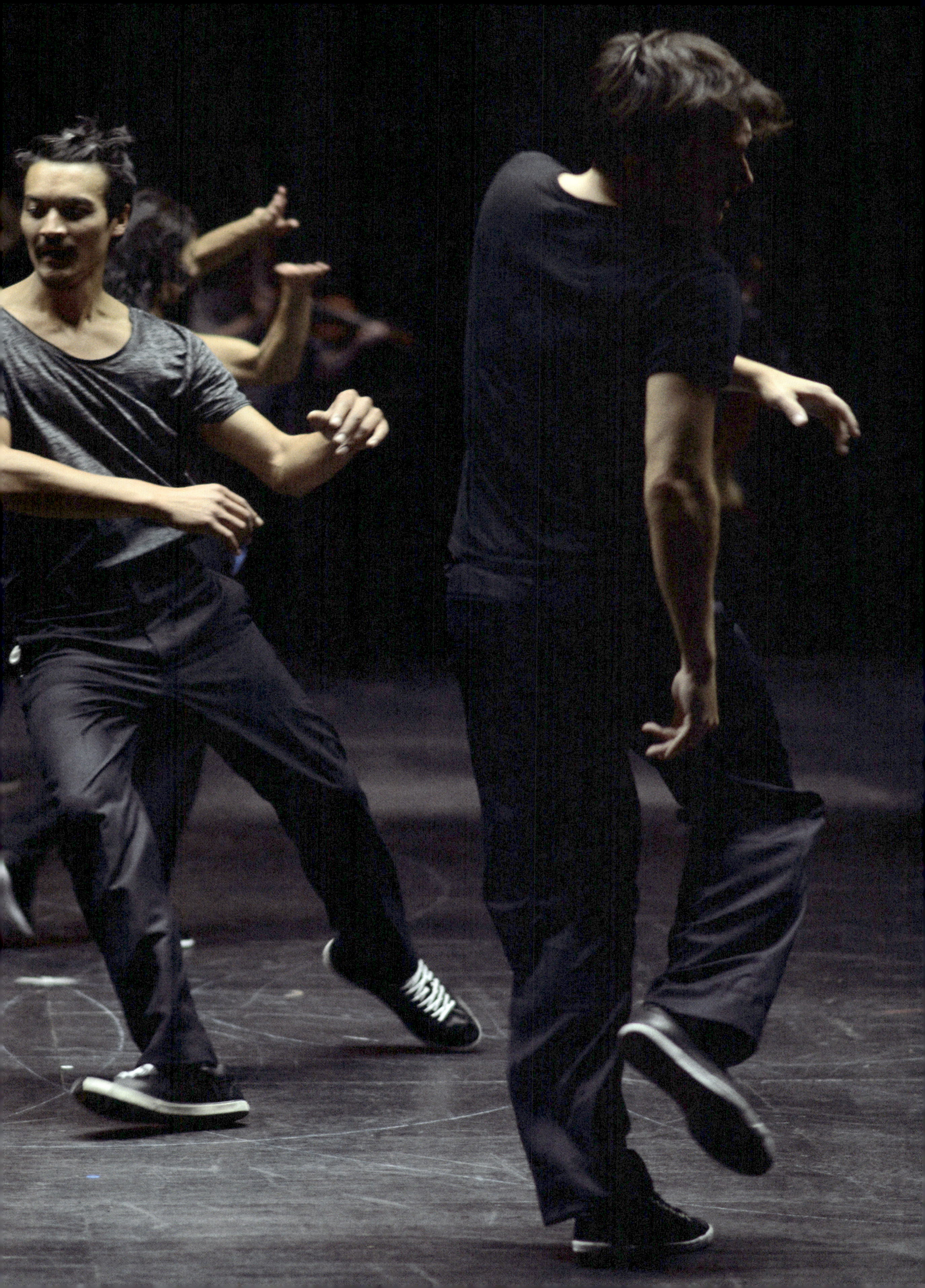

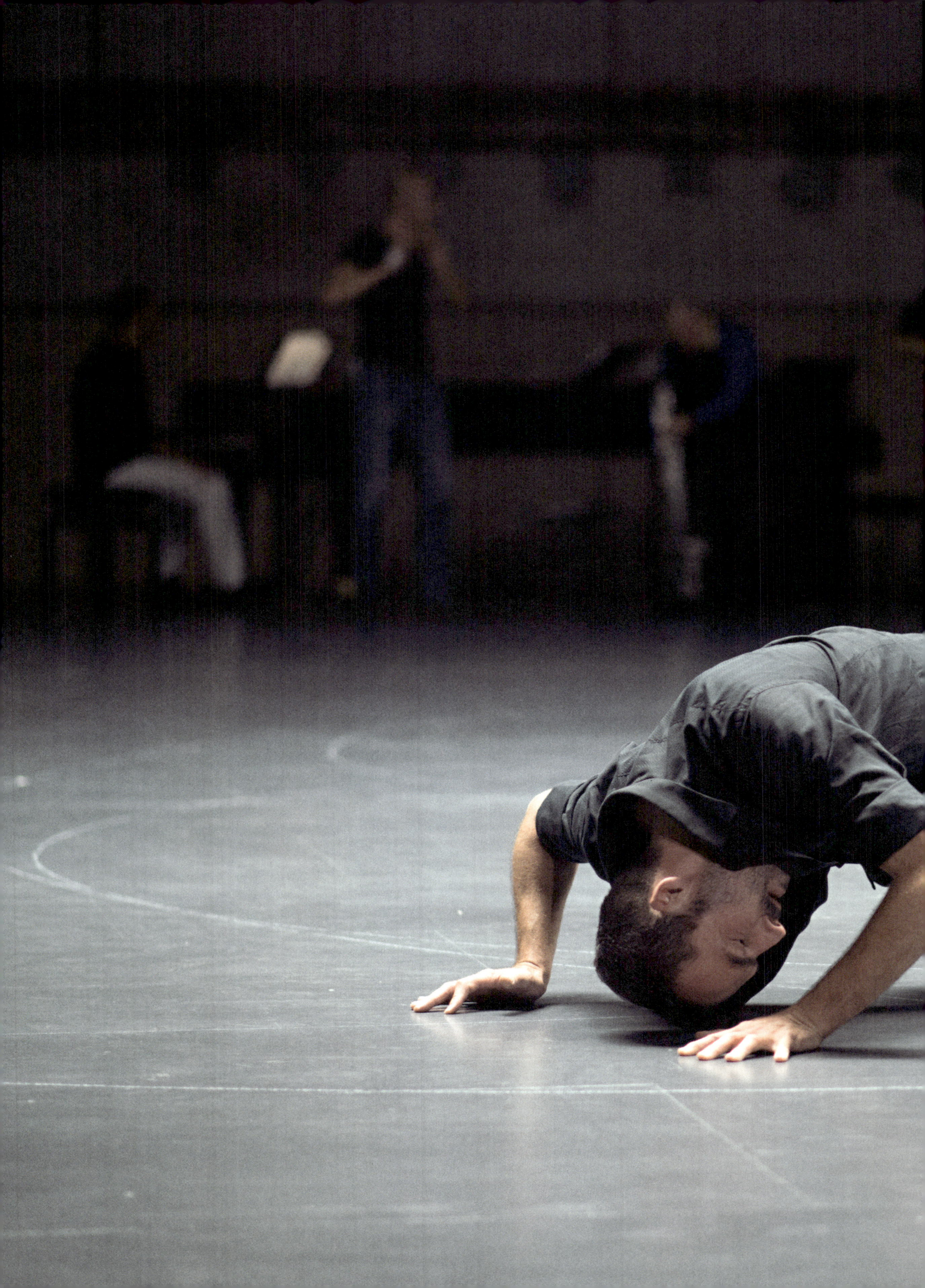

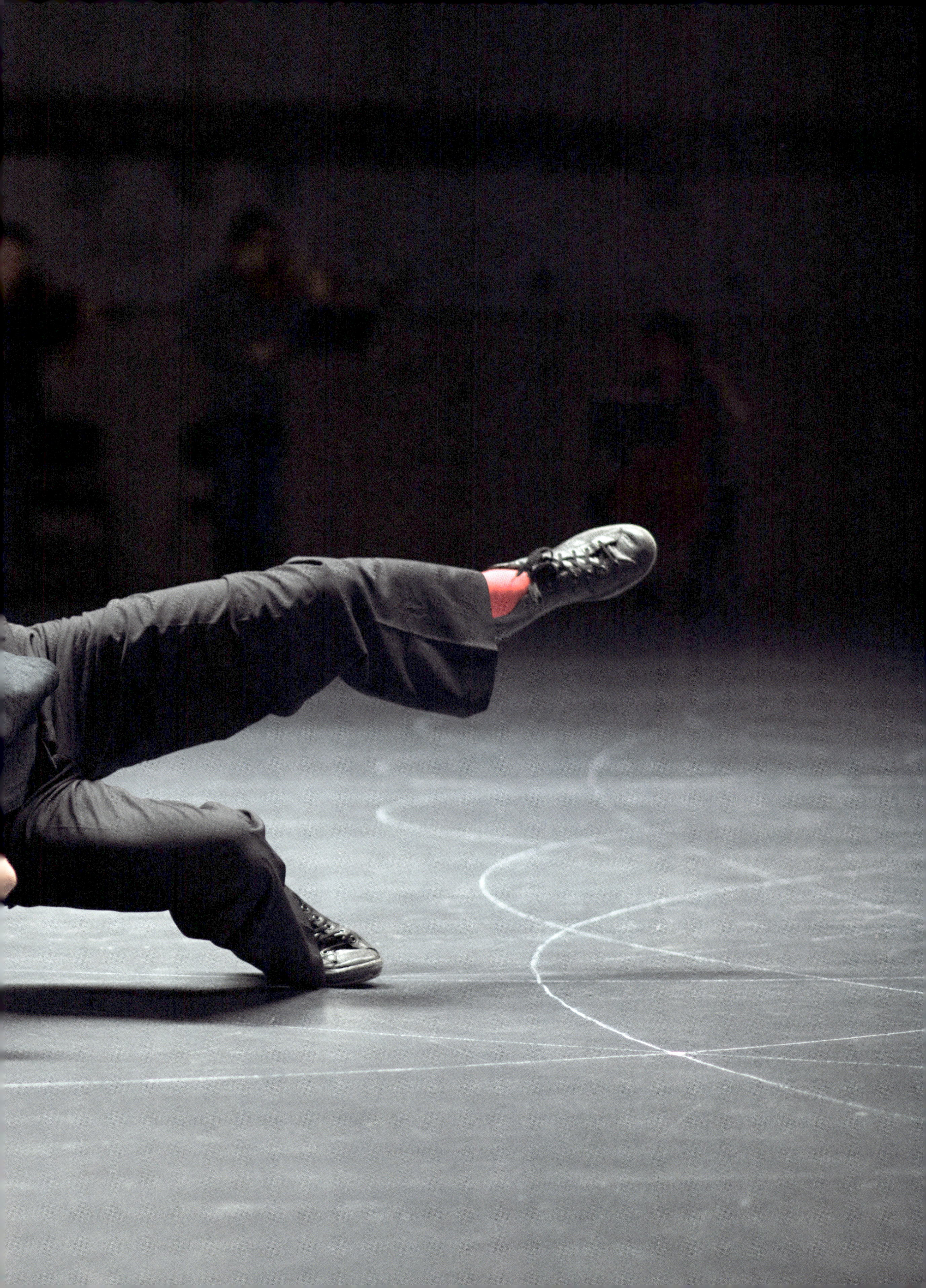

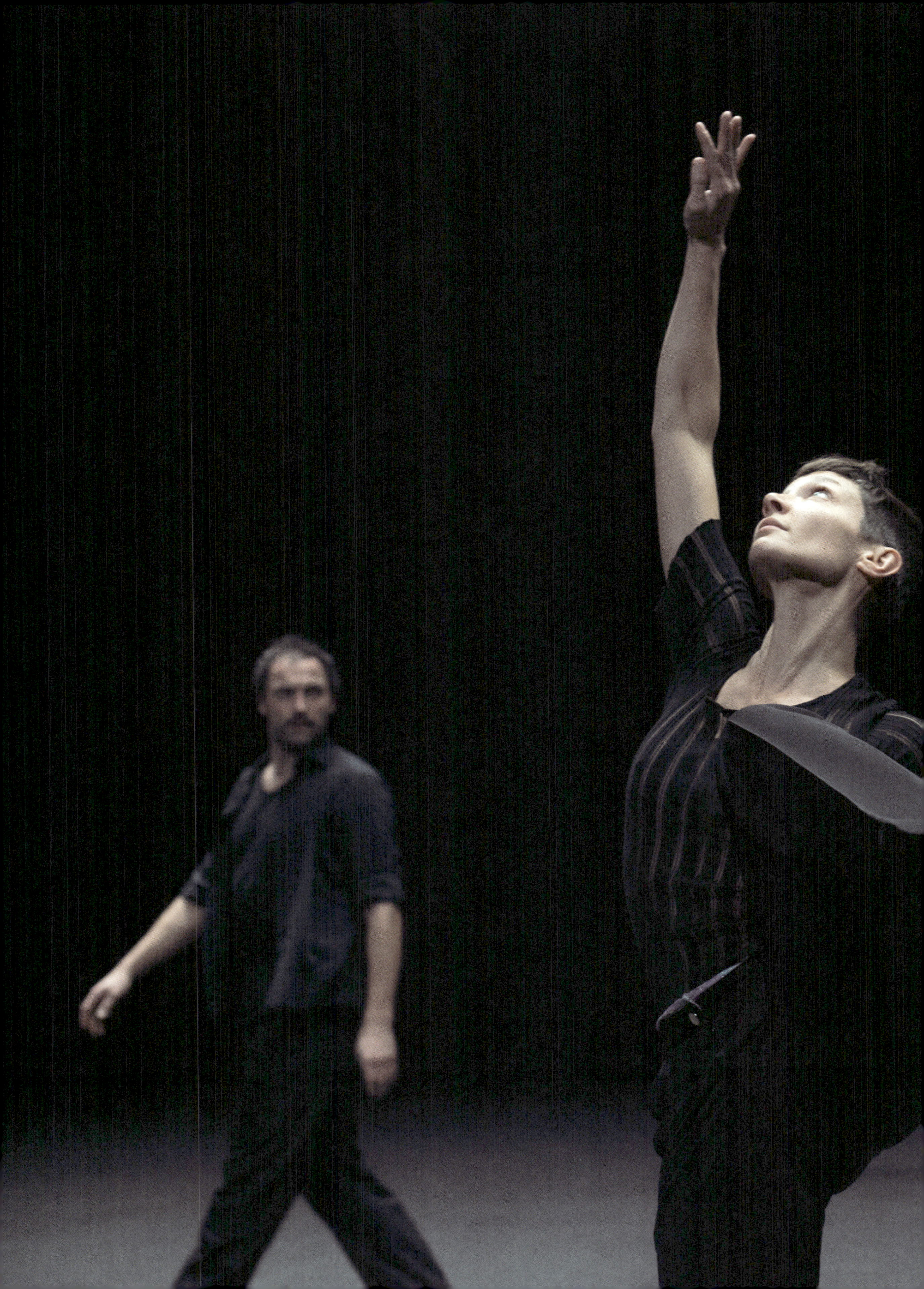

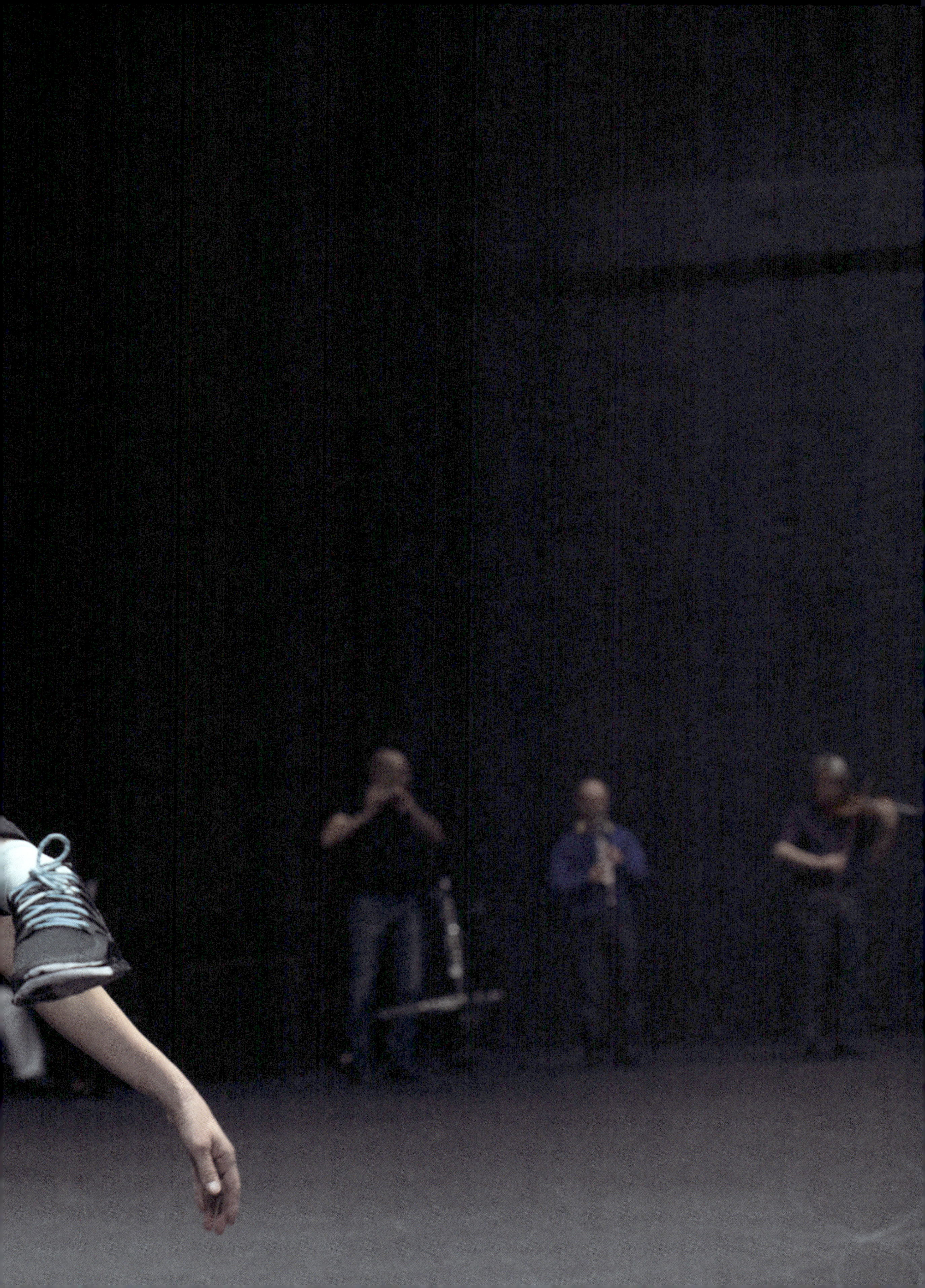

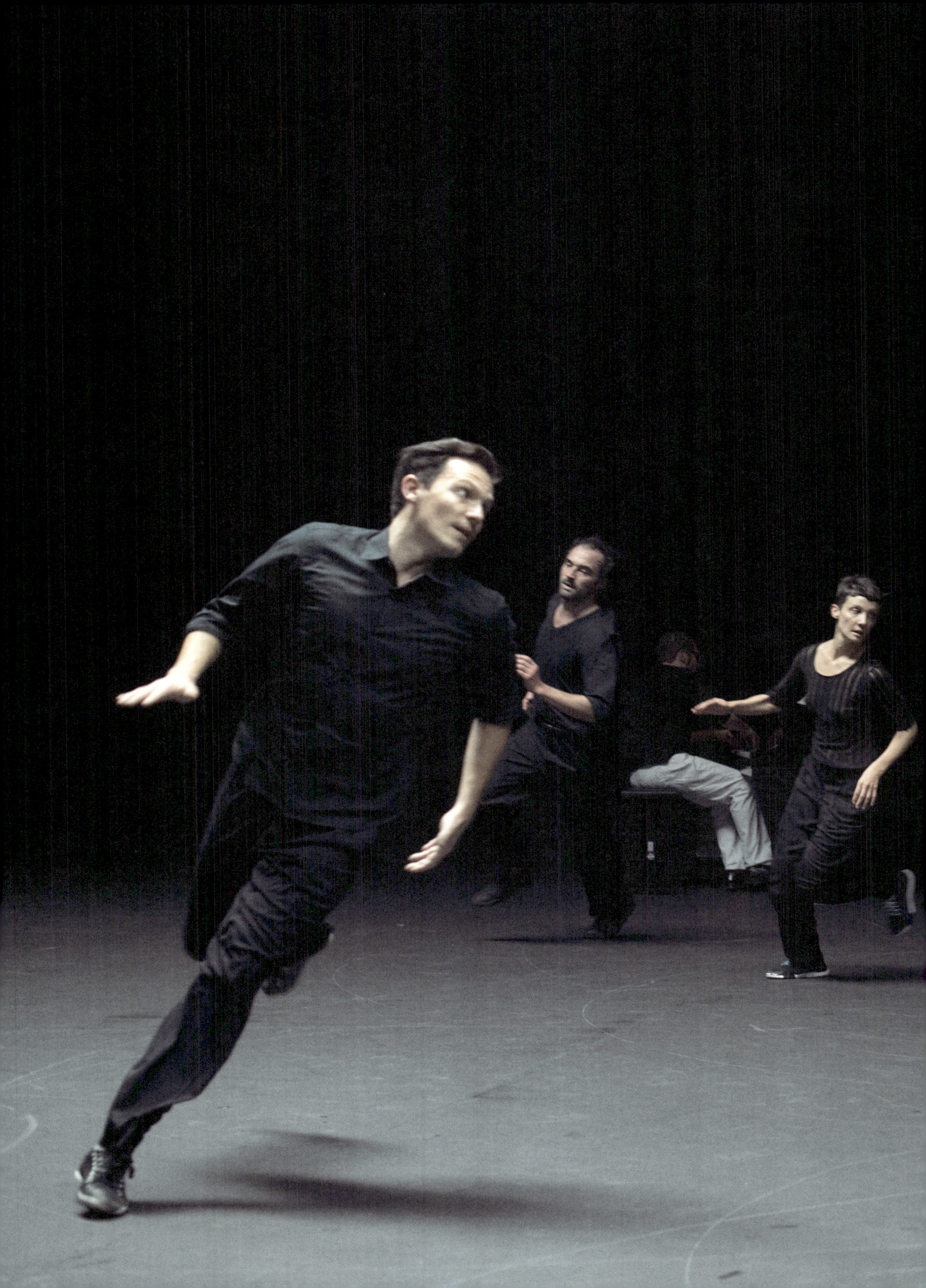

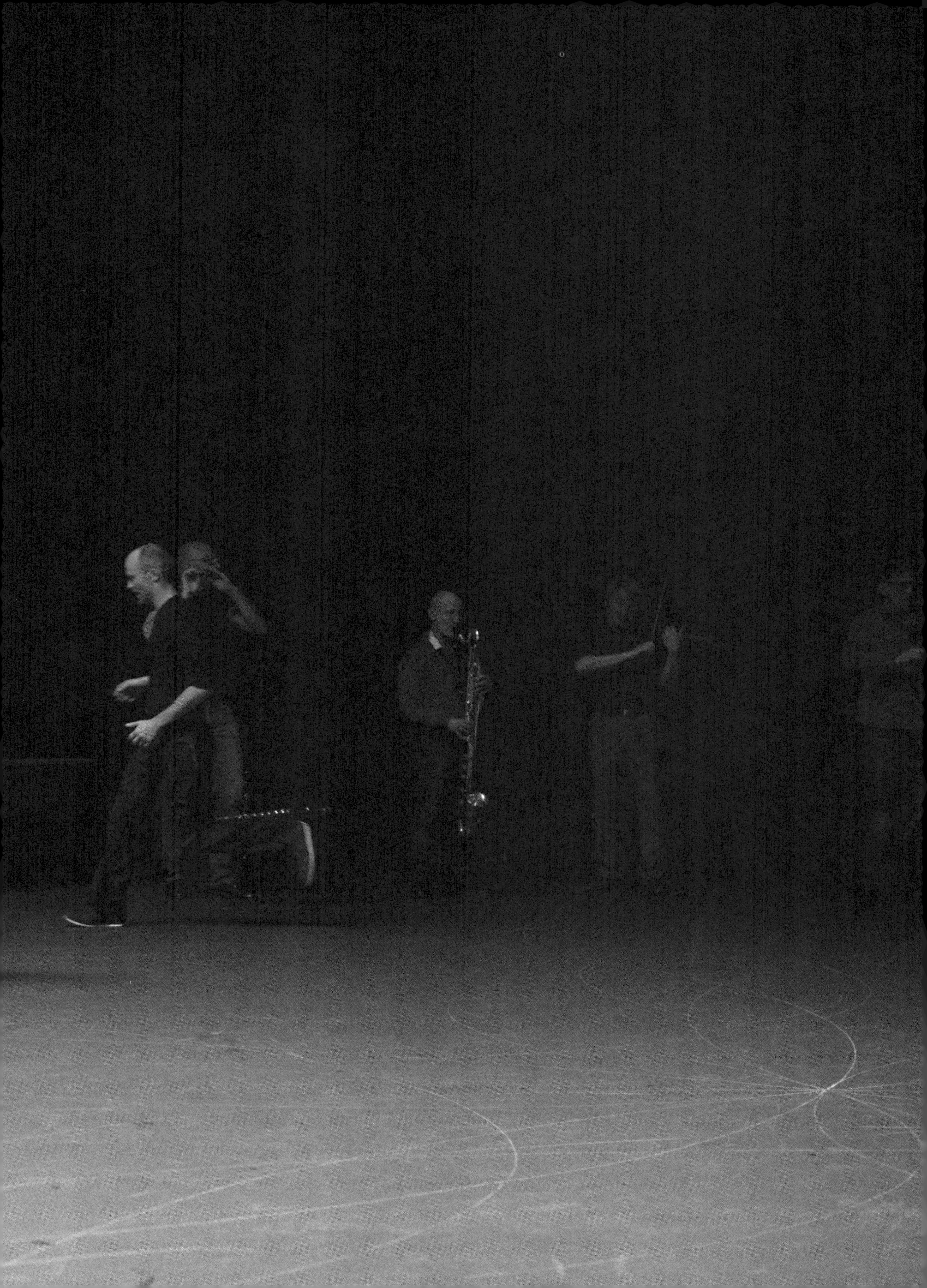

Golden Hours (As you like it) 2015

Concept and choreography
Anne Teresa De Keersmaeker
Created with and danced by
Aron Blom, Linda Blomqvist, Tale Dolven, Carlos Garbin, Tarek Halaby, Mikko Hyvönen, Veli Lehtovaara, Sandra Ortega Bejarano, Elizaveta Penkova, Georgia Vardarou, Sue-Yeon Youn
Music
Another Green World, Brian Eno (1975)
Arrangements
Carlos Garbin
Artistic advice
Ann Veronica Janssens
Dramaturgical advice
Bojana Cvejić
Lighting
Luc Schaltin
Costumes
Anne-Catherine Kunz
Artistic assistant
Femke Gyselinck
Sound
Alexandre Fostier
Production
Rosas
Coproduction
La Monnaie / De Munt (Brussels), Kaaitheater (Brussels), Les Théâtres de la Ville de Luxembourg, Théâtre de la Ville (Paris), Sadler's Wells (London), Steirischer Herbst (Graz), Opéra de Lille, Ruhrtriennale, Concertgebouw Bruges, Festival Montpellier Danse 2015
Premiere
23.01.2015, Kaaitheater—Brussels

Pictures
Anne Van Aerschot

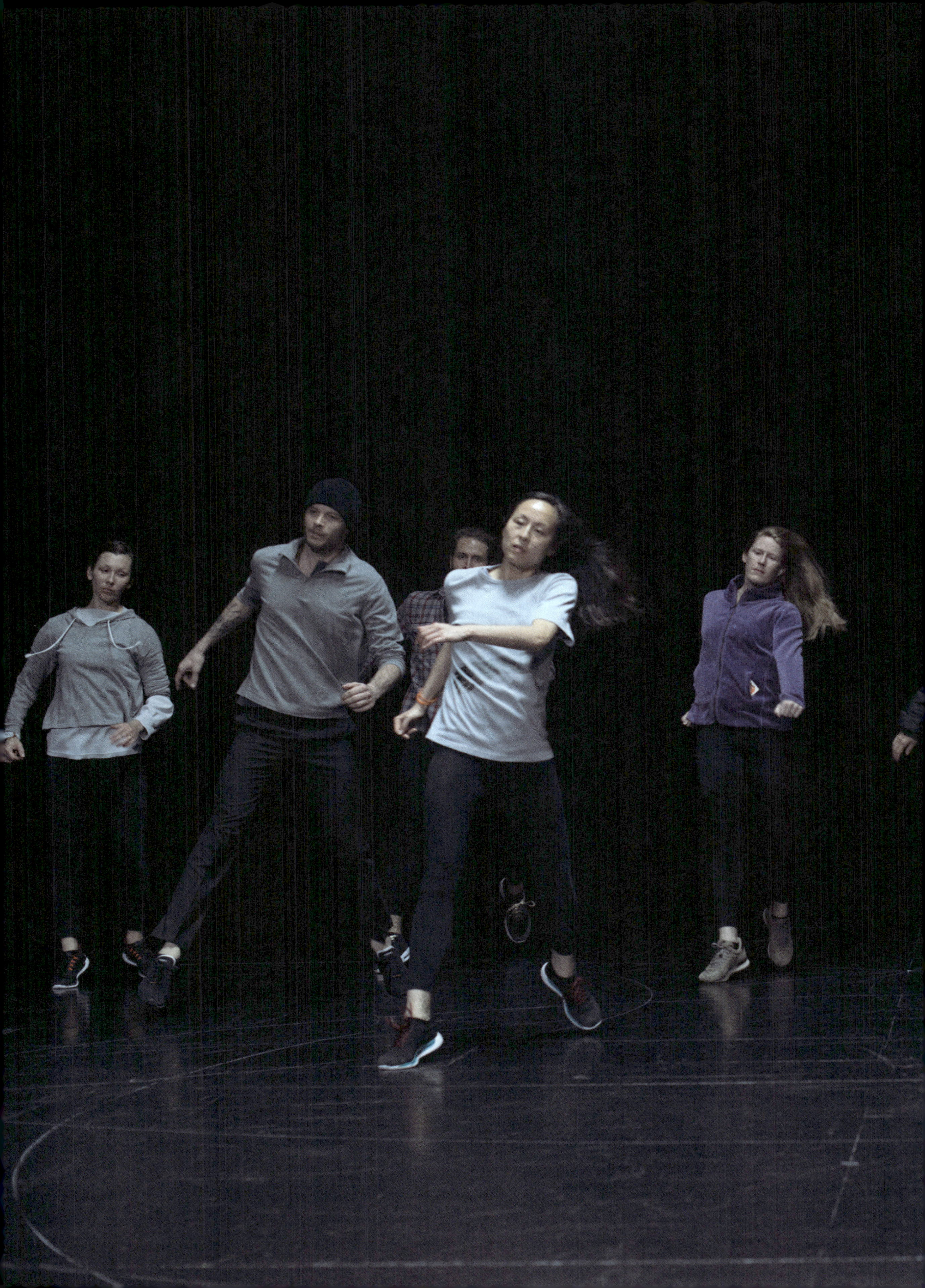

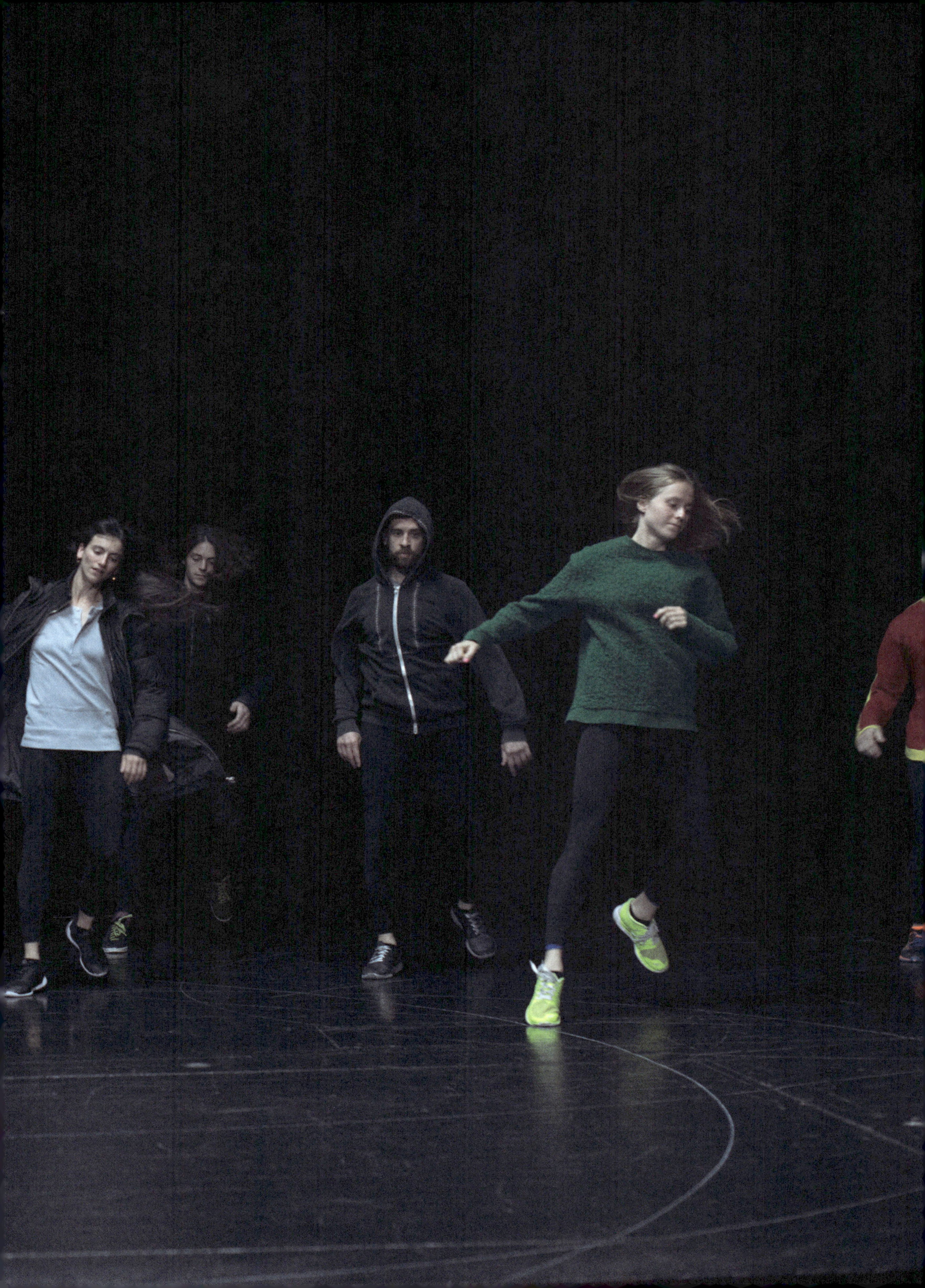

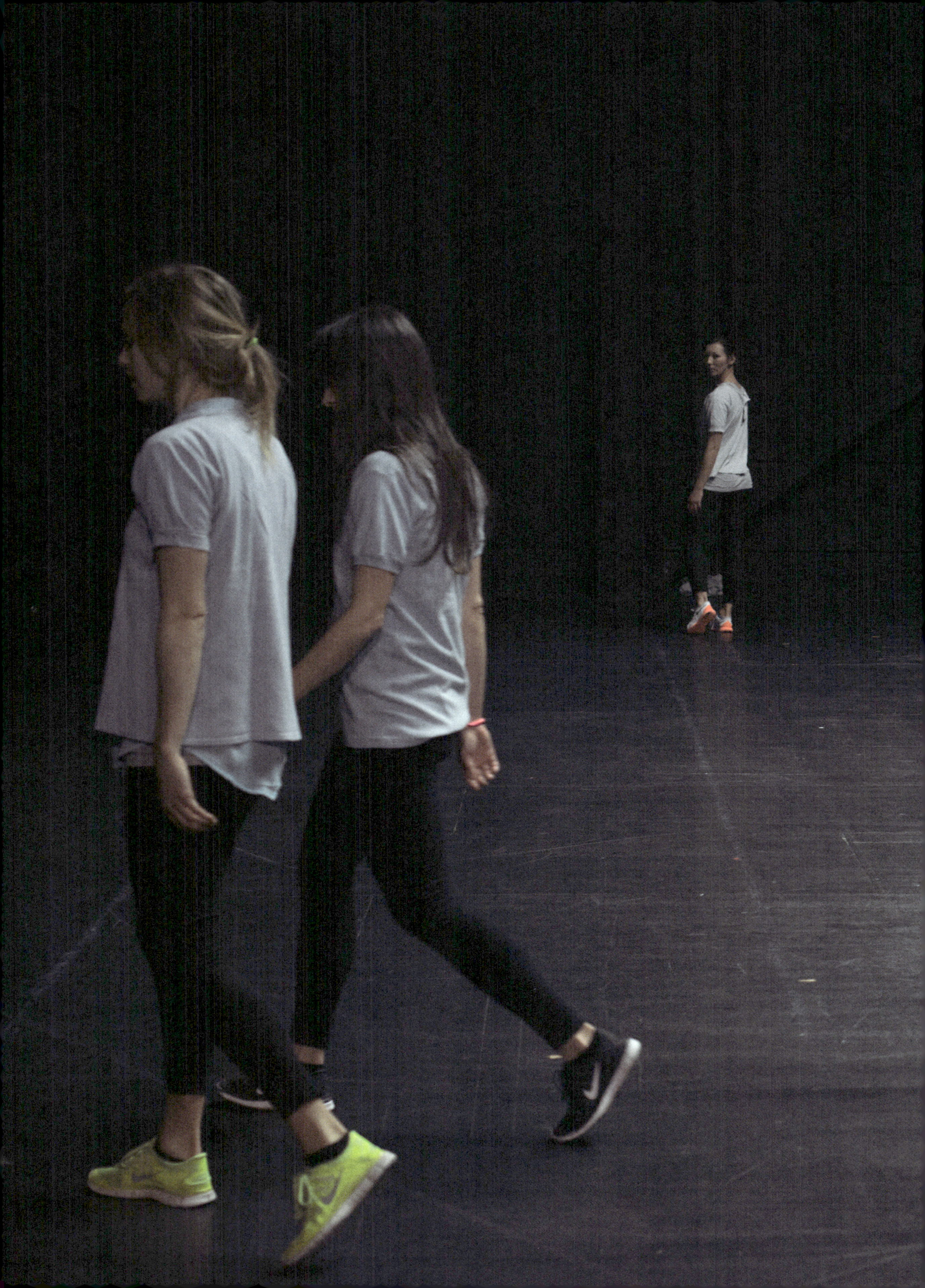

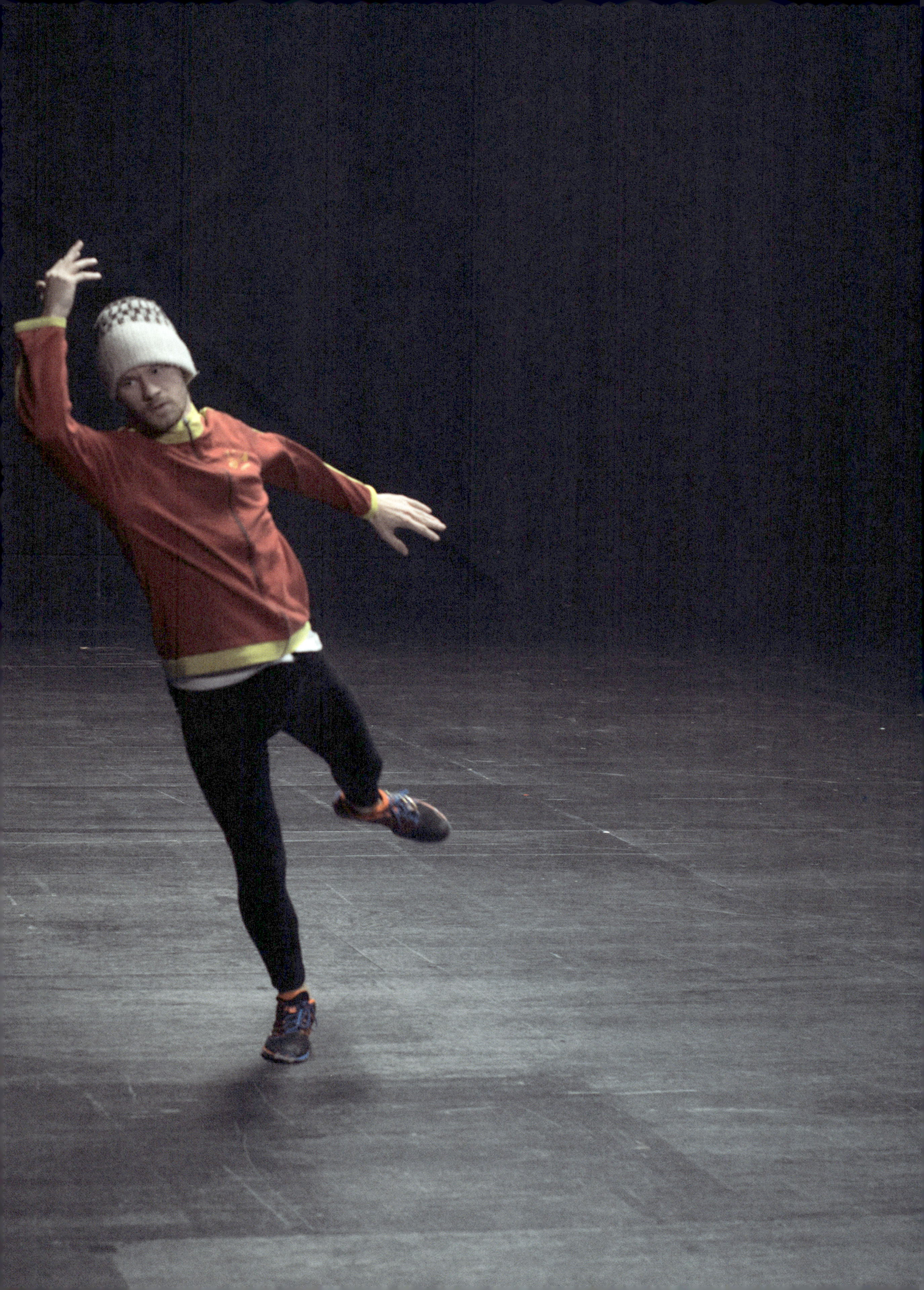

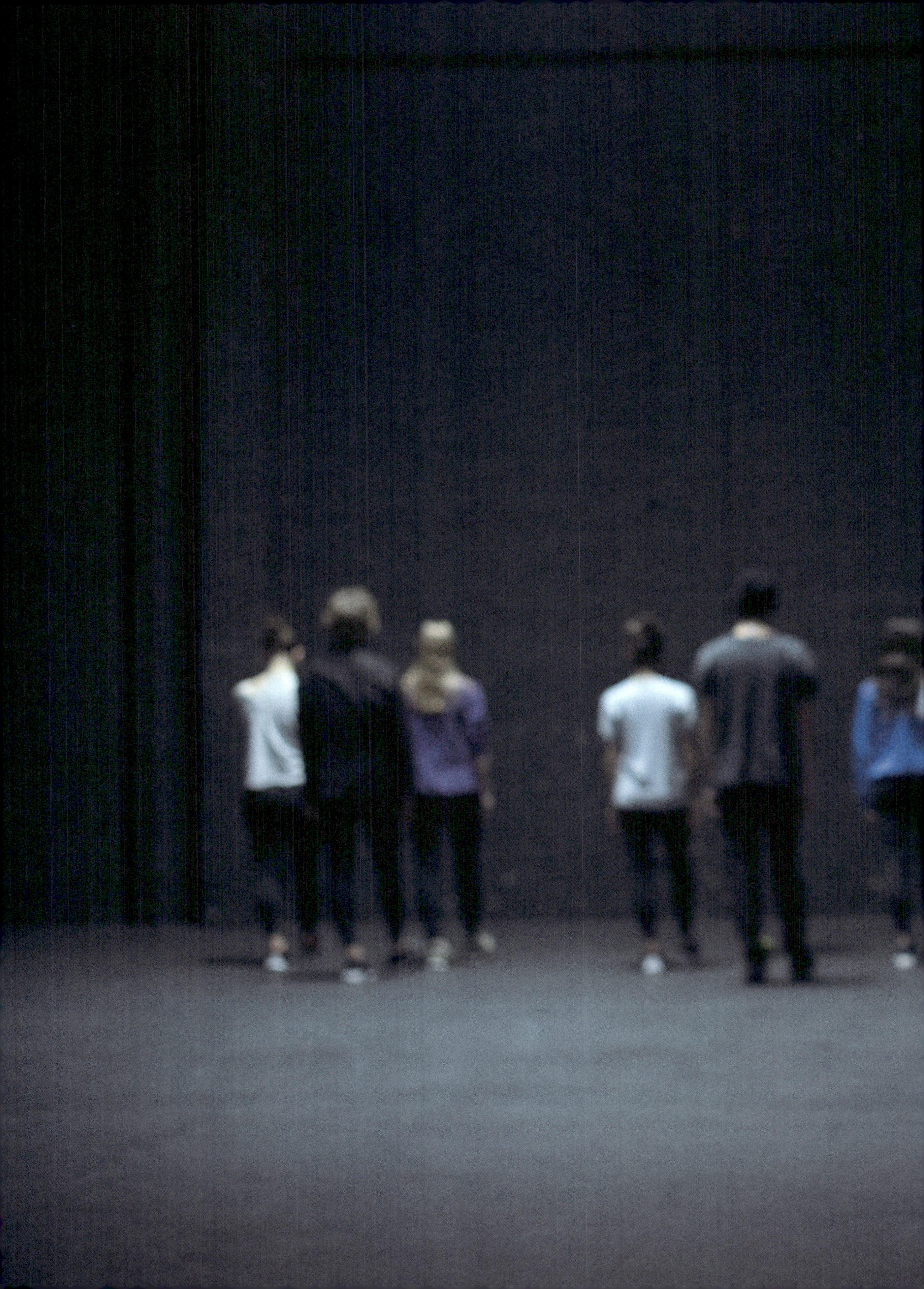

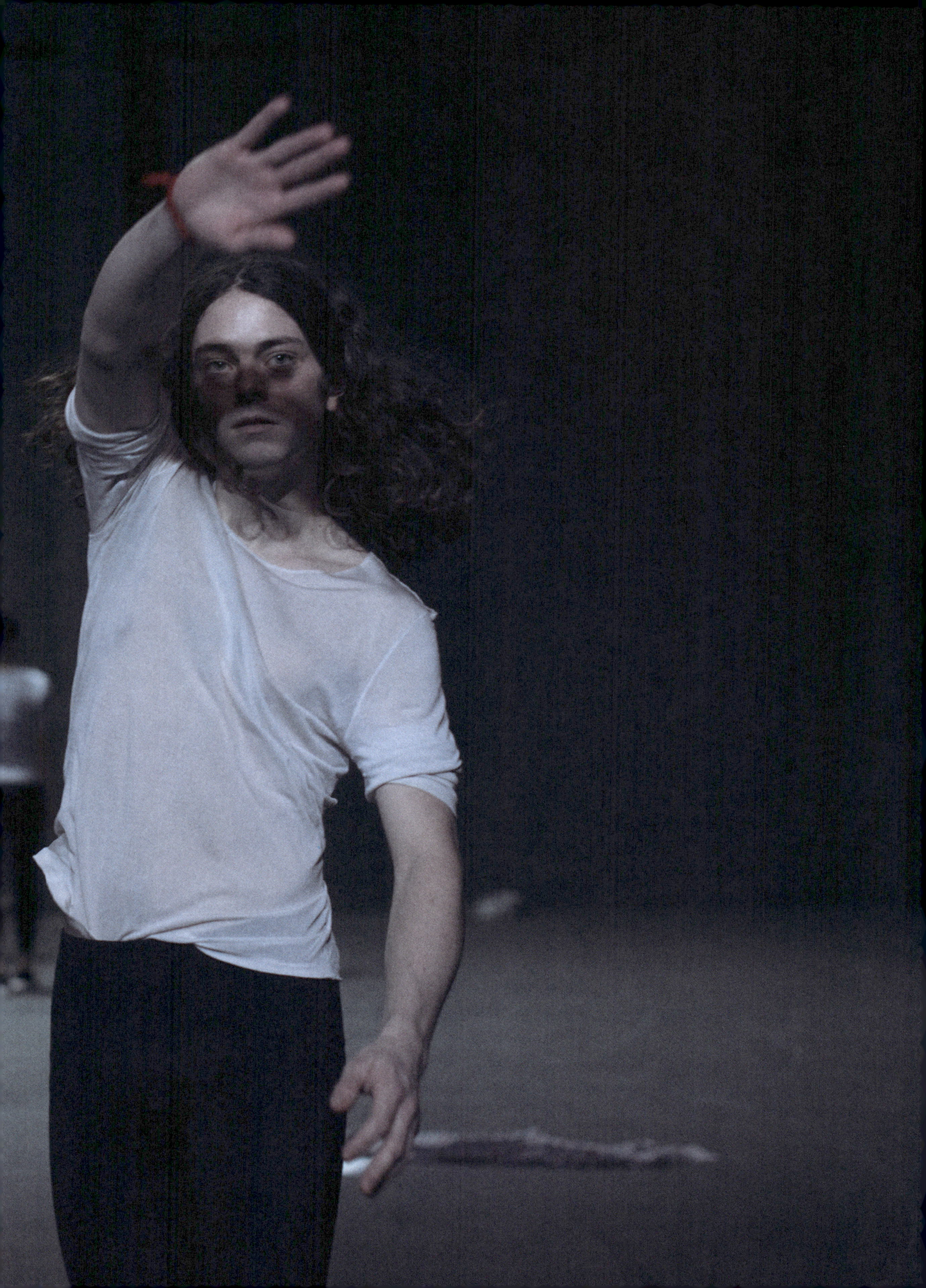

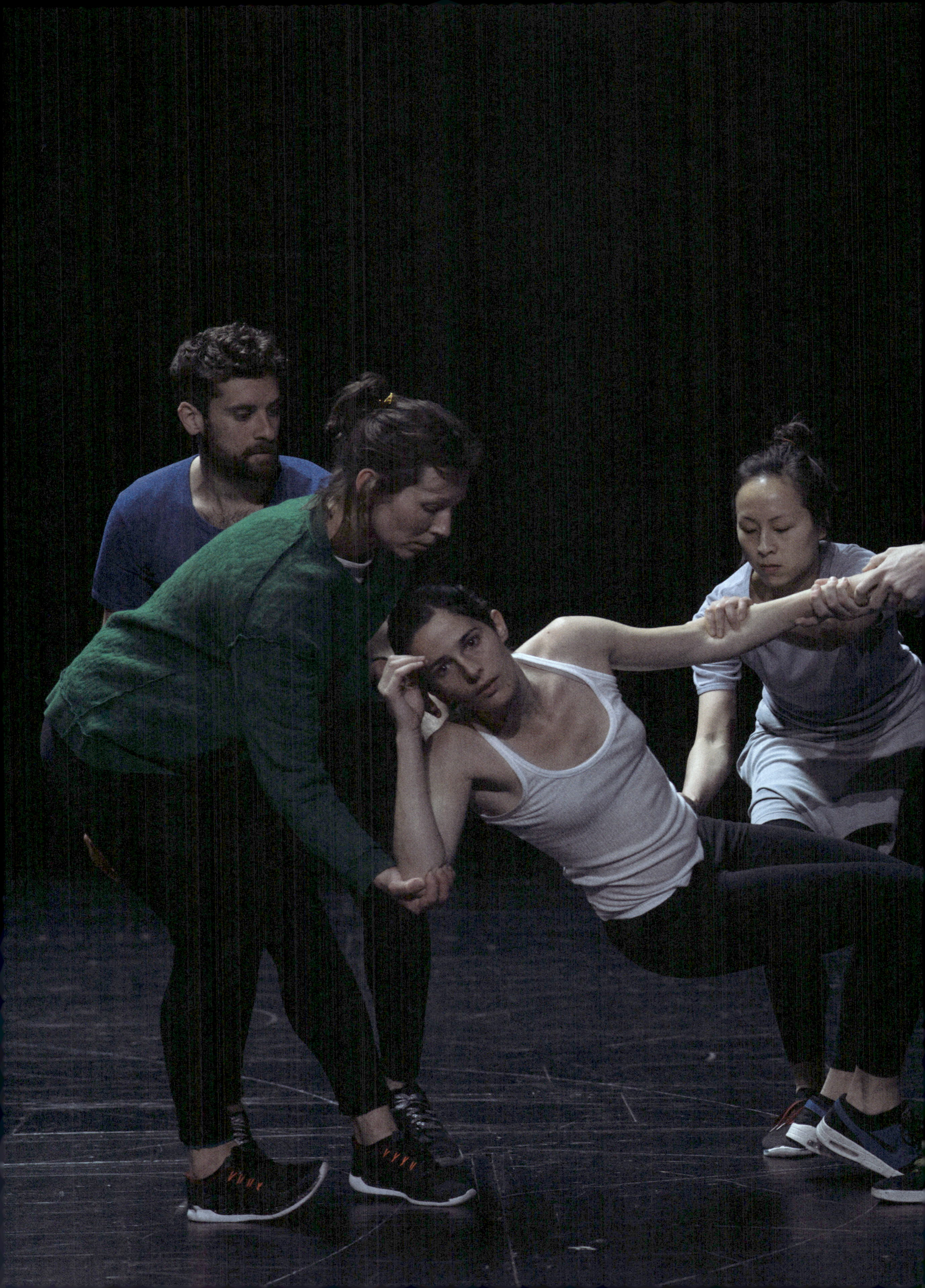

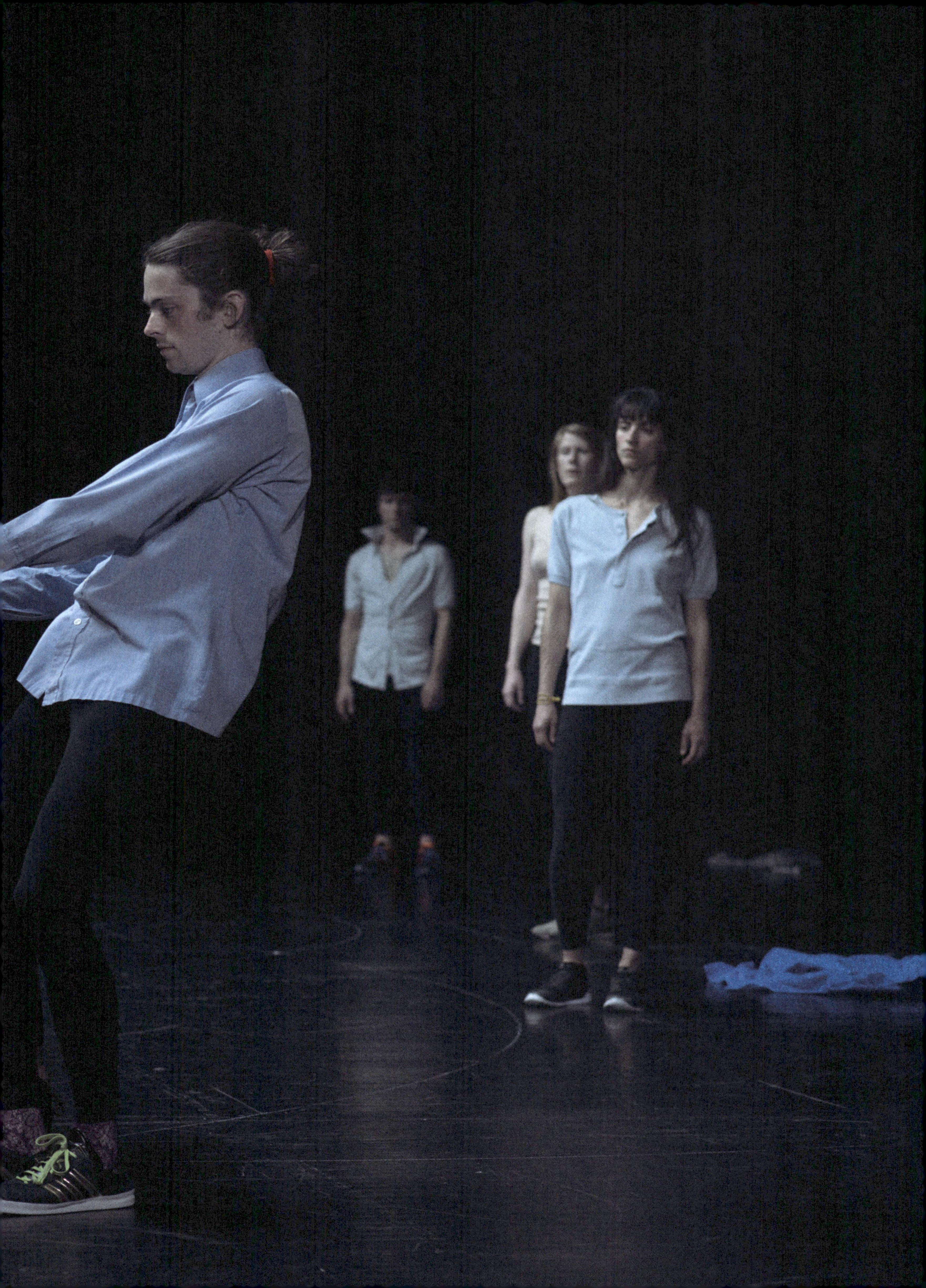

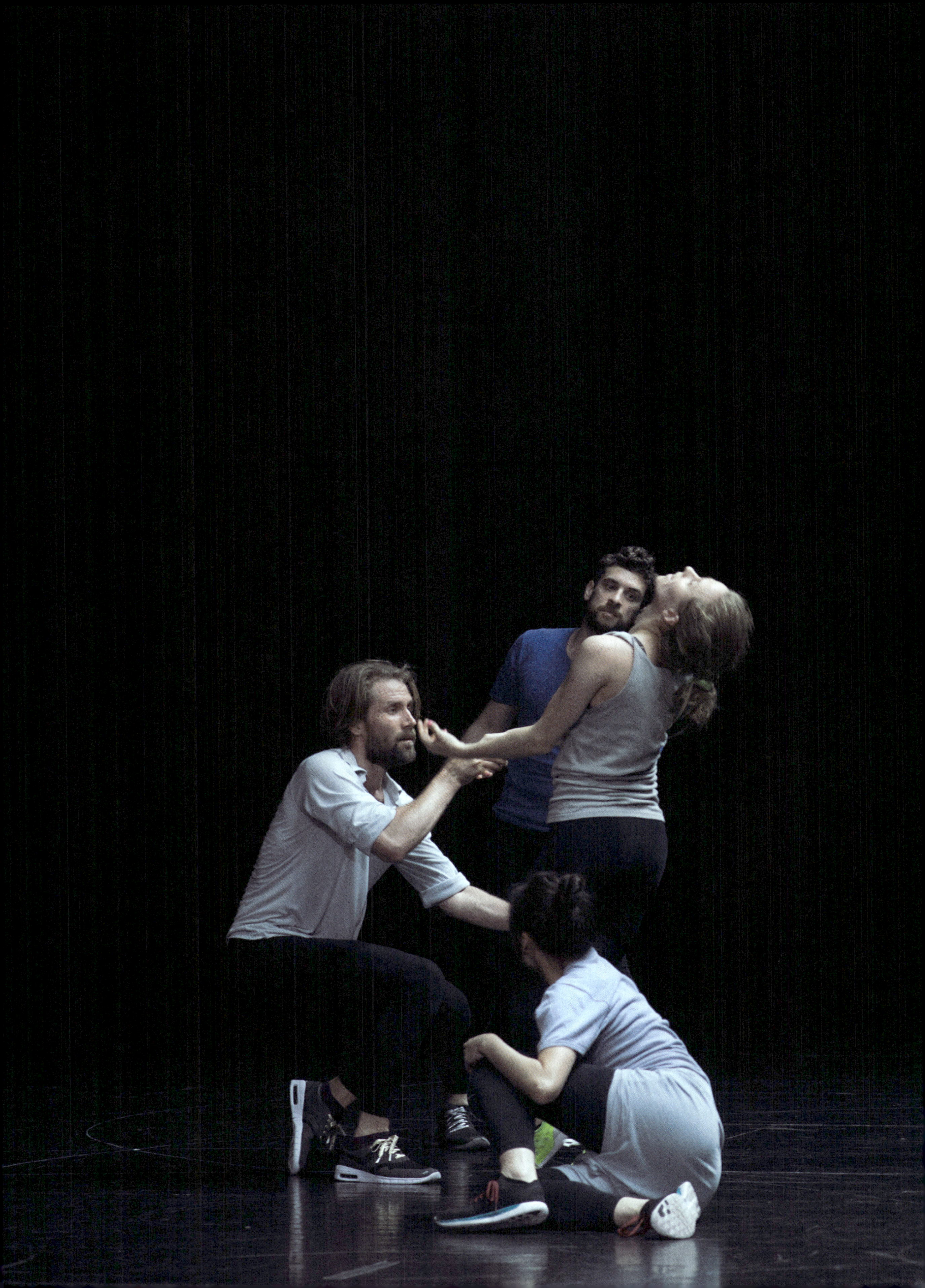

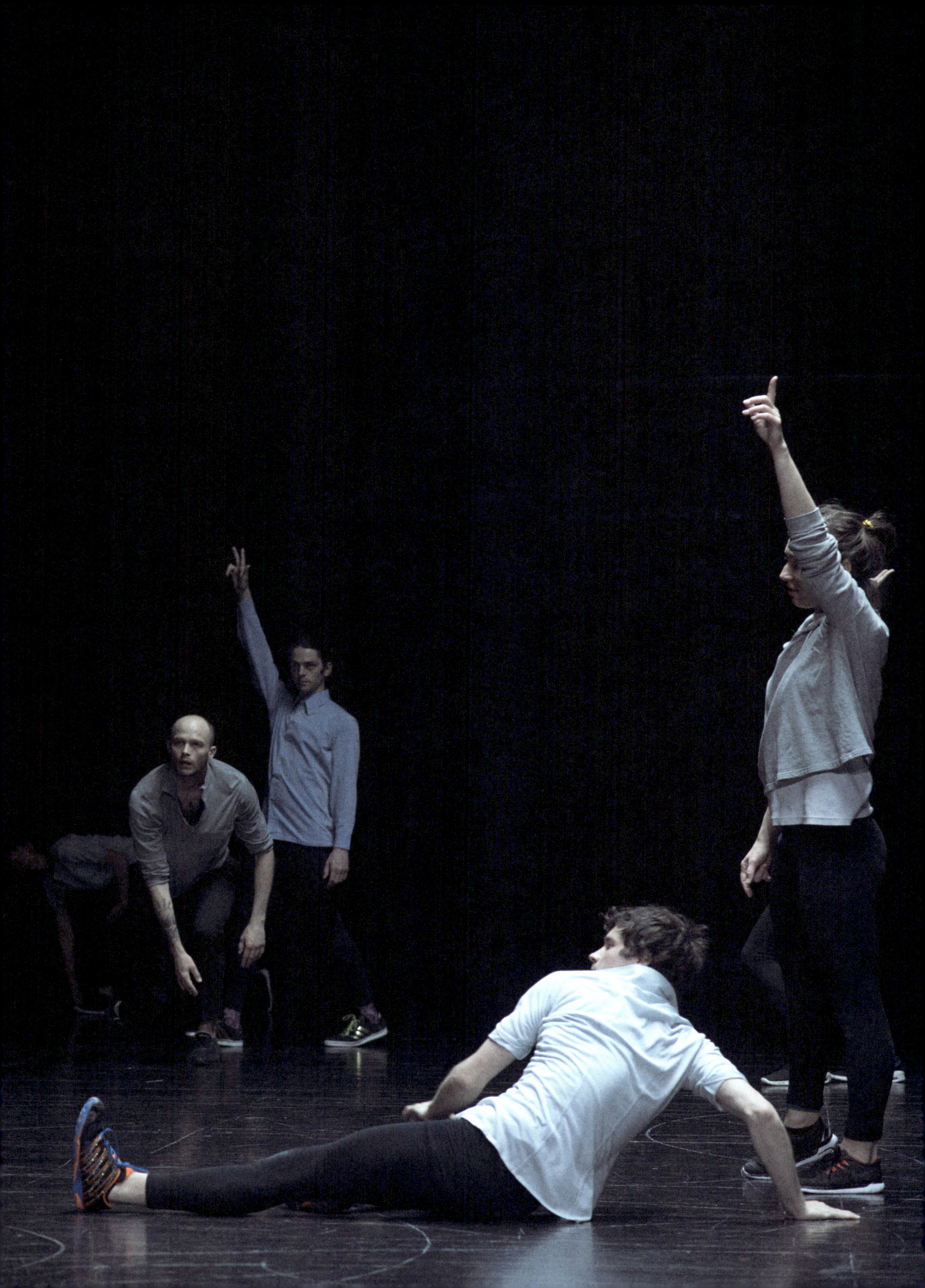

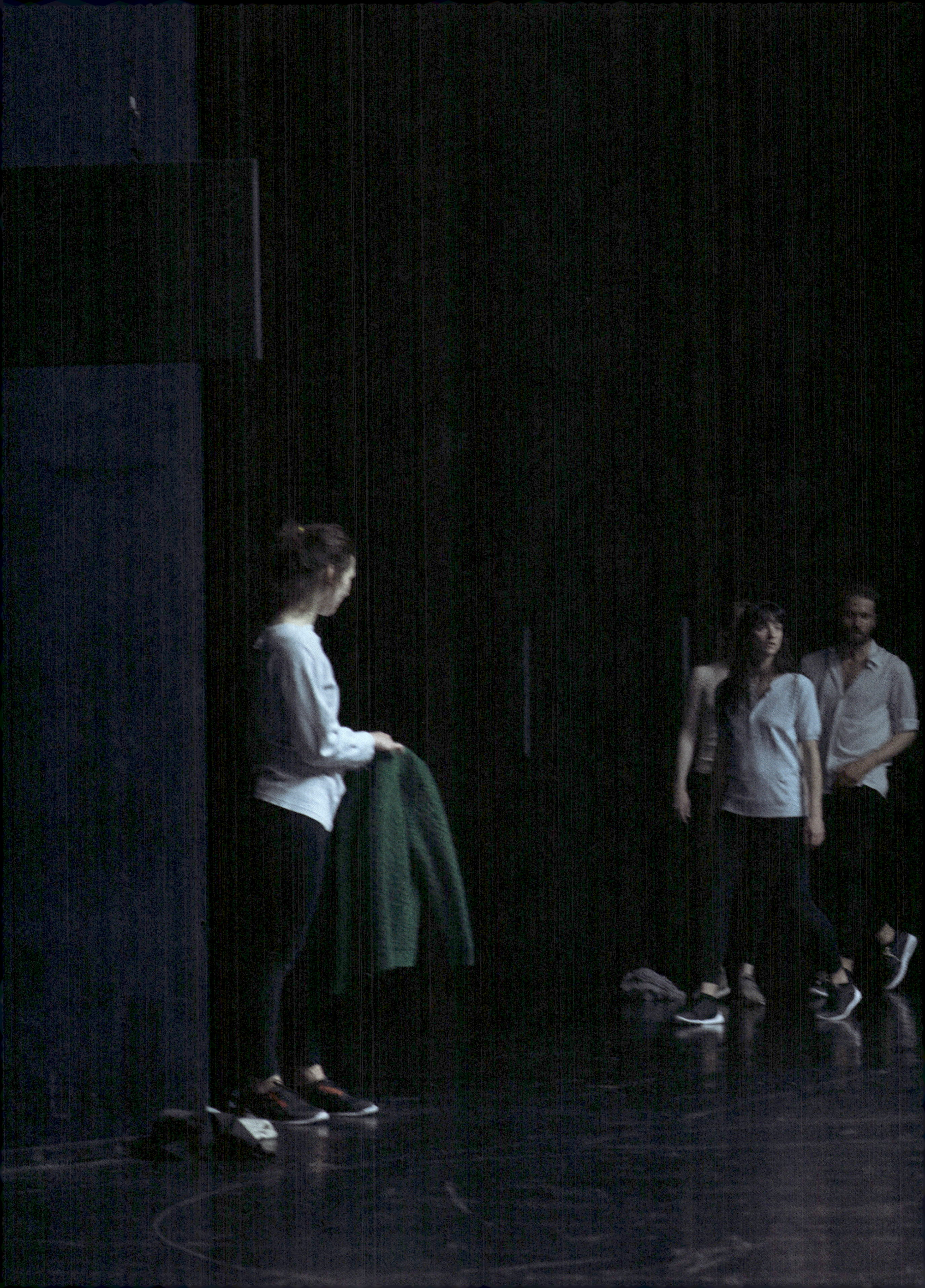

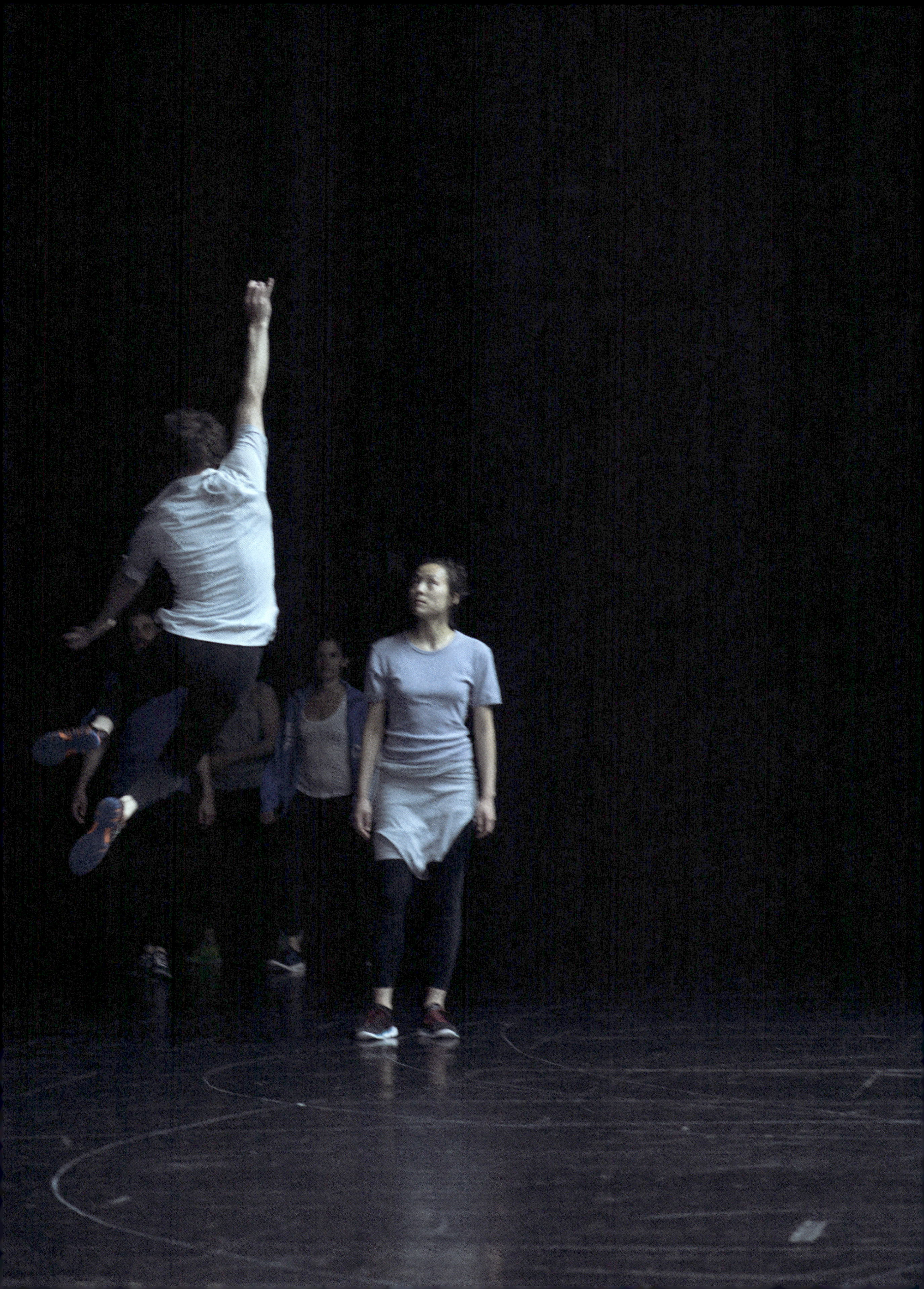

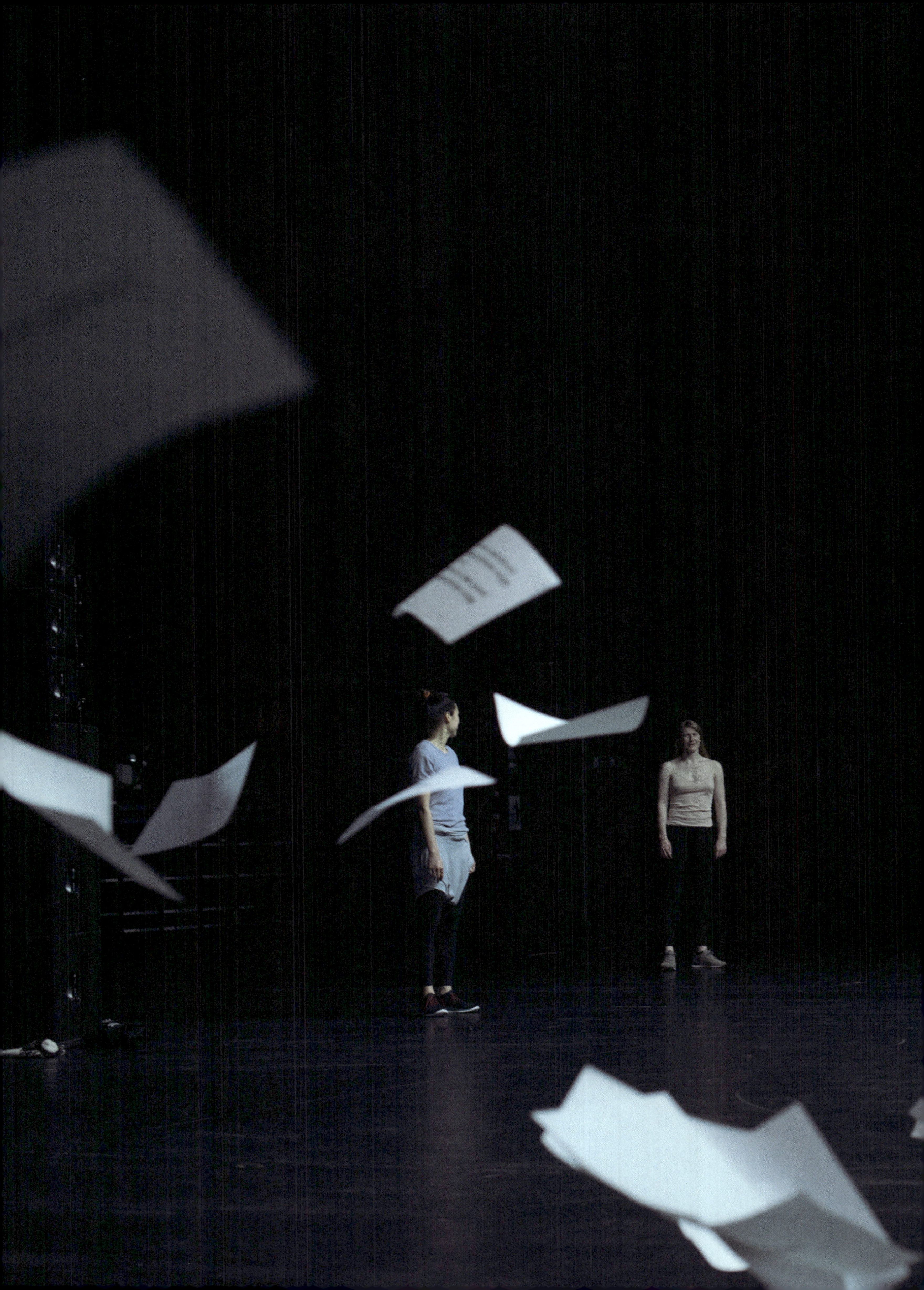

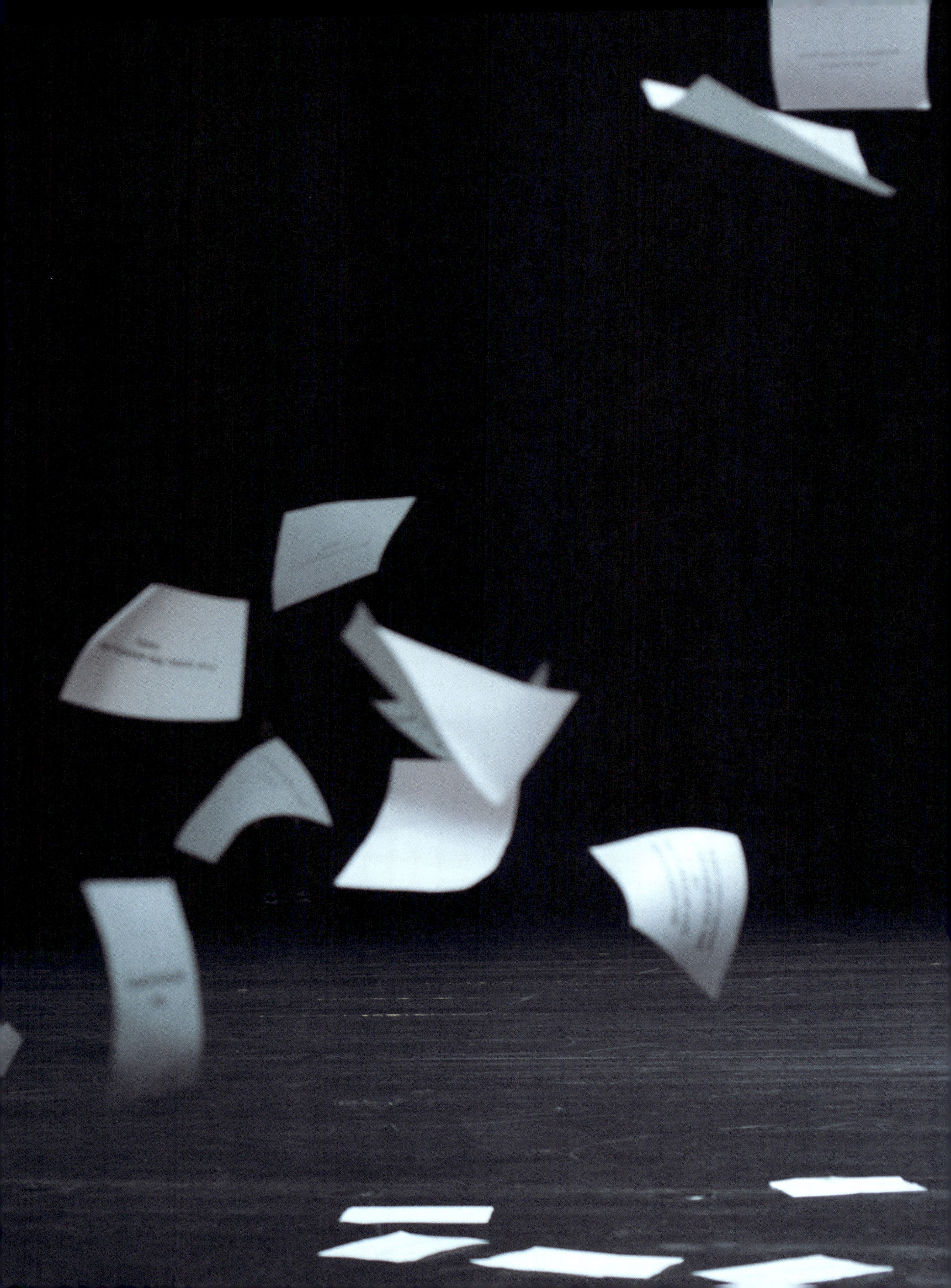

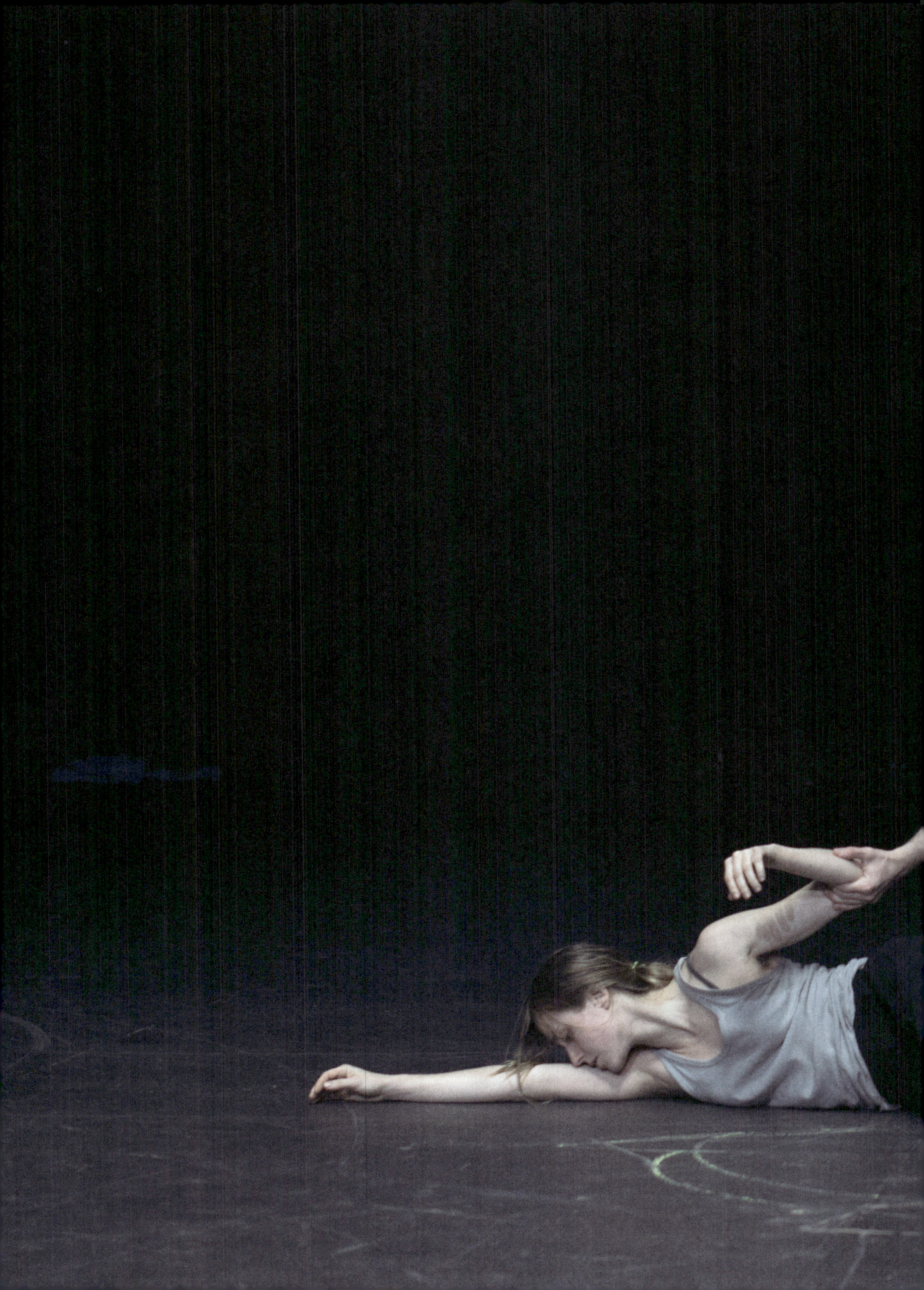

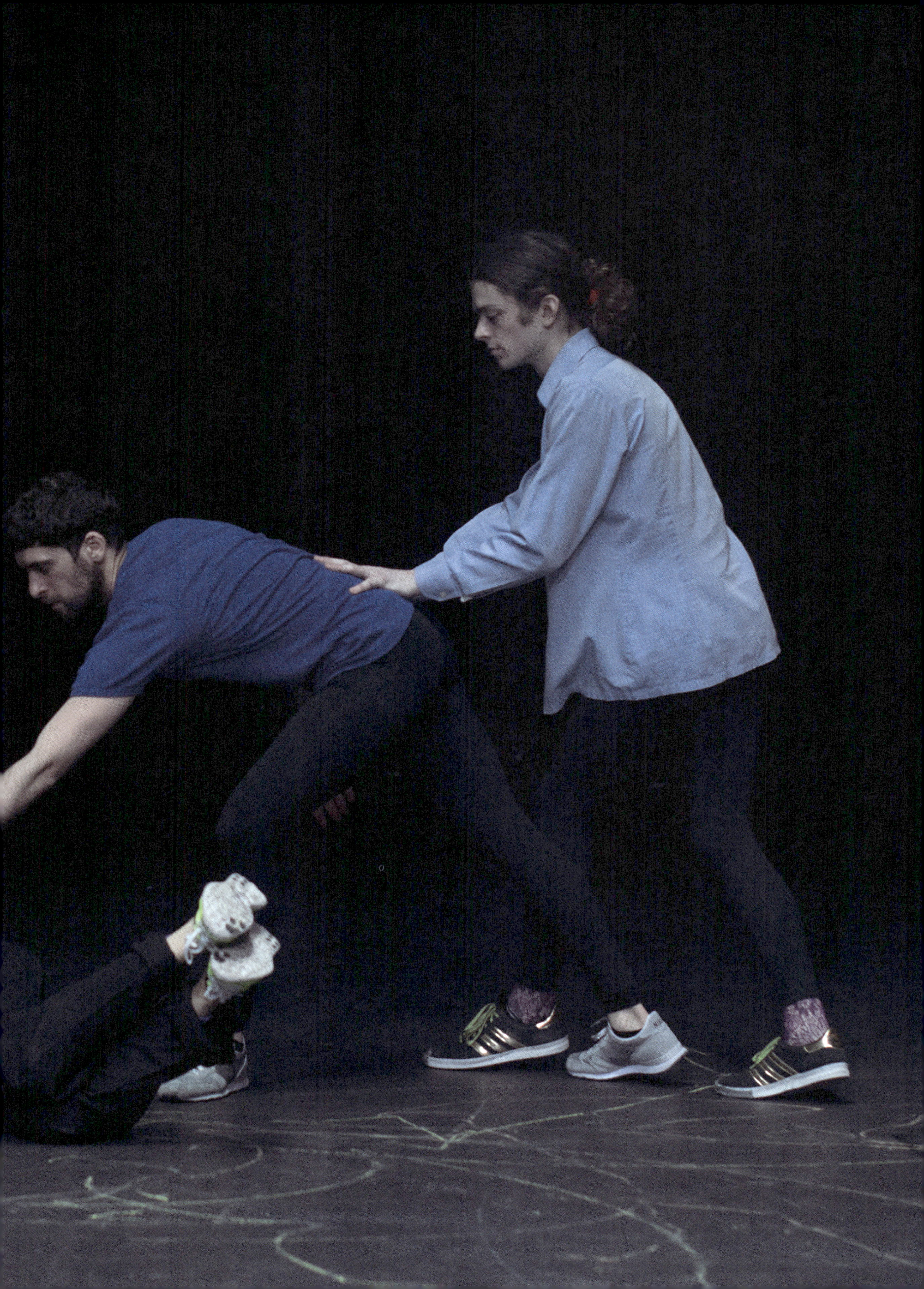

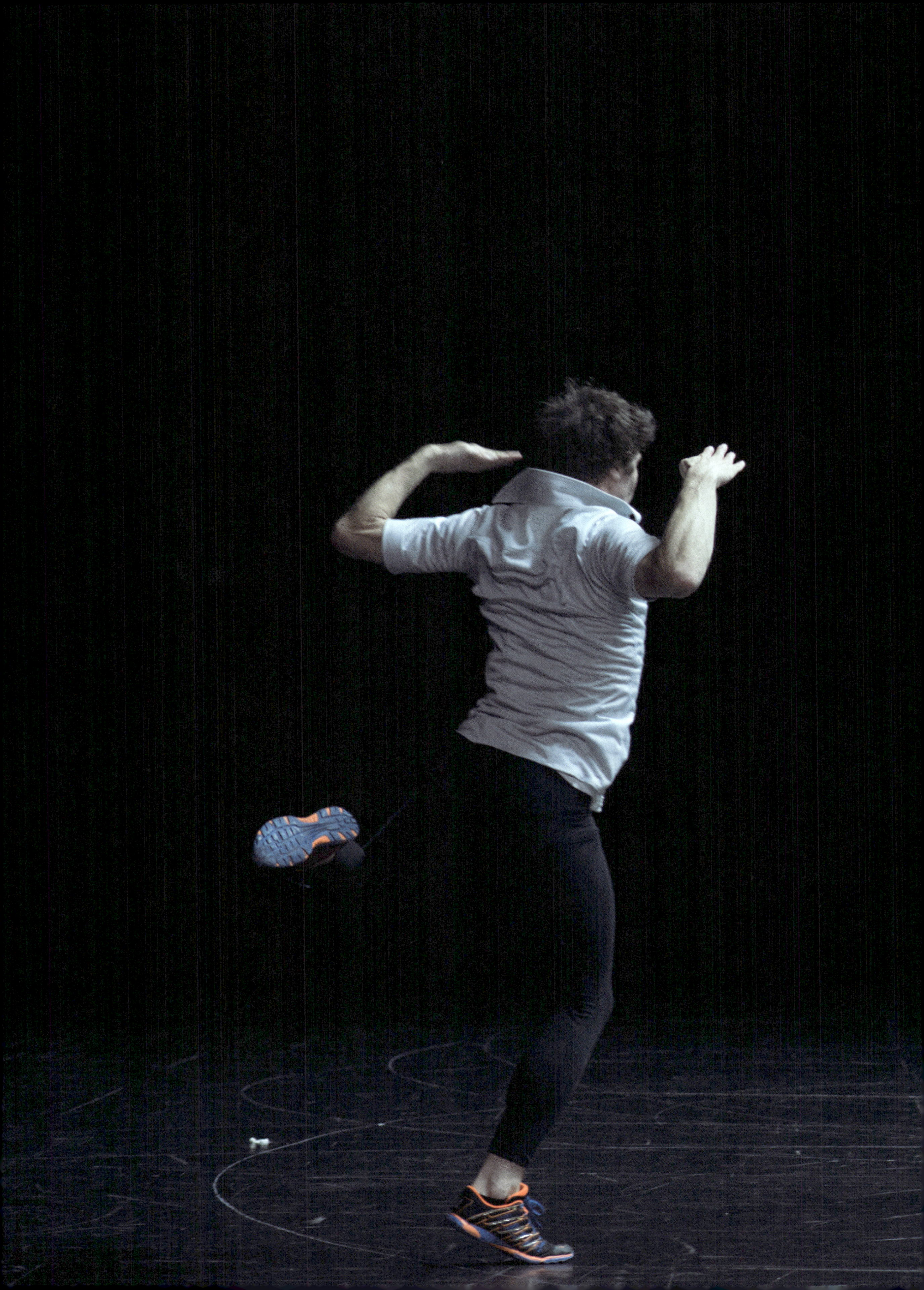

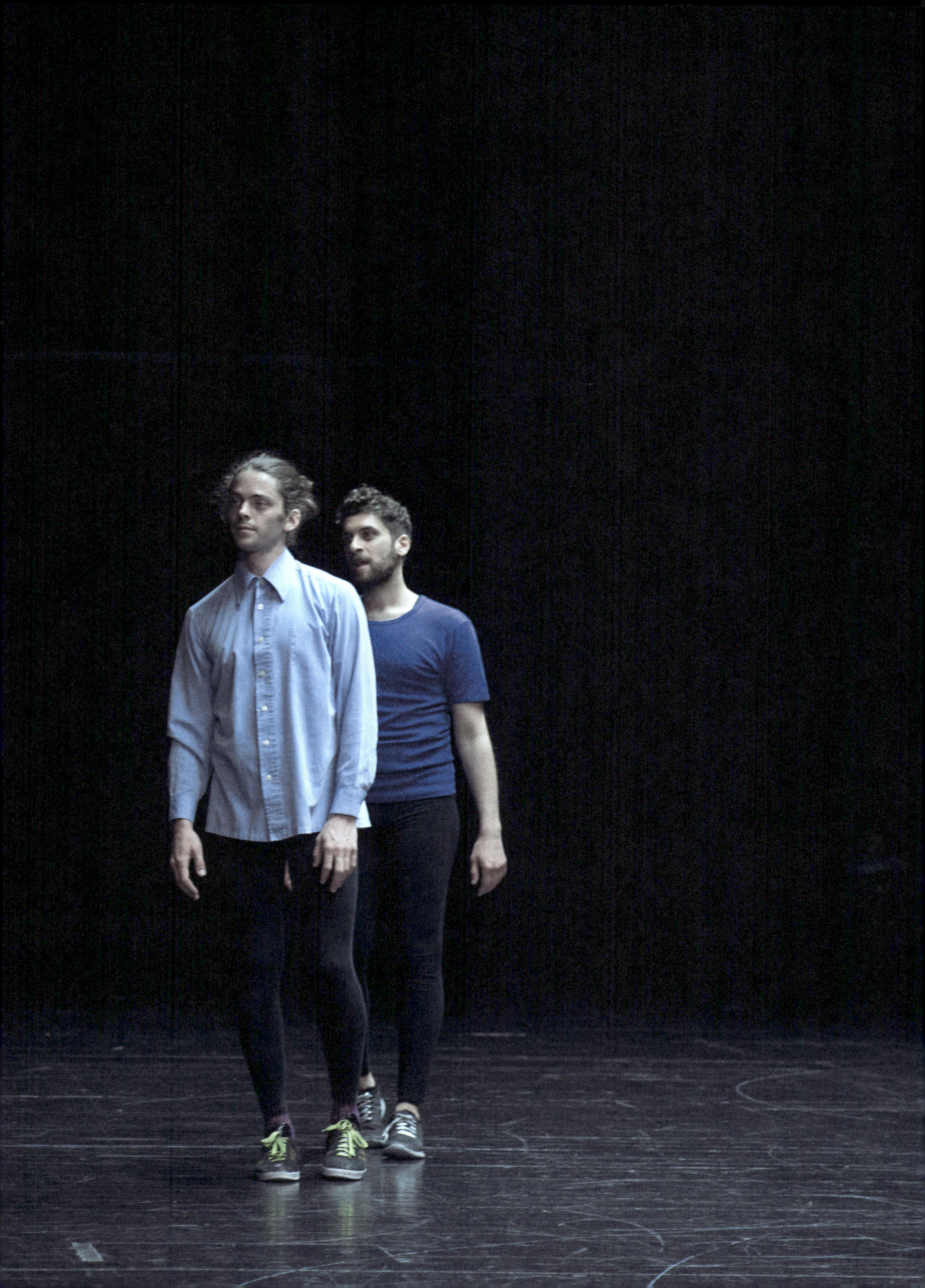

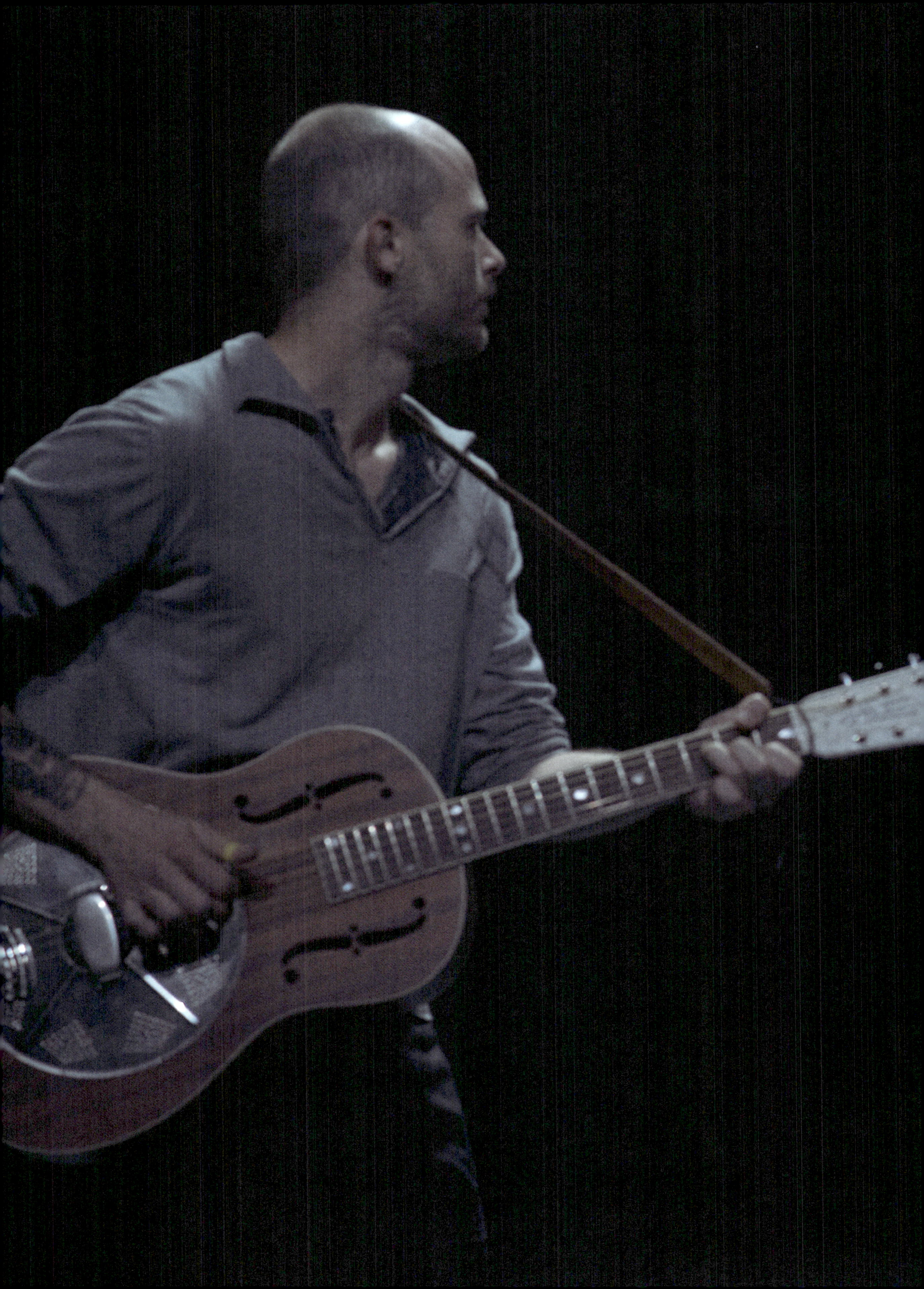

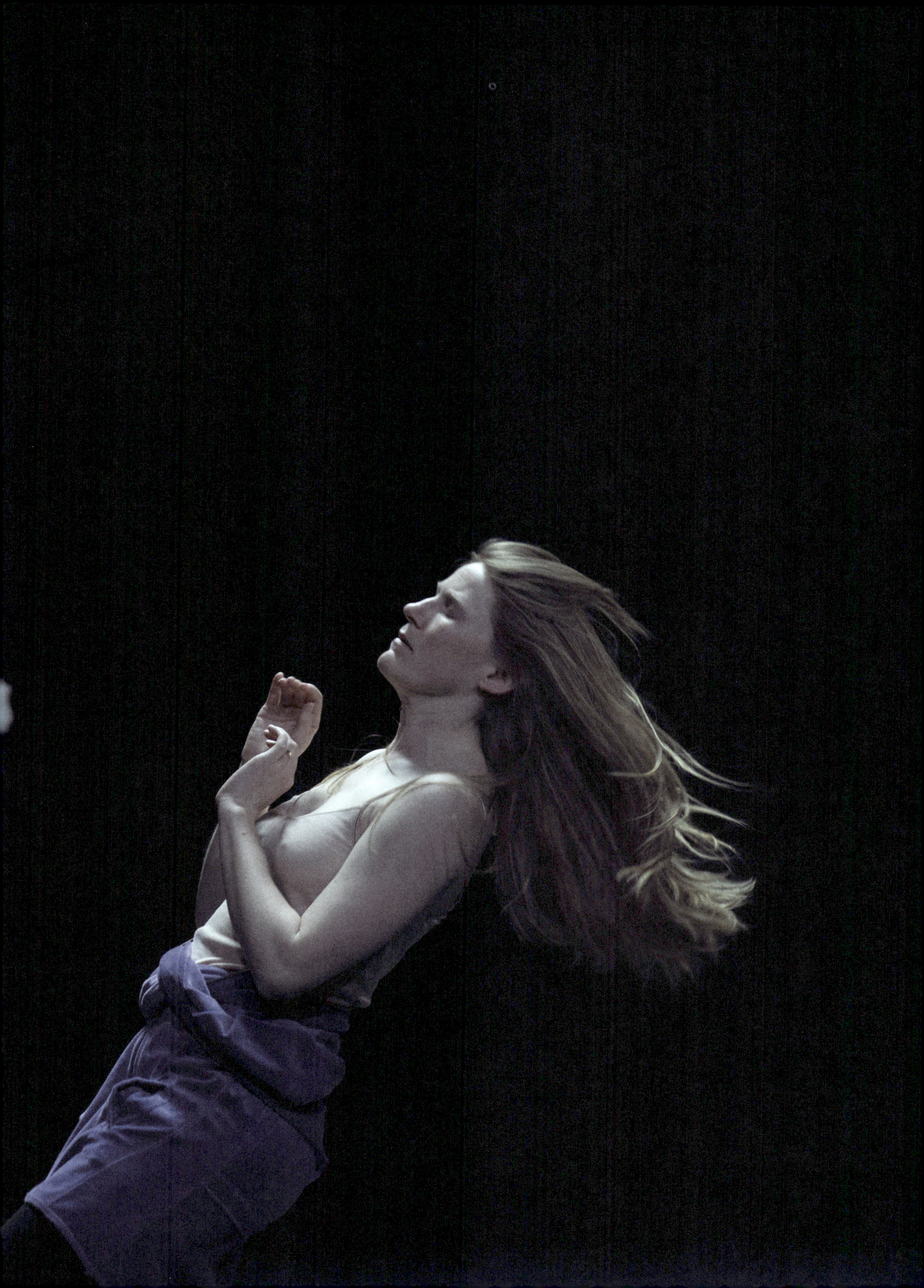

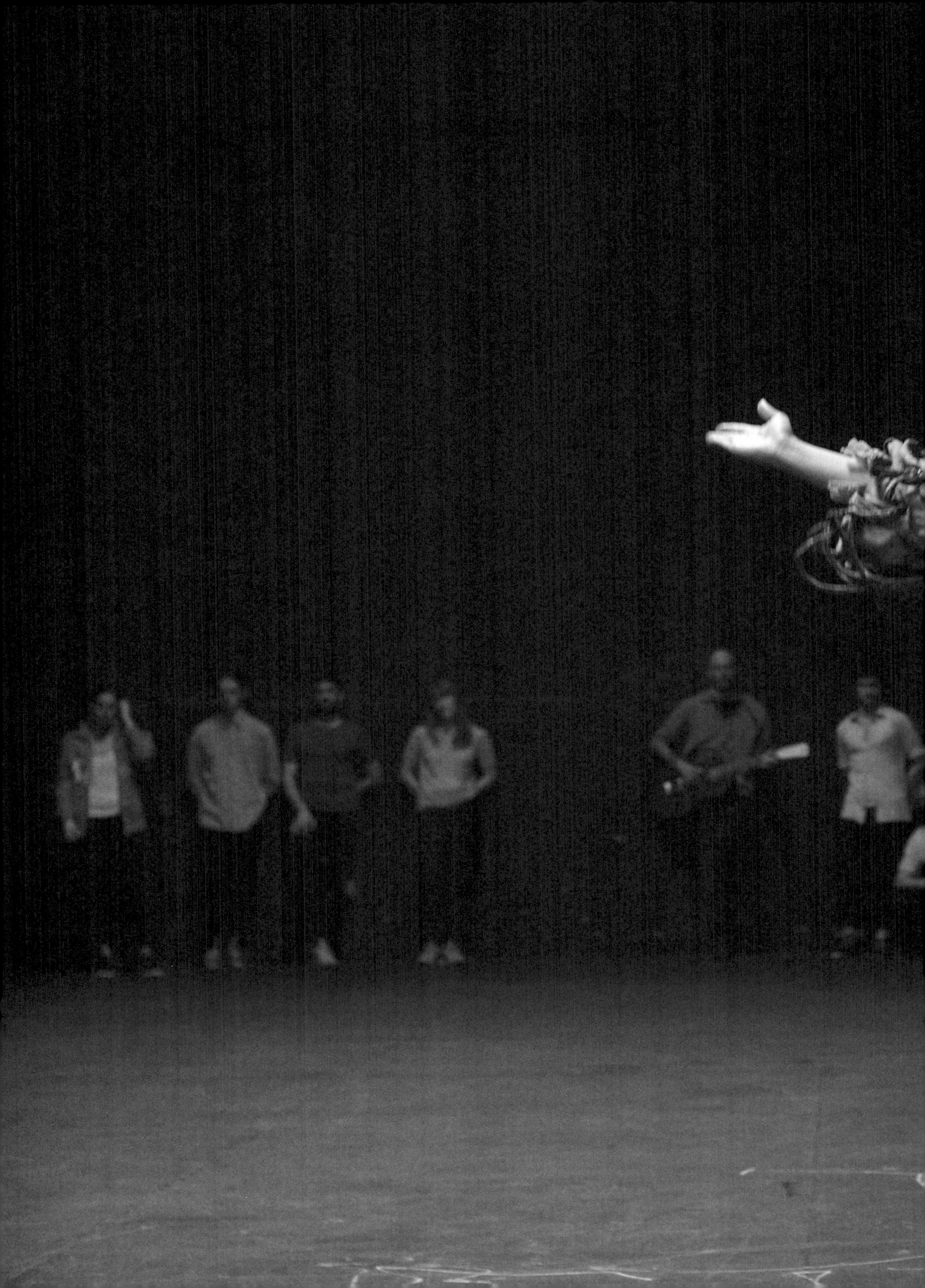

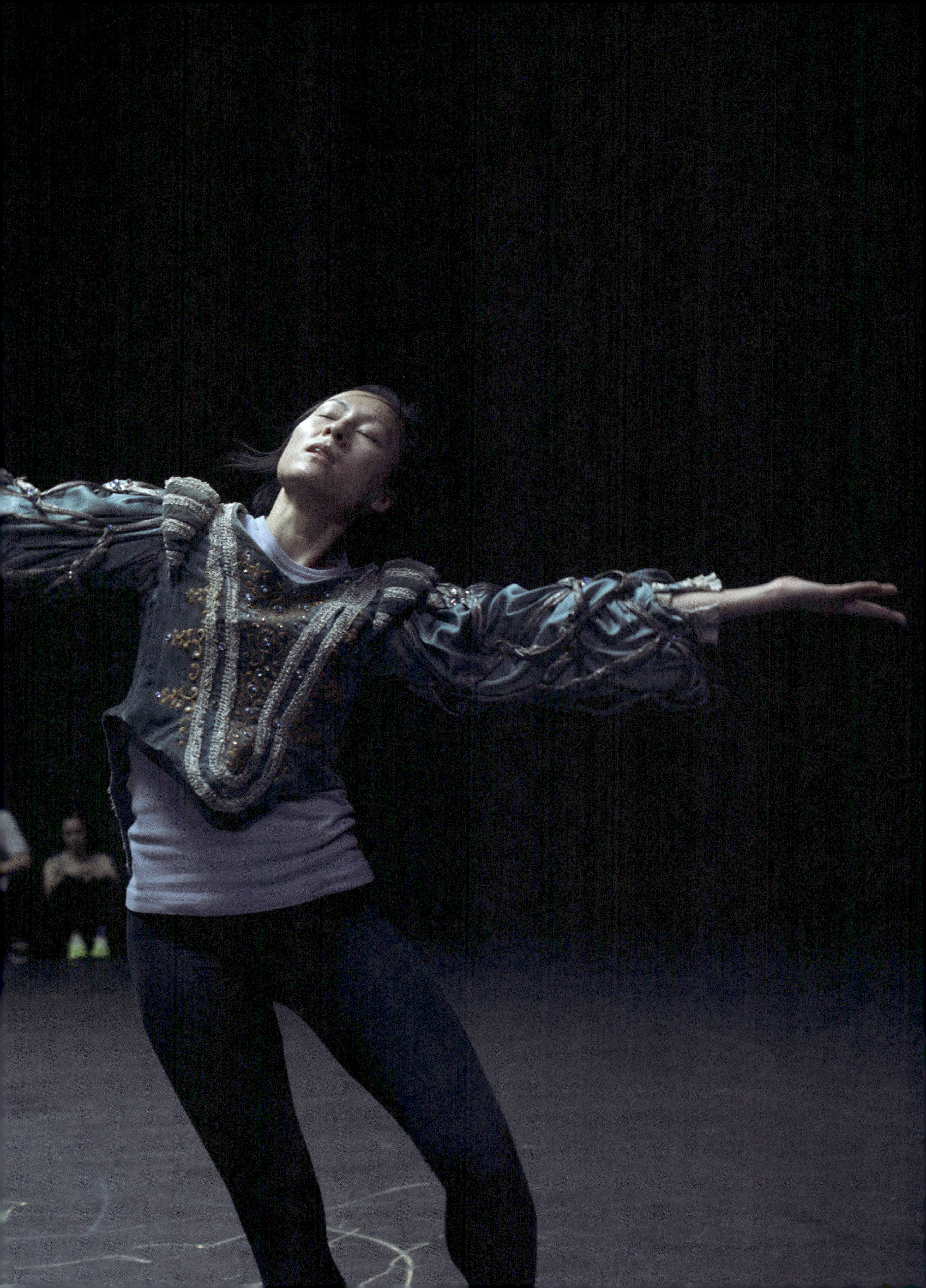

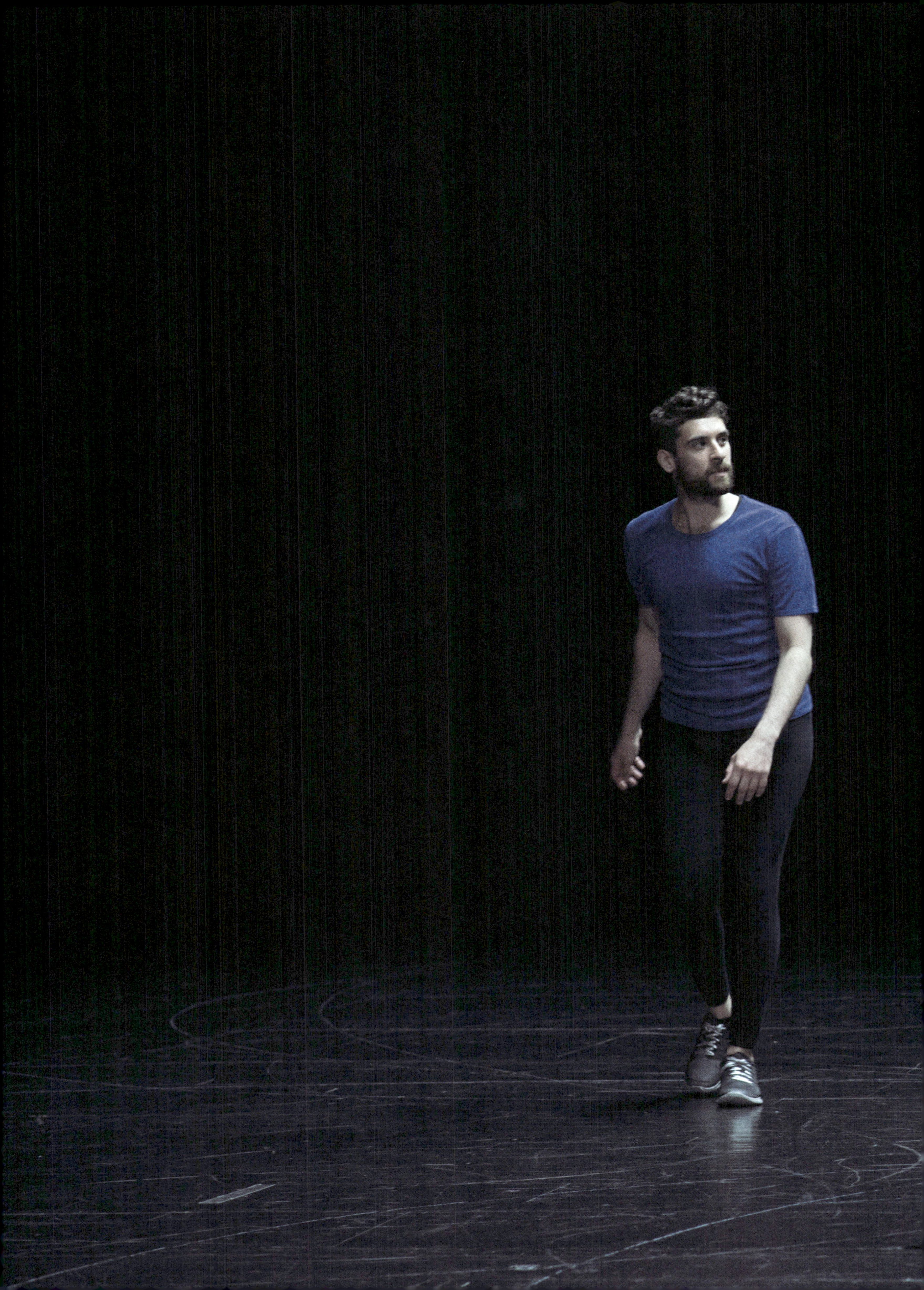

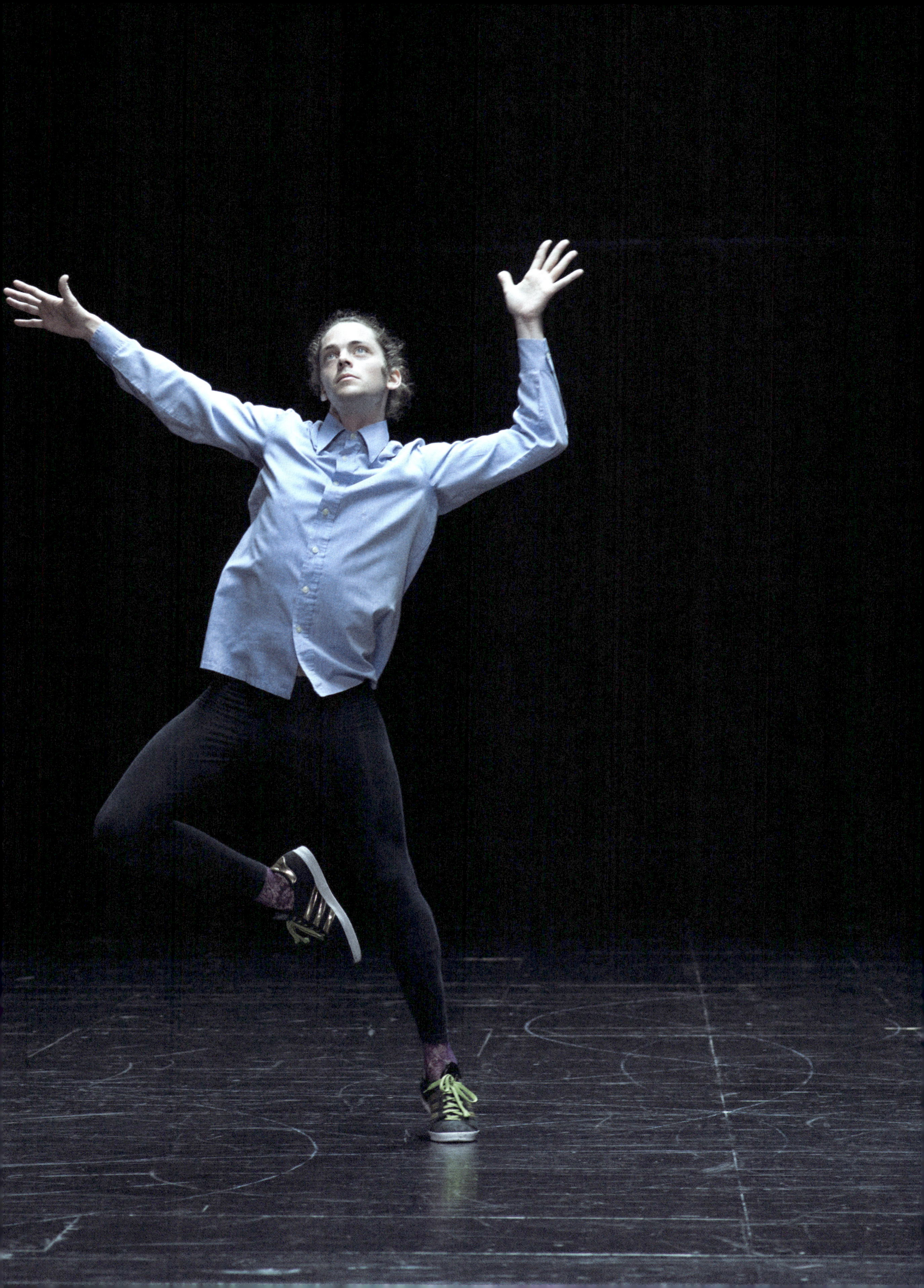

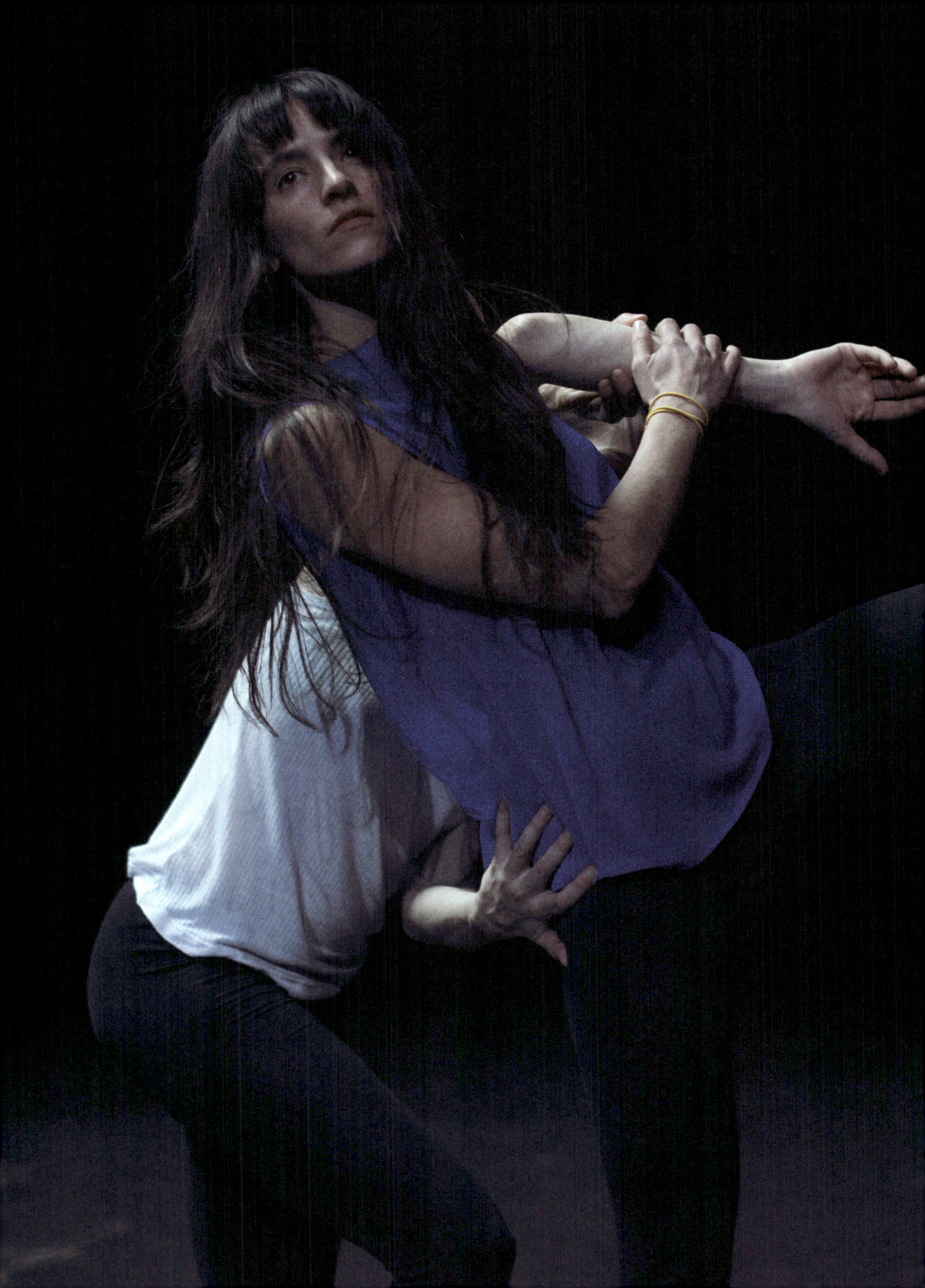

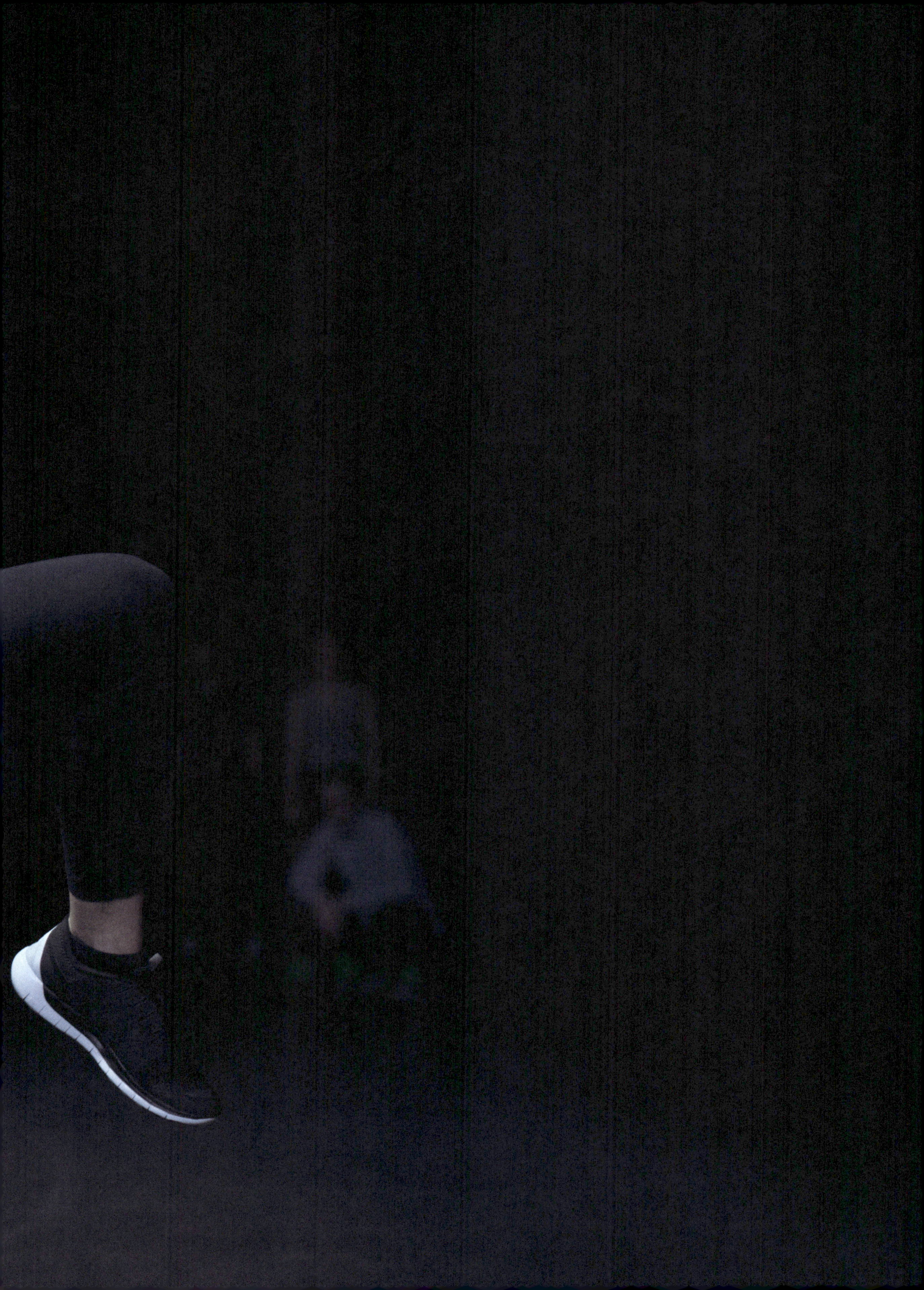

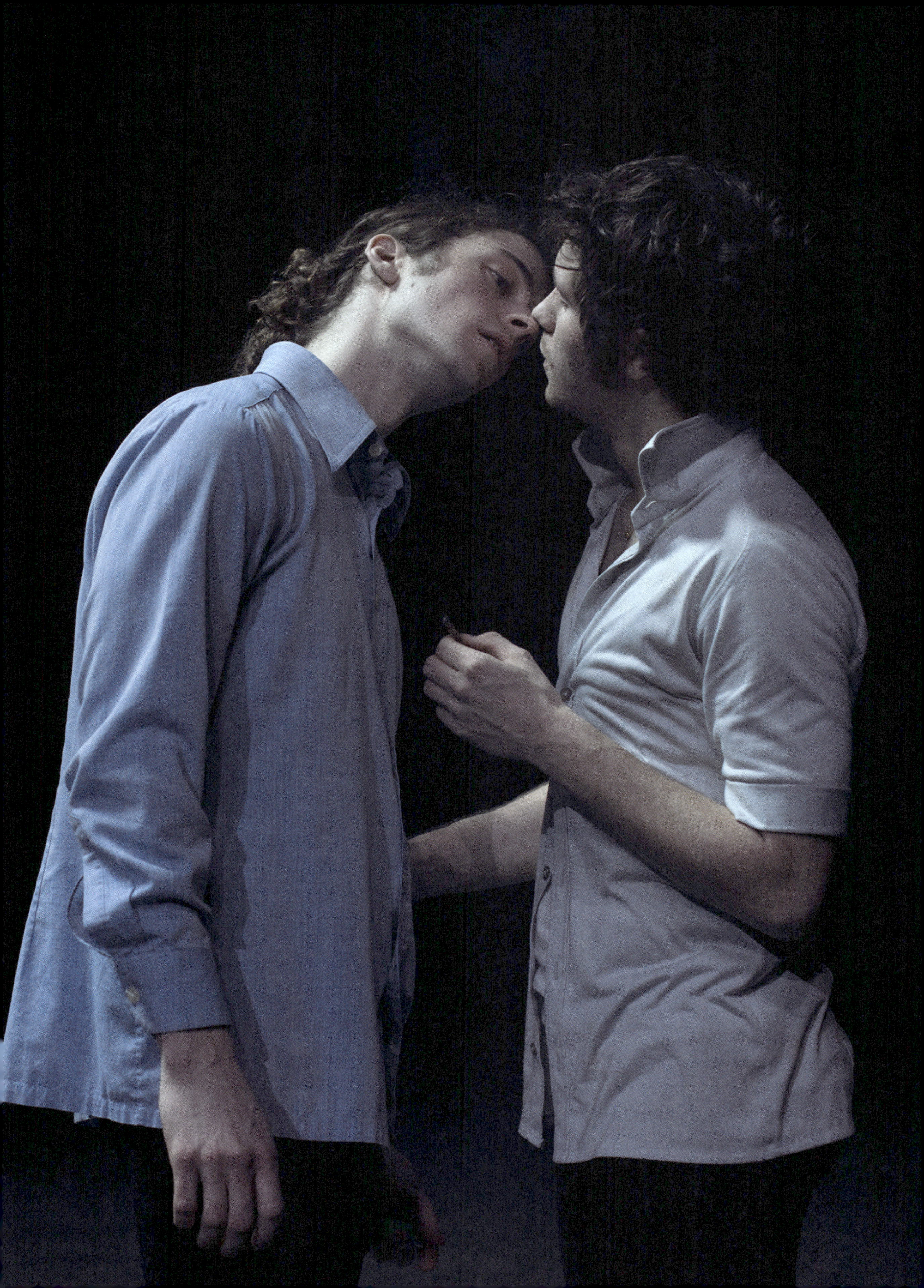

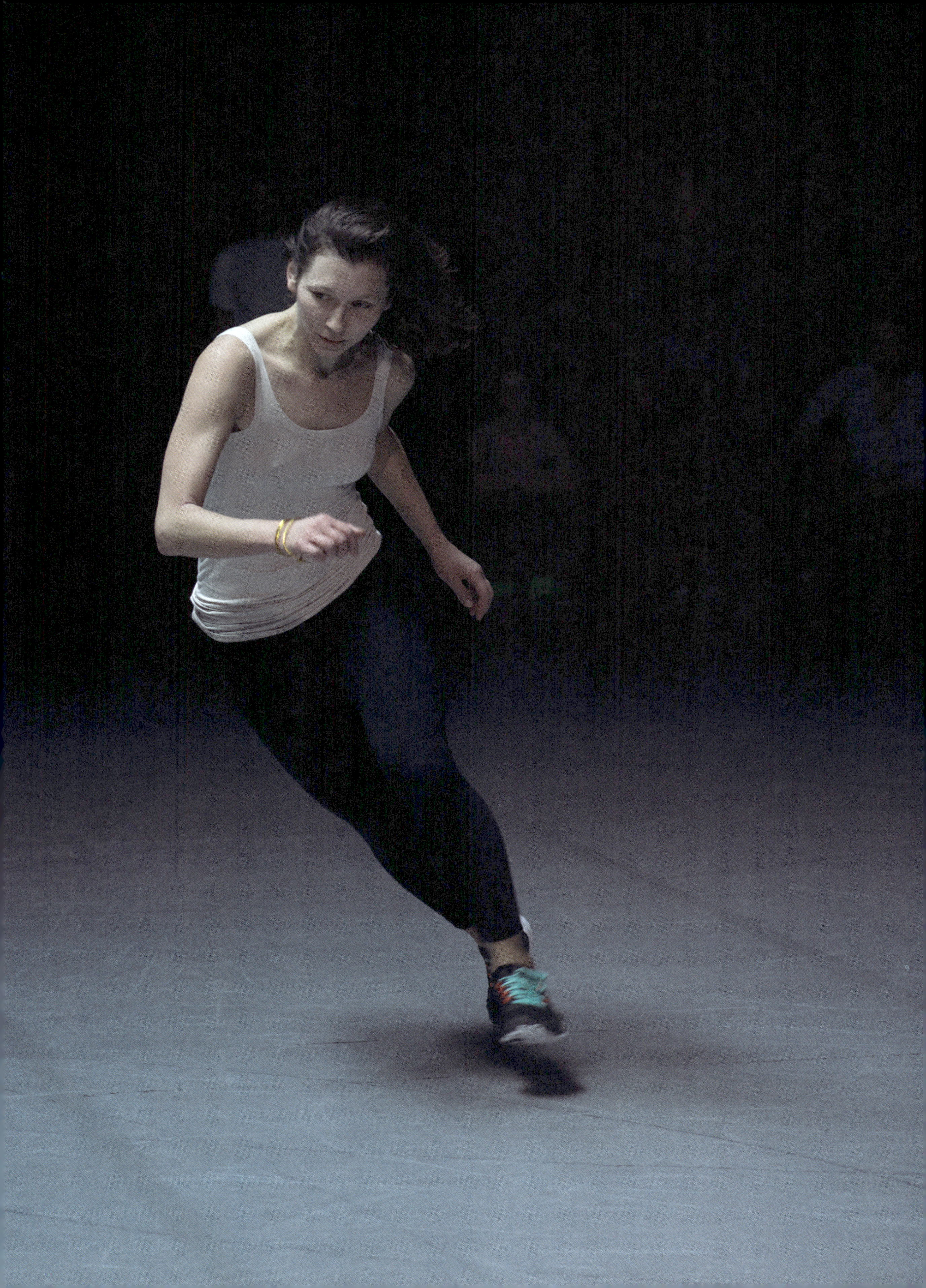

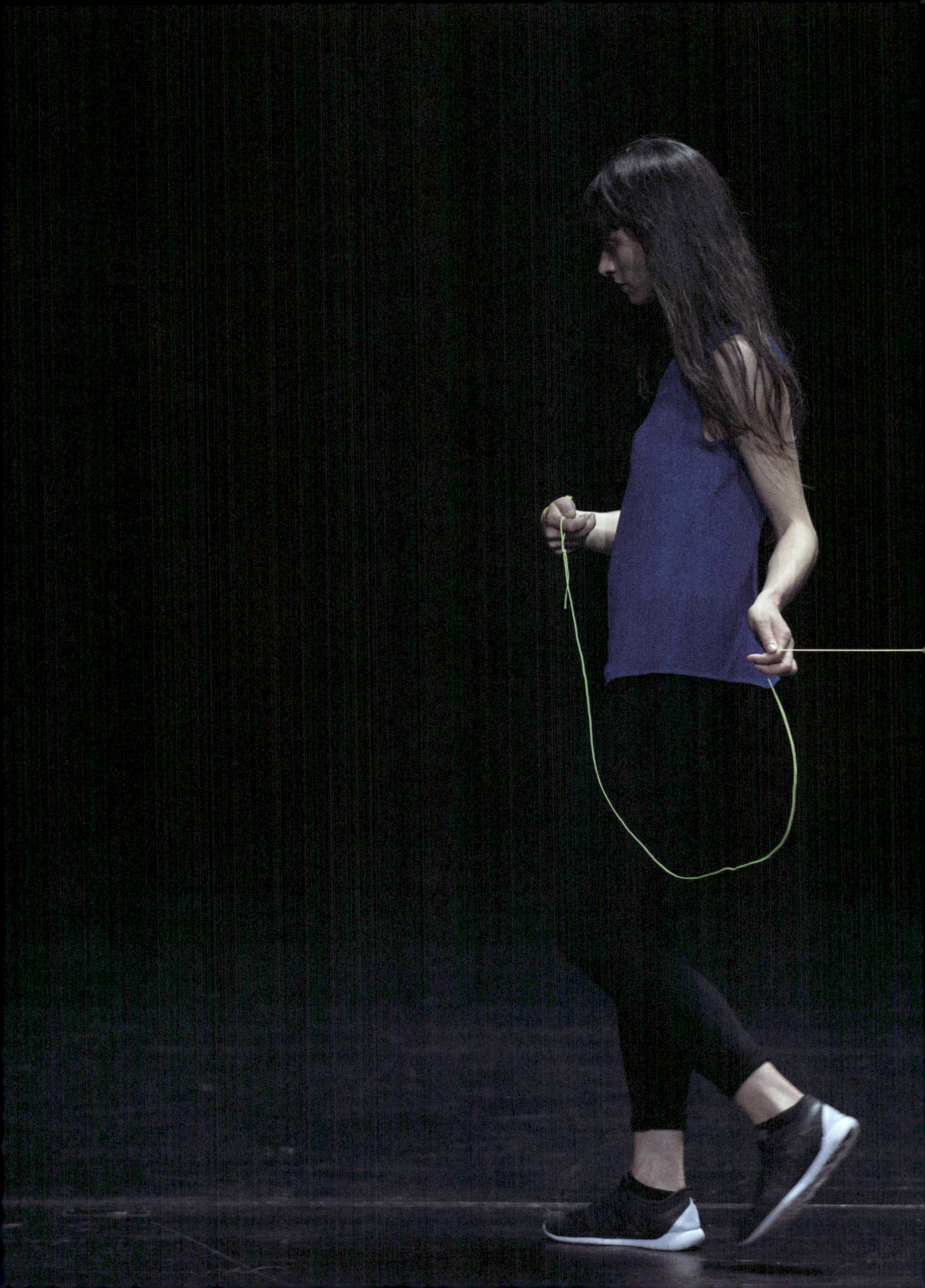

O woman

to like as n

or the love you bear to men,
ch of this play as please you.

Work/Travail/Arbeid 2015

Concept and choreography
Anne Teresa De Keersmaeker
Initiated by WIELS
Curator
Elena Filipovic
Artistic advice
Ann Veronica Janssens
Dramaturgy
Bojana Cvejić
Artistic assistant
Femke Gyselinck
Danced by
Polina Akhmetzyanova, Boštjan Antončič, Balázs Busa, Lav Crnčević, José Paulo dos Santos, Bryana Fritz, Carlos Garbin, Frank Gizycki, Marie Goudot, Robin Haghi, Cynthia Loemij, Sarah Ludi, Julien Monty, Michaël Pomero, Camille Prieux, Gabriel Schenker, Igor Shyshko, Denis Terrasse, Thomas Vantuycom, Samantha van Wissen
Music
Vortex temporum, Gérard Grisey (1996)
Musical direction
Georges-Elie Octors / Diego Borrello
Musicians
Ictus
Piano Jean-Luc Plouvier
Flute Chryssi Dimitriou
Clarinet Dirk Descheemaeker
Violin Igor Semenoff
Viola Jeroen Robbrecht
Cello Geert De Bièvre
Costumes
Anne-Catherine Kunz
Production
WIELS & Rosas

Work/Travail/Arbeid has been made possible with the support of La Monnaie / De Munt, Bozar Centre for Fine Arts, Kaaitheater, Kunstenfestivaldesarts, Ictus, BNP Paribas Fortis, BNP Paribas Foundation, WIELS Patrons, and Rolex Institute.

The *Work/Travail/Arbeid* tour was realized with the support of Centre Pompidou (Paris), the Paris National Opera, Tate Modern (London), the Museum of Modern Art (New York), and the BNP Paribas Foundation.

20.03—17.05.2015
WIELS Contemporary Art Centre—Brussels
26.02—06.03.2016
Centre Pompidou—Paris
08.07—10.07.2016
Tate Modern—London
29.03—02.04.2017
Museum of Modern Art—New York
14.04—15.04.2018
MUDAM—Luxembourg
26.04—29.04.2018
Volksbühne—Berlin

Pictures
Anne Van Aerschot

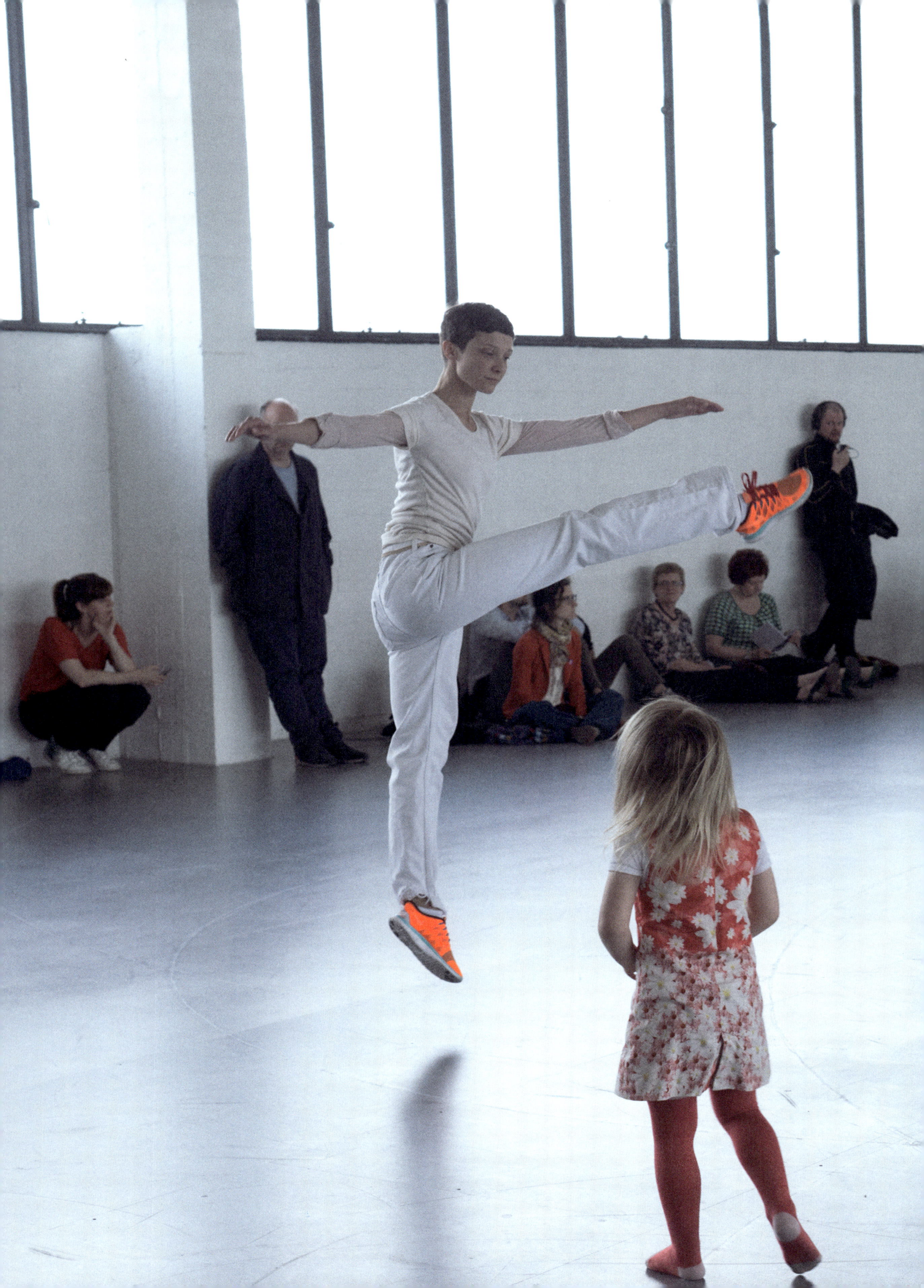

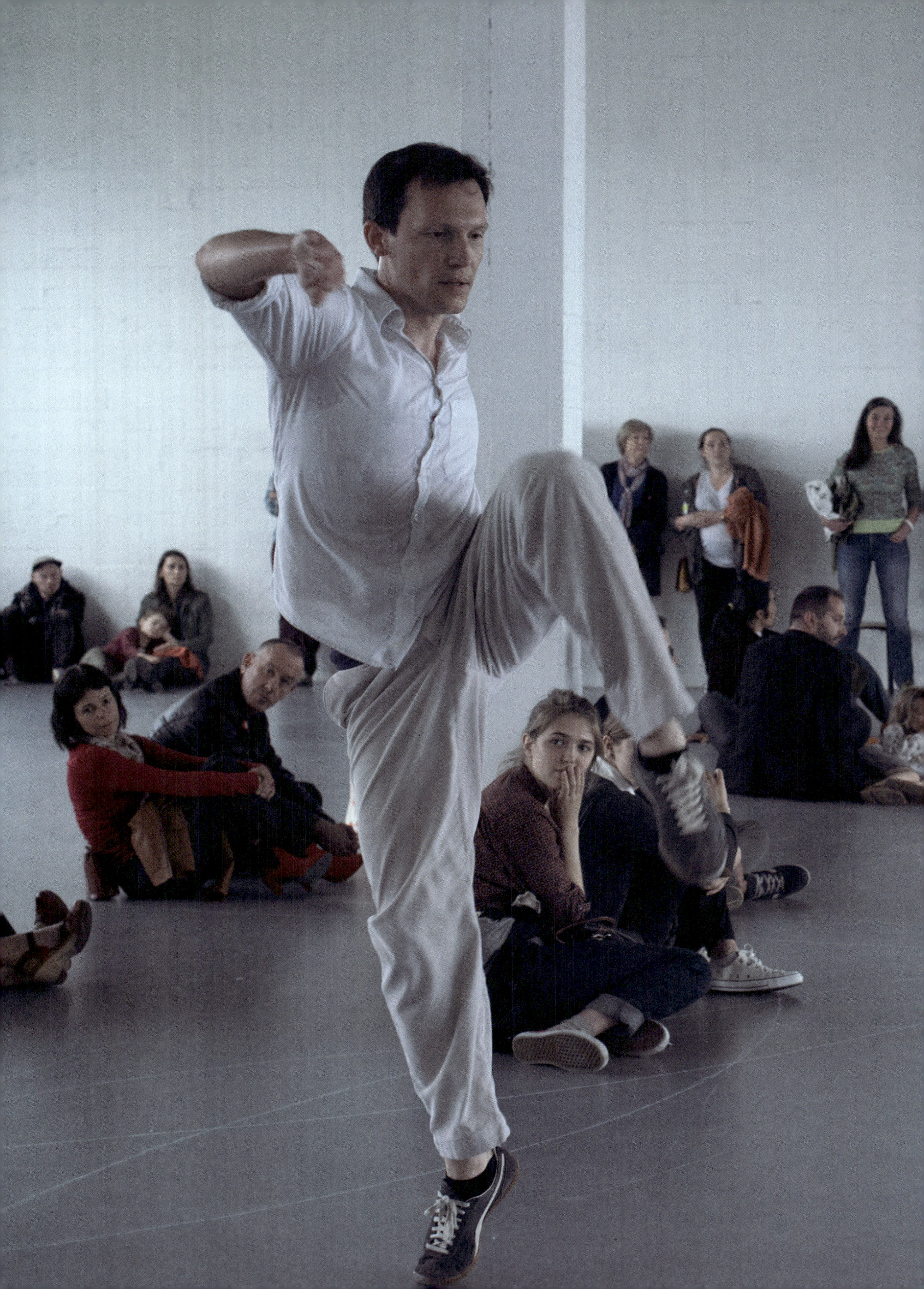

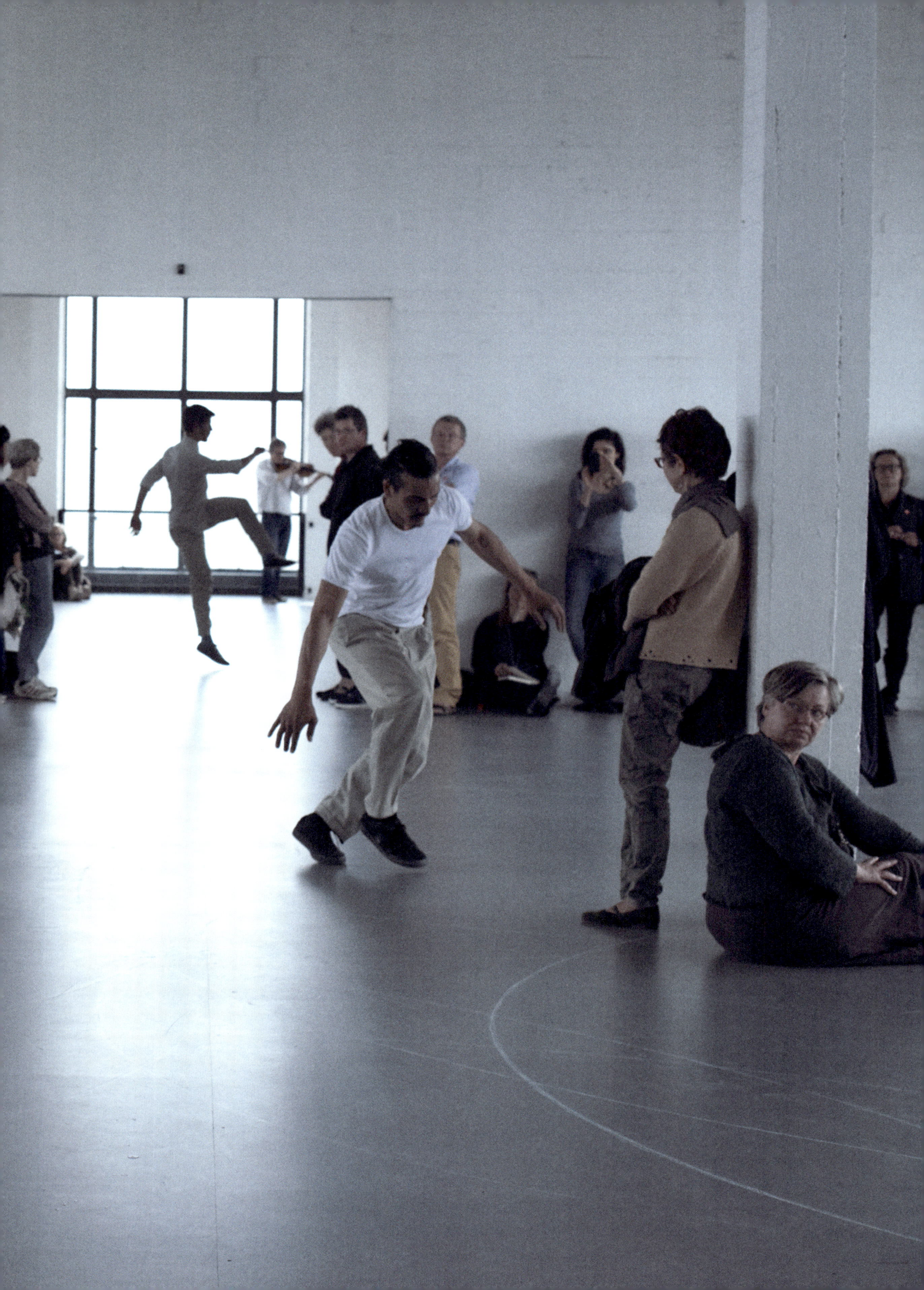

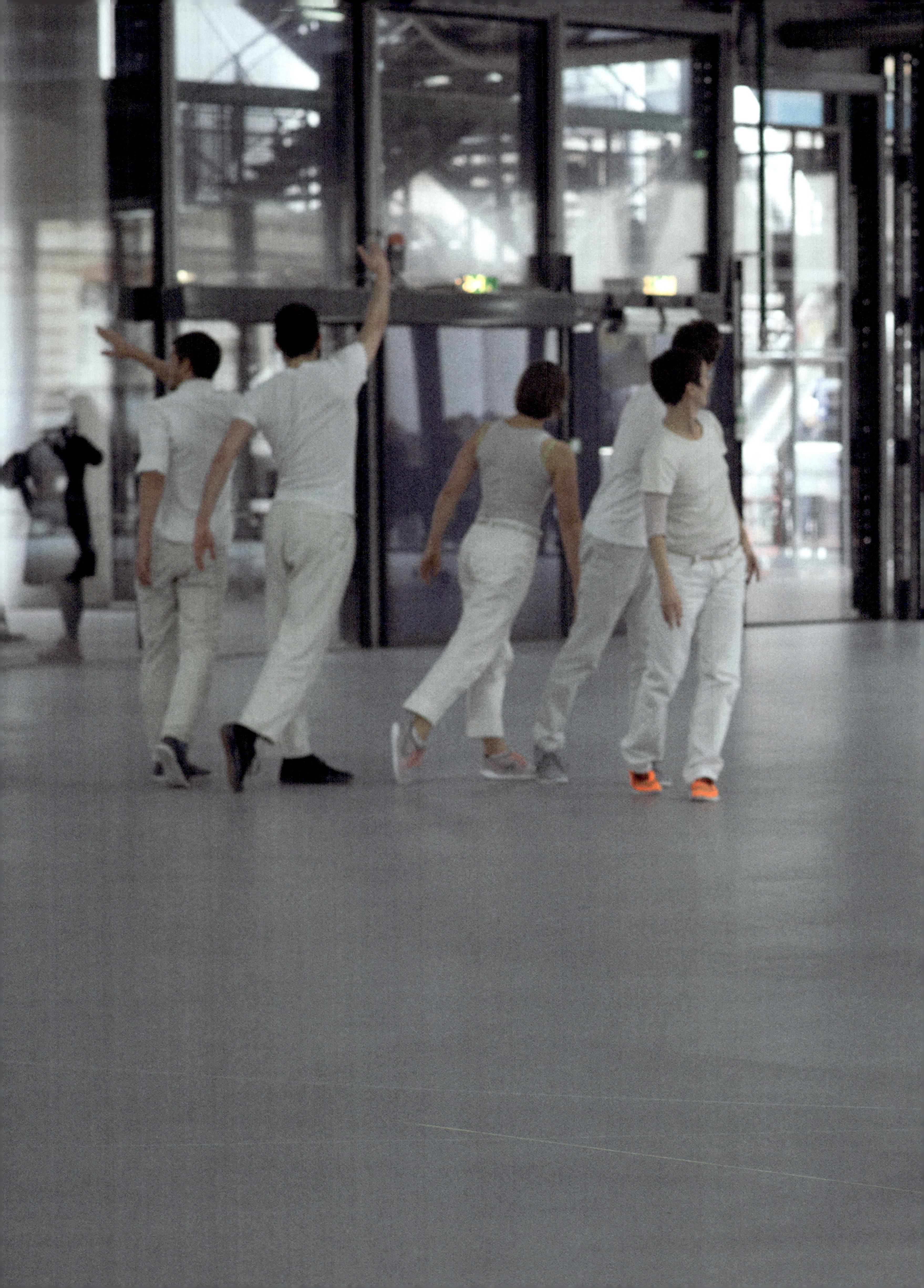

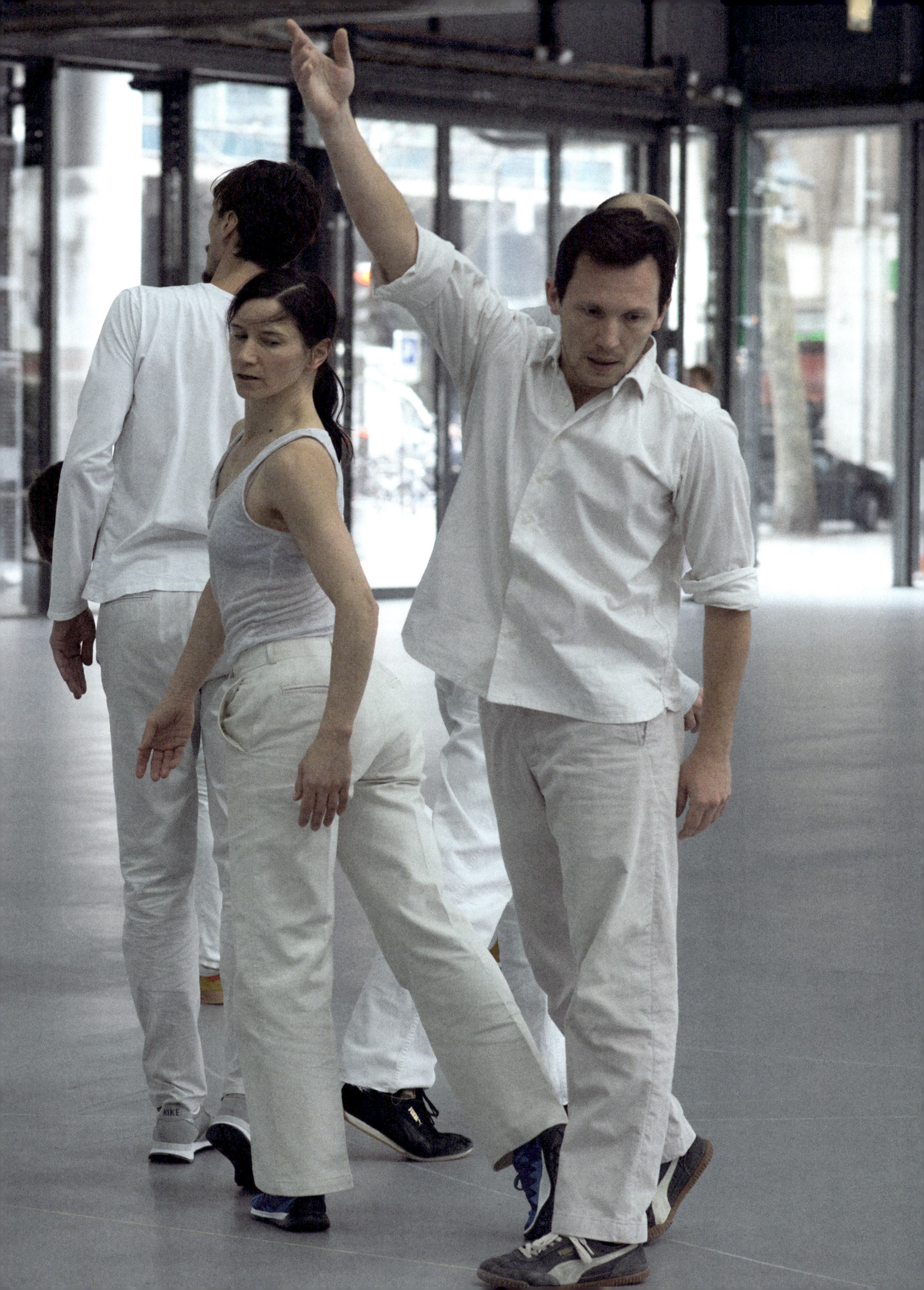
NIKE

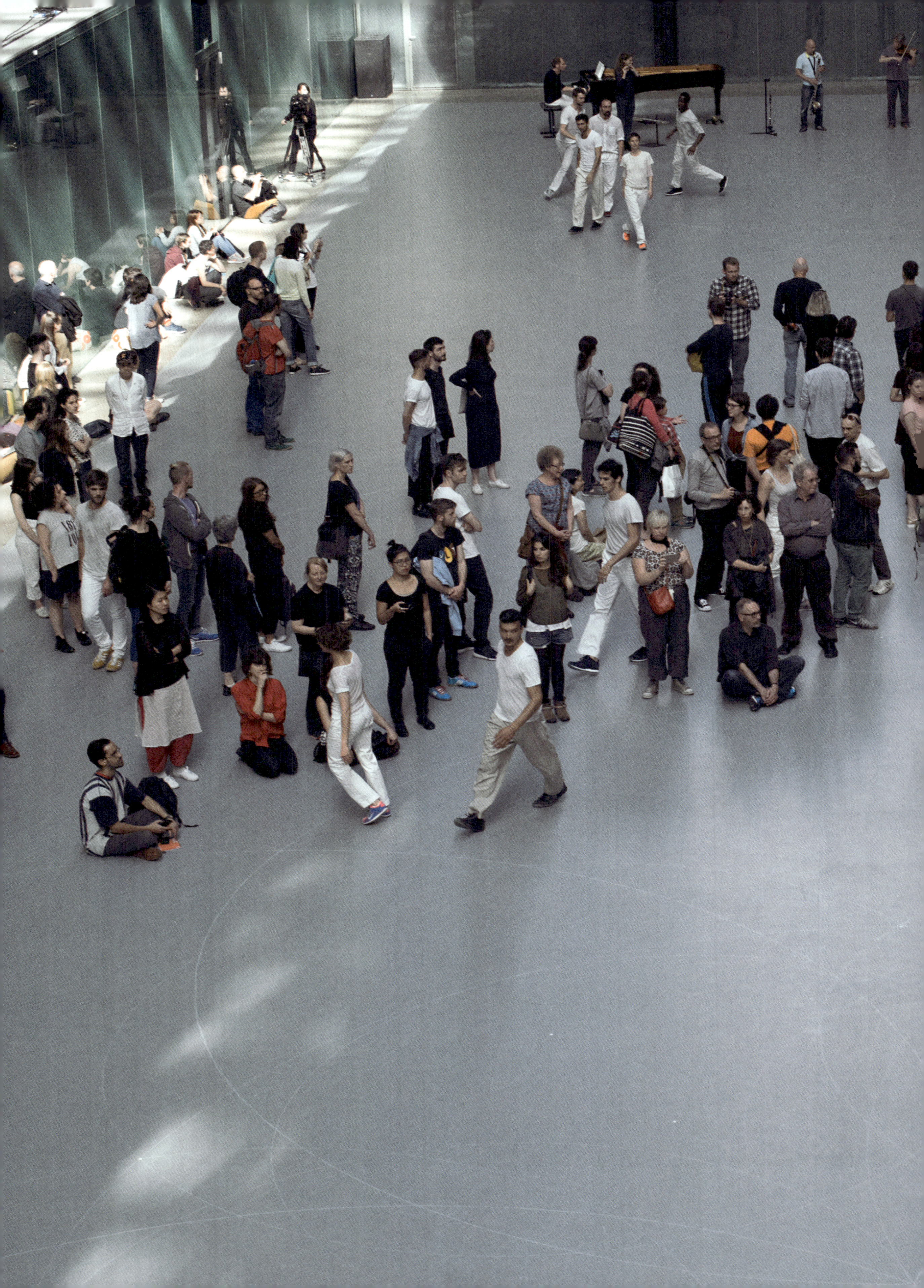

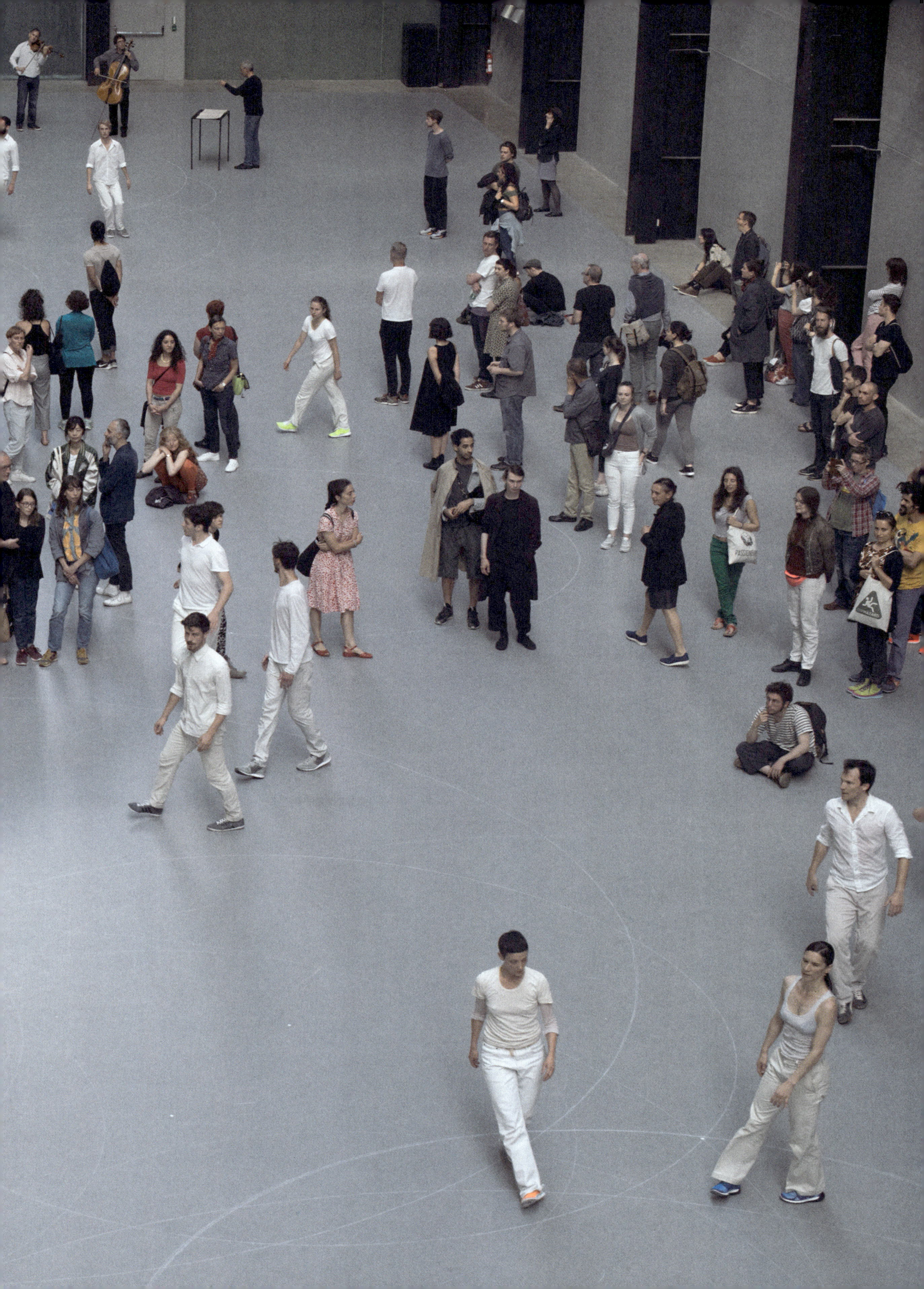

DE KEERSMAEKER
/ARBEID

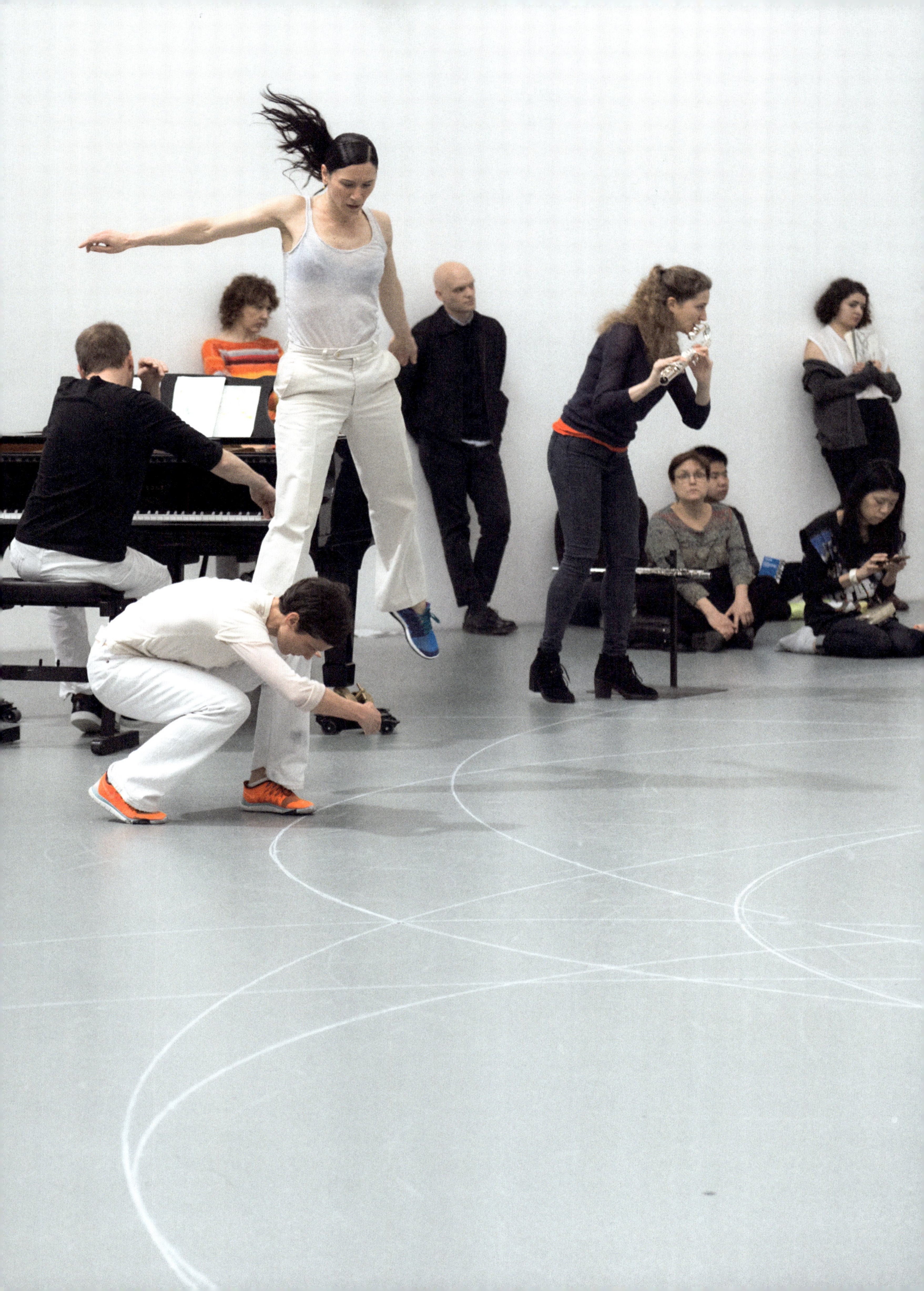

Die Weise von Liebe und Tod des Cornets Christoph Rilke 2015

Concept and choreography
Anne Teresa De Keersmaeker
Created with and danced by
Anne Teresa De Keersmaeker, Michaël Pomero
Text
Die Weise von Liebe und Tod des Cornets Christoph Rilke, Rainer Maria Rilke
Music
Opera per flauto, Salvatore Sciarrino: *Immagine fenicia*; *All'aure in una lontananza*
Flute
Chryssi Dimitriou
Lighting
Luc Schaltin
Artistic advisor—scenography
Michel François
Costumes
Anne-Catherine Kunz
Typography
Casier/Fieuws
Dramaturgy
Vasco Boenisch
German language coach
Roswitha Dierck
Sound
Alban Moraud
Production
Rosas
Coproduction
La Monnaie / De Munt (Brussels), Ruhrtriennale, Concertgebouw Bruges,
Le Théâtre de Gennevilliers with the Festival d'Automne à Paris,
Sadler's Wells (London), Les Théâtres de la Ville de Luxembourg
Premiere
24.09.2015, Ruhrtriennale—Duisburg

Pictures
Anne Van Aerschot

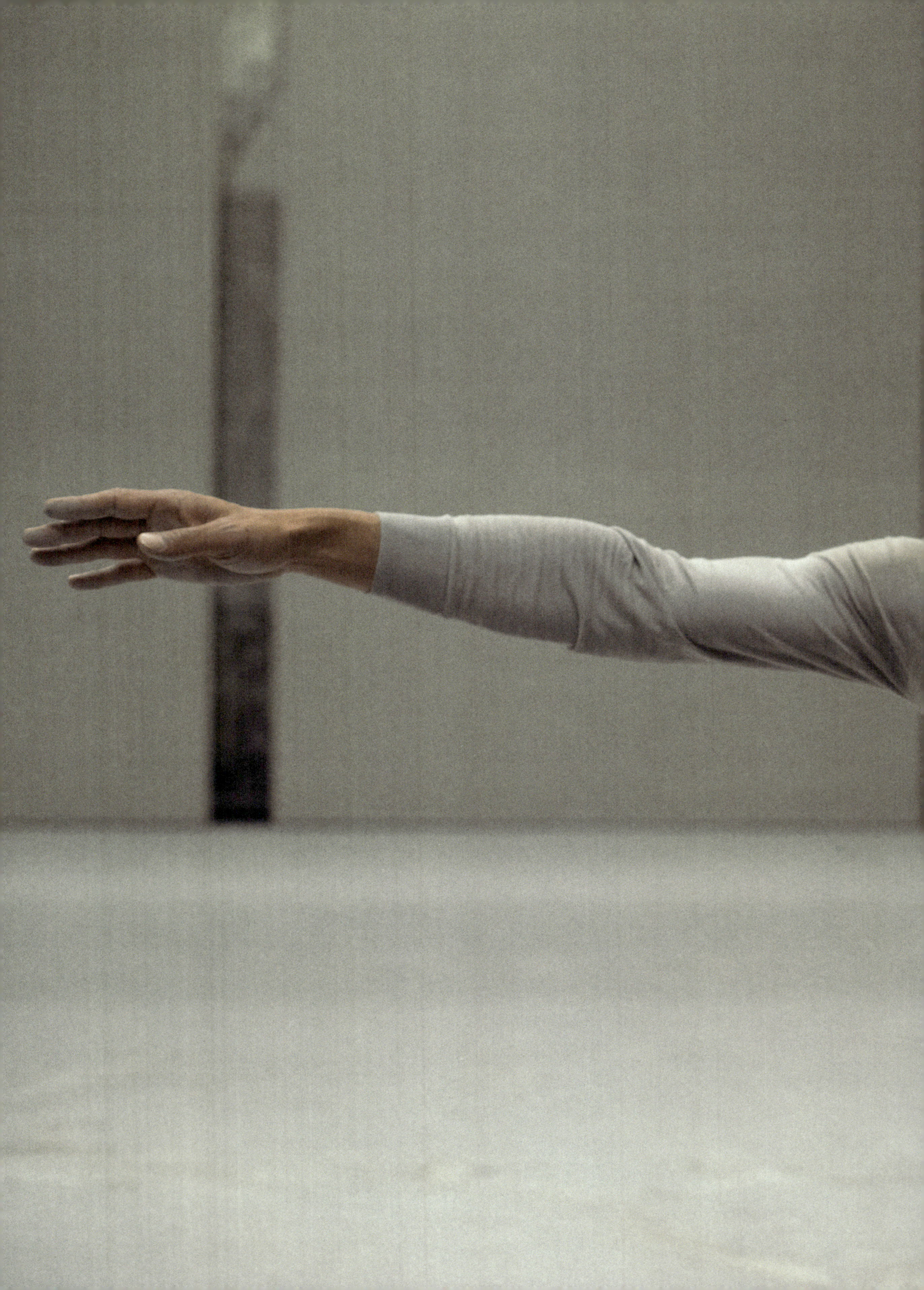

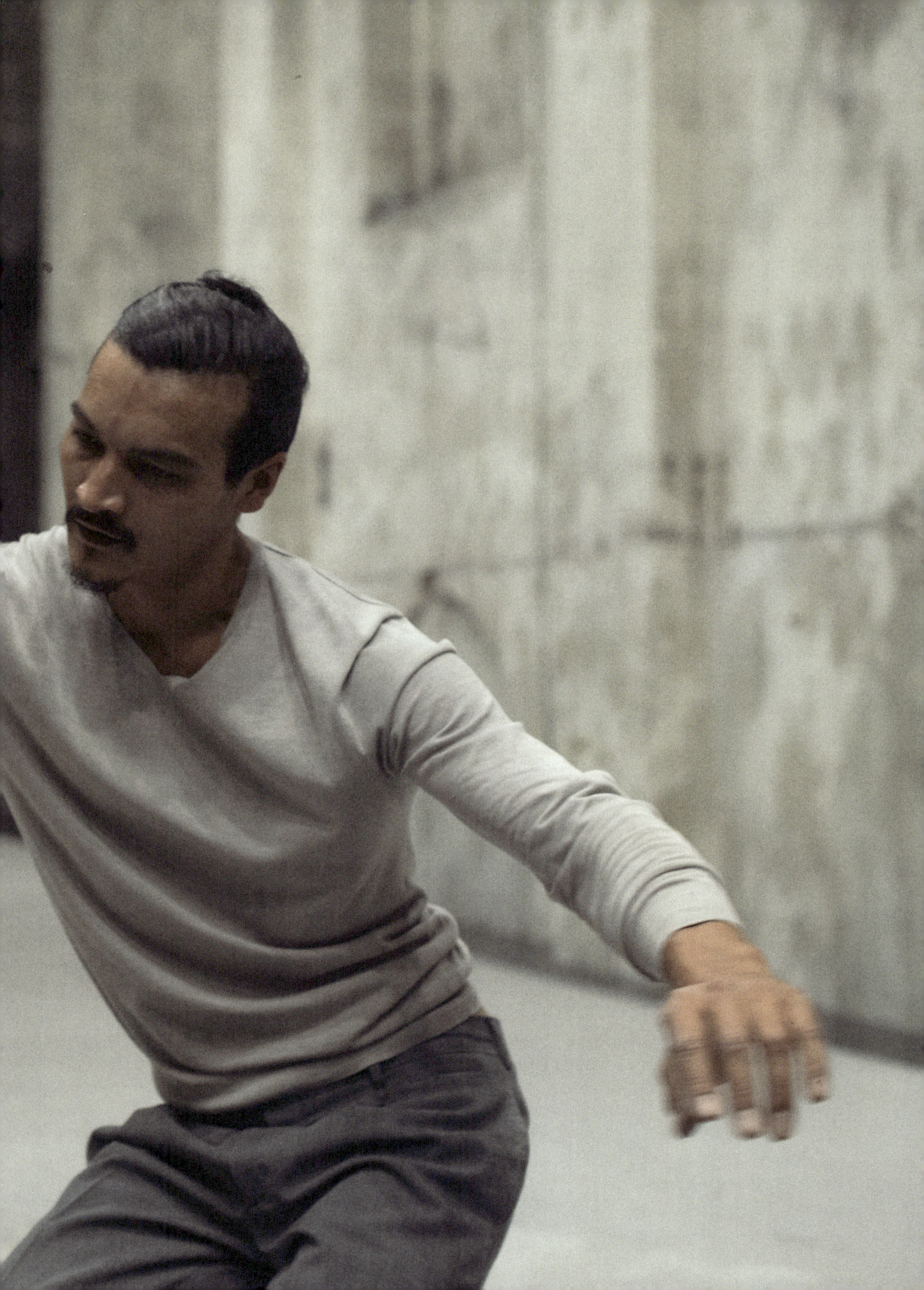

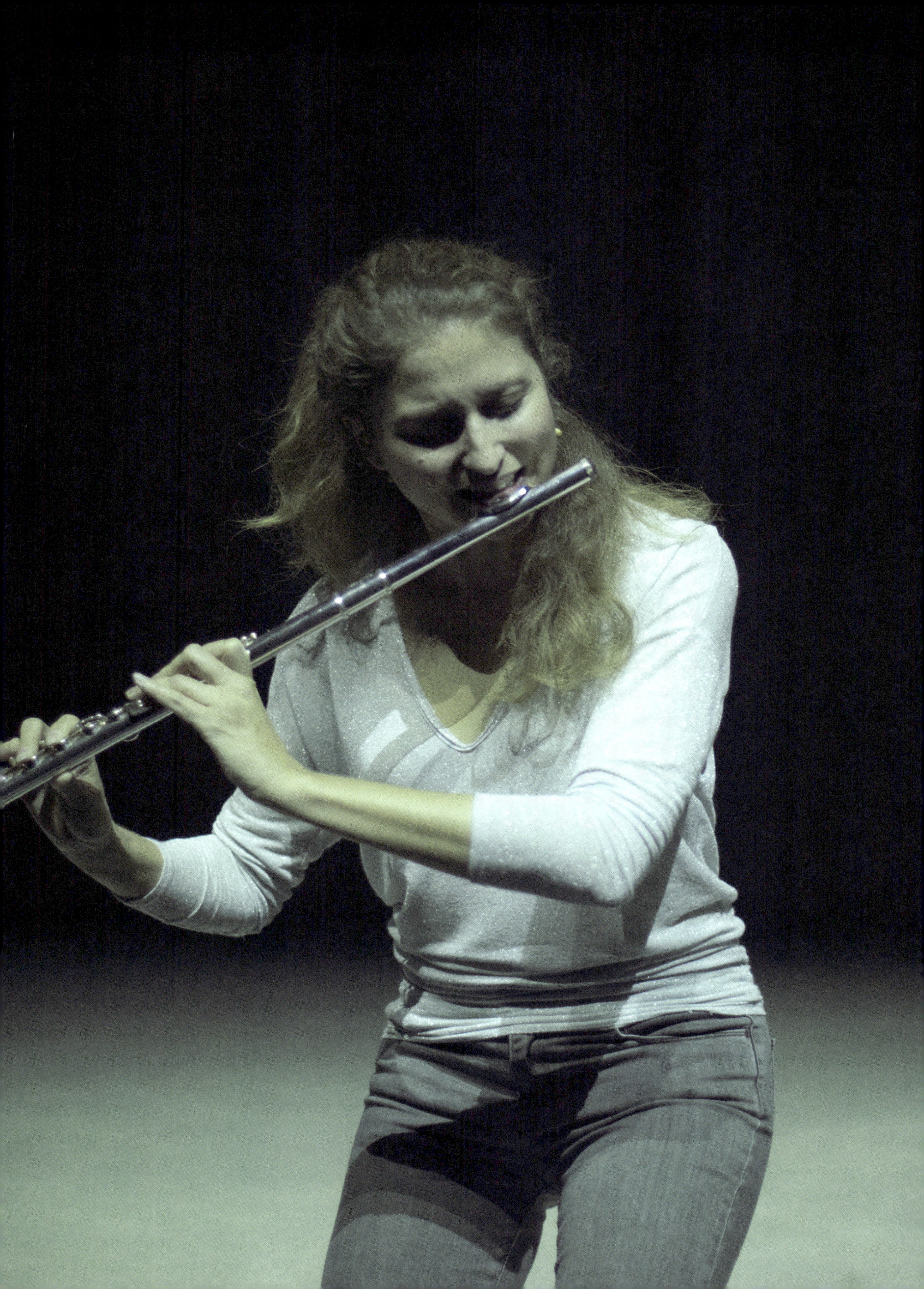

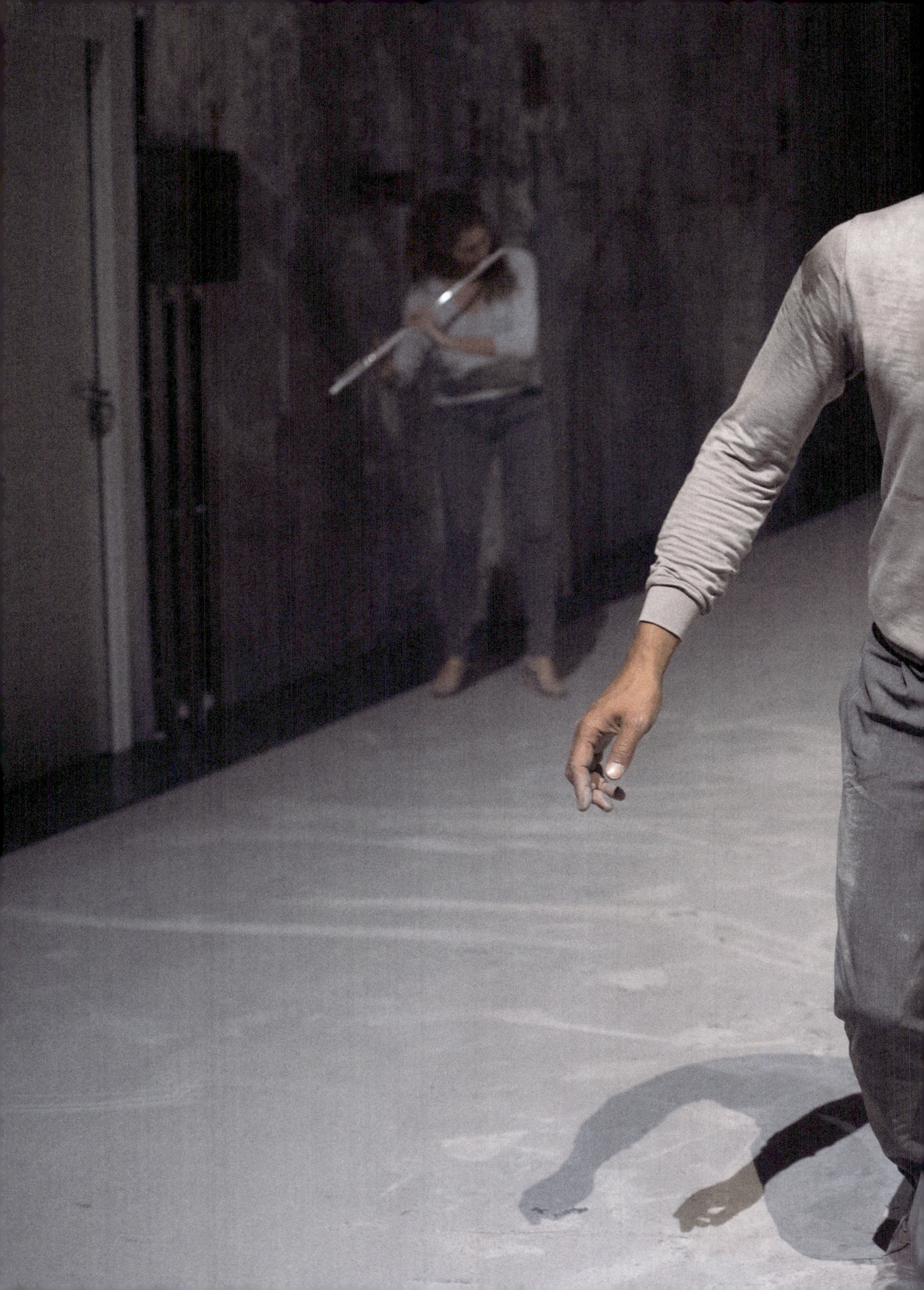

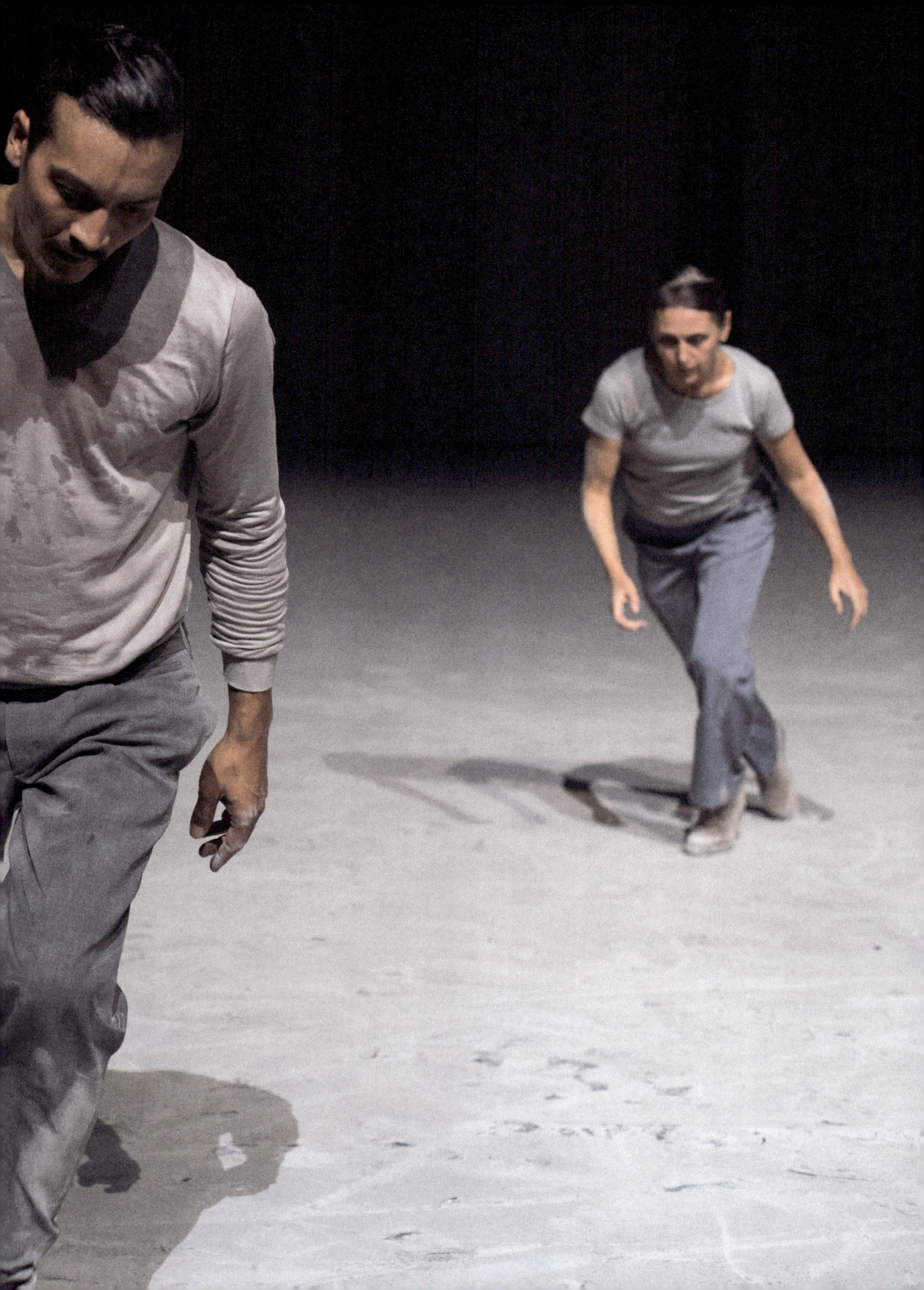

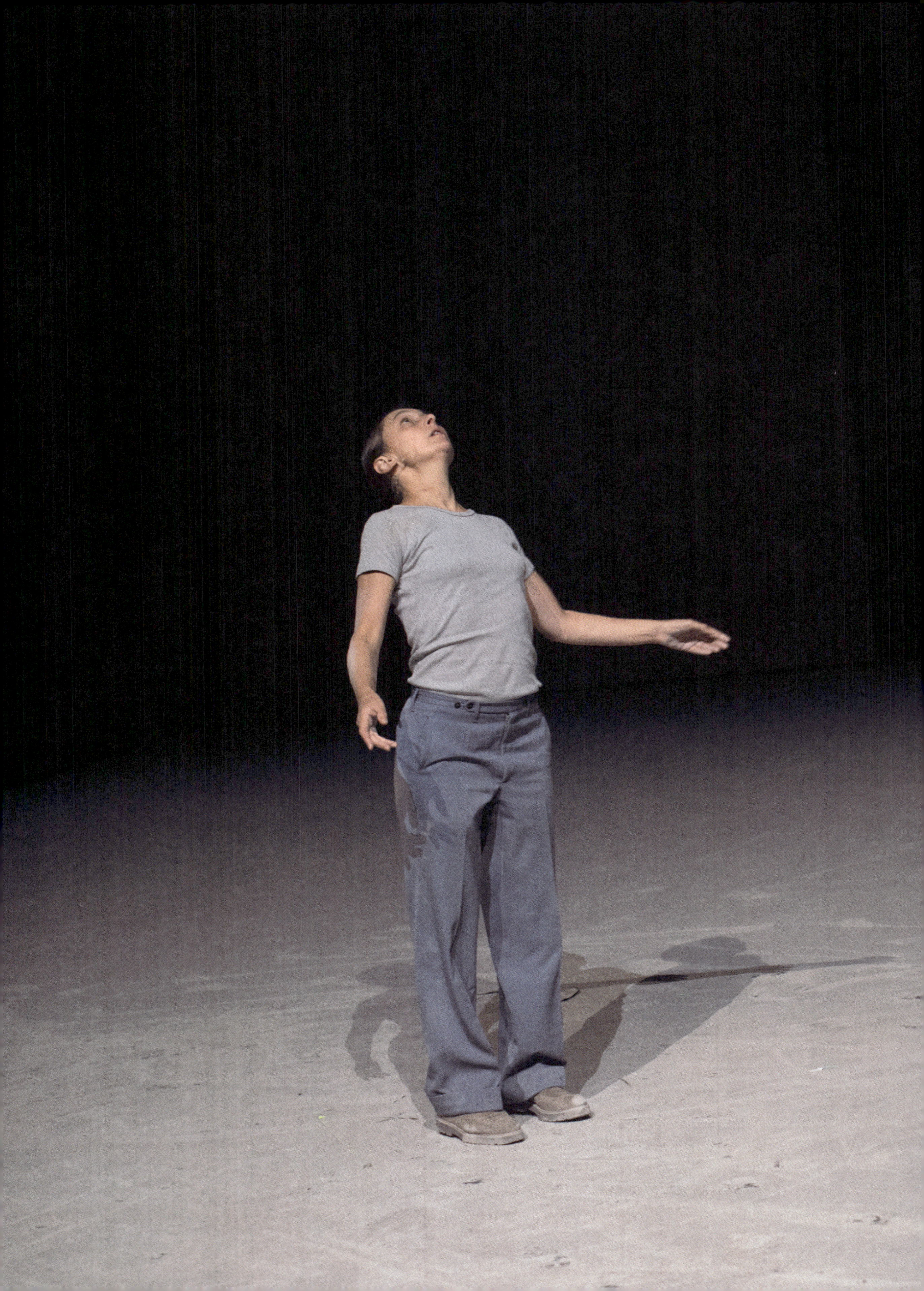

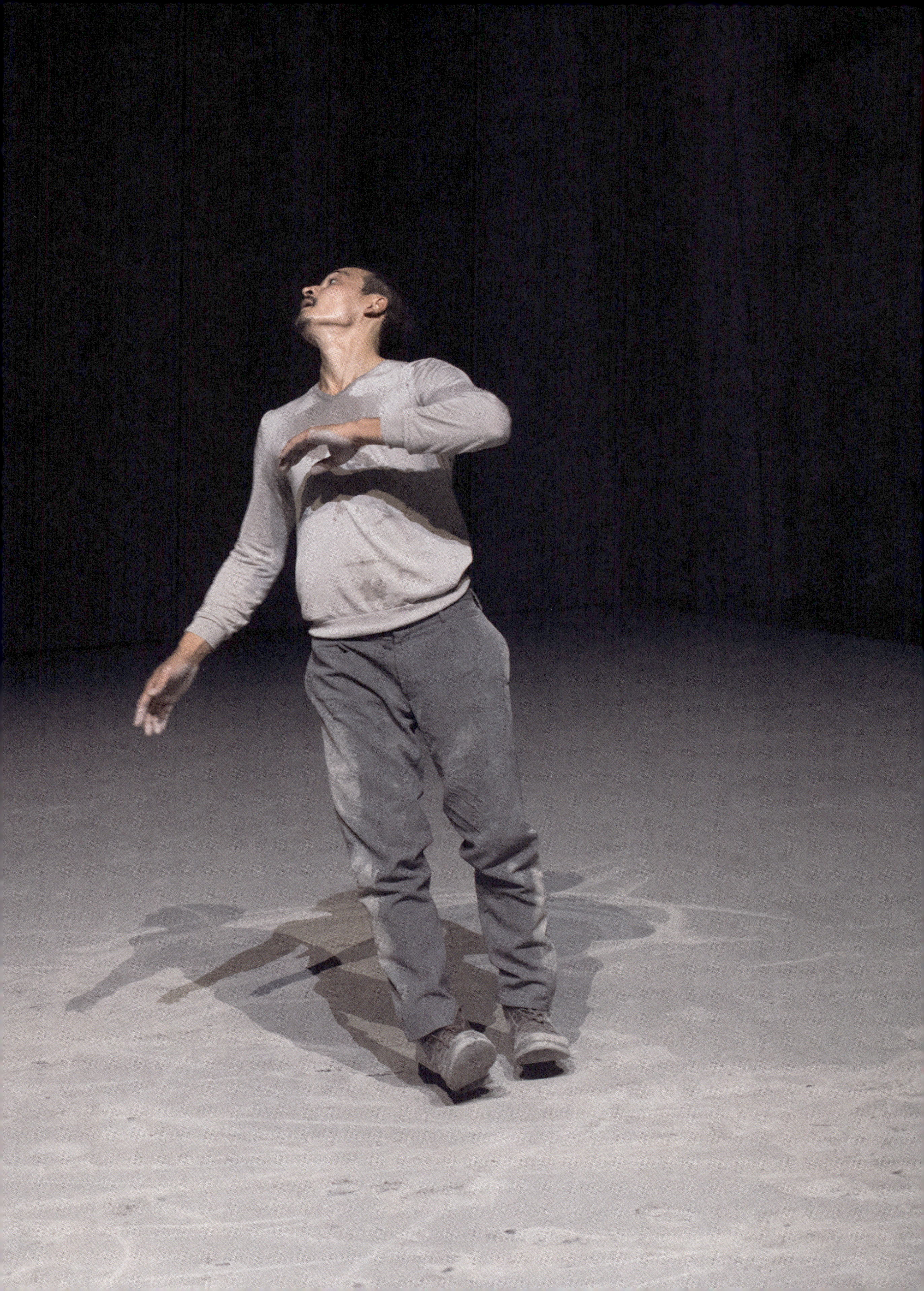

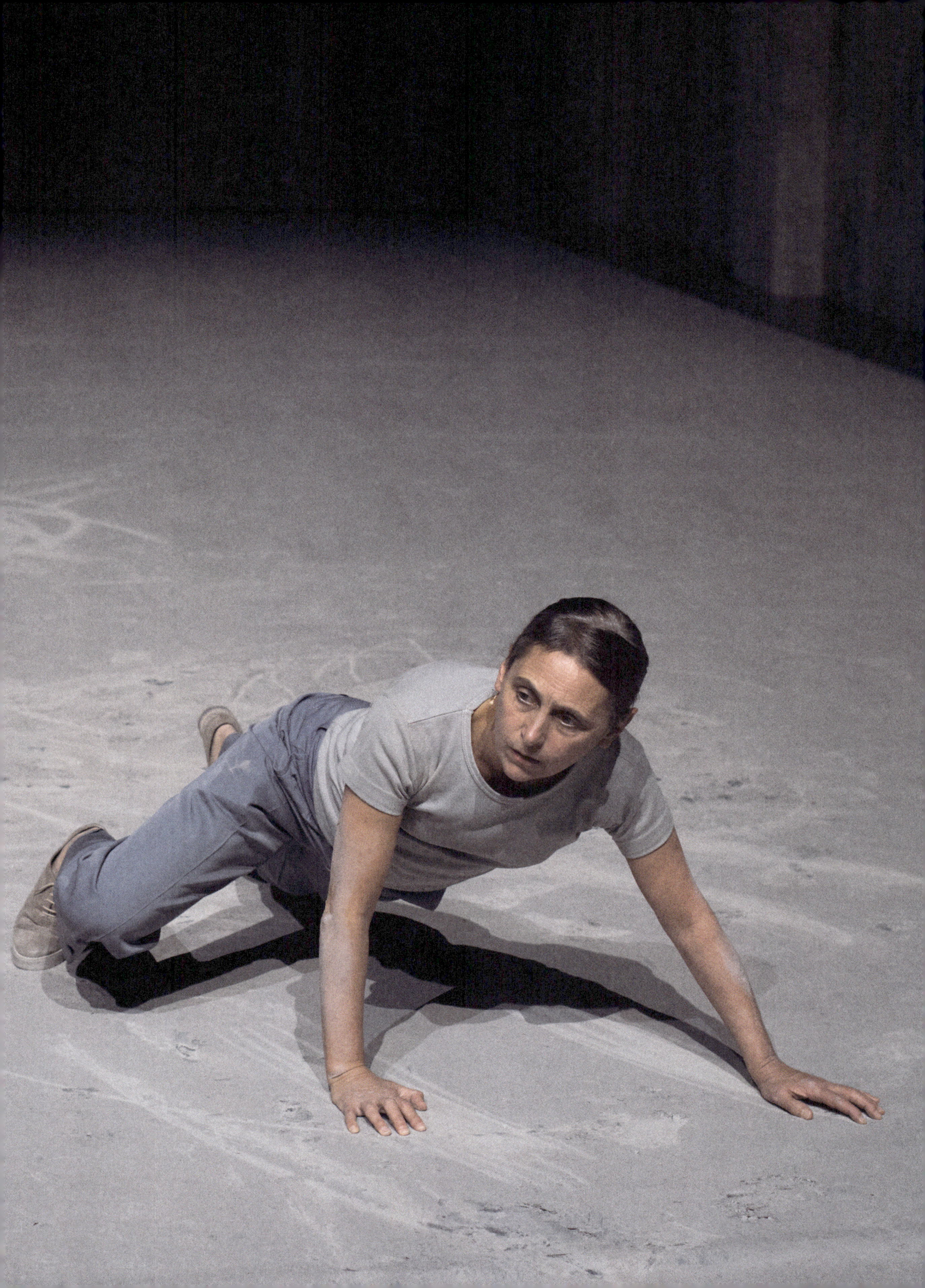

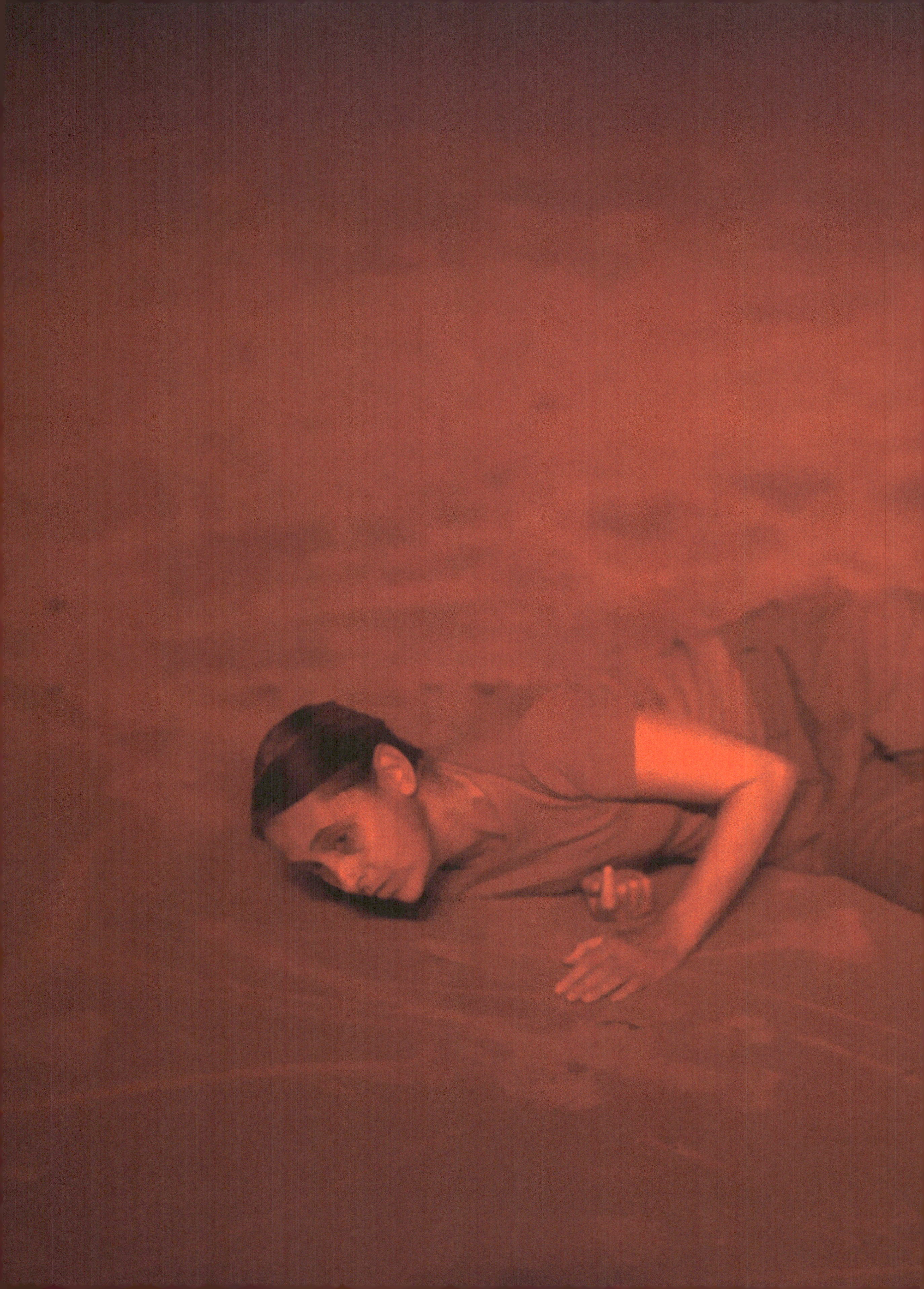

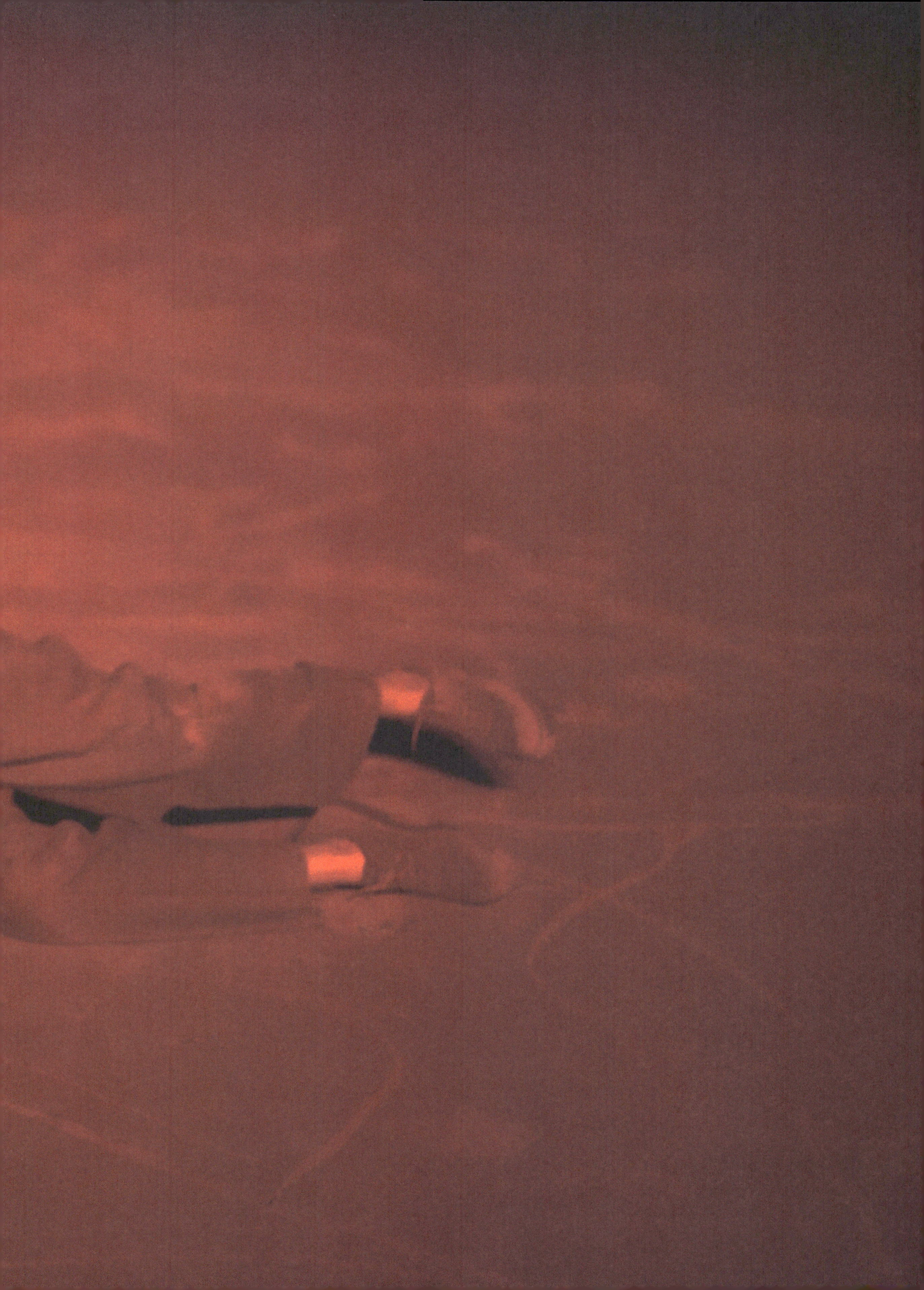

Così fan tutte 2017

Scenography and choreography
Anne Teresa De Keersmaeker
Music
Wolfgang Amadeus Mozart
Libretto
Lorenzo Da Ponte
Conductor
Philippe Jordan / Marius Stieghorst
Decor and lighting design
Jan Versweyveld
Costumes
An D'Huys
Dramaturgy
Jan Vandenhouwe
Choirmaster
Alessandro Di Stefano
Choir and orchestra
Opéra national de Paris
Voices
Fiordiligi Jacquelyn Wagner / Ida Falk-Winland
Dorabella Michèle Losier / Stephanie Lauricella
Ferrando Frédéric Antoun / Cyrille Dubois
Guglielmo Philippe Sly / Edwin Crossley-Mercer
Don Alfonso Paulo Szot / Simone Del Savio
Despina Ginger Costa-Jackson / Mária Celeng
Dance
Rosas
Fiordiligi Cynthia Loemij
Dorabella Samantha van Wissen
Ferrando Julien Monty
Guglielmo Michaël Pomero
Don Alfonso Boštjan Antončič
Despina Marie Goudot / Yuika Hashimoto
Artistic assistants
Carlos Garbin, Femke Gyselinck, Johanne Saunier
Production
Opéra national de Paris
Premiere
23.01.2017, Palais Garnier—Paris

Pictures
Anne Van Aerschot

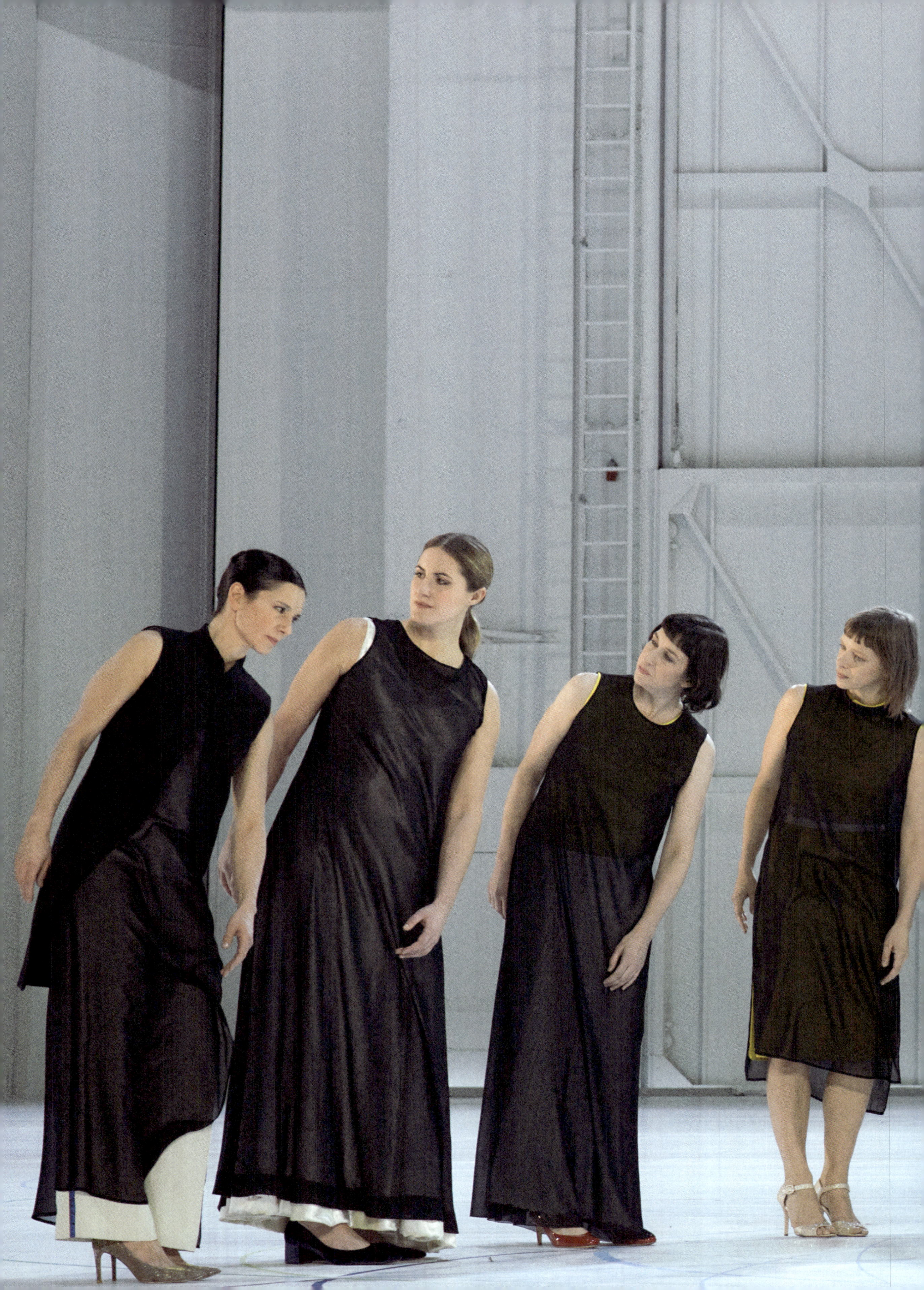

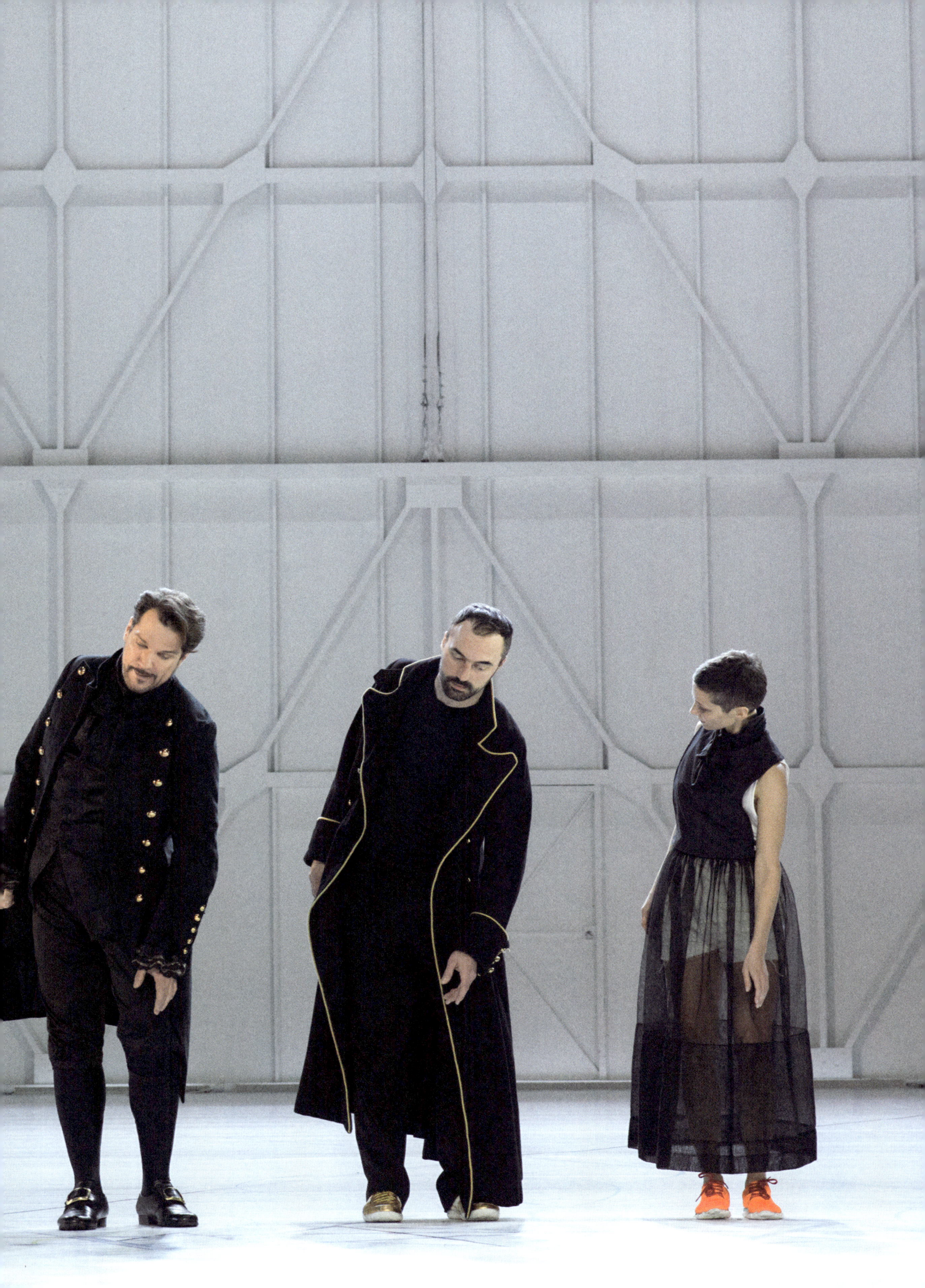

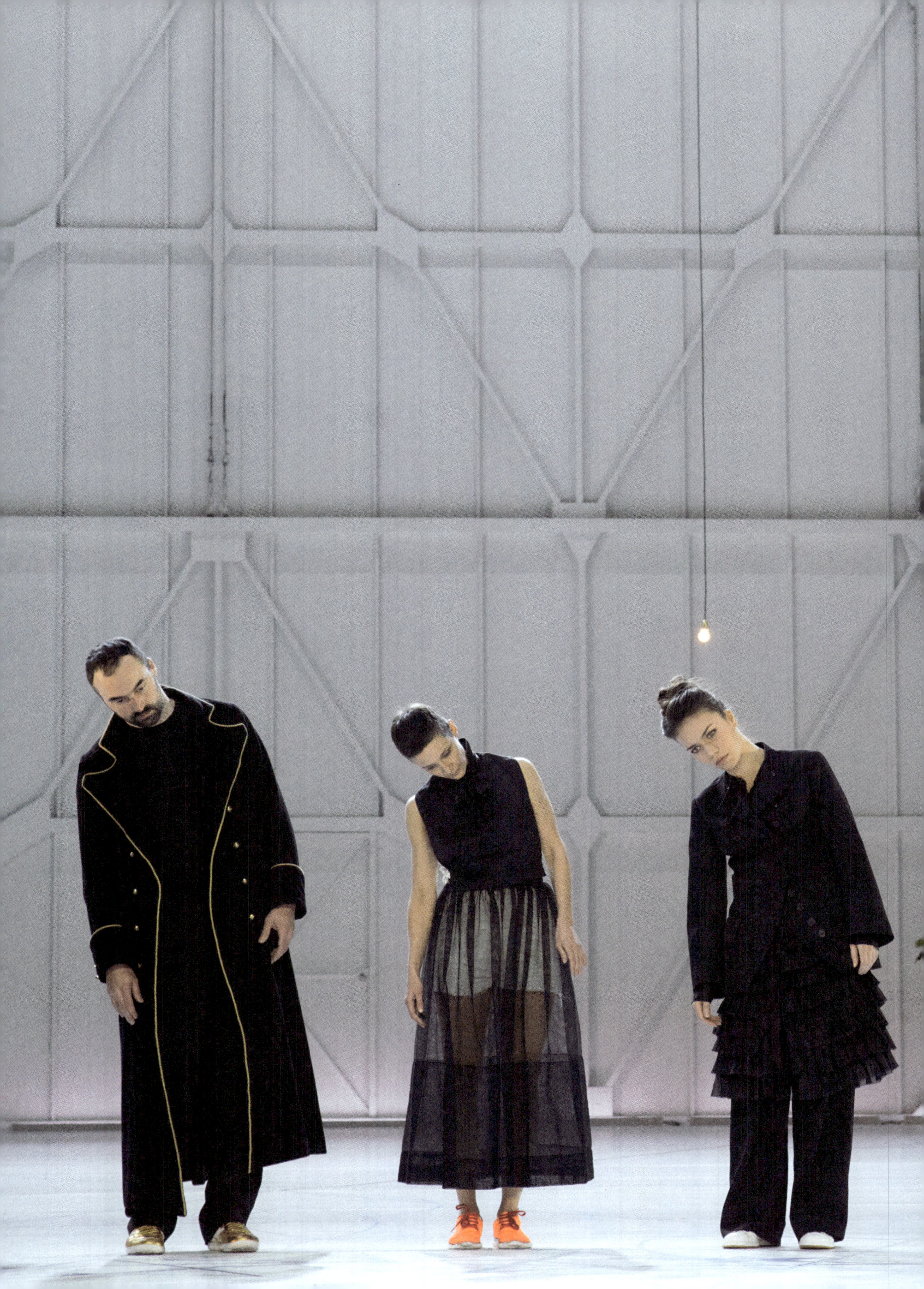

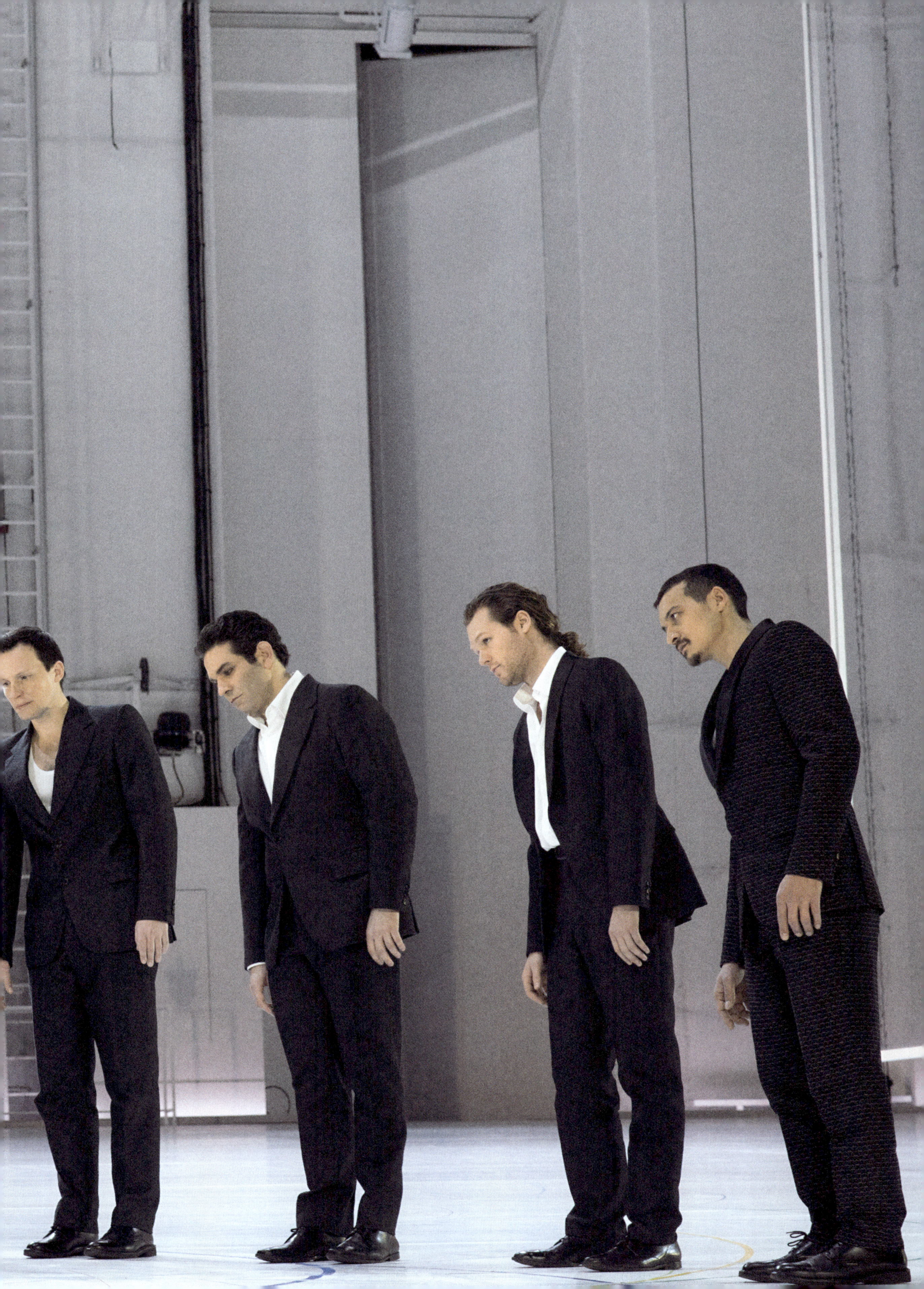

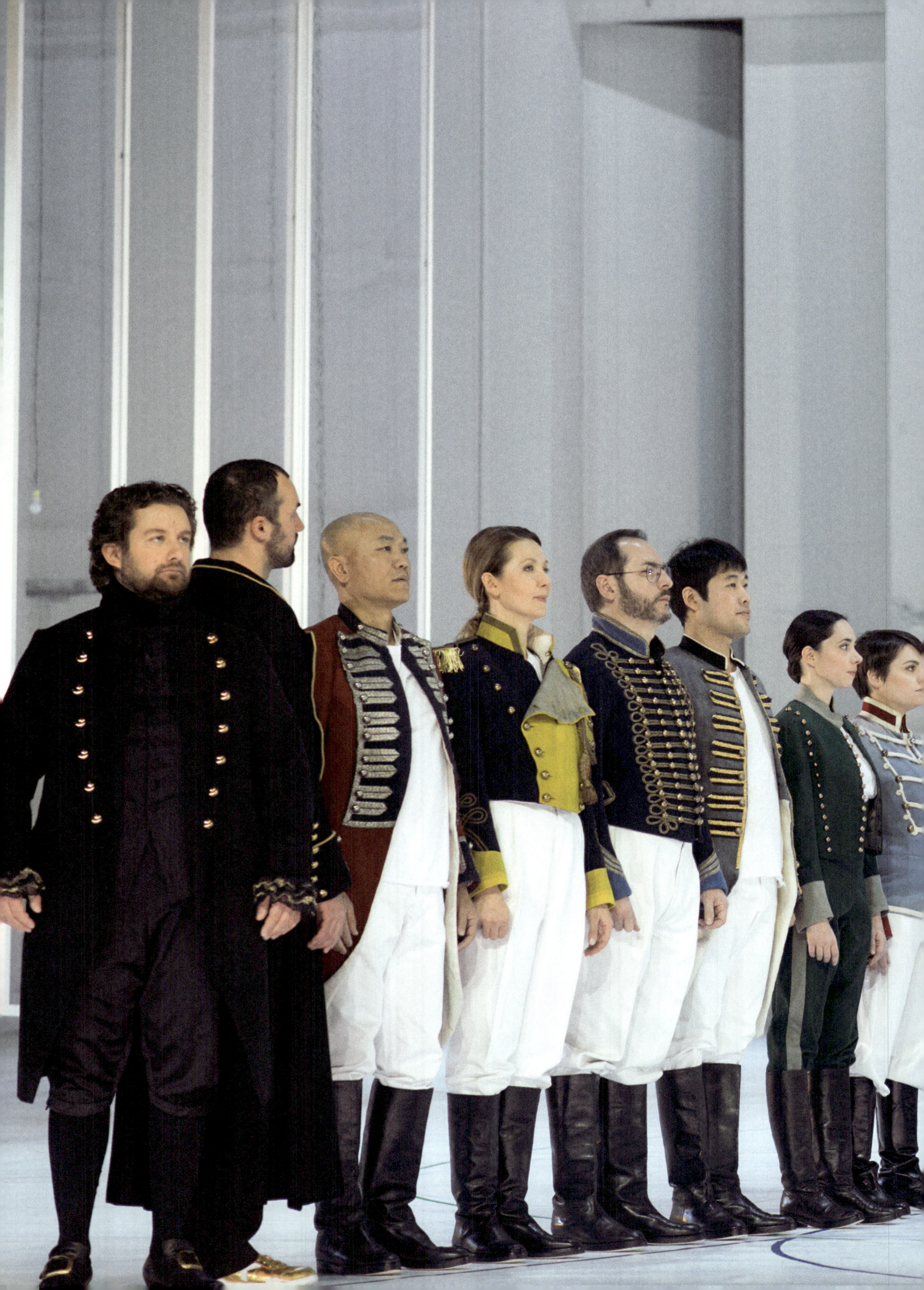

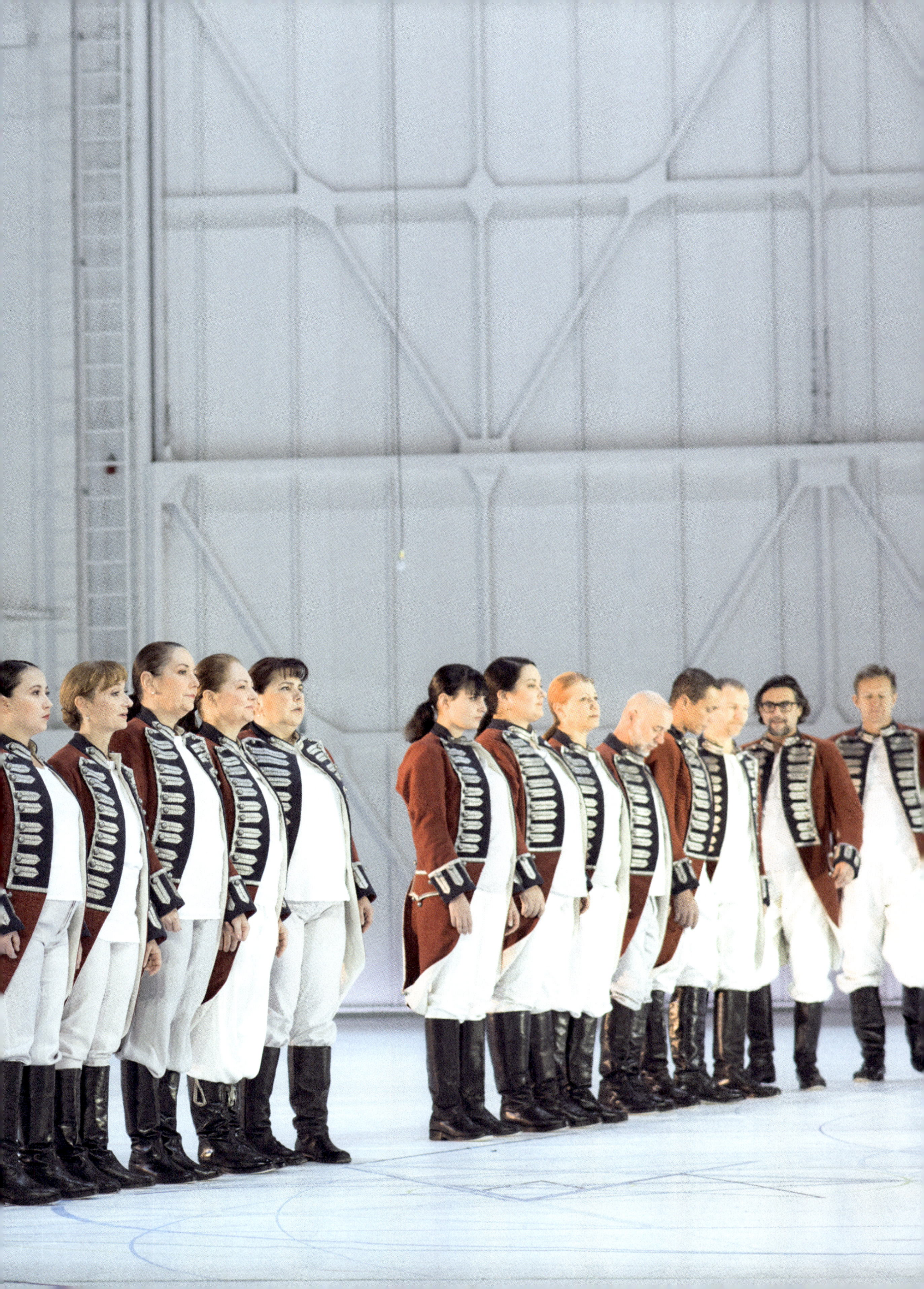

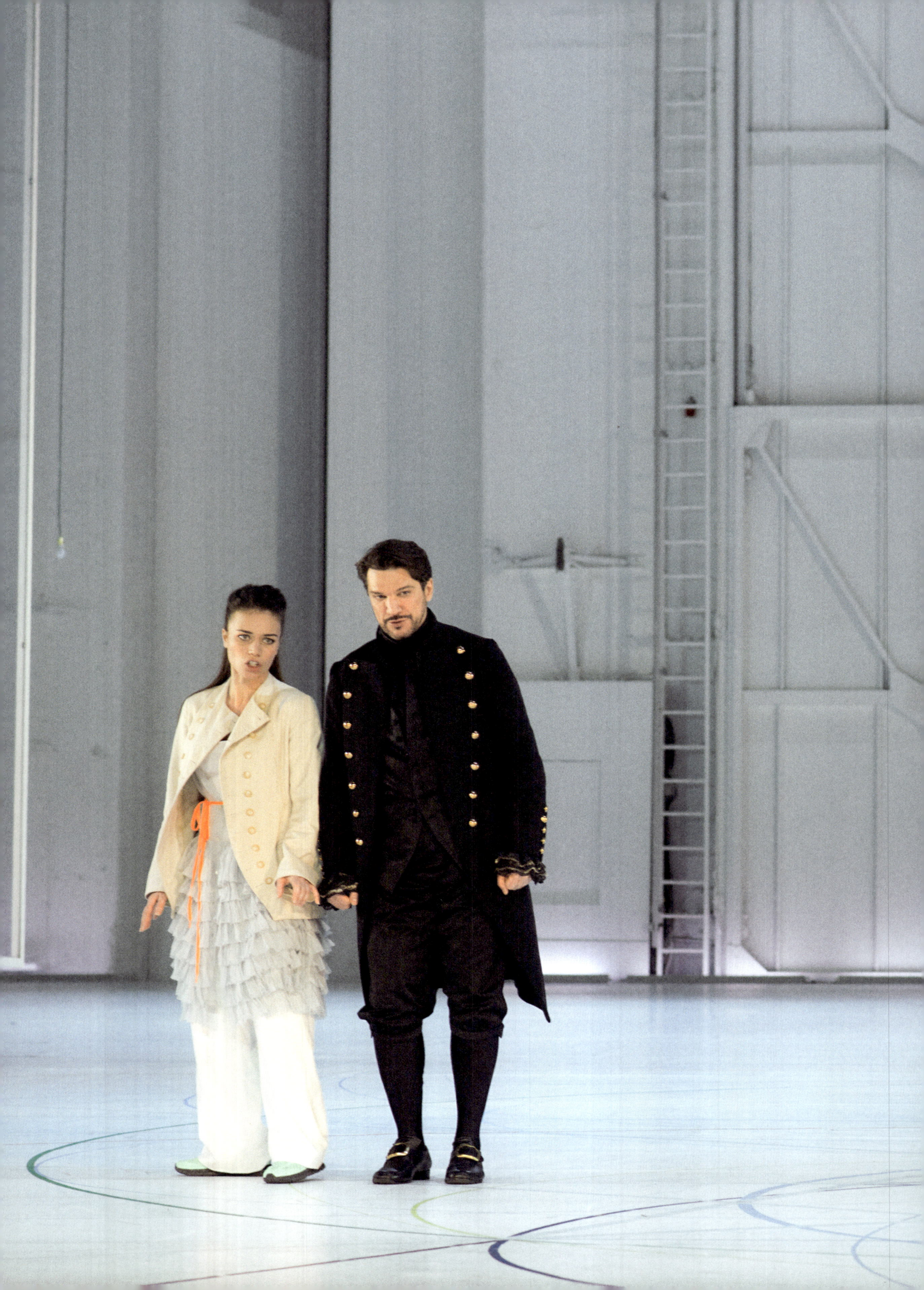

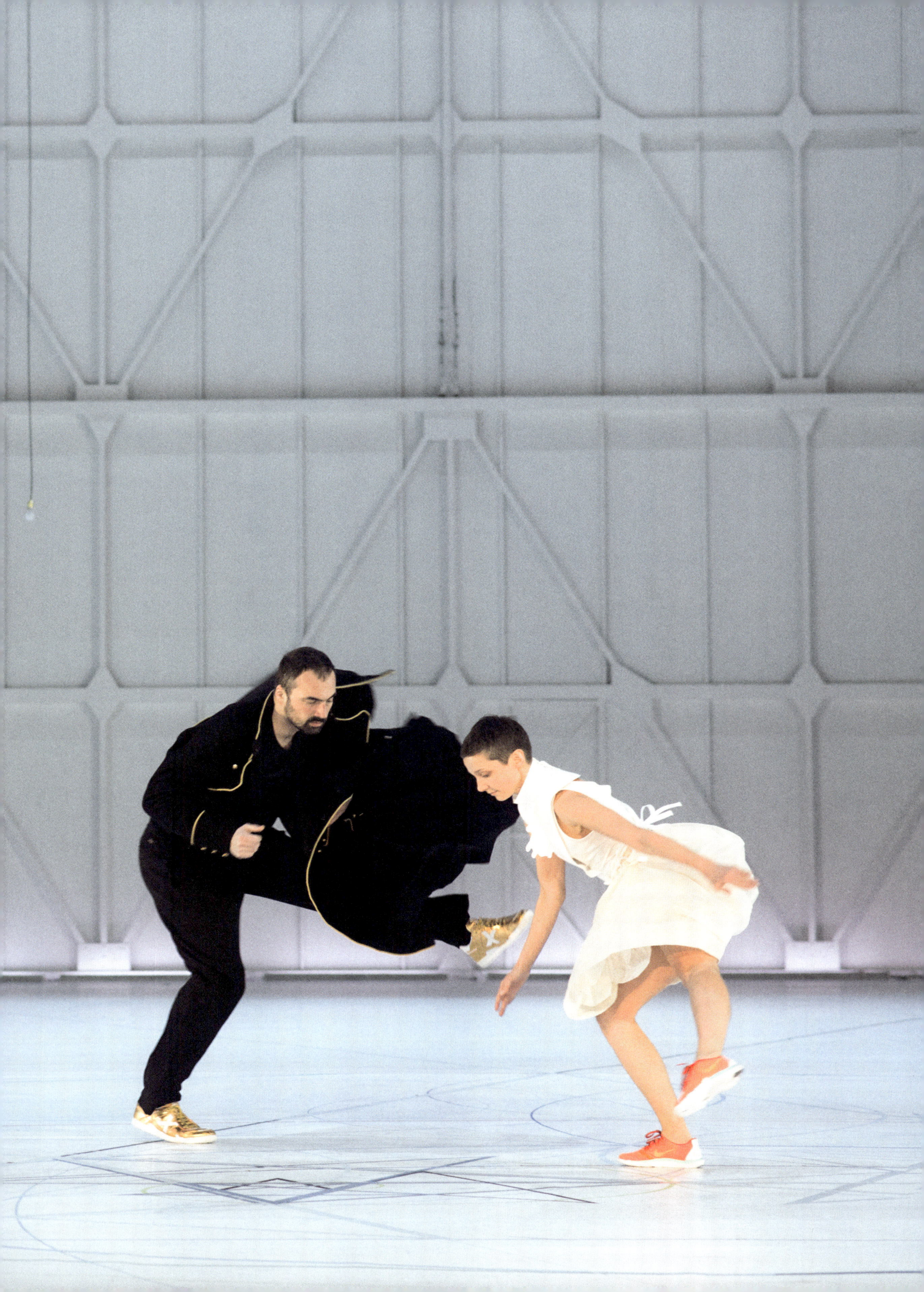

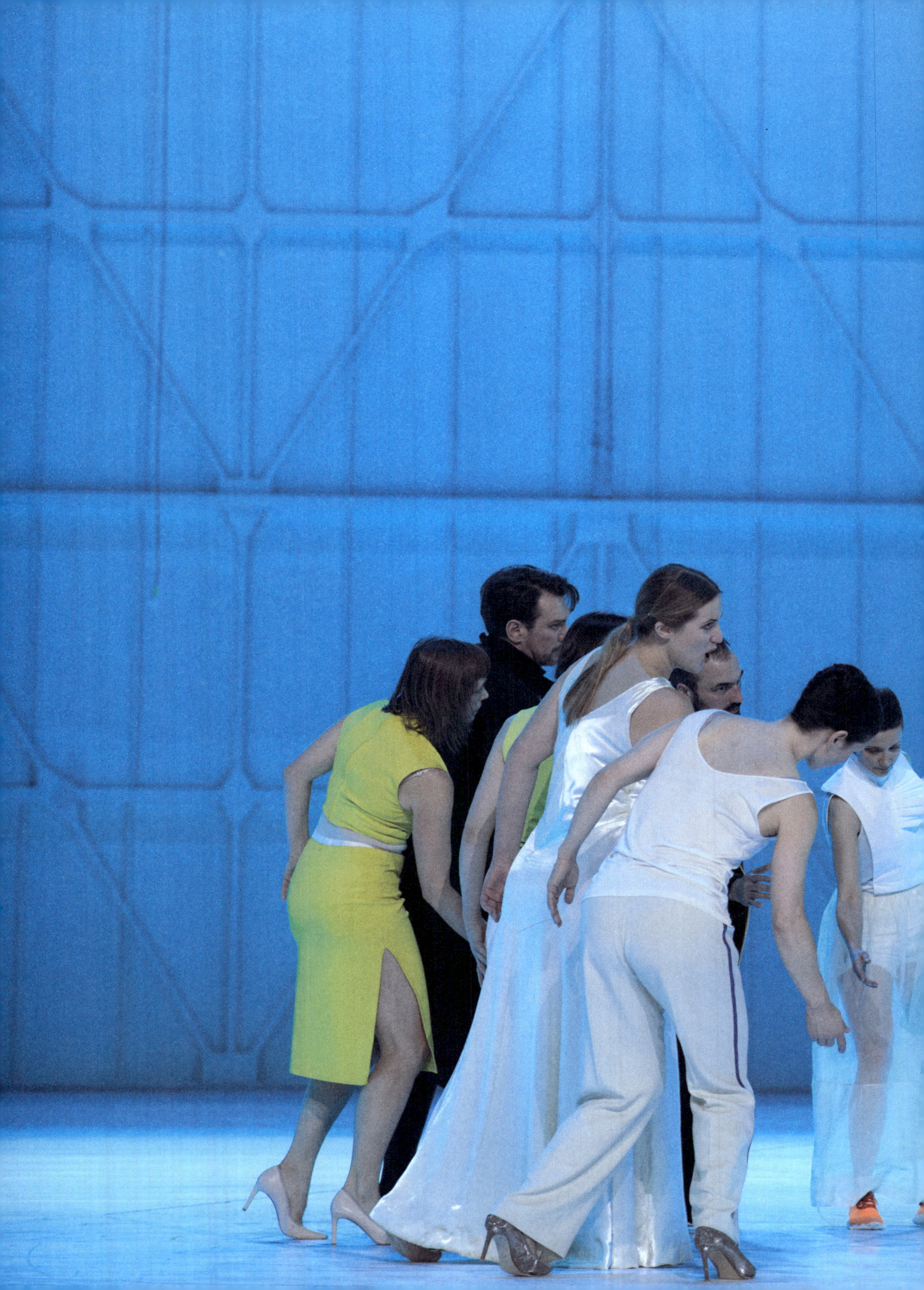

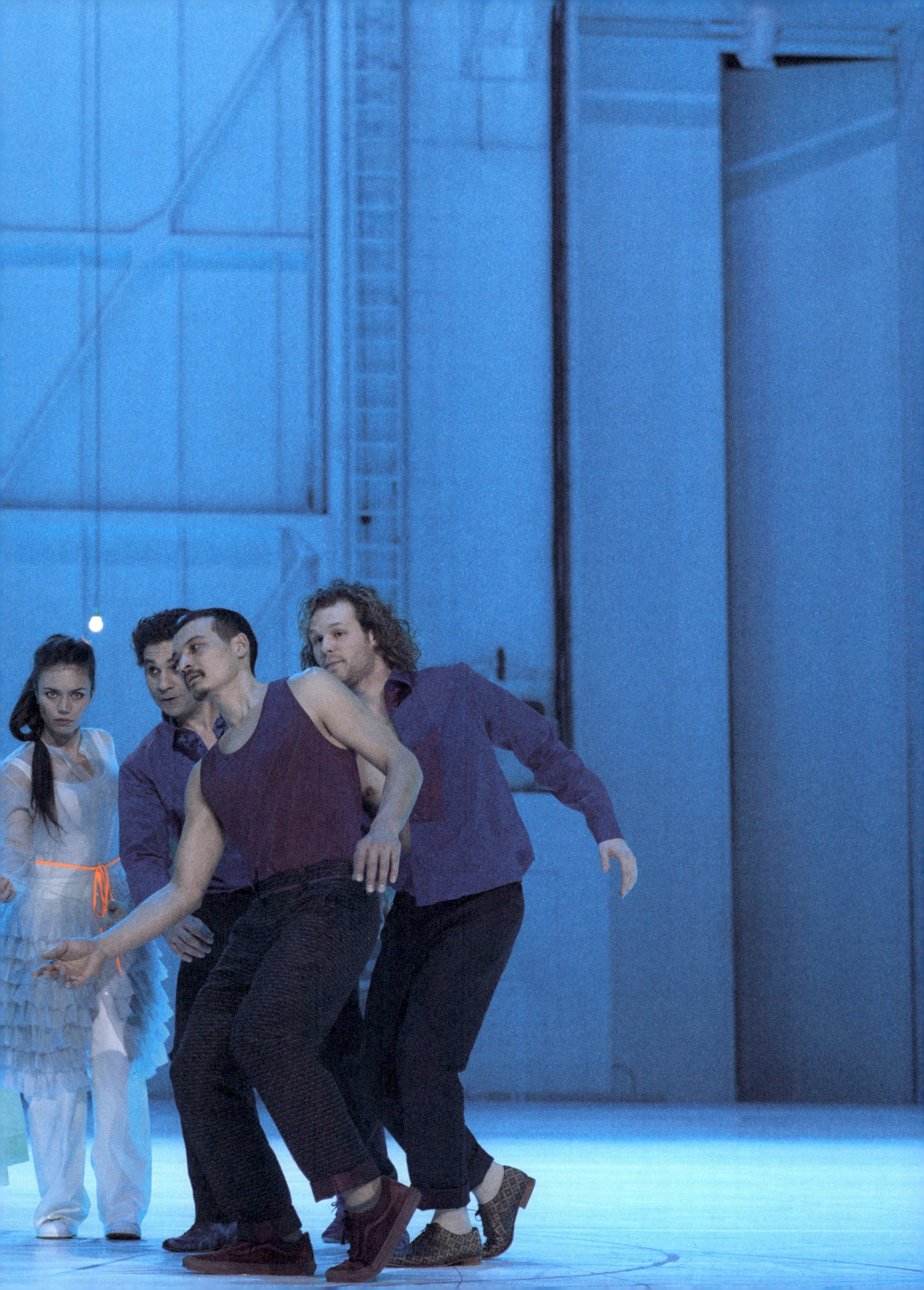

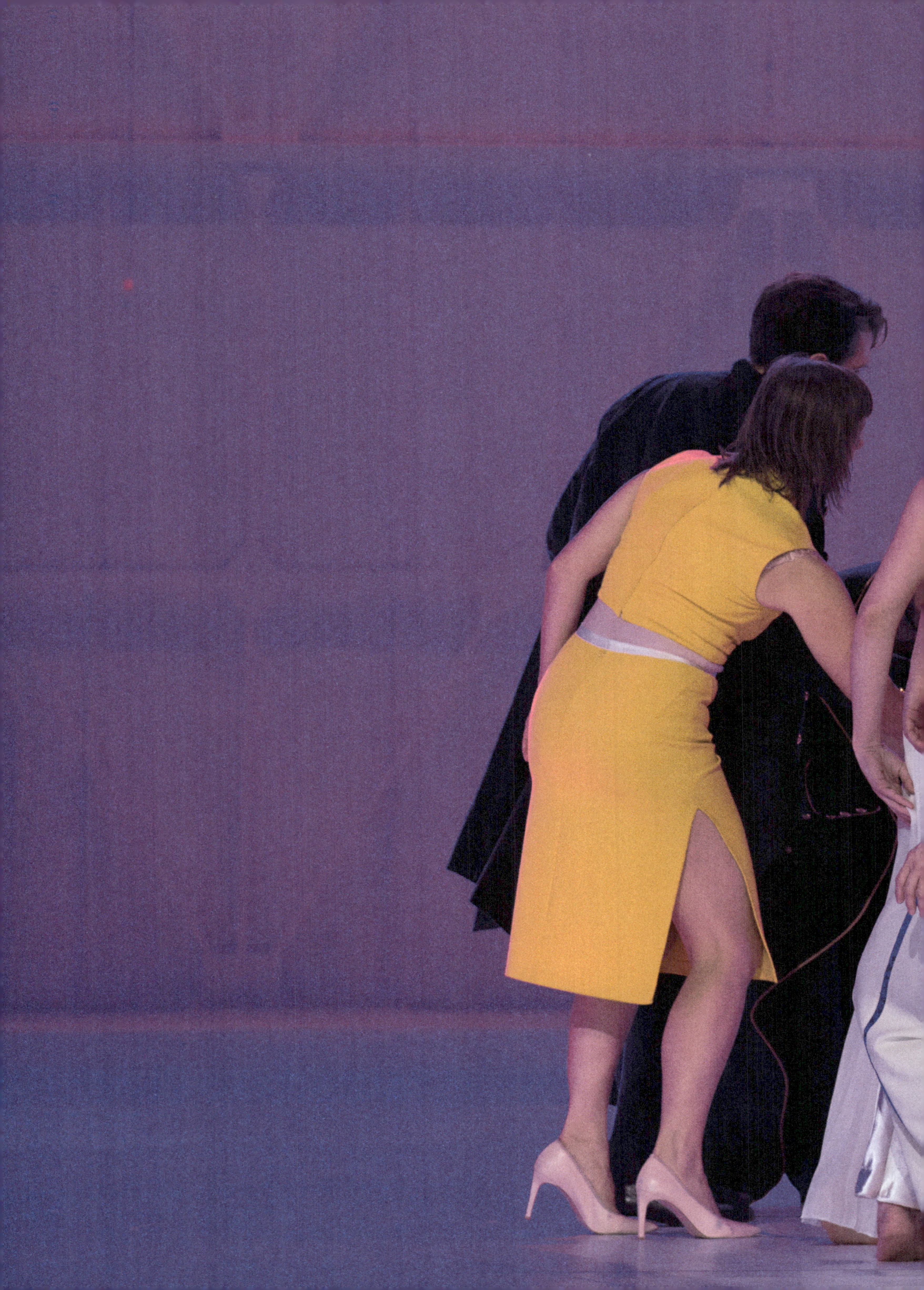

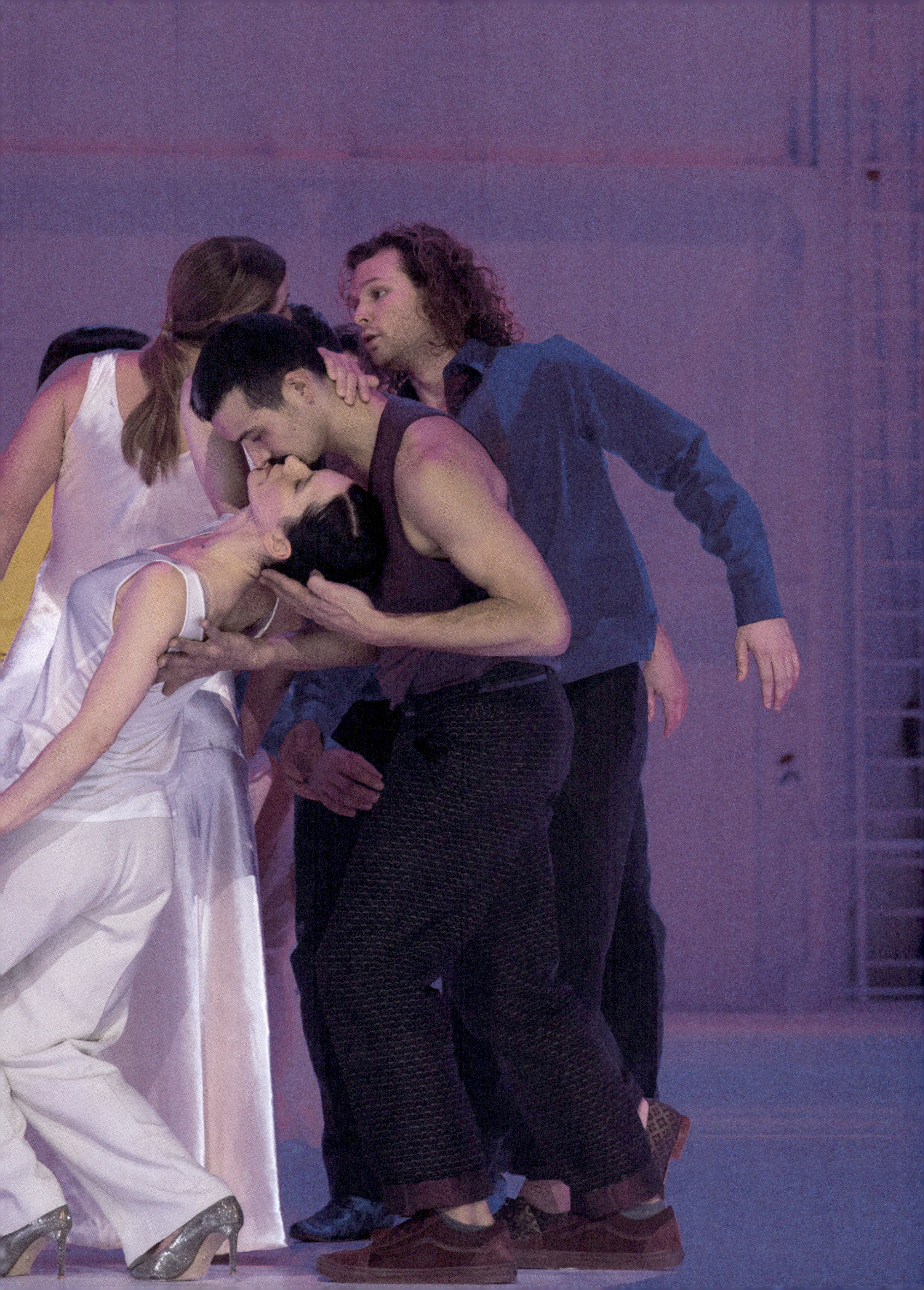

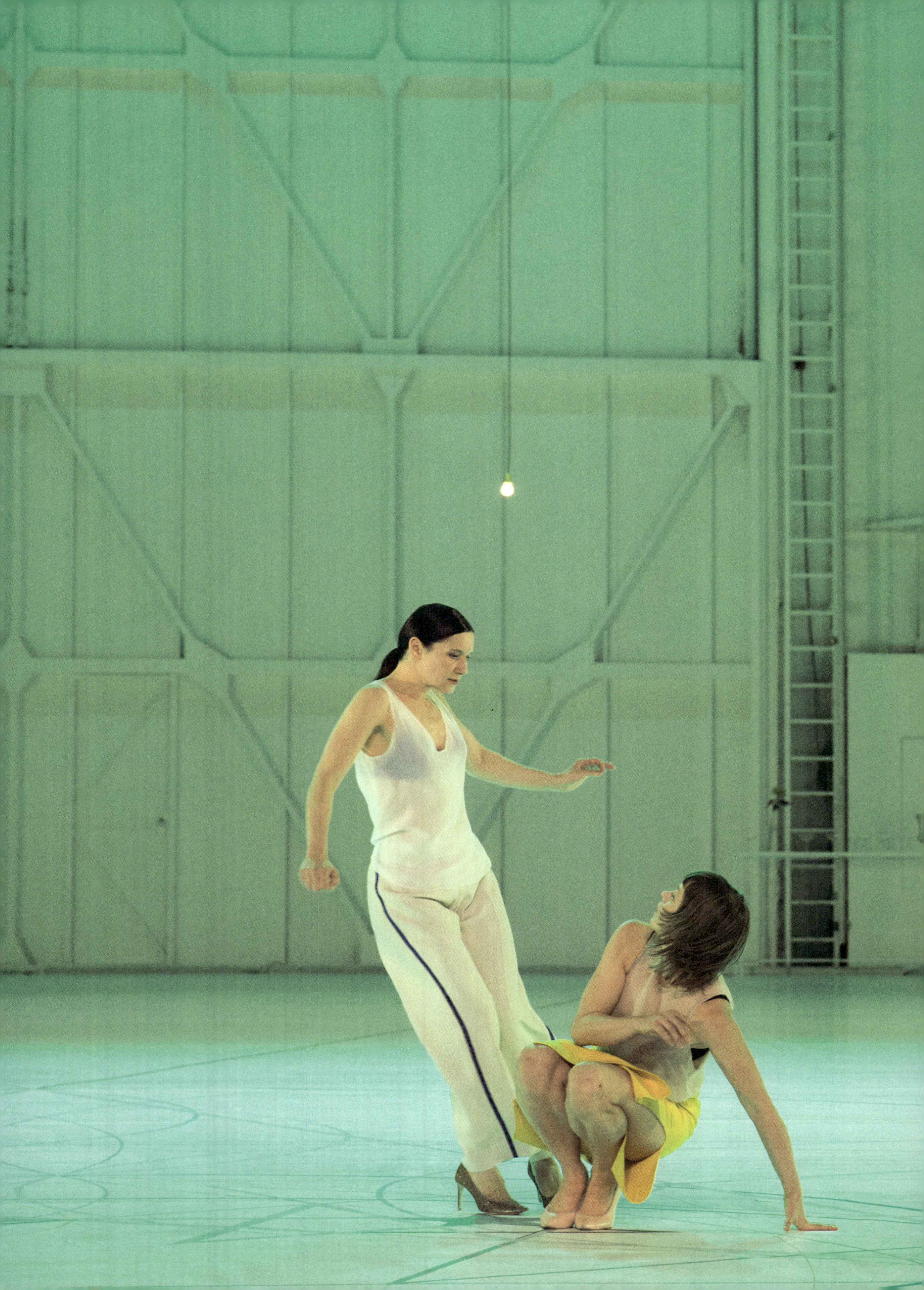

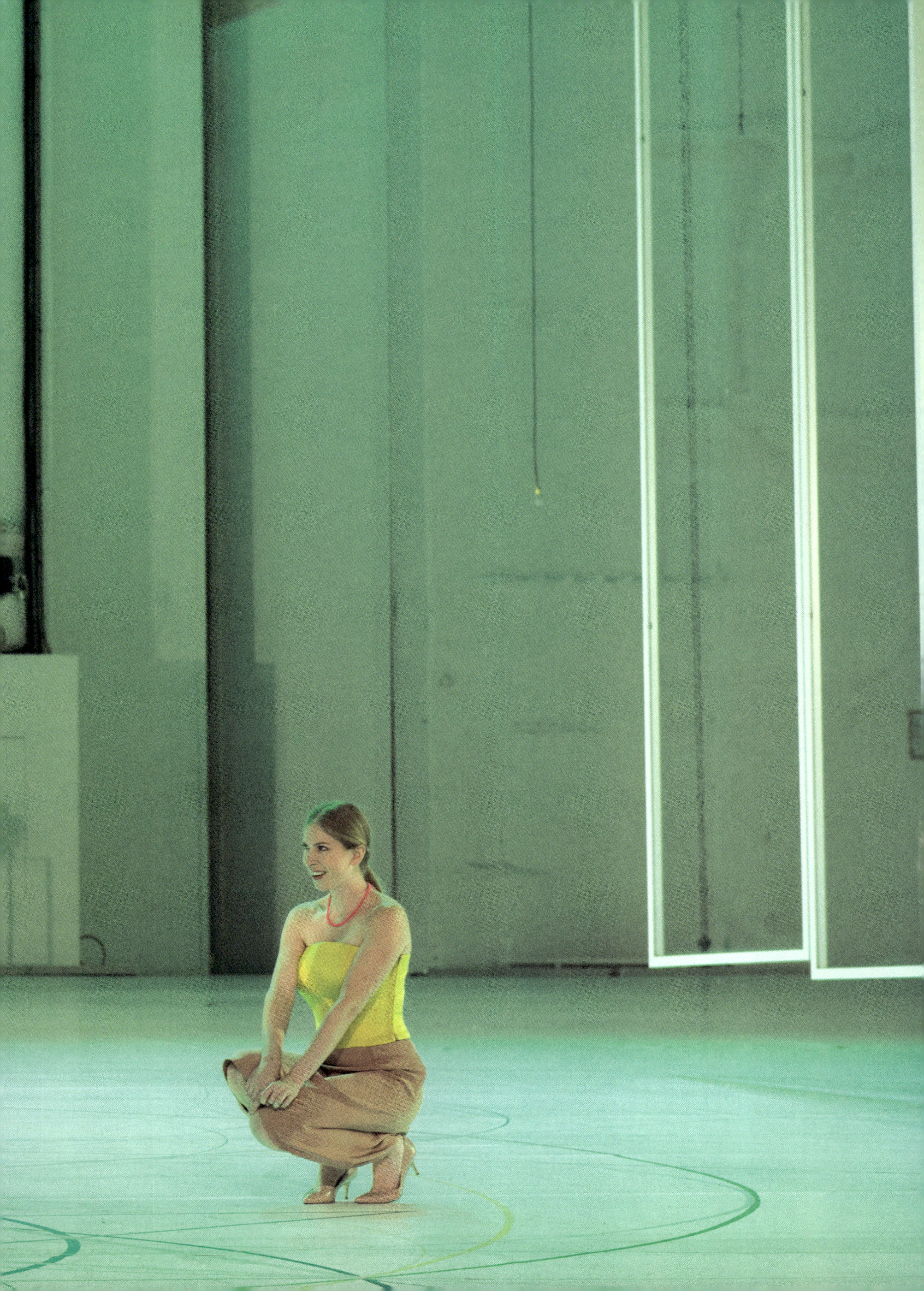

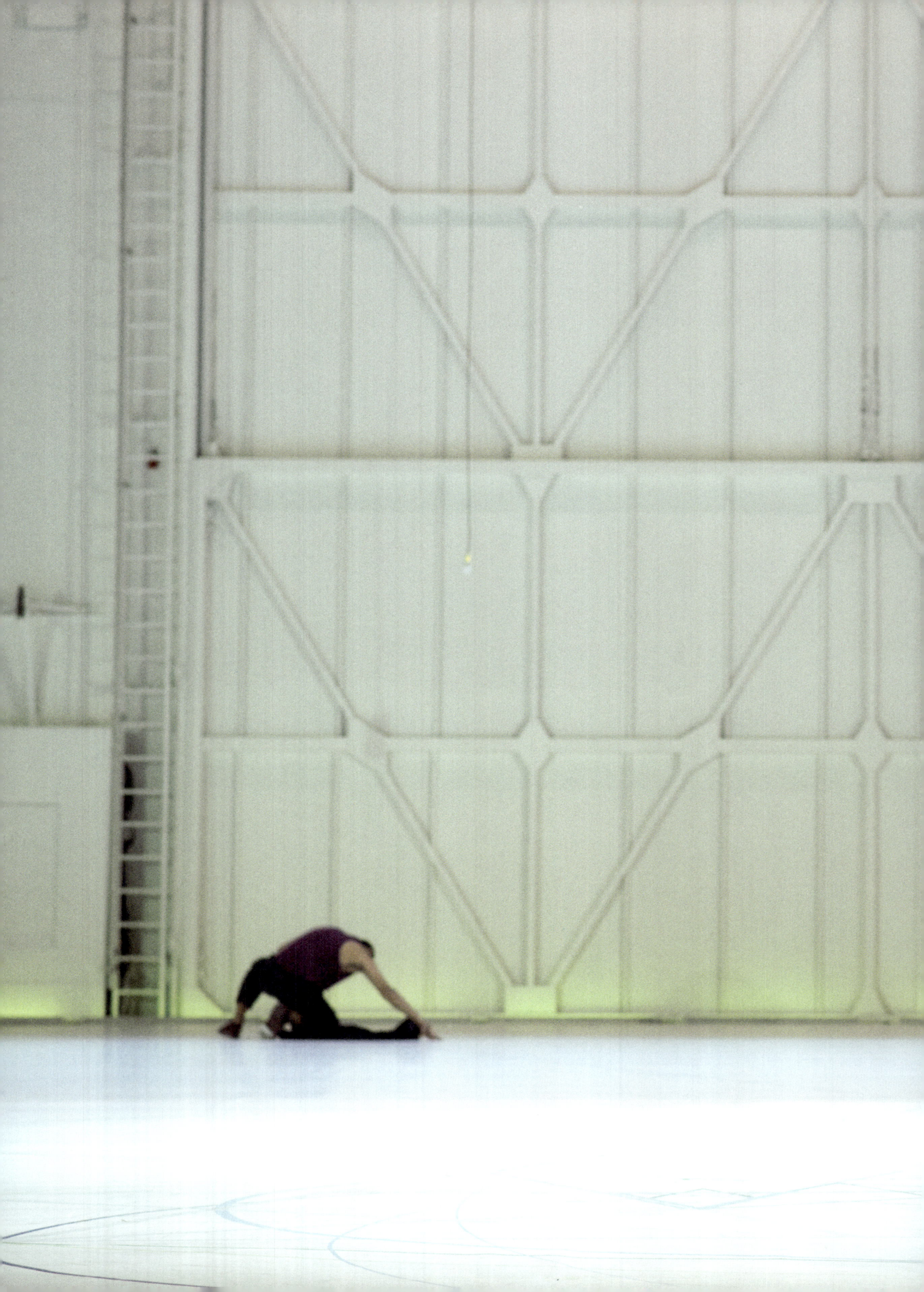

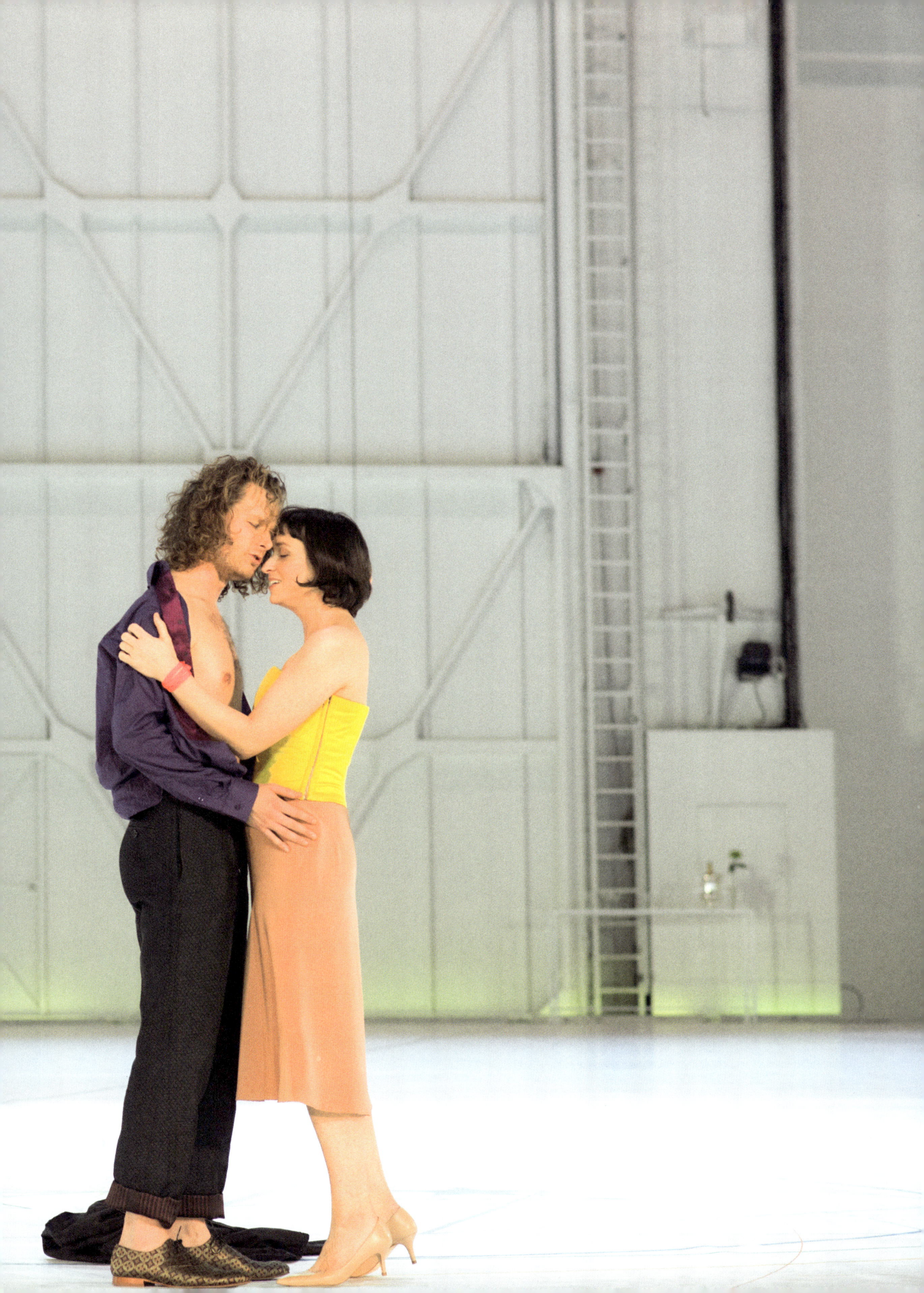

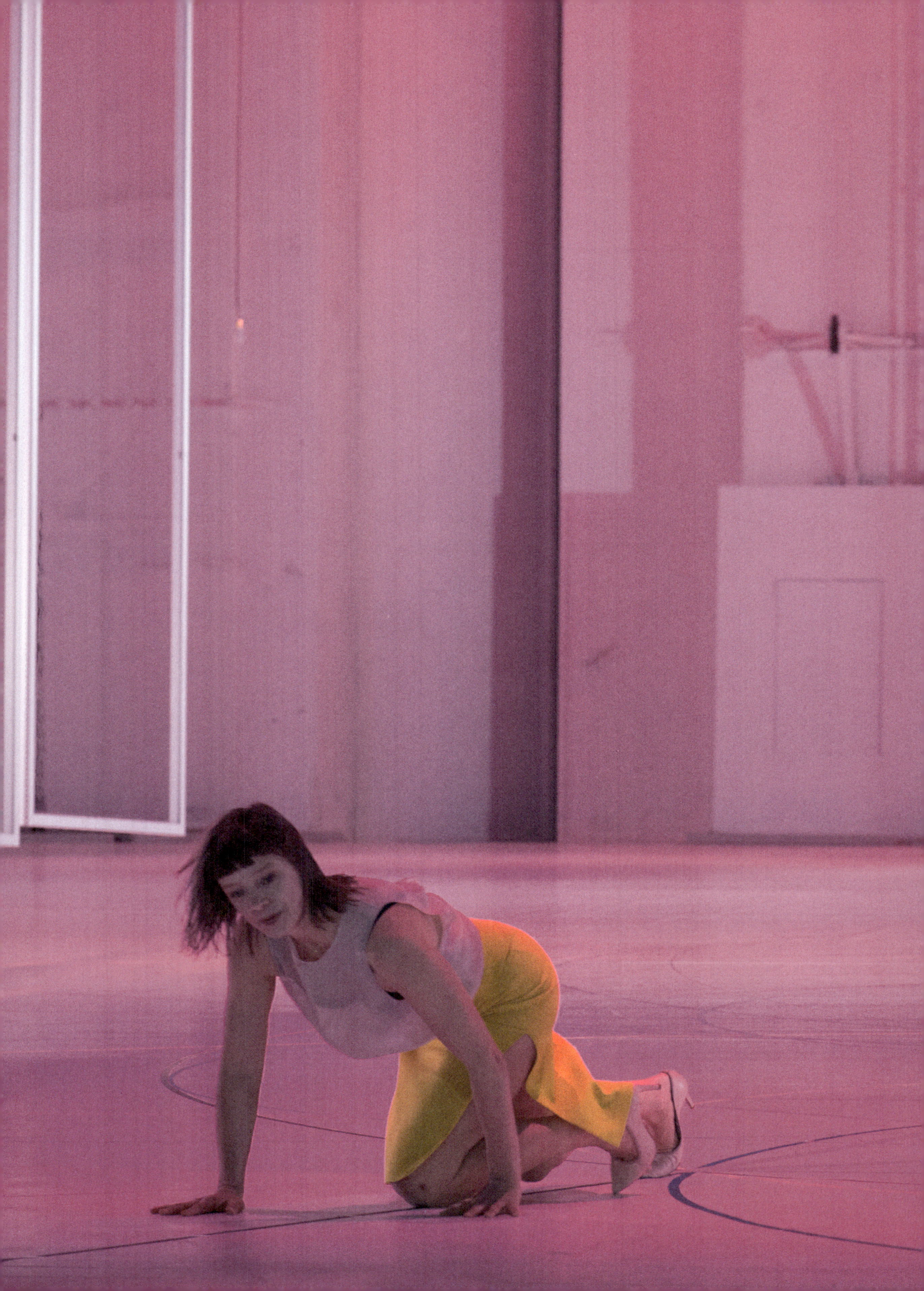

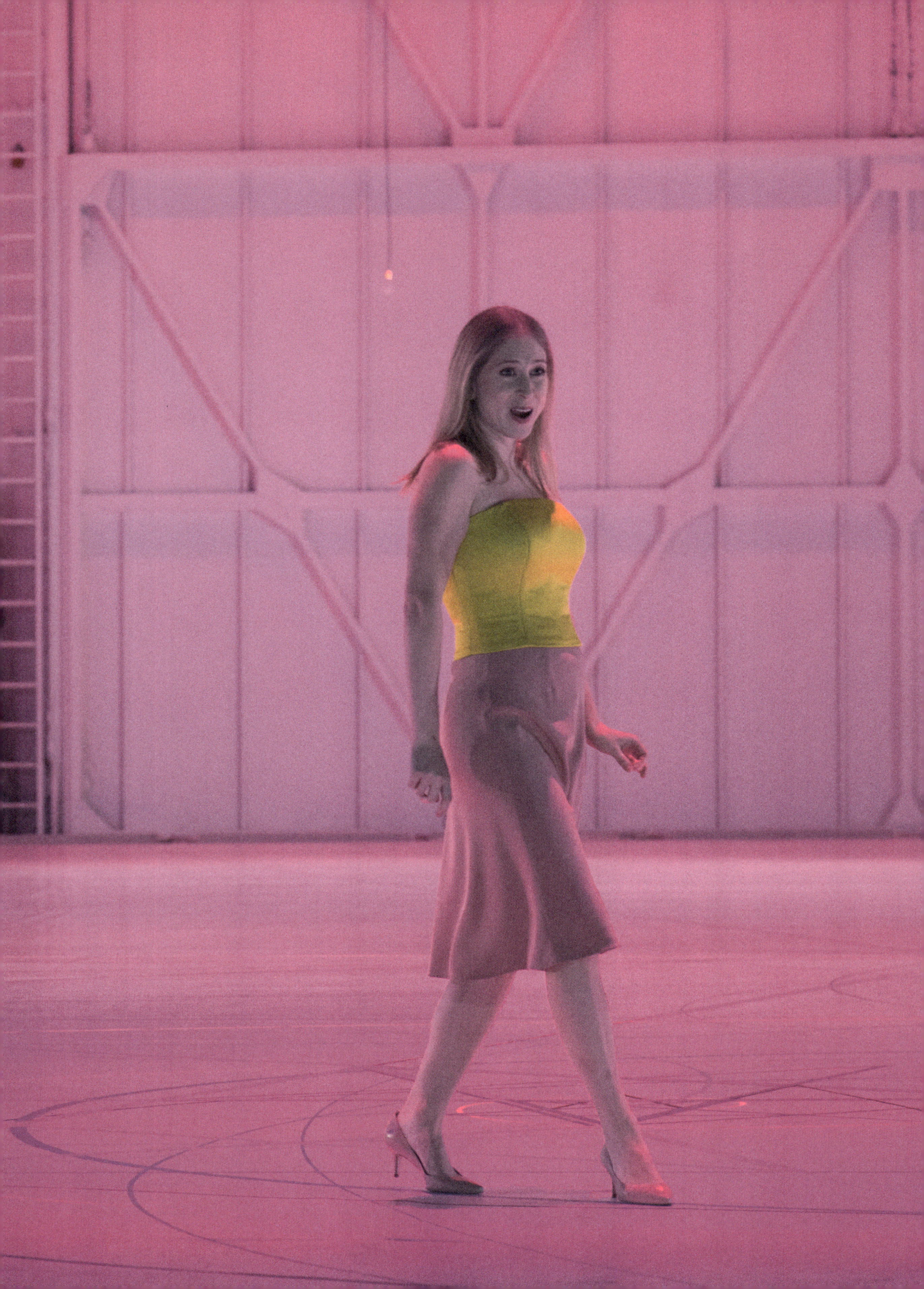

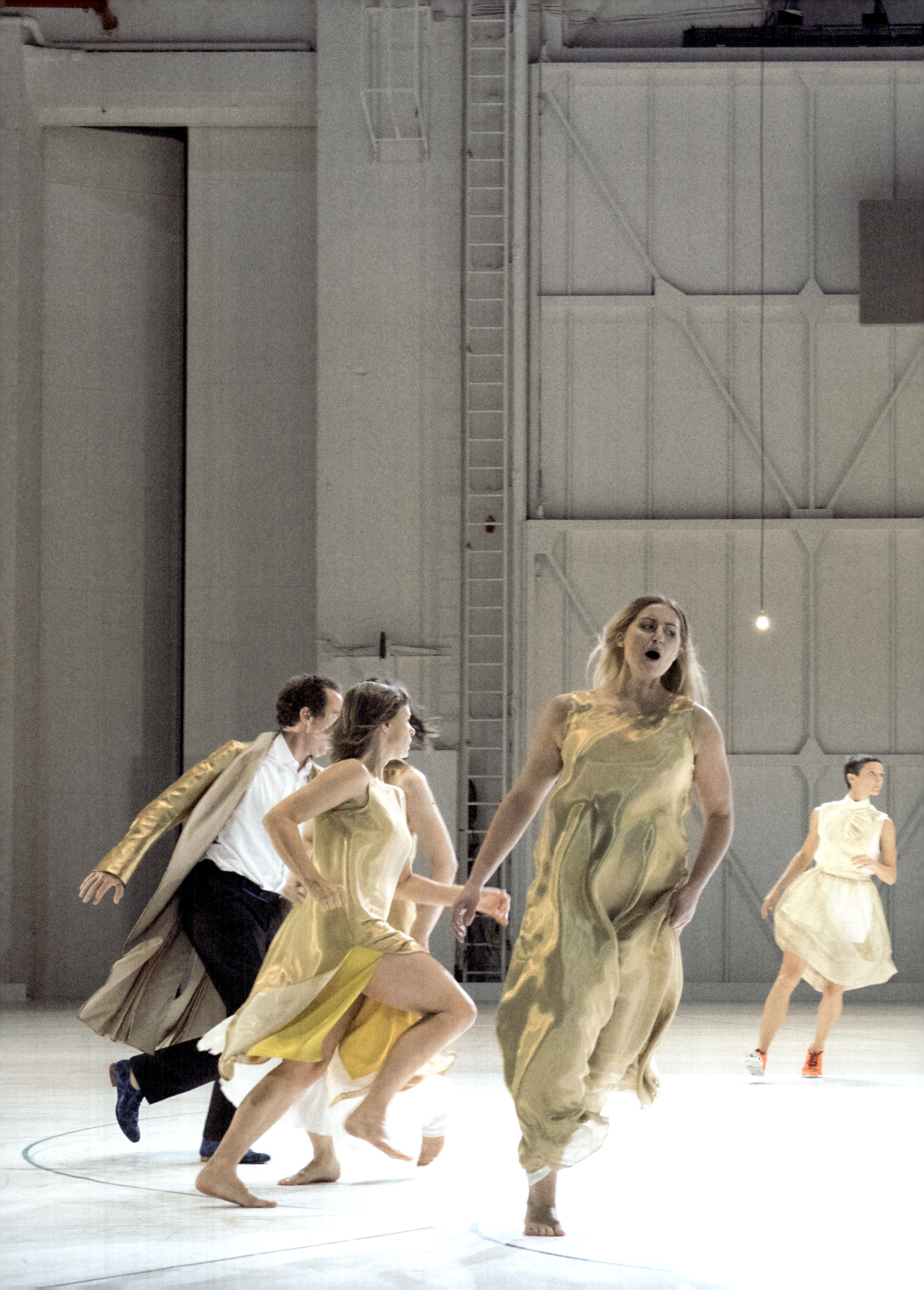

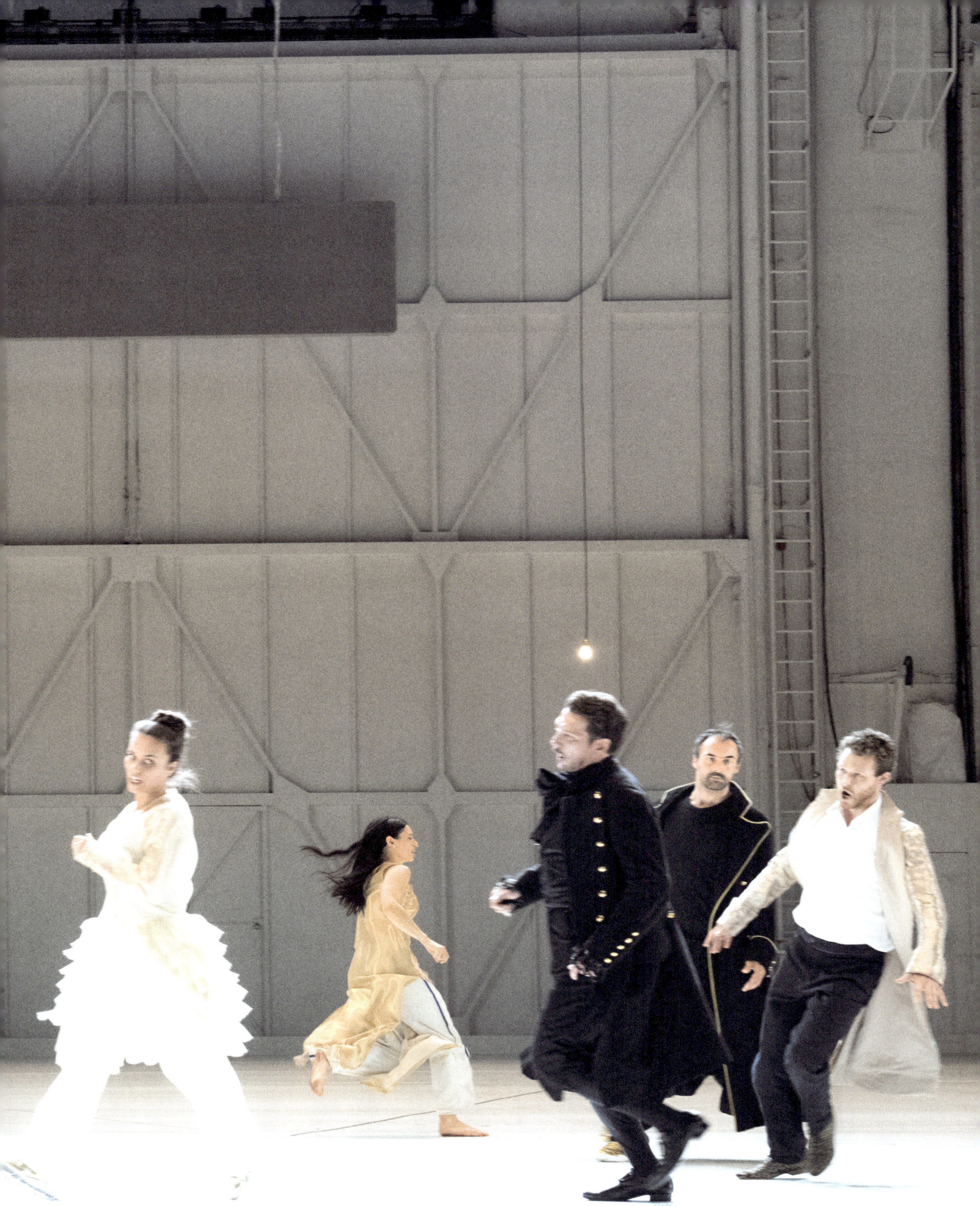

Mitten Wir im Leben sind/Bach6cellosuiten 2017

Concept and choreography
Anne Teresa De Keersmaeker
Cello
Jean-Guihen Queyras
Created with and danced by
Boštjan Antončič, Anne Teresa De Keersmaeker, Marie Goudot, Julien Monty, Michaël Pomero
Music
6 Cello Suites, BWV 1007 to 1012, Johann Sebastian Bach
Costumes
An D'Huys
Lighting
Luc Schaltin
Dramaturgy
Jan Vandenhouwe
Artistic assistants
Carlos Garbin, Femke Gyselinck
Sound
Alban Moraud
Production
Rosas
Coproduction
La Monnaie / De Munt (Brussels), Ruhrtriennale, Concertgebouw Bruges, Philharmonie de Paris and Théâtre de la Ville with the Festival d'Automne à Paris, Sadler's Wells (London), Les Théâtres de la Ville de Luxembourg, Opéra de Lille, Ludwigsburger Schlossfestspiele, Elbphilharmonie (Hamburg), Montpellier Danse 2018
Premiere
26.08.2017, Ruhrtriennale—Gladbeck

Mitten wir im Leben sind/Bach6Cellosuiten was realized with the support of the Tax Shelter of the Belgian Federal Government, in collaboration with Casa Kafka Pictures Tax Shelter empowered by Belfius.

Pictures
Anne Van Aerschot

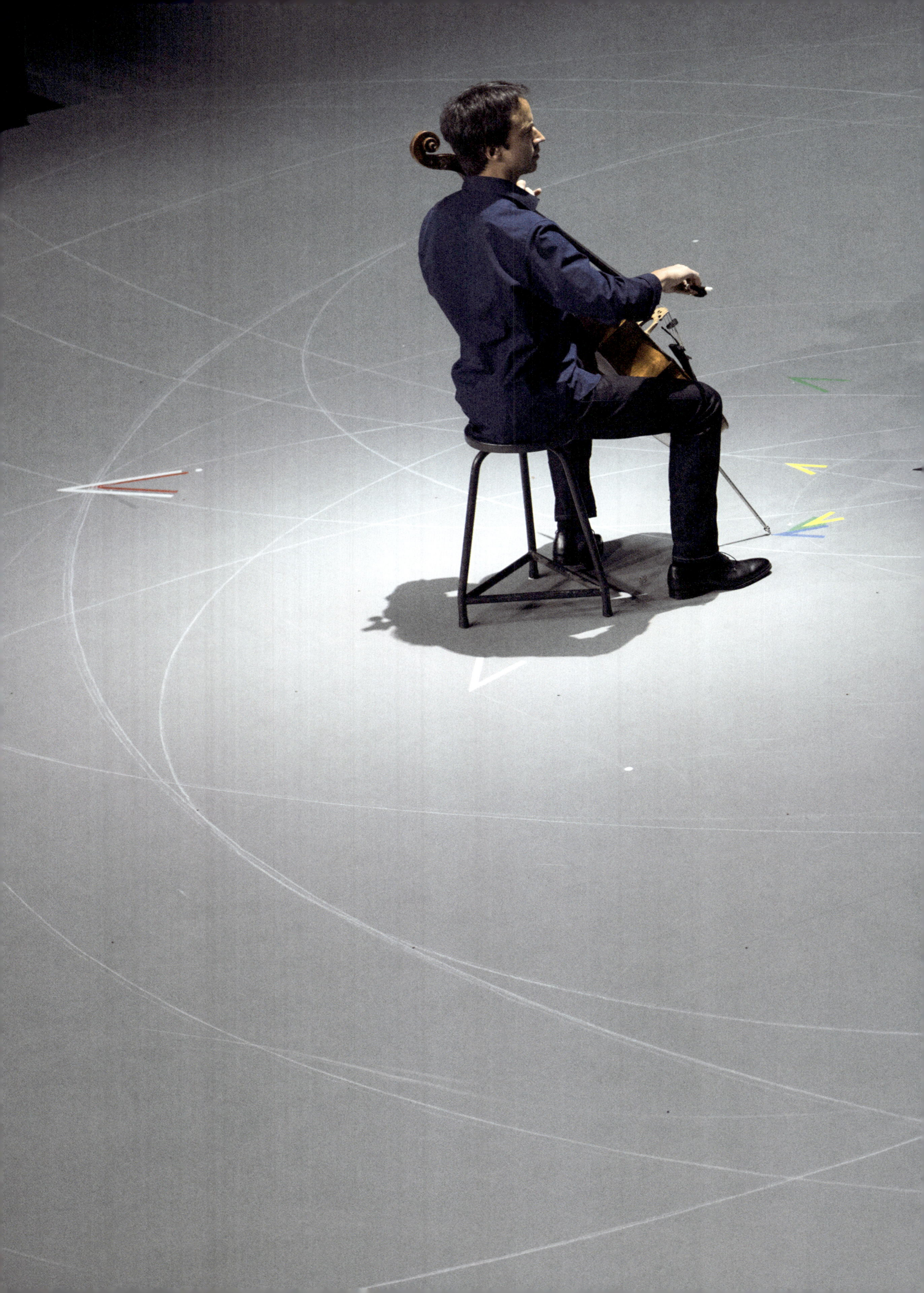

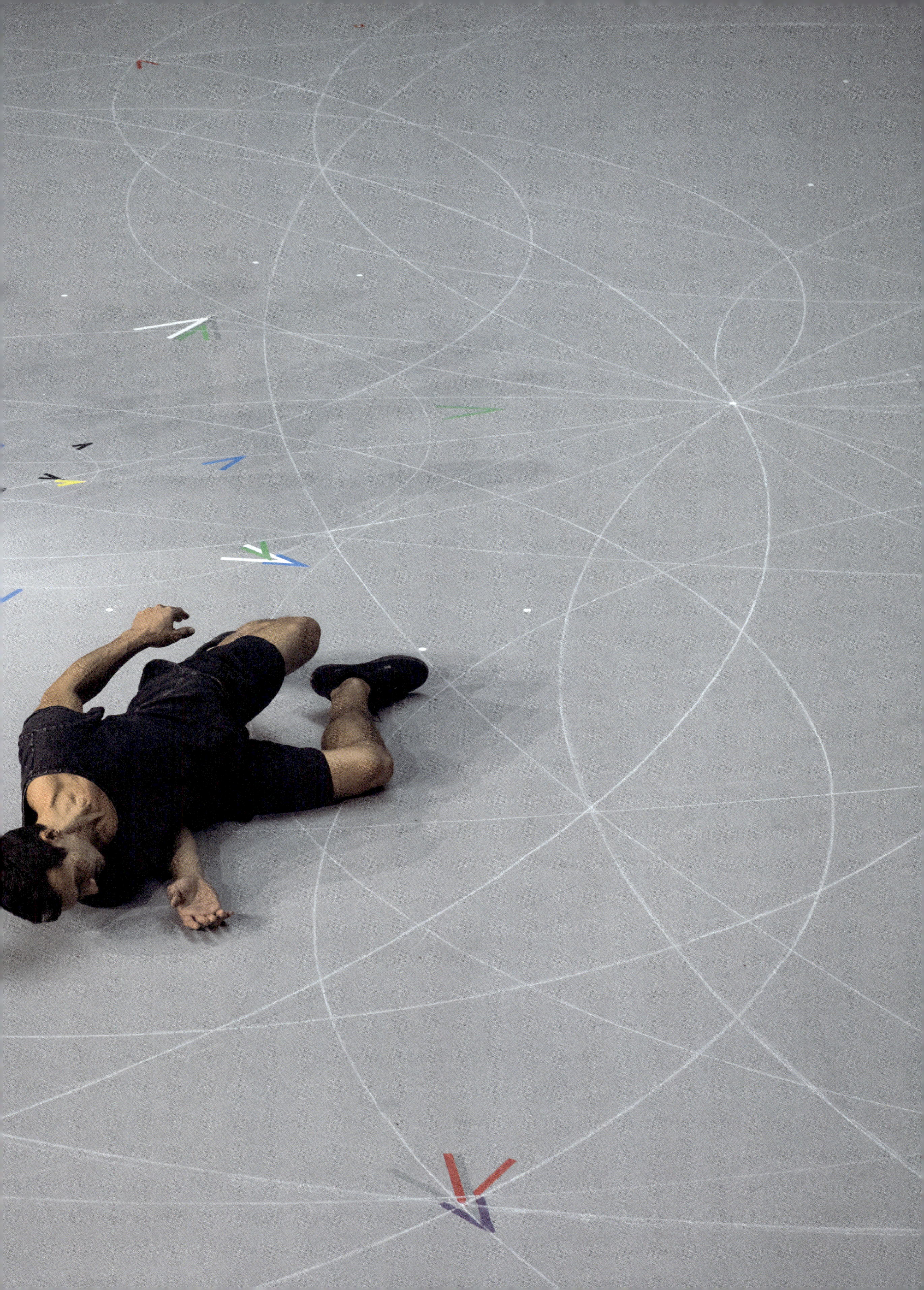

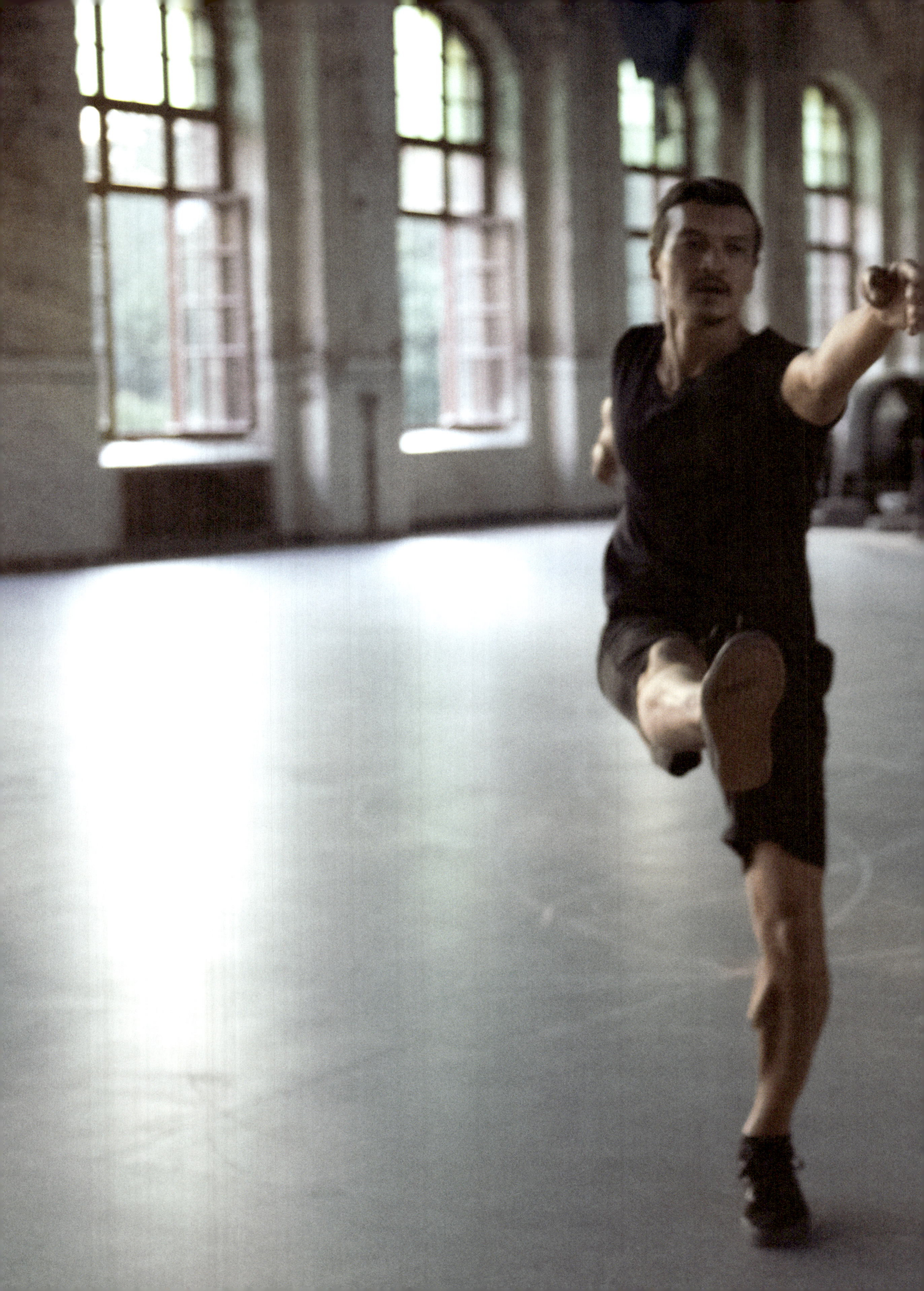

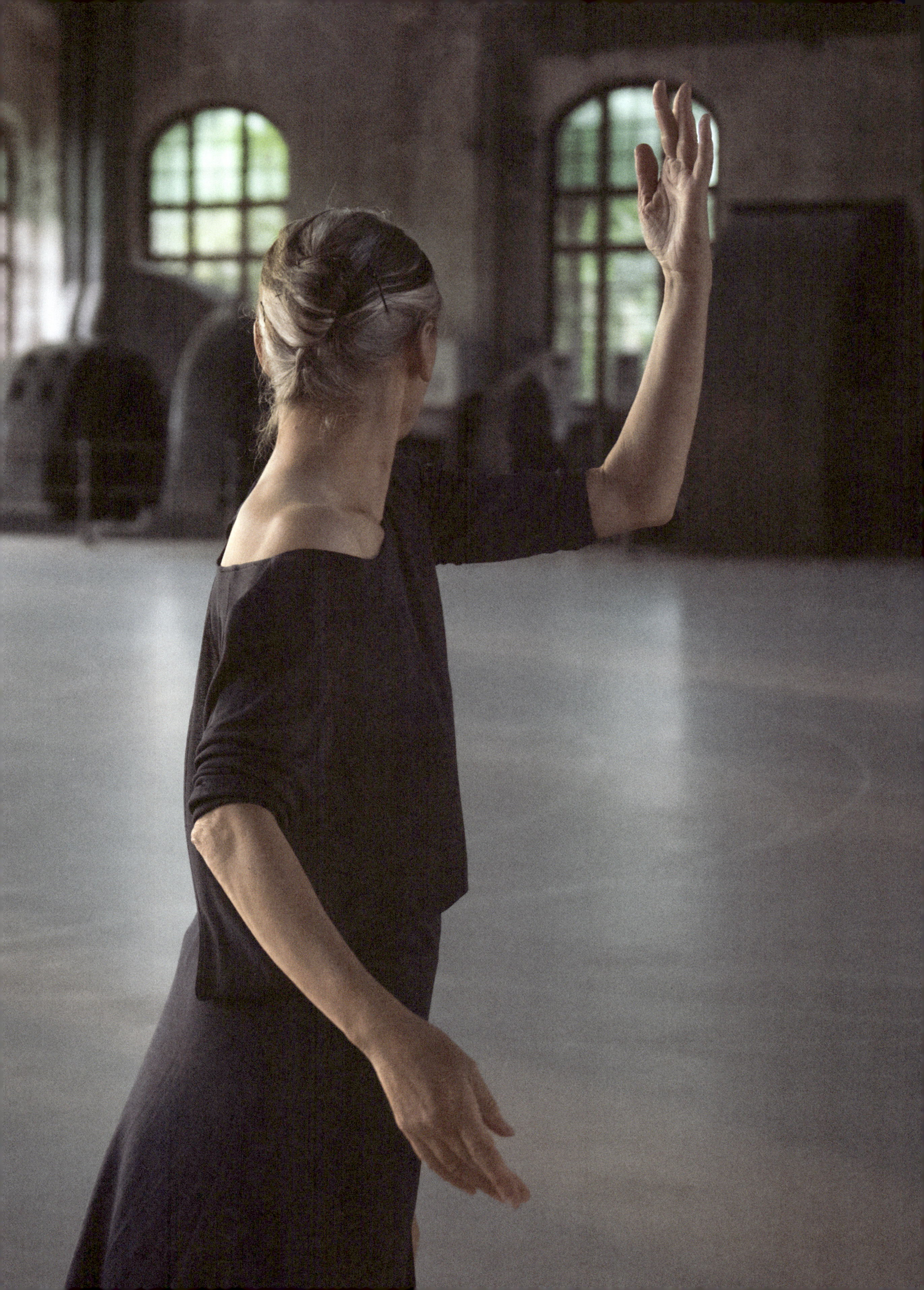

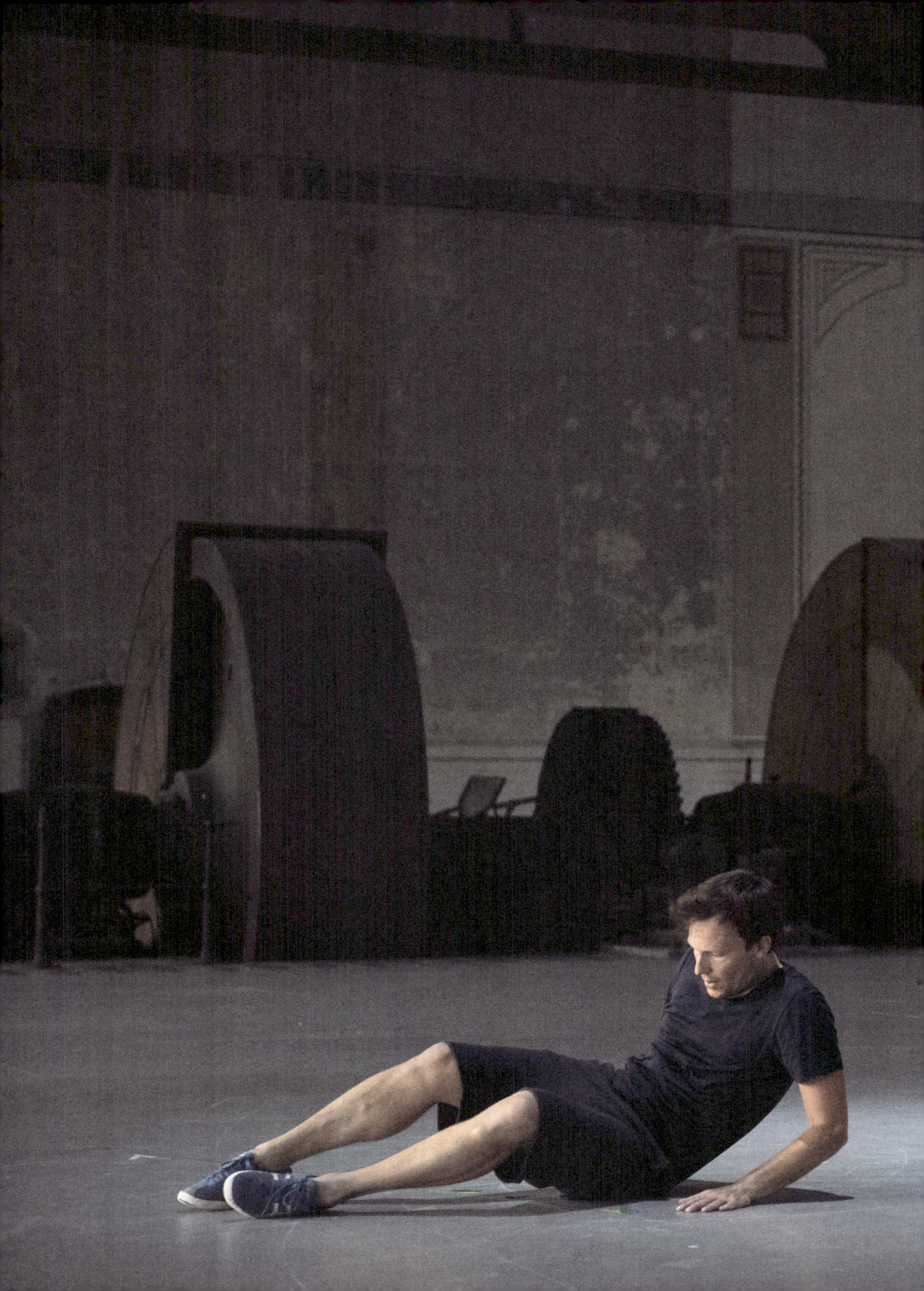

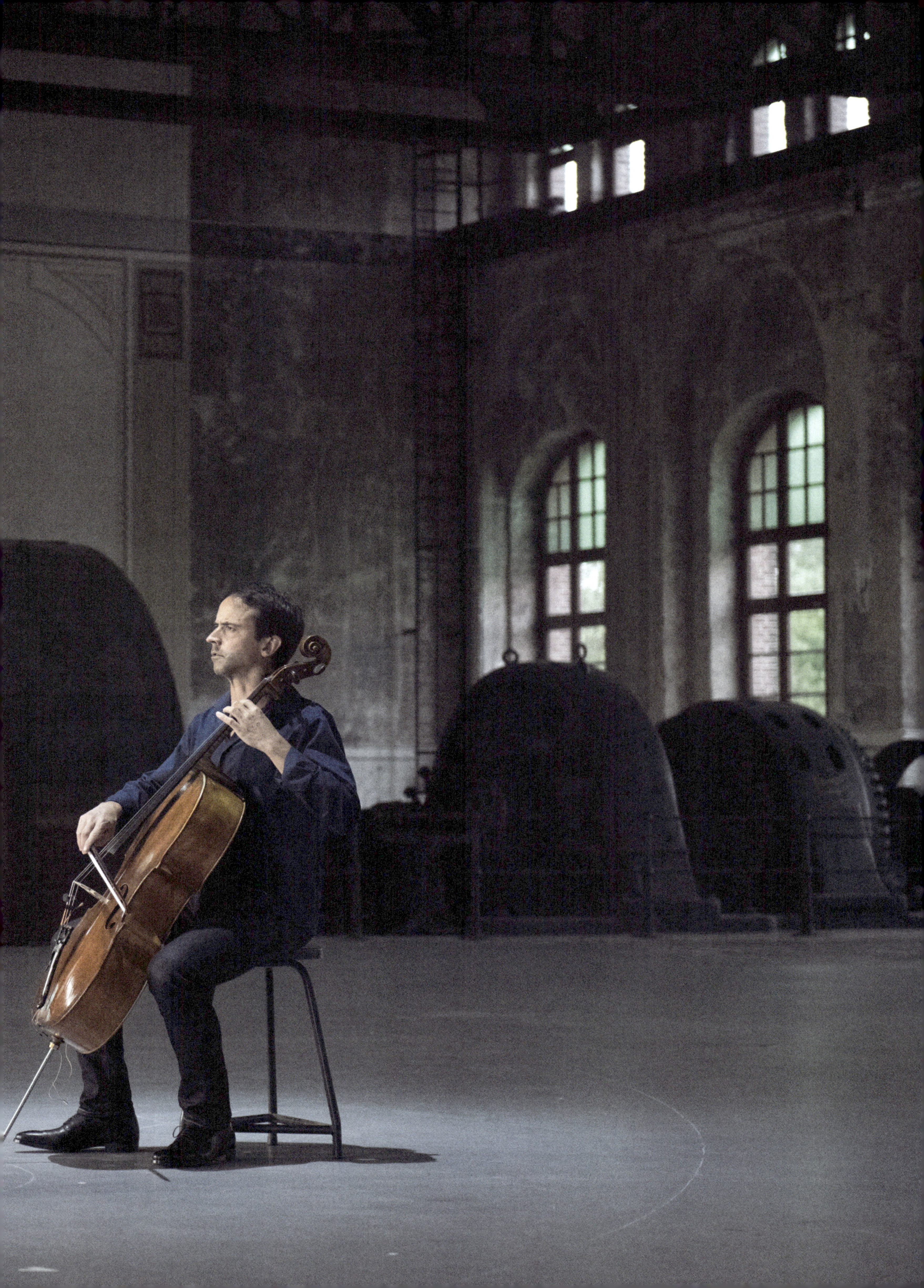

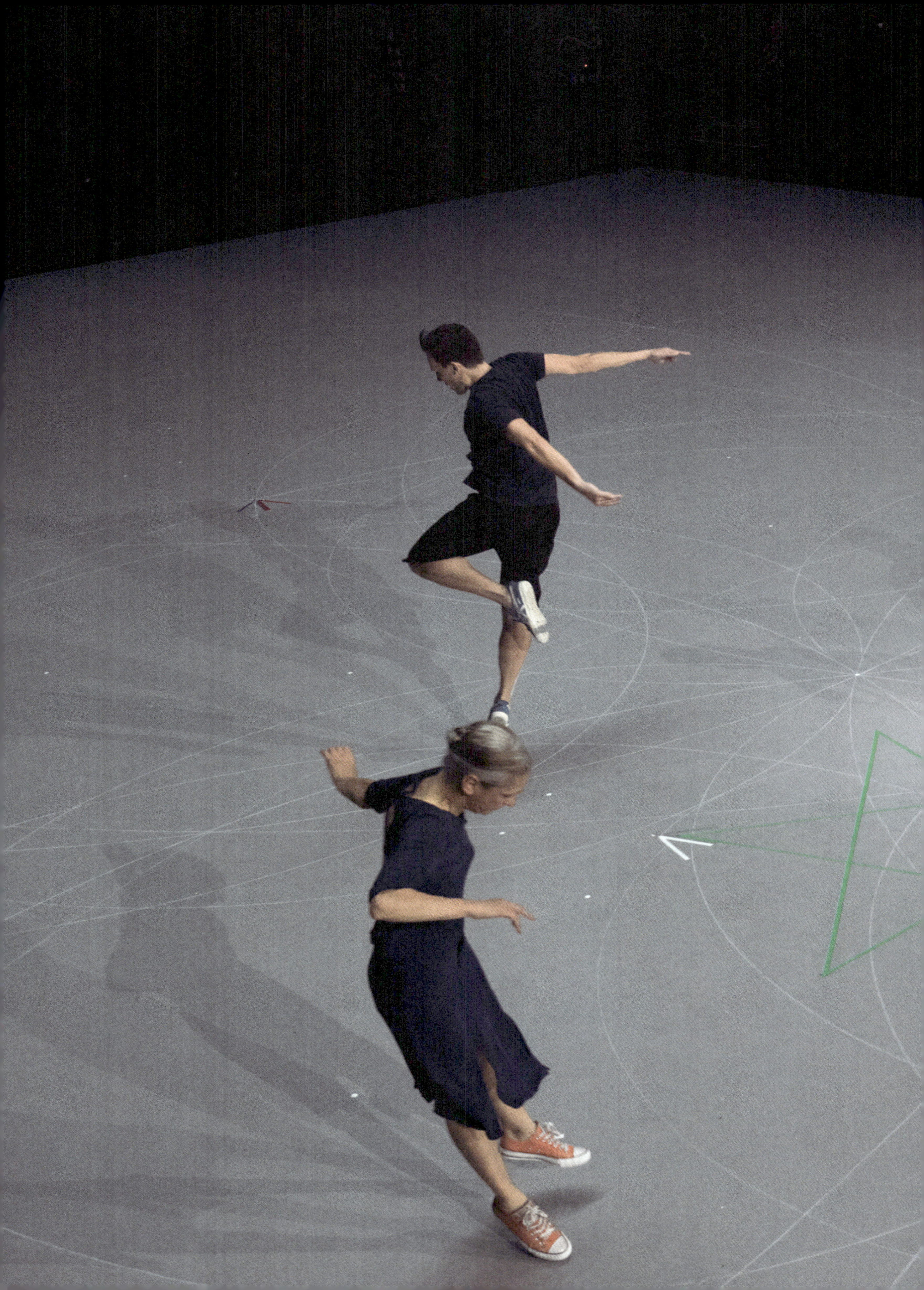

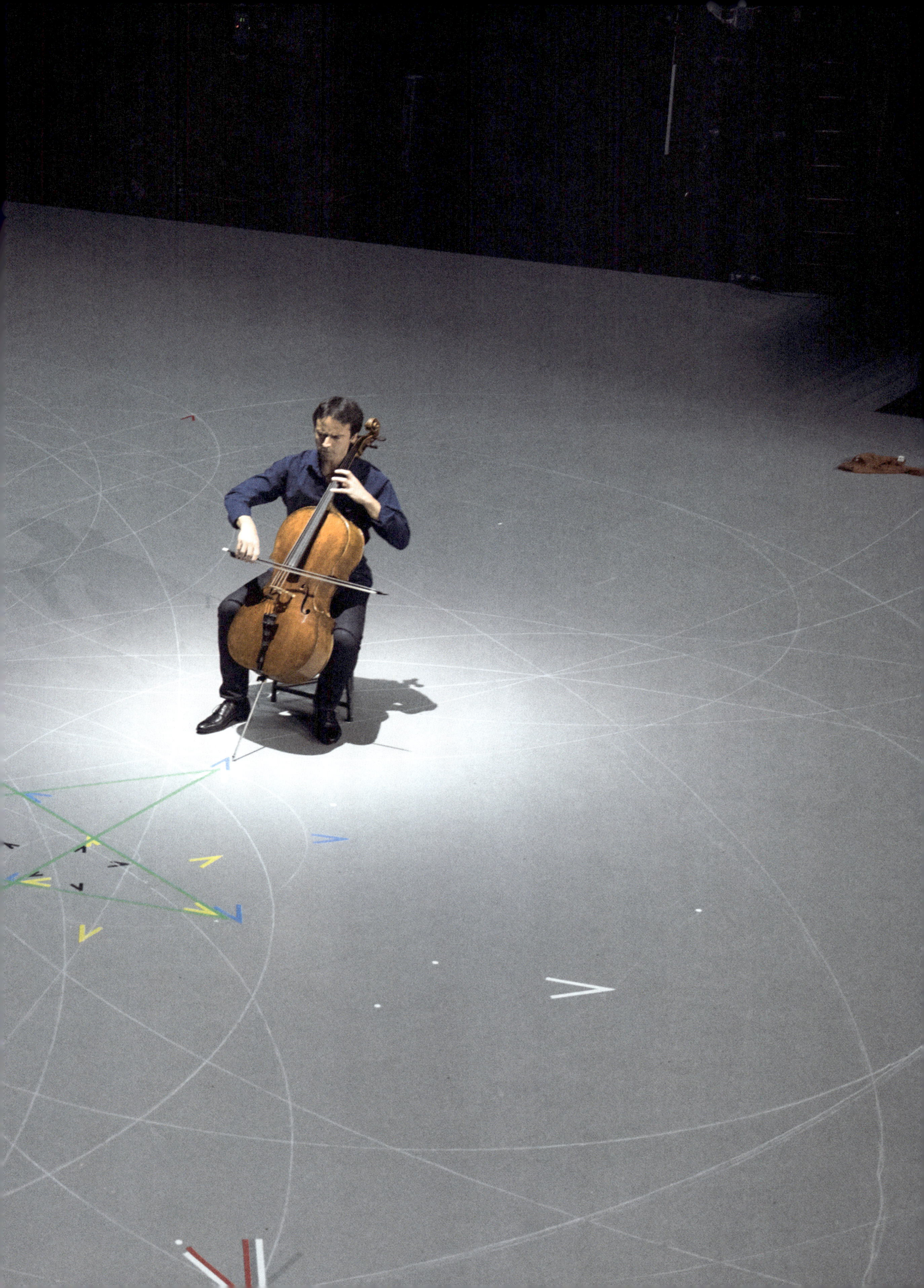

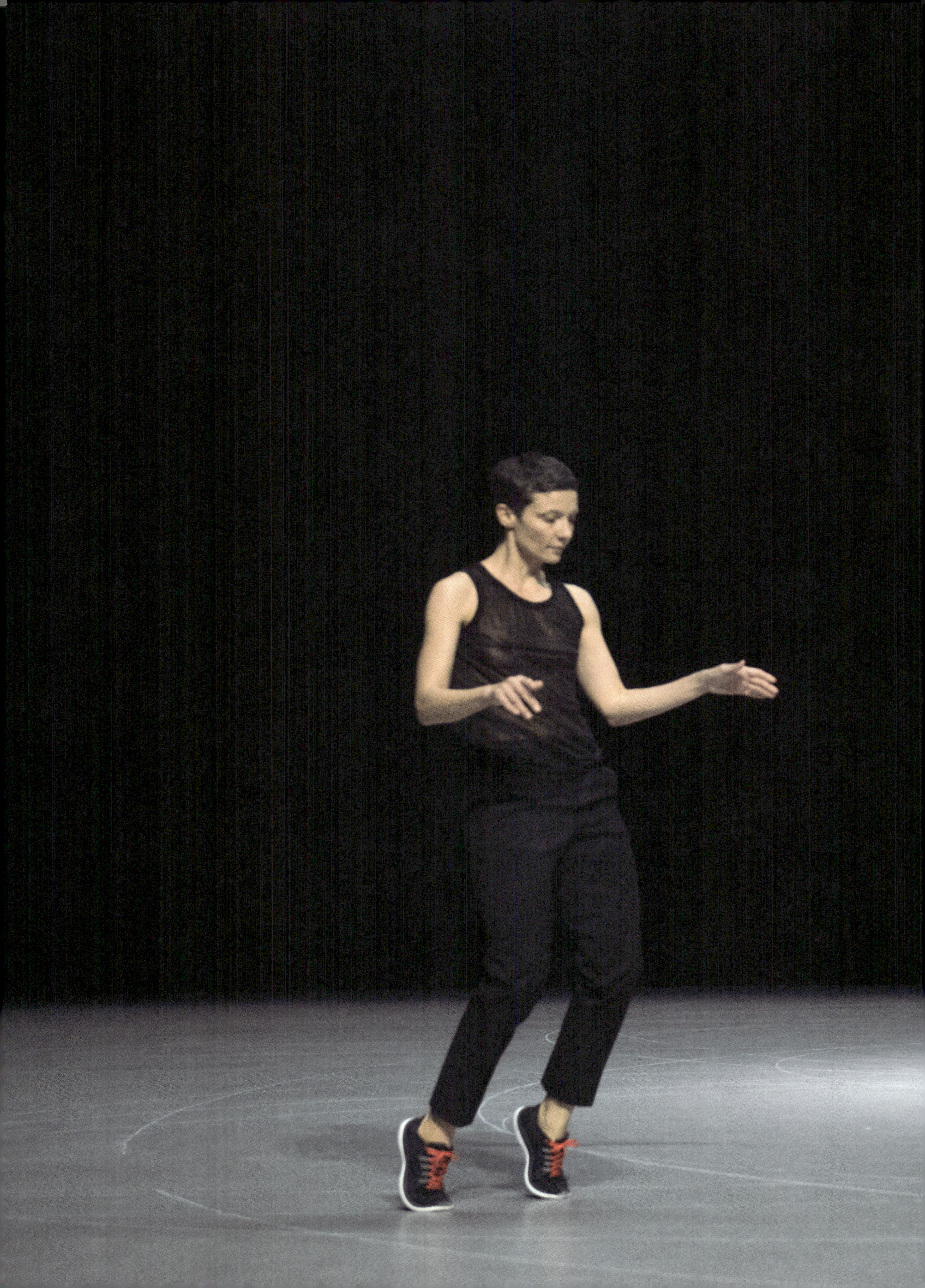

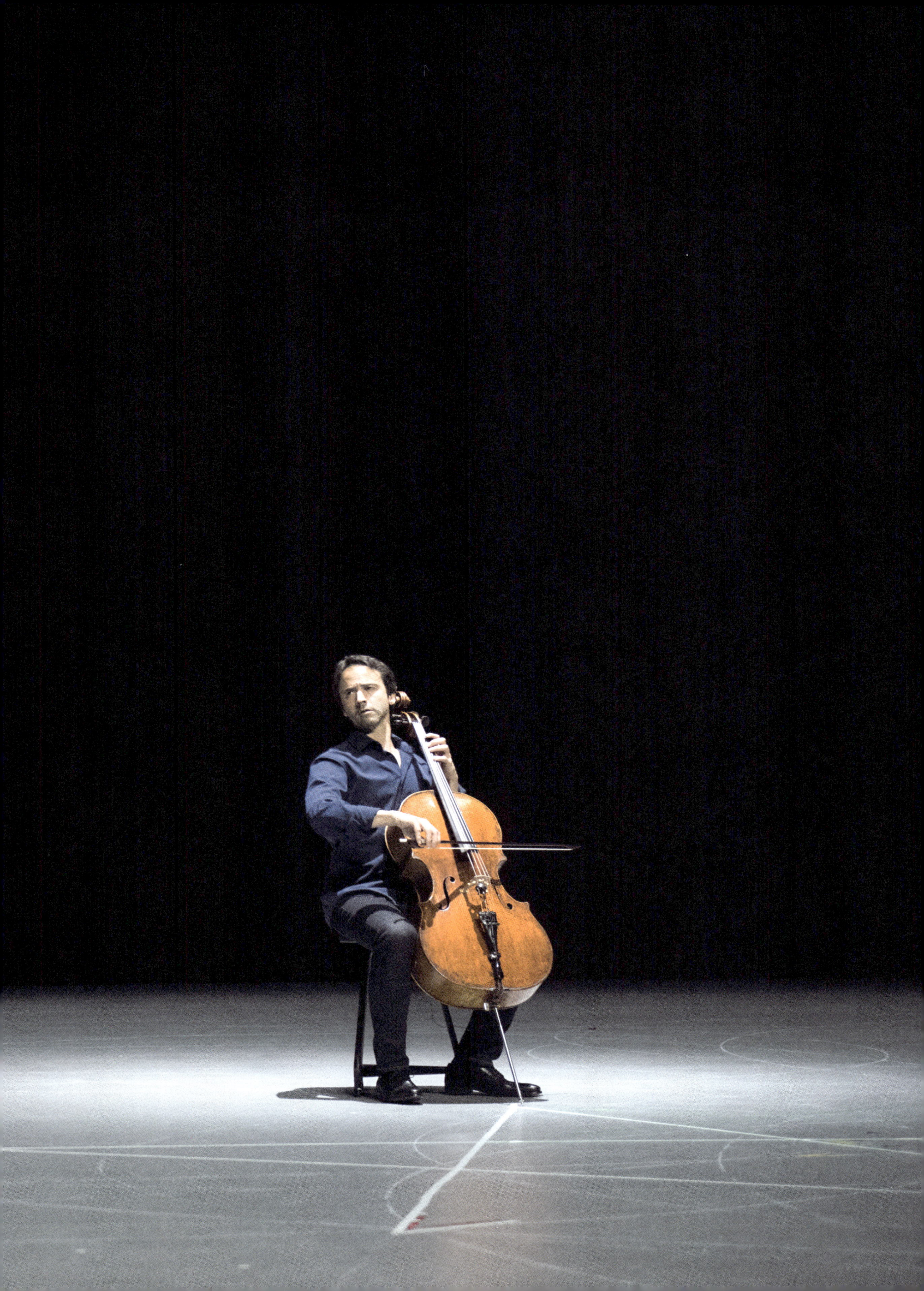

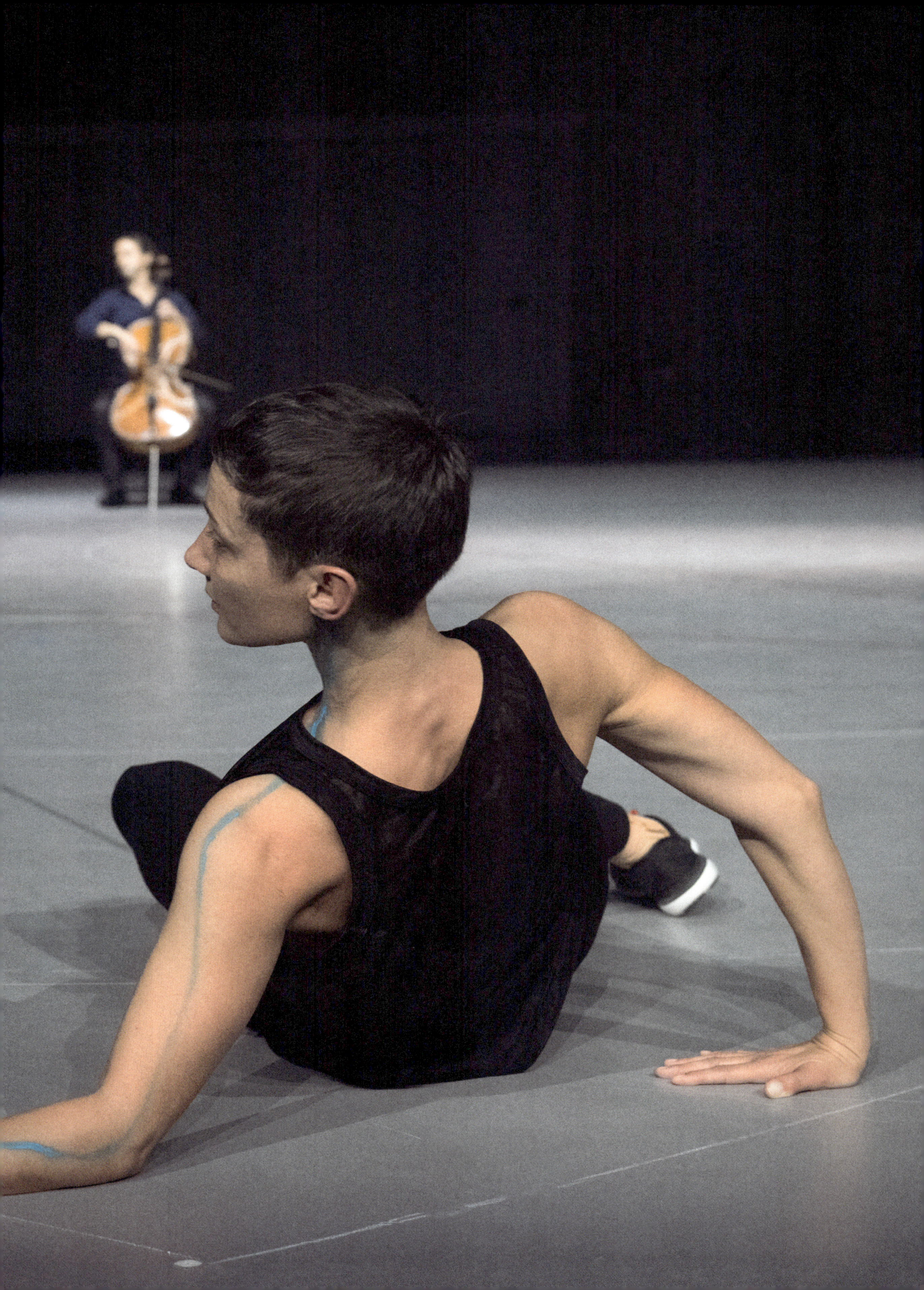

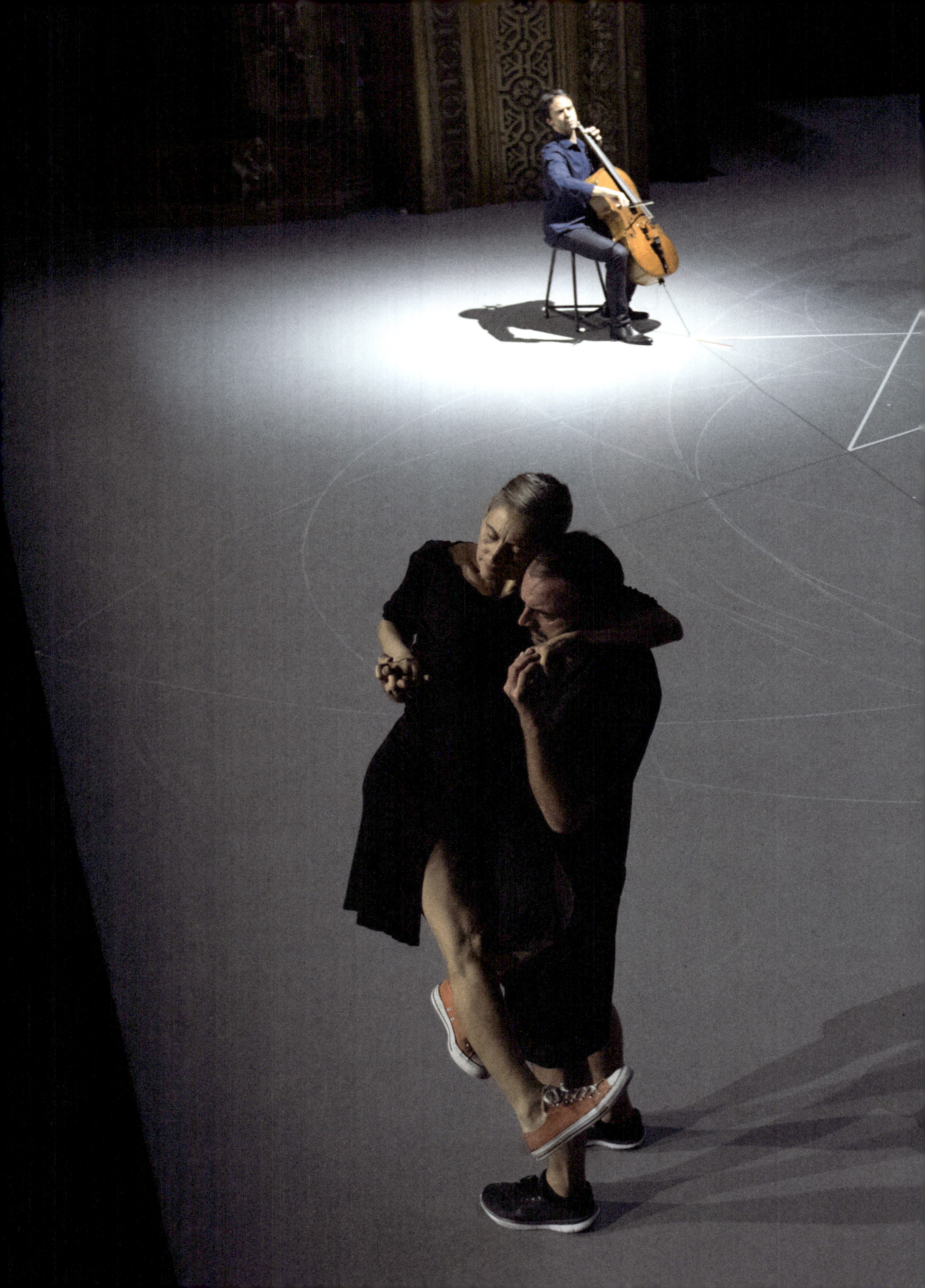

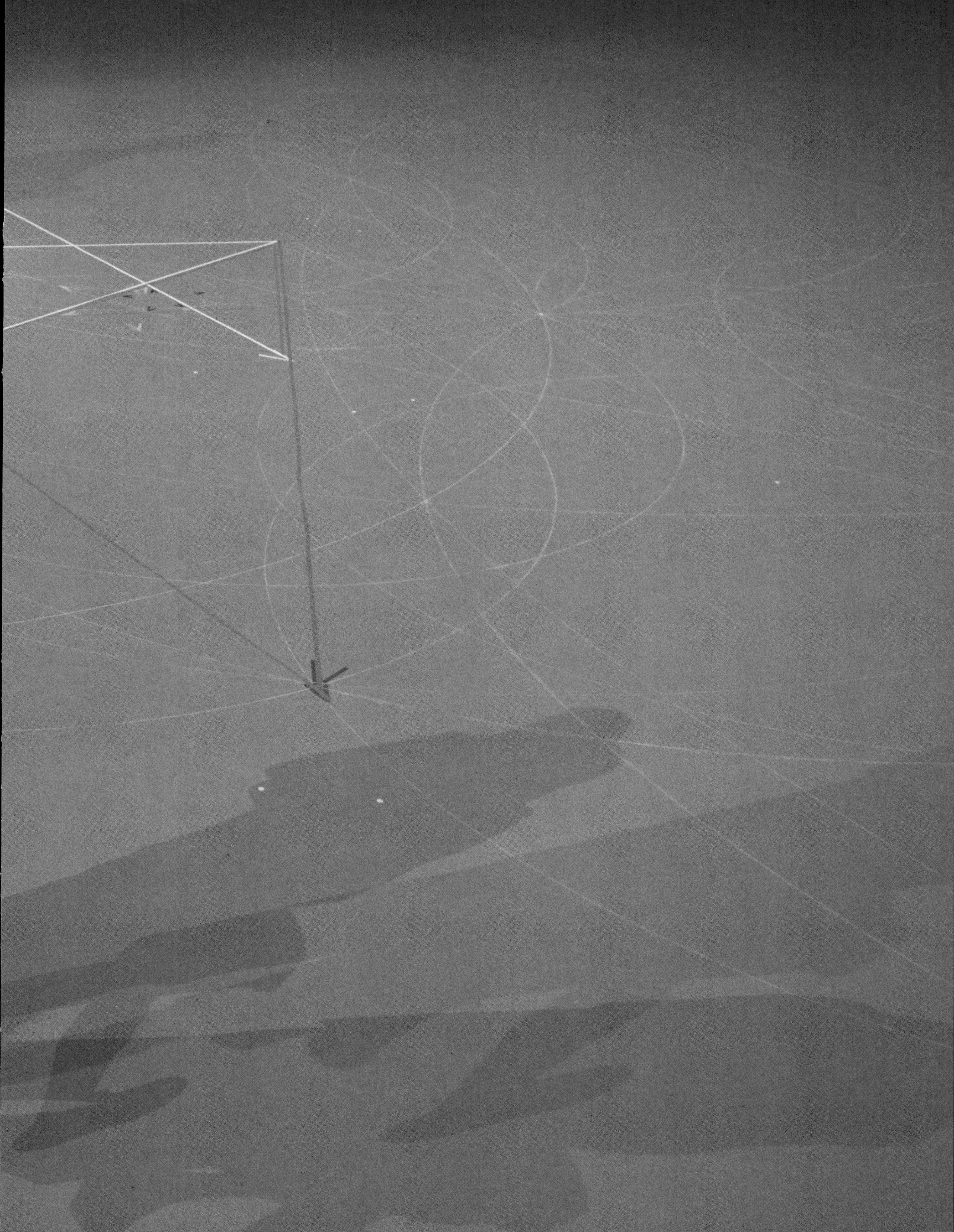

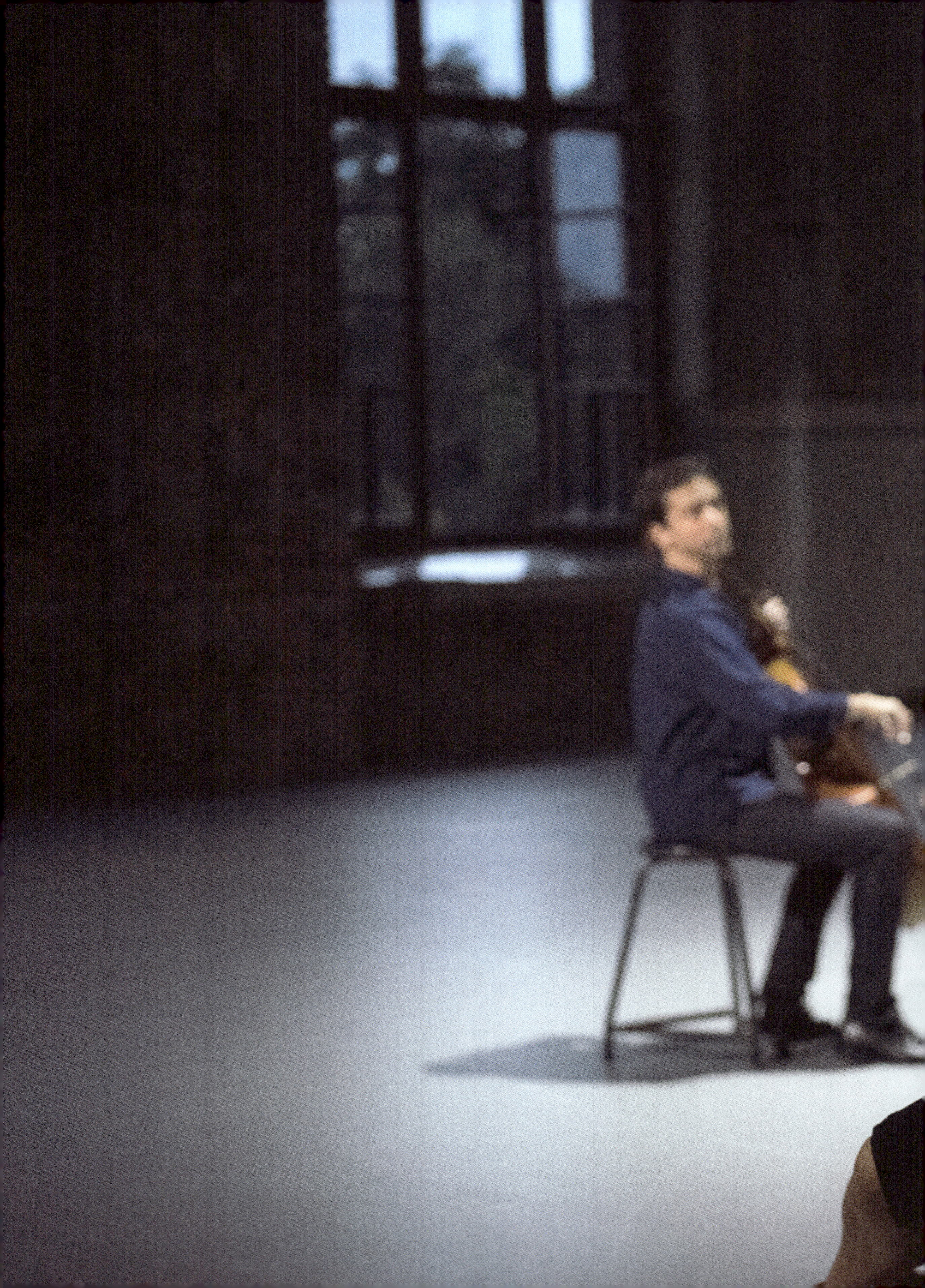

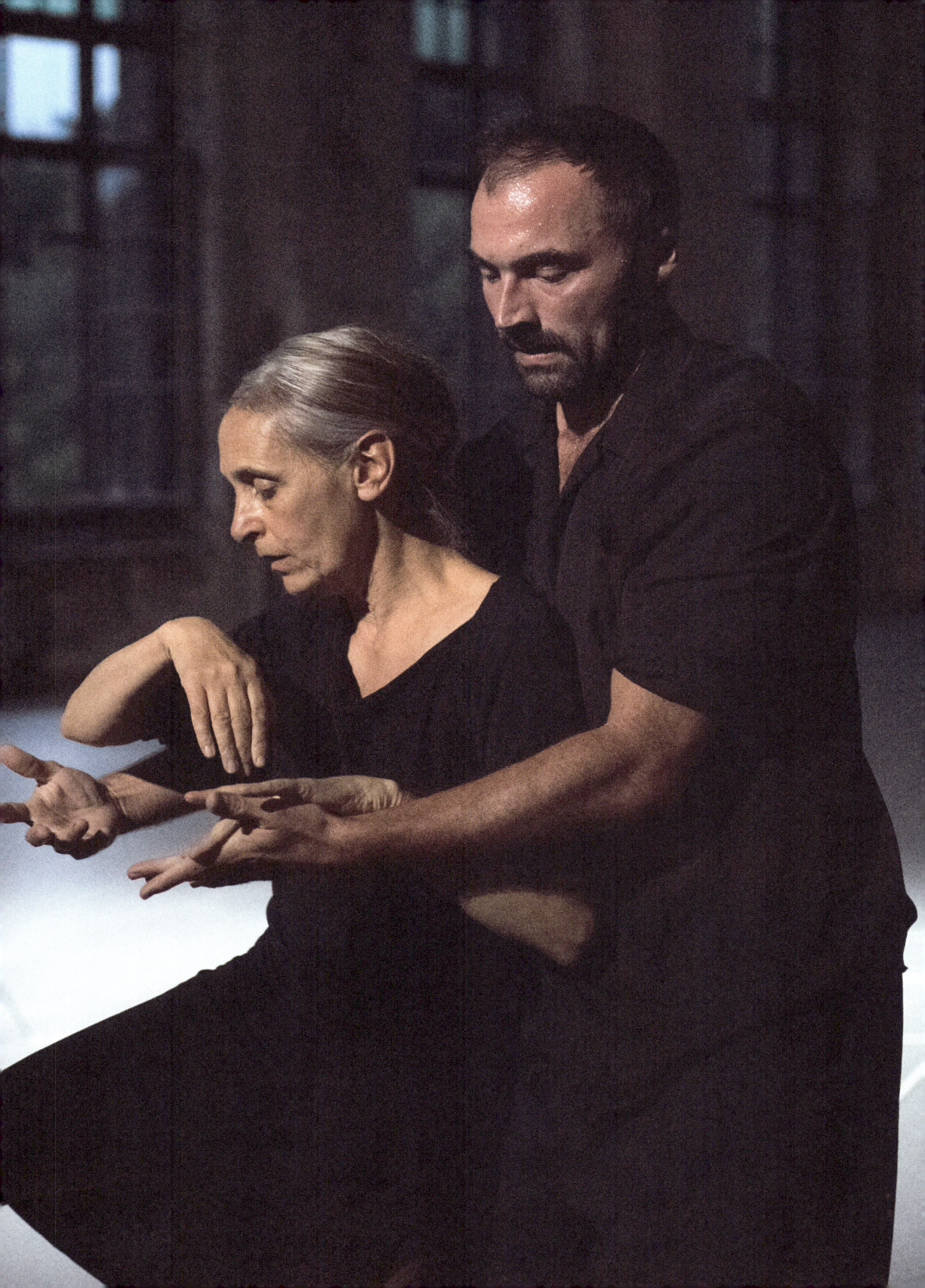

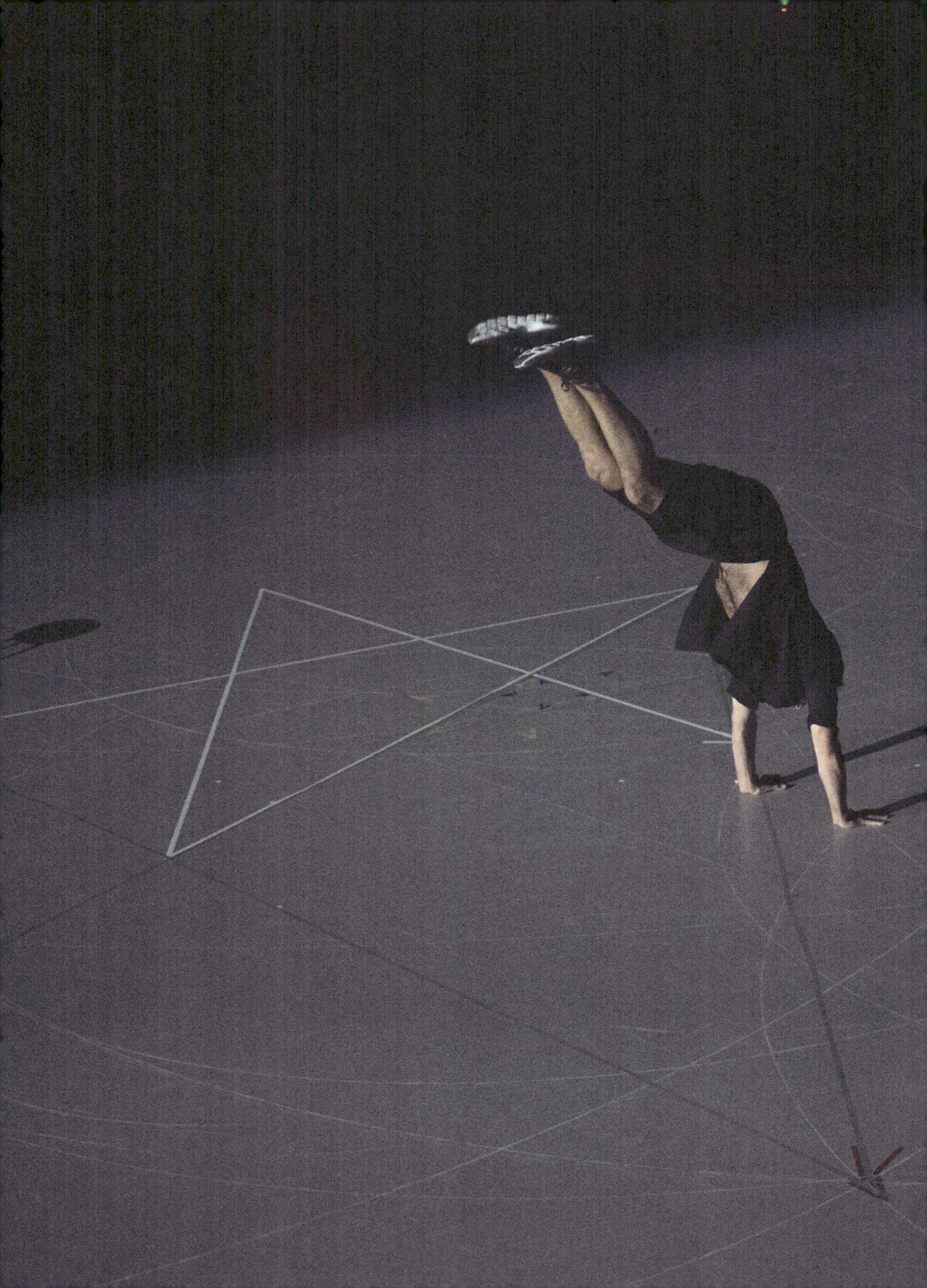

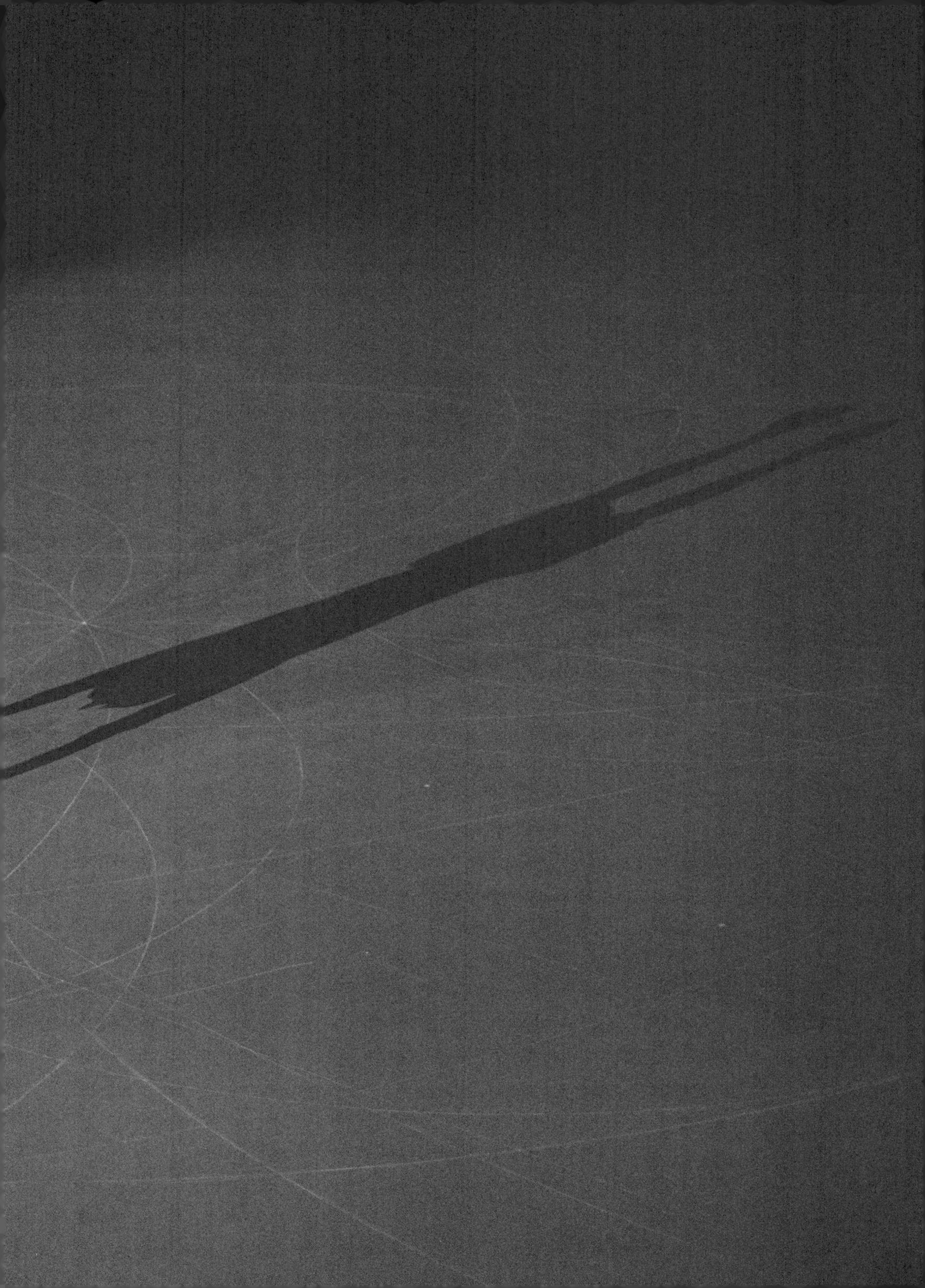

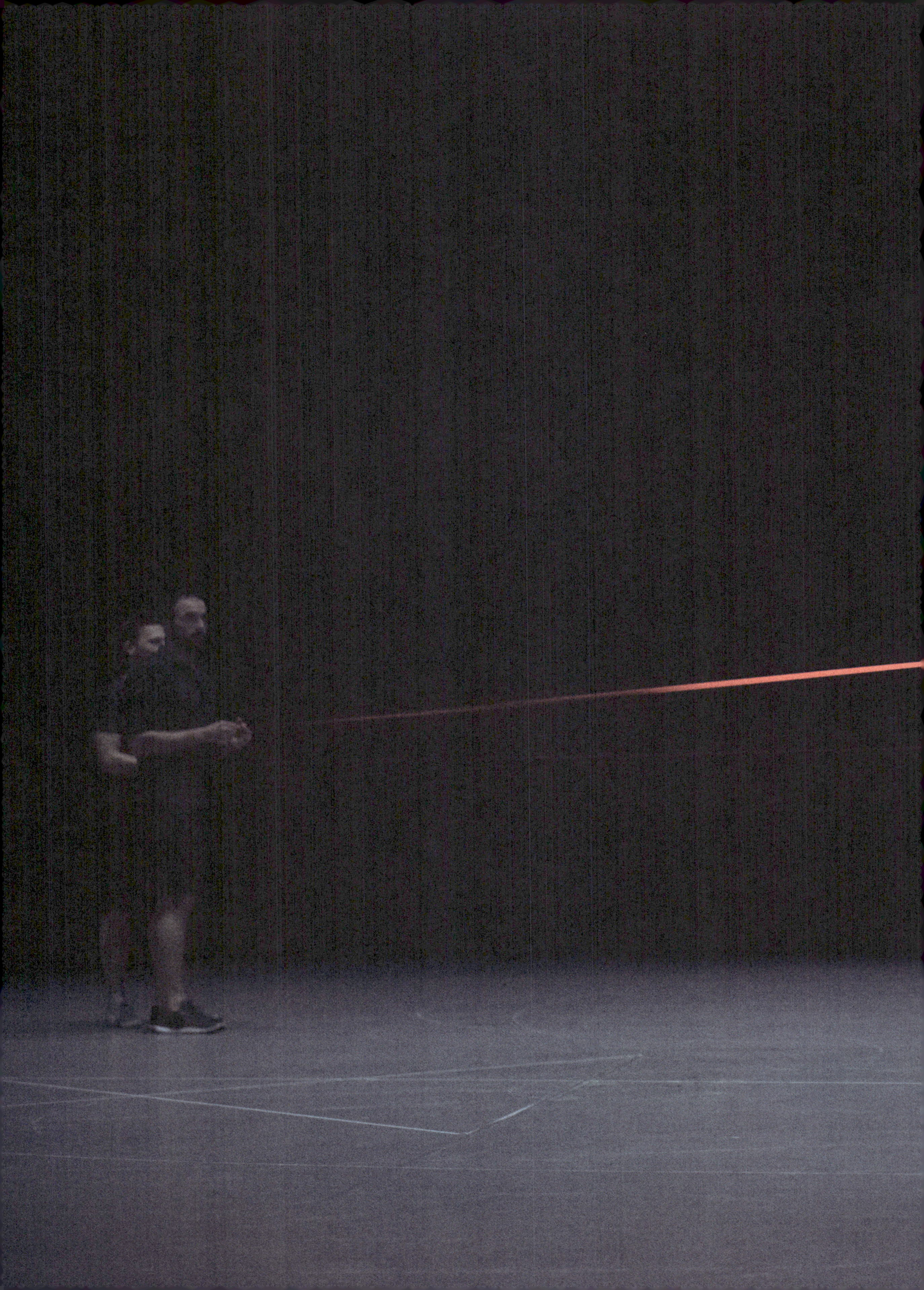

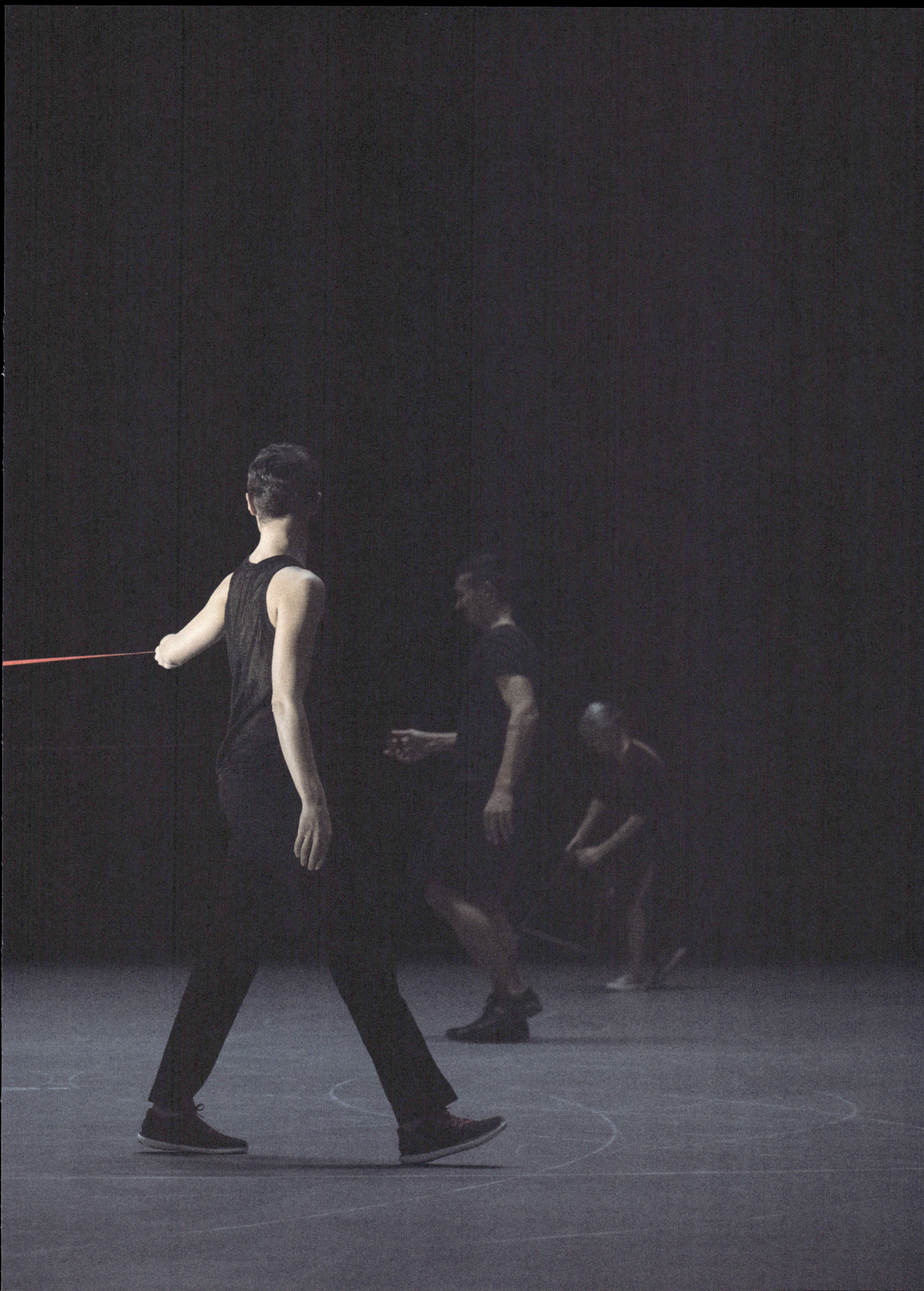

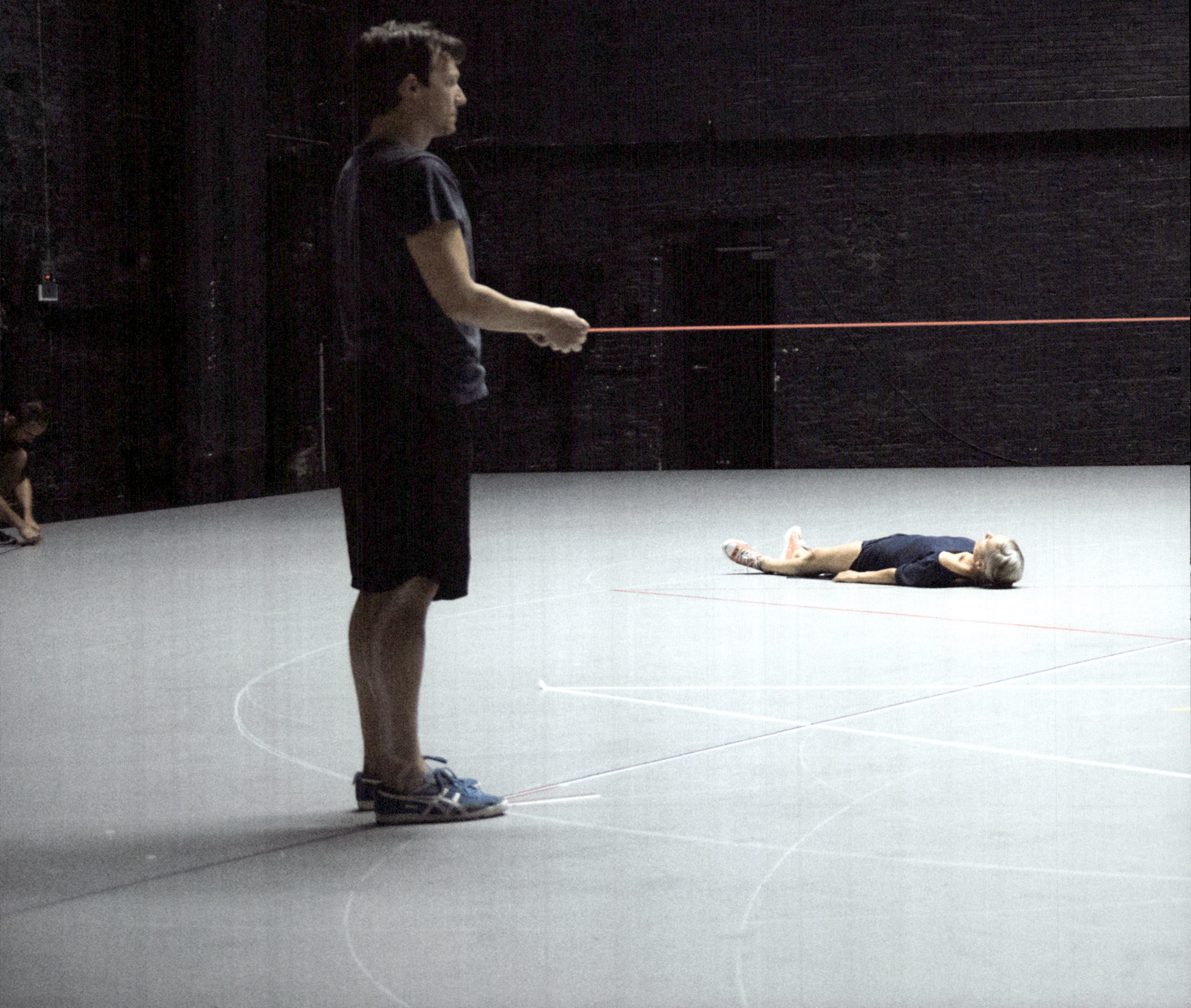

1012

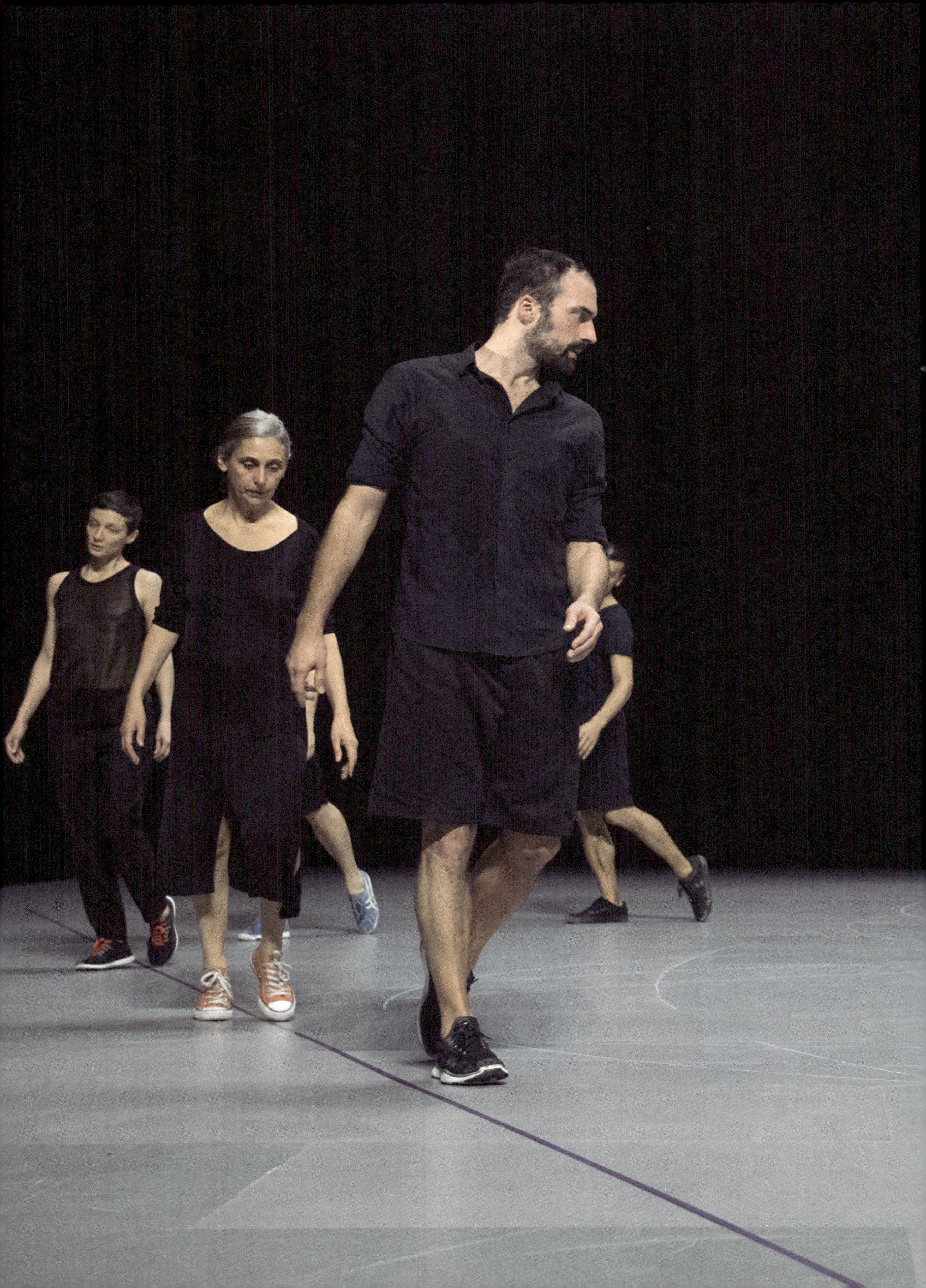

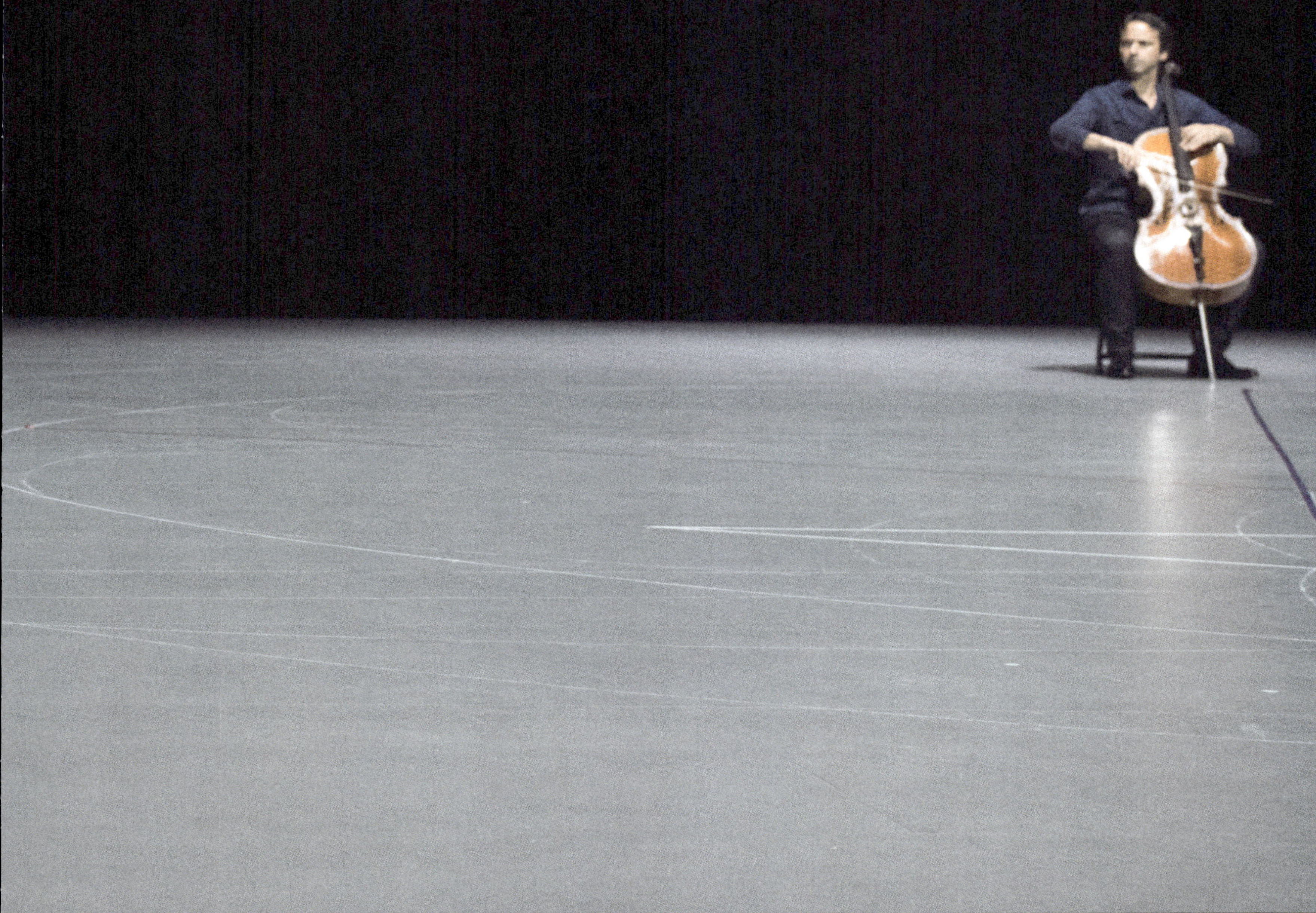

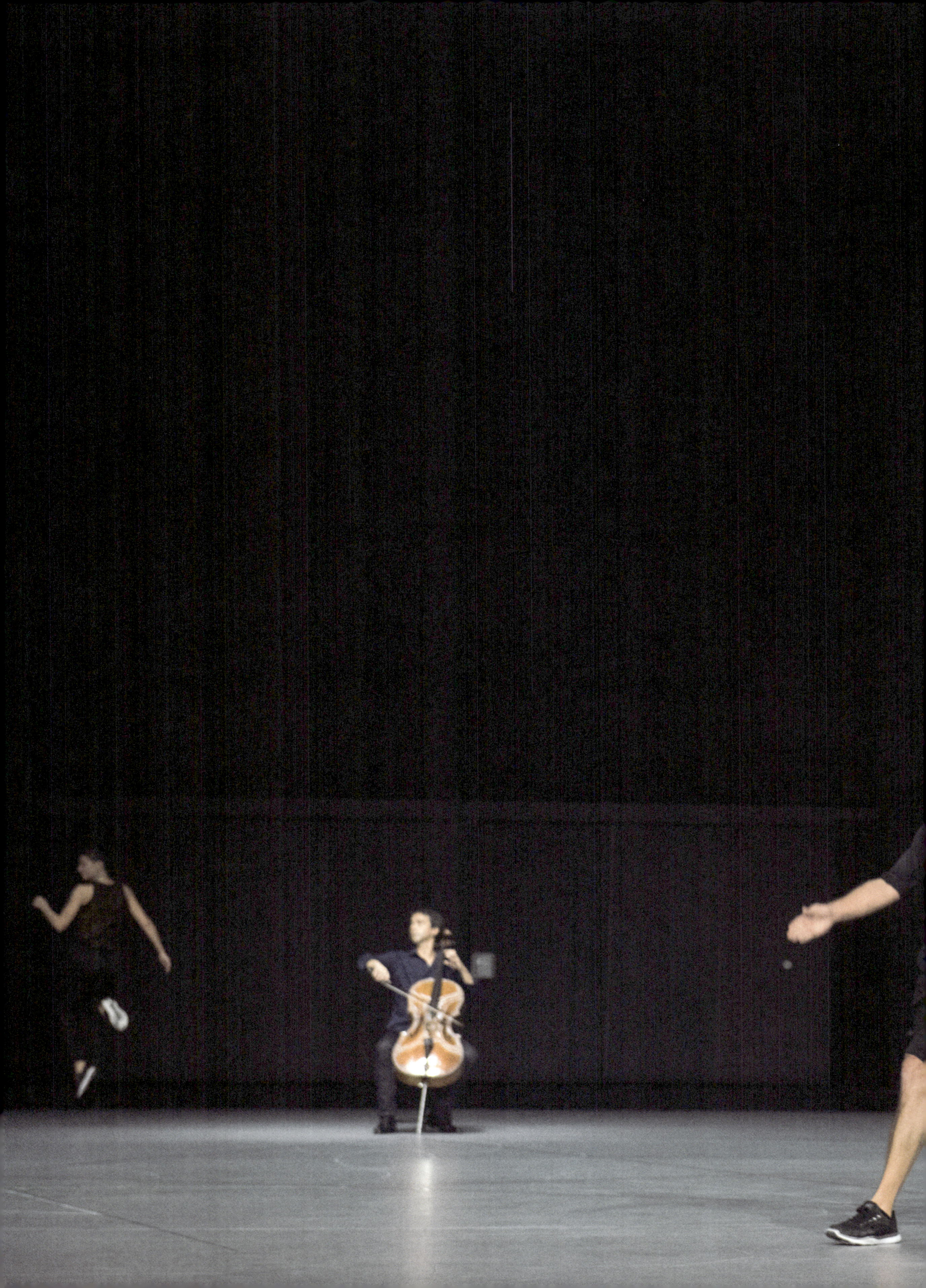

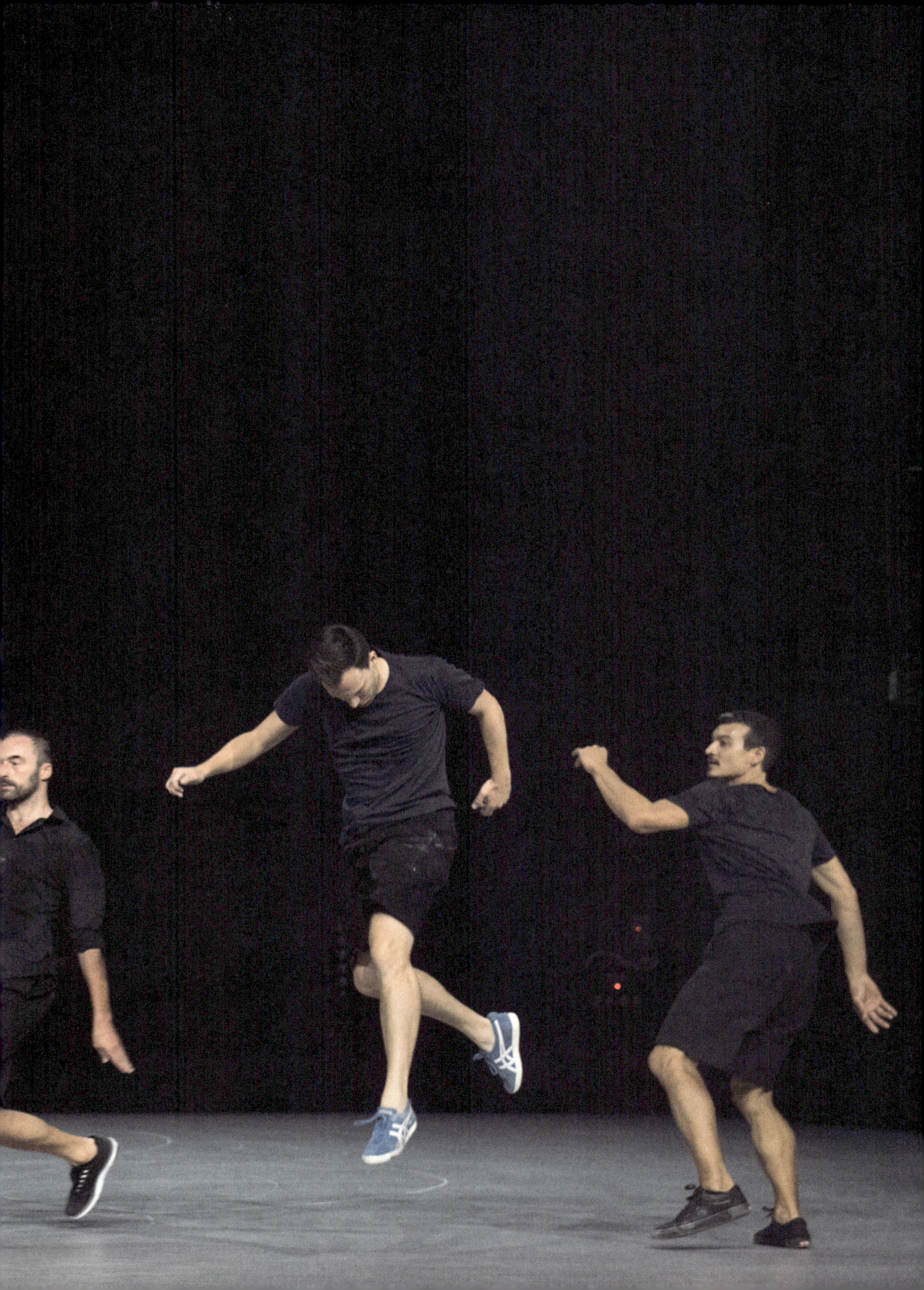

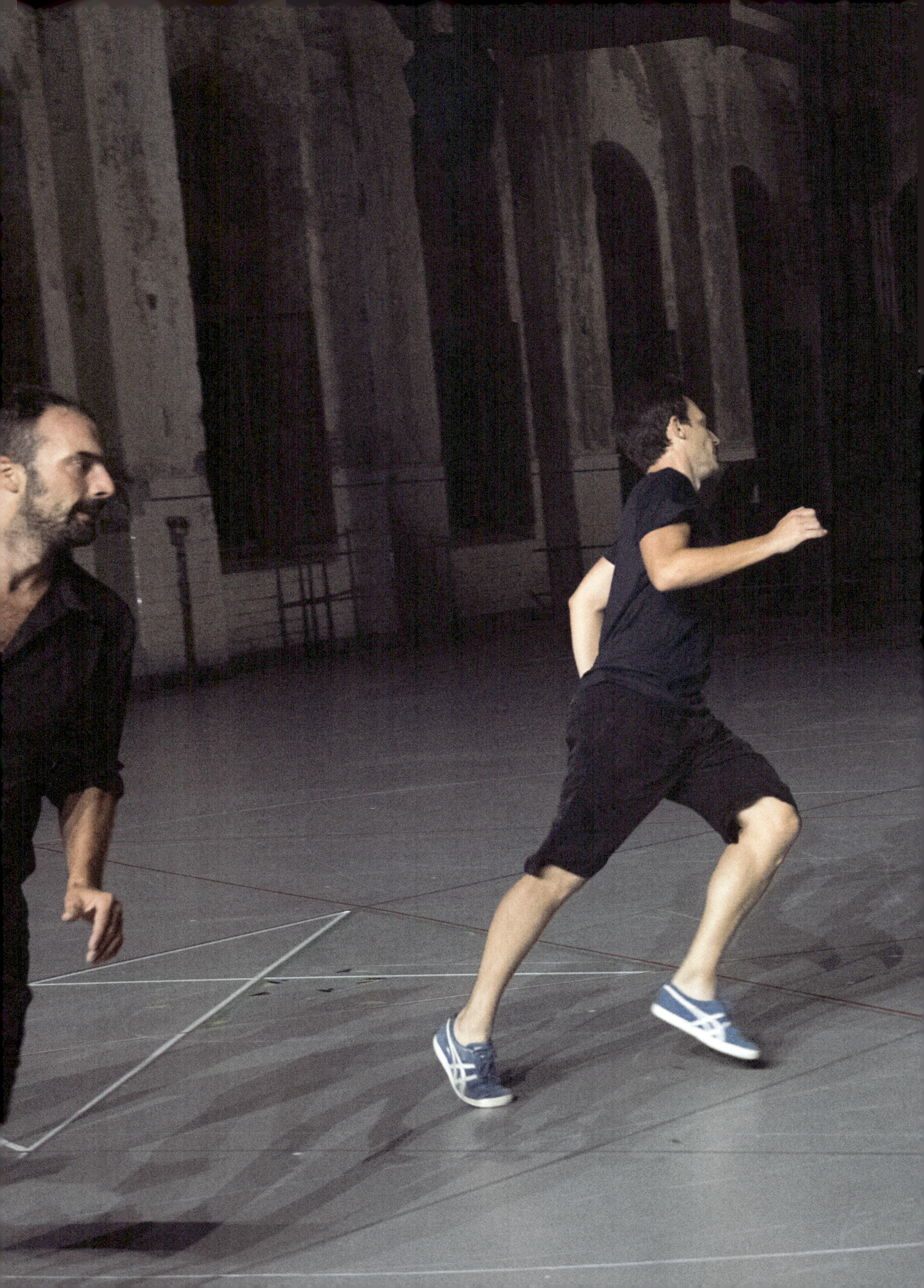

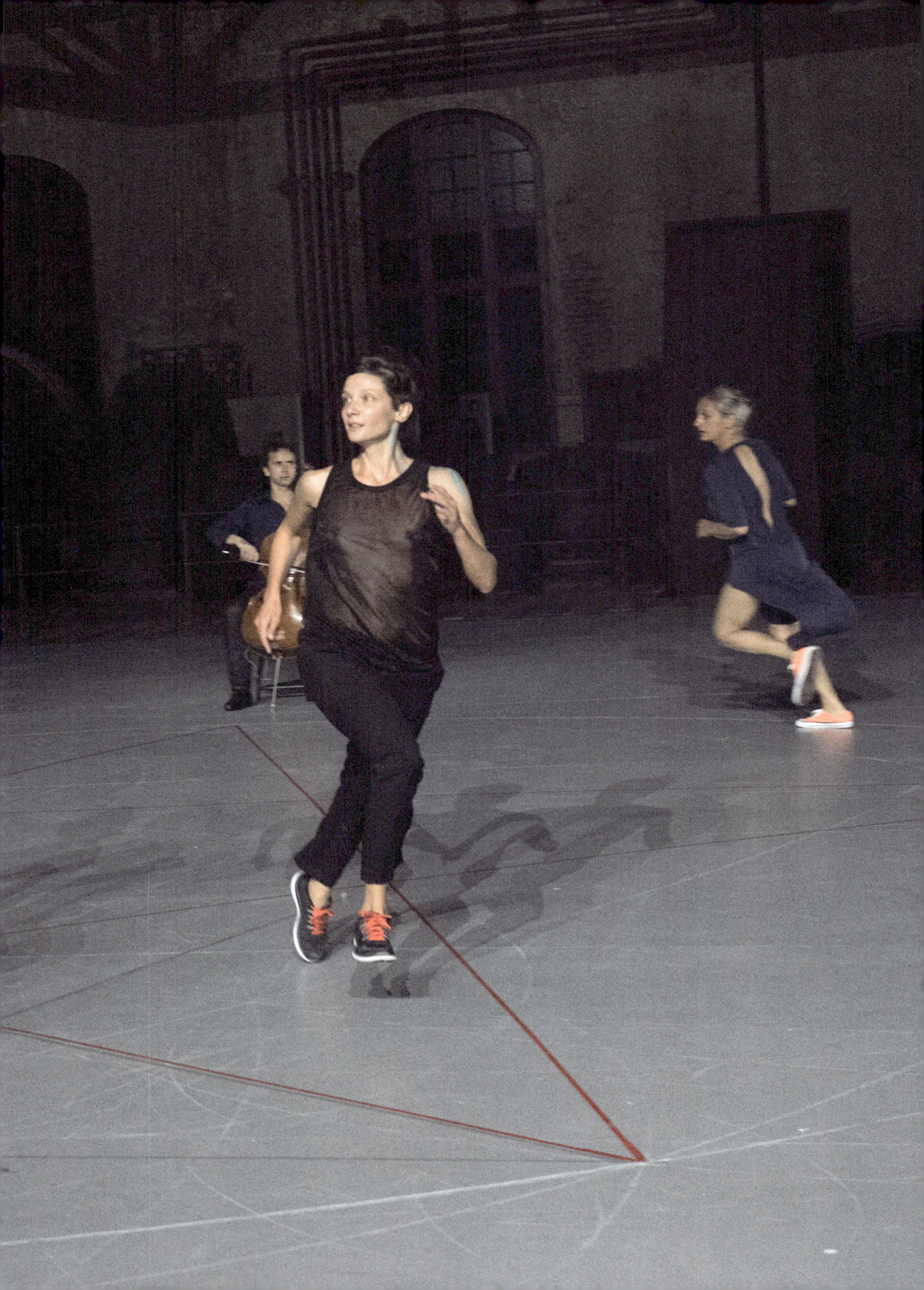

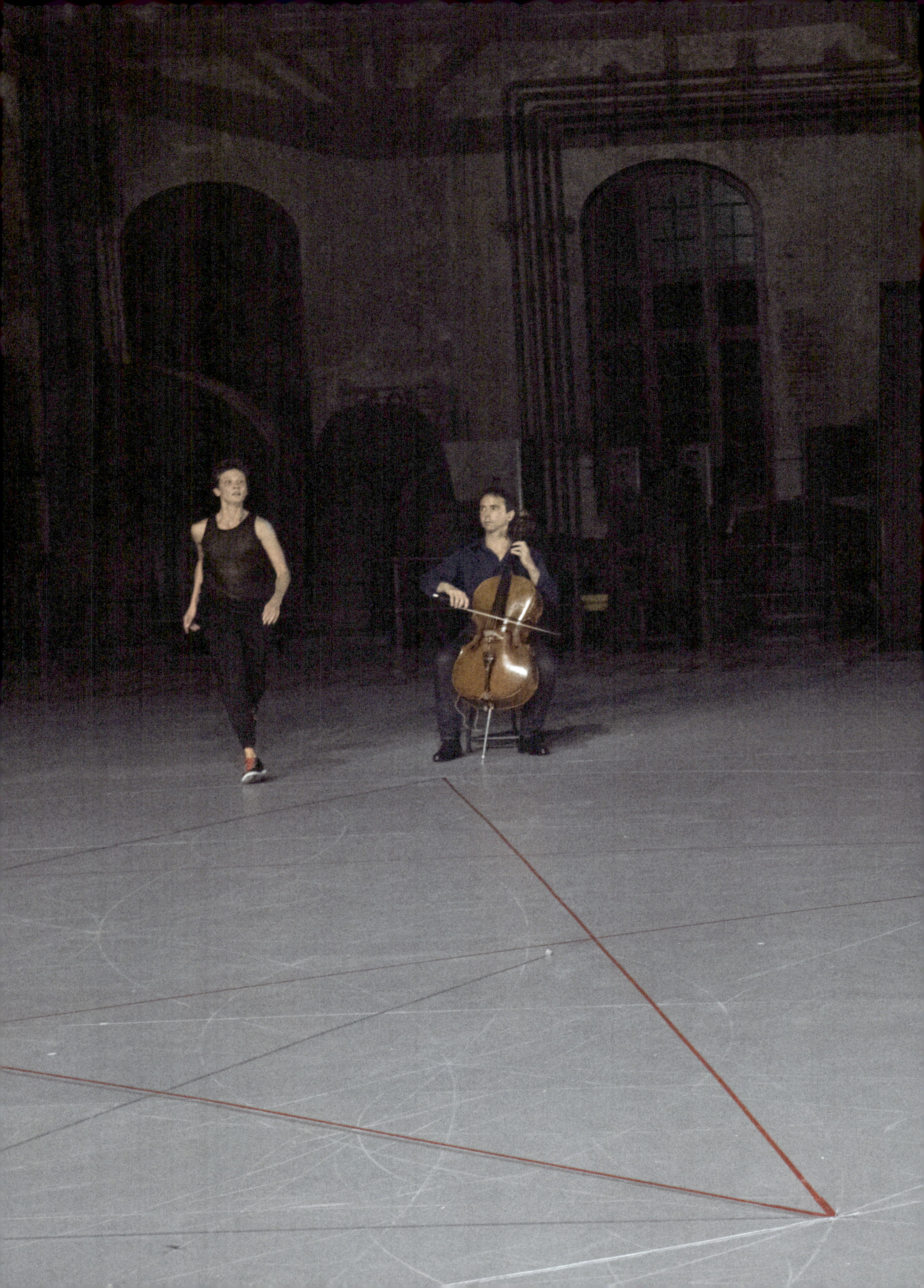

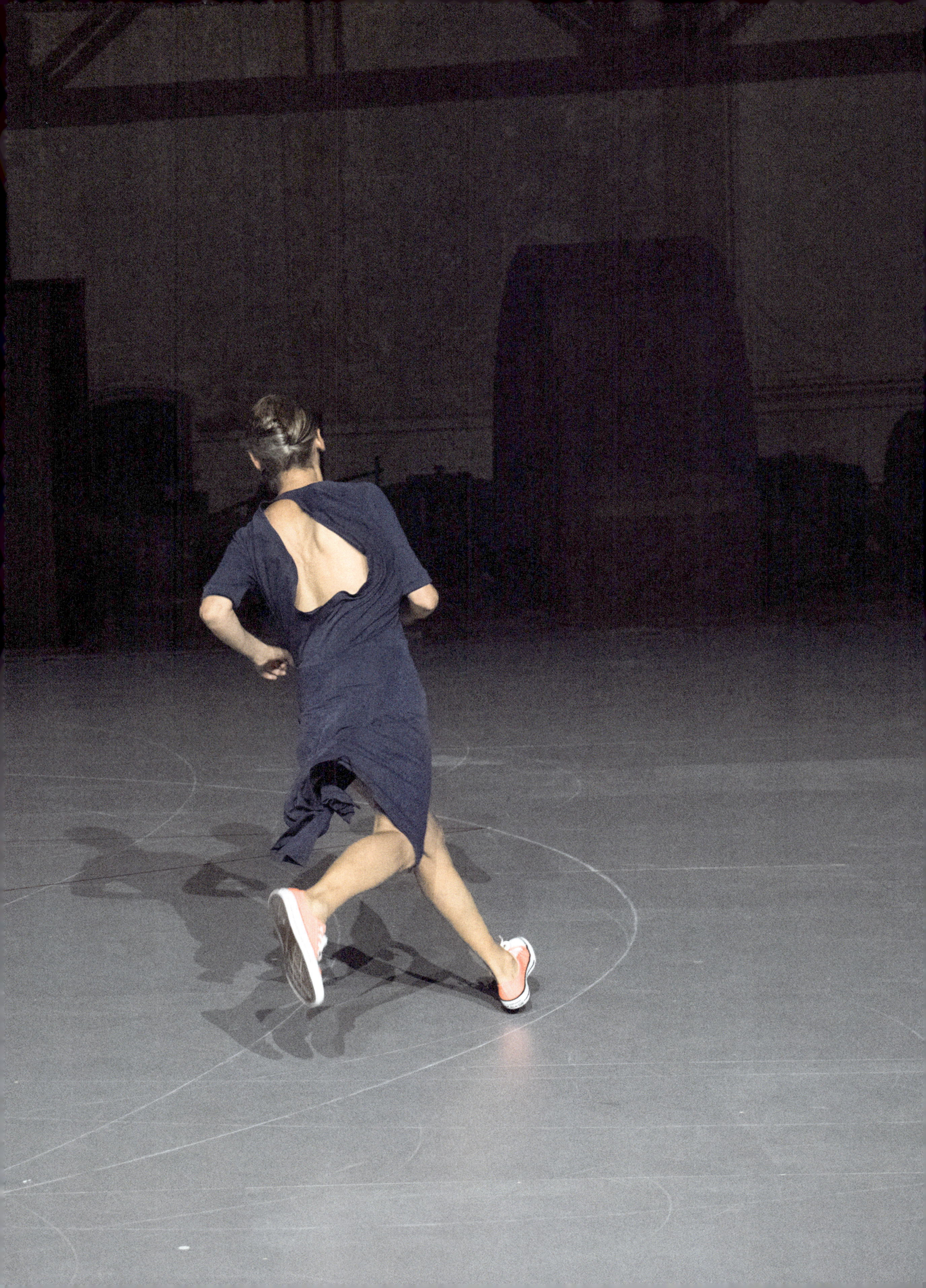

Biographies

Anne Teresa De Keersmaeker
In 1980, after studying dance at Mudra School in Brussels and Tisch School of the Arts in New York, Anne Teresa De Keersmaeker created *Asch*, her first choreographic work. Two years later came the premiere of *Fase, Four Movements to the Music of Steve Reich*. De Keersmaeker established the dance company Rosas in Brussels in 1983, while creating the work *Rosas danst Rosas*. Since these breakthrough pieces, her choreography has been grounded in a rigorous and prolific exploration of the relationship between dance and music. She has created with Rosas a wide-ranging body of work engaging the musical structures and scores of several periods, from early music to contemporary and popular idioms. Her choreographic practice also draws its formal principles from geometry, numerical patterns, the natural world, and social structures to offer a unique perspective on the body's articulation in space and time.

From 1992 until 2007, Rosas was in residence in the Brussels opera house La Monnaie / De Munt. During this period, De Keersmaeker directed a number of operas and large ensemble pieces that have since been performed by repertoire companies worldwide. In *Drumming* (1998) and *Rain* (2001), both with Ictus contemporary music ensemble, complex geometric structures in point and counterpoint, together with the minimal motivic music of Steve Reich, created compelling group choreographies that remain iconic and definitive of Rosas as a dance company. Also during her time at La Monnaie, De Keersmaeker created *Toccata* (1993) to fugues and sonatas by Johann Sebastian Bach, whose music has continued to be a recurring thread in her work. *Verklärte Nacht* (both the 1995 version for fourteen dancers and the 2014 version for three) unfolded De Keersmaeker's expressionist side, bringing the stormy narrative of Arnold Schönberg's late romantic string sextet to life. She ventured into theater, text, and interdisciplinary performance with *I said I* (1999), *In real time* (2000), *Kassandra—speaking in twelve voices* (2004), and *D'un soir un jour* (2006). She highlighted the use of improvisation within choreography in tandem with jazz and Indian music in such pieces as *Bitches Brew / Tacoma Narrows* (2003), and *Raga for the Rainy Season / A Love Supreme* (2005).

In 1995 De Keersmaeker established the school P.A.R.T.S. (Performing Arts Research and Training Studios) in Brussels in association with La Monnaie / De Munt.

De Keersmaeker's latest pieces mark a visible "stripping down" of her choreography to essential principles: spatial constraints of geometric pattern; bodily parameters of movement generation, from the utmost simplicity of walking to the fullest complexity of dancing; and close adherence to a score (musical or otherwise) for the choreographic writing. In 2013 De Keersmaeker returned to Bach's music (performed live) in *Partita 2*, a duet between herself and Boris Charmatz. Also in 2013 she created *Vortex Temporum* to the spectral music piece of the same name written in 1996 by Gérard Grisey. Taking her penchant for writing movements from musical scores to an extreme degree, *Vortex Temporum* had a one-to-one ratio between the Rosas dancers and the live Ictus musicians, bringing the choreography and the music into meticulous dialogue. In 2015 this piece was adapted to a durational exhibition format at WIELS in Brussels under the title *Work/Travail/Arbeid*. Also in 2015, Rosas premiered *Golden Hours (As you like it)*, using for the first time a body of text (Shakespeare's *As You Like It*) as the score for movement, thus allowing the music (Brian Eno's 1975 album *Another Green World*) to recede from strict framework to soft environment. Later that year, De Keersmaeker continued her research into the relationship between text and movement with *Die Weise von Liebe und Tod des Cornets Christoph Rilke*, a creation based on the eponymous text by Rainer Maria Rilke. At the beginning of 2017 she was invited by the Paris Opera to direct Mozart's *Così fan tutte*. In August of the same year she created *Mitten wir im Leben sind/Bach6Cellosuiten* with the cellist Jean-Guihen Queyras.

Anne Van Aerschot
Anne Van Aerschot studied communications and drama at the KU Leuven. She first came into contact with Rosas, Anne Teresa De Keersmaeker's dance company, as an assistant to video artist Walter Verdin in 1992. Between 2003 and 2008 Van Aerschot combined this job with her training in photography. Her first photography assignment for De Keersmaeker was the performance *3Abschied* (2010). In 2013 Rosas published *What appears in the darkness and disappears in the light*, a photo book with stage photographs by Van Aerschot. Her non-Rosas work has included set photography for the filming of Joachim Lafosse's *Élève Libre* (2008) and *À Perdre La Raison* (2012) and stage photography for the productions *Natten* (2016) and *Gerhard Richter* (2017) by the choreographer Mårten Spångberg.

Herman Sorgeloos
Herman Sorgeloos studied film and photography at the Sint-Lukas Institute in Brussels. In 1981 he made his debut as a theater photographer for *Mauser en de Hamletmachine* by Jan Decorte. He would go on to design the sets for several of the producer-director's performances. His collaboration with Anne Teresa De Keersmaeker and Rosas started in 1984, and over the years he has designed sets for *Mikrokosmos* (1987), *Ottone Ottone* (1988), *Stella* (1989), *Achterland* (1990), *Mozart / Concert Arias. Un moto di gioia* (1992), *Toccata* (1993), and *3 Solos for Vincent Dunoyer* (1997). He has also collaborated with the choreographers and directors Jan Ritsema, Tom Jansen, Alain Platel, Fumiyo Ikeda, Benjamin Verdonck, Josse De Pauw, and Pieter De Buysser.

Gilles Amalvi
Gilles Amalvi is an author, dance critic, and sound designer. His works *Une fable humaine* and *AïE! BOUM* have been released by Le Quartanier publishing house. Since *Radio-Epiméthée*, the radio version of *Une fable humaine*, he has devoted his time to exploring the art of writing with sound materials. He is a writer associated with the Musée de la Danse, works for the CND Autumn Festival, and collaborates with choreographers including Anne Teresa De Keersmaeker, Boris Charmatz, Jérôme Bel, Maud Le Pladec, Latifa Laâbissi, Ivana Müller, and Paula Pi.

Floor Keersmaekers
Floor Keersmaekers studied drama and comparative literature at Ghent University. This is where she

started work on her doctoral thesis on comparative literary theory in 2008. During this period, she wrote and published various articles and essays on the literature lectures of the Russian American writer Vladimir Nabokov. She furthermore volunteered as an editor(-in-chief) for various magazines. She has been working for Rosas as assistant to Anne Teresa De Keersmaeker since 2014 and is responsible for archiving and general dramaturgy. In this capacity, she regularly carries out interviews and writes program texts about the company's performances.

Ann Veronica Janssens
Adopting the visual languages of science and minimalism, Ann Veronica Janssens's work suggests that perception is fragile at best. Space, distribution of light, radiant color, and translucent or reflective surfaces all serve to reveal the instability of our perception of time and space. Since 2007, when she first collaborated with Anne Teresa De Keersmaeker on *Keeping Still — Part 1*, she has been a recurring contributor to the choreographer's projects, including *The Song* (2009), *Cesena* (2011), and *Work/Travail/Arbeid* (2015).

Michel François
Michel François is a conceptual artist and maker of sculptures, videos, photographs, printed matter, paintings, and installations. He claims no signature style but creates a web of shifting connections between his works and each different exhibition. François has collaborated with Anne Teresa De Keersmaeker on various productions, including *The Song* (2009), *En Atendant* (2010), and *Partita 2* (2013).

Anne Teresa De Keersmaeker /
Rosas 2007—2017

Publishers
Actes Sud, Arles/Paris
Mercatorfonds, Brussels
Editor
Christian Dumais-Lvowski
Photography
Anne Van Aerschot, Herman Sorgeloos
Additional images
Michel François, Ann Veronica Janssens
On location at
Centre Pompidou, Paris
Cloître des Célestins, Avignon
Concertgebouw, Bruges
De Munt, Brussels
deSingel, Antwerp
Gebläsehalle, Duisburg
Jahrhunderthalle, Bochum
Kaaitheater, Brussels
Museum of Modern Art, New York
Palais des Papes, Avignon
Palais Garnier, Paris
Repetitiestudio's Rosas, Brussels
Rosas Performance Space, Brussels
Tate Modern, London
Théâtre de la Ville, Paris
WIELS, Brussels
The photos of Così fan tutte *were made with the kind permission of the Paris National Opera during the performances at the Palais Garnier in January and September 2017.*
Authors
Gilles Amalvi, Floor Keersmaekers
Editing of the text by Floor Keersmaekers
Hans Galle, Annelies de hertogh
Translation of the text by Floor Keersmaekers
Isobel Mackie, Joris Van Leemput
Translation of the text by Gilles Amalvi
Emiliano Battista
Copyediting in English
Emiliano Battista
Proofreading
Lindsey Westbrook
Coordination
Rosas Hans Galle
Mercatorfonds Ann Mestdag
Graphic Design
Casier/Fieuws
Typefaces Courier, Helvetica Neue Black Condensed
Printing and binding
Graphius, Ghent
Paper Munken Print White 115grs 1.8

© 2018 Rosas, Brussels; Mercatorfonds, Brussels; Actes Sud, Arles/Paris

Distributed in Belgium, the Netherlands, and Luxembourg by Mercatorfonds, Brussels
ISBN 978-94-6230-212-9
D/2018/703/20

Distributed outside Belgium, the Netherlands, and Luxembourg by Yale University Press, New Haven and London
www.yalebooks.com/art — www.yalebooks.co.uk
ISBN 978-0-300-23687-3 — Library of Congress Control Number: 2018954237

www.rosas.be — www.mercatorfonds.be — www.actes-sud.fr

All Rights Reserved. No part of this publication may be reproduced or transmitted in any form or by any means, electronic or mechanical, including photocopy, recording or any other information storage and retrieval system, without prior permission in writing form the publisher.

Rosas is supported by the Flemish Community and by the BNP Paribas Foundation.